D0560568

Is My Armor Straight?

Is My Armor Straight?

A YEAR IN THE LIFE OF A UNIVERSITY PRESIDENT

BY RICHARD BERENDZEN

ADLER&ADLER

Published by
Adler & Adler, Publishers, Inc.
4550 Montgomery Avenue
Bethesda, Maryland 20814

Library of Congress
Cataloging in Publication Data

Berendzen, Richard.
    Is my armor straight?
    Includes index.
    1. Berendzen, Richard.
2. American University
(Washington, D.C.)—Presidents—
Biography. 3. College presidents—
United States—Biography. I.
Title. LD131.A817 1980.A35
1986   378' .111 [B]   85-14214
ISBN 0-917561-01-5

First Edition

Printed in the United States
of America

For Gail, Deborah, and Natasha

FOREWORD

It is an old saying that one looks for the busiest people for the most difficult jobs. Some energetic men and women who entered a particular field because it interested them are drawn into administration when they command sufficient energy, executive talent, public presence, and ambition. In a university, they may, like Richard Berendzen, end up as deans and then as presidents. The American University (AU), unlike its eminent neighbor, Georgetown University, or the highly selective Ivy League-type colleges and universities in the northeast and mid-Atlantic states, is one of a large number of once-Methodist urban institutions that have no wholly assured flow of applicants or donors, given the competitive ecological landscape. Berendzen recognized that to improve, or even to maintain, the relative position of AU, he had to become not only its pedogogical leader but also a cheerleader, tour guide, architectural visionary, and emissary to the well-to-do (and to the go-betweens who lead to them, as well as to the media as the national go-betweens)—all in pursuit of resources for the university.

A president as much in the public eye as Berendzen is under pressure to be an instant expert on almost everything. He has to talk with people of diverse, though often limited, interests. In one area, Berendzen can draw on his background as an astronomer. Indeed, he tells us about the opportunity he had, as a graduate student and teaching fellow in astronomy at Harvard, to assist in a course taught by a then newly recruited professor, Carl Sagan, who was to become famous as the biographer of the universe. And he pointedly refers to the occasion that I have in my own mind always associated with AU: John F. Kennedy's famous address, in the spring of 1963, which helped pave the way for the partial test ban that this writer and many others consider Kennedy's most significant achievement.

Berendzen had the excellent idea of keeping a diary. Although there are moments in the book when he speaks of himself as utterly spent from the periodic combination of diurnal pressures with unanticipated crises, he nonetheless managed to dictate at the end of the day not only what had happened but what he thought about it, often with an admirable memory for colloquy. Flashbacks enable him here to fill in background—for example, to indicate the centrality of the relations of president and provost (Milton Greenberg), one of the many top administrators to whom Berendzen is careful to give full credit for accomplishment, while eschewing criticism.

Berendzen deals at the outset with an ethical question that has preoccupied me also as someone who periodically has kept a diary and later decided to publish parts of it. Is this an abuse of the confidences of others, whether relative strangers or friends? Does the very act of having a conversation knowing one later will record it raise a question concerning one's straightforwardness? Much of our social life revolves around situations in which we hold something back in our relations with others, whatever that "something" may be. There is no ready answer to such scruples. But in the case of Berendzen's diary, I would be astonished if his friends and acquaintances found cause for complaint. He is observant without being caustic, cynical, or censorious. He is critical only when he is being insulted or improperly besieged, and then those whom he criticizes remain anonymous. Surely, the book will only help The American University, revealing as it does the virtuosity, as well as the visibility, of its principal defender.

Berendzen—who actually owns a suit of armor—uses the metaphor of a suit of armor to refer to his own protection against not only the mild hurts of ungenerosity but also the great stress of threats and physical abuse. He is the defender of the university. One of the most dramatic sections in the diary concerns a free, student-sponsored rock concert by the Pretenders, planned for a Saturday afternoon. On the preceding Friday, Berendzen and his administrative associates suddenly realize that the concert is luring thousands to Washington, not to demonstrate but to celebrate. All this comes at the very time when the university's affluent neighbors, never happy about keeping company with students and their cars, have to be cajoled into accepting a zoning change for the university. Berendzen and his student-and-community-affairs staff call in the student leaders. Together they unhappily conclude that the concert must be canceled, for the university can at most accommodate 7,000—an attendance to be expected from its own students—and not the 20,000 to 40,000 now frighteningly anticipated, for whom there is no conceivable place to park or to stand and see the performers. Recognizing impending disaster, virtually all the students leaders advise Berendzen to cancel. He does so, promising that the university will contribute to the cost of the canceled contract and he and a student leader go on the student TV station to report the decision. But Berendzen literally could use his suit of armor when the violence of disappointed students erupts; and what depresses him more than their abuse is that some students who had advocated the decision become sufficiently pressured to turn against him publicly. Berendzen has protected the university. But at the same time, students assail him because a long-sought facility has yet even to be announced, donors equivocate or fail to come forth, and no one—except a few key people—can or will help him. Exhausted, Berendzen considers resigning, asking himself whether an institution that harbors such aggression is worth defending. He recovers his psychic armor quickly, however, particularly when a rescheduled concert with a less-famous band turns into a joyous event.

The psychologist Asenath Petrie, in *Individuality in Pain and Suffering,* divided people by clinical tests into two extreme types: the "augmentors," for whom events resonate internally in amplified fashion so the individuals are overstimulated, and the "reducers," for whom homeostasis is easier, who are less upset by crises, who in fact often seek hazards and pressures because they thrive on external stimulation. Most of us, of course, are blends of these polarities. But university presidents need to be reducers with a built-in suit of armor. In spite of his usually protective armor, the reaction Berendzen had to the vituperation heaped on him because of the cancellation was a rare instance of bitterness and misery.

The problem of mobilizing resources to build a sports and convocation center is a running theme in the diary. Such a facility, in the fierce competition for students, is a factor in recruitment. However, The American University is not out to rival other once-Methodist, urban universities such as Northwestern or the University of Southern California, or even Southern Methodist, as athletic powers. The center would simply facilitate Berendzen's continuing effort to make Washington, D.C.—a city with few patricians and little inherited wealth—a mecca not only for students but for faculty and donors. One target of opportunity is Adnan Khashoggi, Mecca-born, immensely wealthy, a self-made, cosmopolitan philanthropist. Using go-betweens, Berendzen sets out to cultivate this man, who has been referred to as an "Arab arms merchant" possibly "too controversial for a university," yet whom Berendzen brings onto the board of trustees. Adroitly, Berendzen manages to prevent untoward reactions from Jewish nationalists for whom all Arabs are enemies. Indeed, Berendzen seizes opportunities for bringing his Jewish provost, trustees, and friends into contact with potential donors from the oil kingdoms of the Middle East, hoping to make Washington a free port, so to speak, without customs barriers and provincial prejudices of party, race, or religion.

A university president of this persuasion cannot be shy. Berendzen tells a lovely story of how he glimpsed Paul Volcker at LaGuardia Airport, struck up a conversation, and recruited a new potential friend for the university. And Berendzen's wife, Gail, is an equally high-spirited partner in her husband's diurnal round of hosting, soliciting, and celebrating. Parties may be exhausting, their menus unappetizing, and conversations iterative, yet they are usually better than airports for meeting people who can be useful to the university.

In many episodes in the diary, Berendzen impresses me with his ability to avoid self-pity or fury in reaction to the many assaults on his privacy by arrogant, clamorous individuals. When he walks the campus and attends events, he does so with due warning to students —for example, in the dormitories—to make clear that he is not there to inquire into their personal lives. But on these strolls or at receptions, faculty and staff may tug at his sleeve to ask him about a raise, or students may rudely ask: "When will we have our new gym? And, why don't we have it *now?*" A man with an old-fashioned sense of personal space, or one who expects generosity from those whose work and lives he facilitates, would easily become irritated by such behavior and would lose heart in his continuous struggle to raise money for what appears to be an array of demanding, often self-righteous egotists. But Berendzen's wit obviously helps, and he is able to reduce this "noise" and to respond with friendly warmth, especially to faculty, student leaders, and editors of the student paper who accept responsibility and care about the institution.

Berendzen admits to one arena of intense vulnerability, namely his wife, Gail, and their daughter, Natasha, just entering her teens at Georgetown Day School. He has almost no time to be with them. This is characteristic of the lives of many people with large responsibilities, but it is especially poignant for a university president whose wife has newly taken up the career of presidential partner—i.e., social coordinator, community volunteer, all-purpose stand-in—so that she too is often pulled away from their daughter. The diary makes clear, however, that Natasha's life, like Gail's, is not without rewards, in terms of meeting people who are both famous and interesting; and since many of Natasha's schoolmates are also children of influential people, she does not feel singular in her deprivation.

I believe that the stresses on a university president are comparable to those on a big-city mayor, at least if one is at an institution like The American University, large enough to present an array of crises and too small to be subdivided into separate arenas with which the president need be only intermittently involved—although it is hard to imagine Berendzen ever being wholly uninvolved, even were he to head a splendidly endowed and comfortably federated institution.

Many students of higher education, including myself, have written about the allotment of a university president's time. Clark Kerr has criticized presidents because so few spend substantial time on academic affairs, especially on the general education of undergraduates, leaving curriculum, faculty recruitment and tenure, and the intellectual coherence of the undergraduate college in the hands of academic deans and provosts. Berendzen aims to be more than the crisis manager and arbitrator, more that the avid university defender he plainly is, more than the ingenious fundraiser. This book is an attempt to say something that is not simply about himself but that will illuminate better than research reports or college histories what it is like to be in a world of scholars and wheeler-dealers, politicians, and media celebrities, simultaneously.

In the year prior to the particular year of the diary, enrollments at AU had dropped unexpectedly while tuition had not been raised to make up for the shortfall. There were empty beds—as happened that year at many private colleges and universities—of students who had paid deposits but due to economic pressures had subsequently transferred to public institutions where they would be more handsomely subsidized. A union protested AU's consequent firing of its custodians and its contracting with a custodial firm. This yielded all the drama of sentimental students and professors supporting the demonstrators, such as we witnessed in 1984–85 at Yale—a situation where the president of the university and his top administrative staff are gagged by their lawyers from saying anything against allegations of exploitation and "union busting." In Yale's case there was an additional charge of sexism, because of the demand by white-collar women for "comparable worth," whereas in The American University's case the explosive issue of racism was involved, since the custodians were black.

For most trustees, their volunteer activity is a sometime thing. The most responsible ones will have periods of stress, as when they search for a new president or when they face pressure for contributions beyond what they would prefer to donate or might raise from others. Trustees are on occasion the goalies of a university. They must look to its long-term future as against the demands of its immediate constituencies, often filtered through extremist advocates. It is plain that Berendzen is able to depend on some very dedicated trustees among the forty-six on AU's board, although some can be as arrogantly importuning as any student or faculty member—there is at least one such example in the diary. Berendzen not only cultivates his trustees but, through having faculty members address them on occasion and through other cross-cultural modes, he tries to make them more aware of the university as well.

I hope that *Is My Armor Straight?* will be read widely by trustees. It should help them become more sensitive concerning the stresses on a president and on his family. The term of presidential incumbencies has been decreasing. Since it takes time for a new president to learn the ropes (though somewhat less so when, as in this case, the president is recruited from within), and since interregnums tend to be costly, trustees have every incentive to learn how to become more solicitous of the president without being intrusive. The Association of Governing Boards of Universities and Colleges works constantly at the education of both neophyte and experienced trustees. *Is My Armor Straight?* might serve not only The American University, but that larger purpose.

Professor David Riesman
Harvard University

PROLOGUE

"What do you do?" I am frequently asked. When I explain that I am president of The American University in Washington, D.C., the questioner will reply, "But what exactly does a university president do these days?" Of course, each president is different, just as each university is different. But all of us must be concerned with the curricula, the faculty, and the students. And most of us must raise funds, meet with alumni, oversee the finances, speak publicly about education, and attempt generally to advance the institution. But how can I explain this? For the past few years, such matters crossed my mind. Quickly, however, I put them aside as I rushed to my usual tasks.

One of those is to discuss education. And never has there been a more apt time. In April 1983, the U.S. Department of Education published a thin, blue book that stunned the nation. Its prose rang; its facts jolted. "[The] educational foundations of our society are presently eroded by a rising tide of mediocrity that threatens our very future as a Nation and a people," *A Nation at Risk* declared. "If an unfriendly foreign power had attempted to impose on America the mediocre educational performance that exists today, we might well have viewed it as an act of war."

Because I give addresses about educational reform, a friend introduced me to Trevor Armbrister, a senior editor at *The Reader's Digest* in Washington, D.C. Over lunch one day in the summer of 1983, I explained to Trevor what I thought was wrong with our educational system. He prodded me with questions, at first about public schools and then about my own university. As we left, he asked me to send him something in writing about what we had discussed. I had wanted to summarize my thoughts about public education anyway. This was a good excuse. So I sent him a sixteen-page letter.

Four days later he called: "You've got a book here." I replied that the letter might contain the core for an article but not a book. What he had in mind, he explained, was not an essay on education; it was the story of my life as a university president. Not a summary of my meetings and memos, it would be a sampling of what I do and what I have done. Despite my protests that I had no time for such an endeavor, Trevor persuaded me to think about the matter. Reluctantly, I agreed to do something for a few weeks that I had never done before: keep a journal. Those weeks evolved into months and finally into a full academic year: 1983–84.

Early in this undertaking I realized potential difficulties. If I told people I was keeping a journal, they might act differently. But if I did not tell them, would I violate a confidence? Finally, I convinced myself that I would not, for I did not intend to harm anyone or to disclose privileged information.

But how was I to keep accurate records? I could not take notes during meetings or record conversations; so I jotted notes, if possible, within a few hours of an event. Then late each night, I dictated a day's segment into my desk recorder; on a trip, I did so into a portable recorder. My recitation is not that of a journalist with a pad; nor are this book's quotations a transcription. The details and the dialogue are as I remembered them; nonetheless, I believe my recall was good. On weekends and after her usual long day, my secretary/assistant, Joan Leach, transcribed my dictation. Later, I edited that draft into the final manuscript.

This is not a scholarly treatise on education nor a complete chronicle of my professional activities. It is a personal account of my life as a university president and as a man.

Gratefully, I acknowledge Trevor Armbrister's editorial assistance and Joan Leach's clerical assistance.

Richard Berendzen
Washington, D.C.

Is My Armor Straight?

TUESDAY, AUGUST 30

"Education," wrote philosopher Alfred North Whitehead, "is discipline for the adventure of life." If so, I wonder as I walk to my office this morning what education, what discipline, what adventure my life will have this academic year.

With anticipation and anxiety, I await the opening of the term tomorrow: anticipation because this could be a decisive year for The American University; anxiety because the term last year began badly, with the enrollments down and the budget squeezed. For days, we have readied the campus: repaired dorms, removed litter, painted curbs. Today it shines. But is the university's greater structure strong: its finances, faculty, curriculum, and reputation? Yes, although we have much yet to do.

And we have major needs. Our looming, pressing challenge is to build a sports and convocation center—a comprehensive facility that will be the core of the campus from a student's registration day to his graduation day. From major speakers to major sports events— all will occur there. For forty years, The American University has needed such a center, and every day we wait the cost rises.

My first meeting this morning is with Don Triezenberg, the vice-president for development and university relations. At six feet three, he is an imposing figure, with a youthful face topped by wild curly hair. He looks like a professor and thinks like the physicist-turned-administrator that he is. For nine years he has been one of my closest colleagues. Our discussion topic: how to build the center.

The costs are an astronomical $20 million—$12 million for the center itself, $4 million for a mandatory parking garage, and $4 million for an adjunct services building. The last, which will include stores, will be self-financing, as will be about half the cost of the garage from parking fees. But we still need $14 million. To date, we have obtained $4 million in pledges; thus, we have $10 million to go.

To get it, we need support from many people, including the students, alums, and others who complain loudly that we do not have the center yet give virtually nothing themselves. Truth is, however, that one donor with $5 million will make it possible. That person must be joined by others in the $100,000 to $1 million range. When it is finished, fewer than two dozen people will have provided 80 percent of the funding.

But where can we find these critical supporters—and especially the single big one? For two hours, Don and I plan our next efforts. Of our vital two dozen, so far we can name only two or three and certainly not the large one. Where can we find them? And how fast? The campus cry to end this four-decade-long need has reached a crescendo. We hear it and join it. But where are the donors?

Frustrated, I leave Don and rush to the WRC studio to be a guest on a radio talk show. Interviewer Joel Spivak introduces me by saying that I am the president of AU and also an astronomer. Our topic today is the space shuttle. Repeatedly, he asks why anyone would want to support it. The discussion is lively. But what is the subject? He roams from the space shuttle to the newly discovered "galaxy." As the show progresses, I realize that he does not understand the difference between a solar system and a galaxy. Such misunderstandings about political science, say, would be embarrassing. But the public's knowledge about science is so poor that any blunder is socially acceptable. Meeting me for the first time, Washingtonians often ask: "Oh, you're an astronomer. I was born in June. What's my horoscope?" Once when I did a national TV show in Canada, the host told me during a break, "When we return, we'll have only a moment left. Be brief." The show resumed and he said: "Please explain for us the origin of the universe." All in sixty seconds.

After a commercial break, Spivak remarks that many AU alumni would like to know when our sports and convocation center will be built. What, I wonder, does this have to do with the space shuttle? I tell him we have made progress; the project now looks promising. There are several seconds of silence—a rare thing on radio—and then he says I have not given him the exact date when the center will be built. All of this live, of course.

I appear on such shows because they generate visability for AU. That in turn helps us with student applications, alumni support, and job opportunities for our graduates. Hence, it is in the university's best interest. But is it in mine?

WEDNESDAY, AUGUST 31
Shortly after noon, standing in an open amphitheater, I welcome the freshmen and their parents to the university. Of the many talks I give each year, this one is special. For the freshmen, it is an introduction to the university; for the parents, it is a time to let go.

I begin by introducing my wife, Gail, and our twelve-year-old daughter, Natasha. Then I address the young men. "Let me warn you about something. Last year, Gail was eating a hamburger by herself in the student dining room. A young man came up and sat down next to her. 'My name is John,' he said. 'What's yours?'

"She told him and he said, 'Look, Gail, if I can have your number, maybe we can get together some time.'

" 'That wouldn't be a good idea,' Gail replied.

" 'Why, are you married?'

" 'Yes, I am.'

" 'That's all right.'

" 'No, I don't think so.' Gail shook her head.

" 'Is your husband around?'

" 'He works at AU.'

" 'Is he a professor?'

" 'Yes . . . and the president.'

"At that point the young man said, 'Did I tell you my last name?'

" 'No.'

" 'Thank God!' he exclaimed, running from the dining room."

Gail blushes, the audience roars, and I wait five seconds.

"Students," I continue, "develop a sense of humor about yourselves, a sense of humanity about others, a sense of history and your place in it, and, finally, a sense of humility."

And I tell them about a radio show I was on in 1970, when I was a professor at Boston University. As an astronomer, I was to describe the birth of the universe and the formation of earth; as a biochemist, Isaac Asimov was to describe biological evolution. To make the show more lively, the producer had students interview us. Everything went well until there was only about a minute left. The student interviewers exchanged knowing glances and then asked: "Dr. Asimov, what do you think about the warnings we young people get about mind-expanding drugs? Are they valid or just scare tactics?"

Aside from being a prolific writer, Isaac is an iconoclast, who takes contrary views on many things. No doubt the students expected him to do so about drugs. His reply surprised us all.

"Of the things I own, perhaps the most delicate is this fine Swiss watch," he began, as he held up his wristwatch. "And it was expensive."

I wondered where he was going with this. And so did the students, as they frowned. Seconds ticked by.

"Do you know what's even more precise, complex, and valuable to me than this watch?" Isaac went on. "It's my brain. Now, I wouldn't smash my watch against a tree just to make it tick funny, and I'm not about to pump drugs into myself just to make my brain tick funny."

Click! The show ended. The stunned interviewers had no chance to rebut.

I tell our students today: "There's a moral here. If you're tempted to take drugs, just bang your head against a tree. You'll get the same result and save the money.

"Parents," I go on, "do not be embarrassed if you feel a tug today or if you call your son or daughter a few days from now. That's to be expected. It's as it should be. Cut the cord, but keep the connection; let the child go, but keep the tie of love."

At least a dozen handkerchiefs come out, as parents and children clasp hands. In our jaded world, these youngsters might not want others to know their sentimentality, yet it is real and visible. A few months from now, they may think they know how to run the university, the nation, and the world. Everything prior to their arrival was incompetent, some of them will say. But today they abound in humility and family affection. I close by welcoming them "home."

Afterwards, we form a receiving line on the campus quadrangle. Several hundred students and parents file by. They shake our hands and tell us about their hometowns and their hopes. True excitement lights students' eyes. And the parents look proud and anxious simultaneously. A golden moment, this afternoon is one of the reasons I find academic life so rewarding.

THURSDAY, SEPTEMBER 1

The university's top administrators and I meet to review the opening of the term, a possible pay increase for employees in January, and many other issues. The most unusual concerns a single student. Rarely do we focus on individuals during these meetings, but this one is exceptional: an outspoken, charismatic black student leader with financial and academic problems. If his grades are too low, he cannot serve in any student organization. The rules apply to everyone. Yet if we ask him to resign, it could be traumatic for him. We want to help him, not oust him. For an hour, we try to determine how best to do so. No matter what we do, the student or the news media may claim that we are discriminating against him. The meeting ends with the issue unresolved.

Andy Sherman, the head of the student lecture series this year, is my next appointment. He tells me that he is thinking about asking Walter Mondale, Jesse Jackson, and Petra Kelly, the head of the West German Green Party, to appear at AU. At many East Coast universities, liberal speakers are popular; conservatives are condoned. Nonetheless, Andy plans to have a balanced program. If Petra Kelly comes, I note, we may lose contributions. But academic freedom is strong at AU and we will ride out any storm. He looks pleased to hear that.

After Andy leaves, I return calls and wade through mail. As I dash out the door finally to have lunch—at 4:00 P.M.—and get a haircut, Joan Leach, my secretary/assistant, tells me that "the strange caller" has been at it again. While I was on the radio show the day before yesterday, he called to declare that Spivak and I are insane, that we were defying God's will, and that science is rubbish.

FRIDAY, SEPTEMBER 2

I begin the day by meeting with the provost, Milt Greenberg, and the two vice-presidents, Don Myers and Don Triezenberg. Talented and dedicated, they aid me enormously. Our intense discussion today ranges from the current budget to long-term plans. We schedule meetings for the board of trustee's committees, review personnel matters, and conclude that this academic year is starting extremely well —in contrast with last year, when an unexpected enrollment drop torpedoed our budget and plummeted campus morale. Like most private universities, especially ones with small endowments, AU depends heavily upon tuition for revenue.

Then I sort my mail. Intermingled with two job applications, an invitation for me to speak, and a complaint about the university is a letter from Paul Volcker, chairman of the Federal Reserve. He agrees to address our winter commencement in January 1984. Long ago someone told me to use opportunities because they will not come my way often. So it was that I happened to be waiting at LaGuardia Airport in New York to board the shuttle to Washington when, above the crowd, I spotted Volcker's domed head and ever-present cigar. Pushing aside my reticence, I told him that I admired his achievements. He thanked me and we had a delightful conversation about the economics of higher education. As we entered the plane, I asked him to be our commencement speaker. Naturally, he could not make a commitment that far in advance without checking his calendar. A few days later, I bumped into him again at a White House function. Soon thereafter, our board authorized awarding him an honorary doctor's degree. I wrote to him and today I received his acceptance.

This evening is family time: Natasha's twelfth birthday party. On her actual birth date, July 20th, her friends were out of town. They can come tonight, and what a delightful group they are. Not quite girls, yet not quite women, they still play while wondering about the ways of the world.

Gail and I drive them to two of Natasha's favorite places—a pizza parlor, followed by a bookstore. When we return home, the girls roast marshmallows and then bundle into sleeping bags. As an adventure, they are going to sleep outside. Our fenced backyard seems secure. Still, Gail and I worry. Fortunately, so do the girls. By 10:30 P.M. they are inside.

SATURDAY, SEPTEMBER 3

On this day with a blue sky, soft breeze, and low humidity, we hold our annual barbecue for entering students. Gail, Natasha, and I join Milt and his wife, Sonia, in serving on the food line. The freshmen are startled, then delighted, to see us here. An upperclassman passes me, beams, and says, "Hi, Prez." When I took this job, I assumed it would be dignified, like Ronald Colman with elbow patches. It is—but with a human touch, too.

Soon we rush home to change clothes and drive to Potomac, Maryland, where we attend a surprise birthday party for Sondra Bender, a supportive trustee and a driving force to build the sports and convocation center. Though she is fifty, she looks thirty-five, with a broad smile and youthful figure. The party, done with style and taste, is set in an expansive backyard. The Benders are Jewish, as are most of the guests. And as the orchestra strikes up "Hava Nagila," I think what a special heritage they have. As soon as they hear the first notes, everyone—from the youngest to the oldest—breaks into smiles and leaps up to dance. The sense of family and bonding is profound. In the cynical 1960s, many people thought traditions were outmoded. But they were not then and they are not now.

After chatting with several trustees, Gail and I drive home to change clothes again and join students at their late-night dance. Another opening-of-the-term event, it is wondrous, with perfect weather and a grand mood. Held in a parking lot, the dance's ambience is less than romantic. But the freshmen do not care. For them, this is the "great beginning." And they are excited.

In due course the inevitable happens: a boy nervously asks Gail to dance and an equally jittery girl asks me. We join the hopping, clapping throng through a seemingly unending rock piece. If someone had announced that tonight's event was to be an aerobic exercise, no student would have attended. Call it a dance and hundreds appear. As we gyrate to and fro, I shout to my partner: "You are a good dancer." The girl, whom I presume is a freshman, smiles and says, "Well, my father taught me. He was born way back in the forties, so he knows all about dancing." Way back in the forties! And he can still walk? Gail and I hobble home.

SUNDAY, SEPTEMBER 4

Months ago I was invited to speak at the forty-first International Science Fiction Convention in Baltimore, Maryland. I would have declined, but I thought Natasha might find this an eye-popping experience. So this afternoon we drive to Baltimore. As we enter the convention center, we pass several dozen Darth Vaders, numerous Princess Leias, a few Wookies, a Tarzan, an orange woman, and a teenage girl wearing a fur bikini. As I head to the podium, I wonder if my talk on the scientific search for extraterrestrial life will go over well. The audience, though, responds enthusiastically.

Afterwards we go to the vending area, which is filled with stalls selling a bewildering array of items—posters and photos from science fiction movies; swords and clubs; clothing out of *Star Wars;* buttons espousing every imaginable cause. As we leave, Natasha sums up the day: "I'd like a button that says, 'I represent normal earthlings.' "

Is My Armor Straight?

TUESDAY, SEPTEMBER 6

This morning I meet with Nouha Alhegelan, wife of the ambassador of Saudi Arabia. A brilliant and beautiful woman, she is a lawyer and public speaker. Also she has been a leader on the Washington social scene and has helped several philanthropies. Last year, she became a trustee at AU.

Before she was elected to the board, the trustees had wondered: Could she help us secure Arab money? Arab students? On the other hand, might her being on the board disturb other supporters? The board, a self-perpetuating body that elects its own members, ultimately voted: unanimous. And this was a prudent decision, for she has helped AU substantially.

My meeting with Nouha this morning is sad. Some months ago, she was stricken by a mysterious ailment. Despite repeated tests, no one can find its cause. In addition, her husband has been assigned to another diplomatic post. As we talk in her living room, the house remains but its charm is gone. The embassy belongs to the home country, but the items that make the house a home belong to the ambassador. The Alhegelans have packed to leave. As Nouha tells me she must resign from the board, I think back to the last gala I attended here. Today the house is empty and cold.

When I return to my office, I indulge in cake and ice cream: today is my forty-fifth birthday. My staff has prepared a luncheon and some two dozen administrators stop by. A fine and talented group, they dedicate themselves to the university—even enough to attend this ritual.

This afternoon I must fly to New York because I give an address early tomorrow morning in New Jersey. A friend has insisted that I stay as his guest at the Helmsley Palace Hotel. With magnificent common rooms, the Palace deserves its name. But as I sit alone at dinner and later look out my window across Saint Patrick's Cathedral, I remember that what counts is not where you are but whom you are with. I call Gail and Natasha and try unsuccessfully to reach my twenty-six-year-old daughter, Deborah, who works in Dallas.

WEDNESDAY, SEPTEMBER 7

Up at six o'clock, I walk to the Avis office, pick up my rental car, and head to Woodbridge Senior High School in New Jersey. Nowhere is interest in education greater than in New Jersey. On this first day of school, I have been invited to give the keynote address to some twelve hundred teachers. The hot, humid air hangs over the auditorium. Despite the heat and despite how teachers feel put-upon by outside critics, they are vibrant and optimistic. I tell them that although much of the criticism is justified, the root problems of U.S. education go deeper than just teachers—they lie in the home and in our national sense of values. When a profession becomes a job, when living for today towers over preparing for tomorrow, the foundation for self-respect deteriorates. What is needed—not just in education but in all American life—is a rededication to an individual, institutional, and even national sense of pride.

Back in Washington again, I rush home and shower. Then I put on television makeup. Network shows provide makeup artists, but local ones often do not and tonight I am to tape a program locally. With powder on my pants and rouge on my tie, I remember how easy the makeup salesman promised it would be. And I remember my experience after taping the "David Susskind Show" a few years ago. I decided to walk back to my Manhattan hotel. At the first stoplight a man eyed me and said: "Hi. Can I buy you a drink?" At another stoplight, a different man invited me to his hotel. Then I remembered my makeup. And people claim New York is not friendly.

THURSDAY, SEPTEMBER 8

I leave home early for the U.S. Chamber of Commerce headquarters to be on "Ask Washington," a call-in interview show on cable TV at 9:00 A.M. Although I have long made some radio and television appearances, the recent excitement over education has increased greatly the number I do now. With Foxhall Road jammed, I nervously creep in the traffic, finally arriving at 8:59. Bounding two steps at a time to the studio, I drop in my seat just as the show begins. The topics hop from cosmology to educational standards to the role of parents to the impact of TV on children to the need for positive female role models. Last year I cohosted a similar call-in show over C–Span cable TV. It, too, was remarkably lively, although it was watched, I believe, only by bedridden people who were unable to change channels. ("Nurse, get him off. I want the game show, not this dull guy.")

While gulping down a hamburger at my desk, I read the mail and dictate letters. Then the calls start, three arriving simultaneously. Later, I meet with the uncle of Climis Lascaris, a new trustee. The uncle—an elderly immigrant from Greece—is a prosperous, self-made man of deep convictions and strong ethnic pride. We discuss revising his will to endow scholarships for deserving Greeks. "We must give back to the world," he says. His accent is thick, but his message is clear.

FRIDAY, SEPTEMBER 9

The morning evaporates rapidly, as Milt, the Dons, and I study the enrollment data, which are excellent. But the early numbers last year were so misleading that we are reluctant to celebrate until we have final figures. Watching fall enrollments is like watching election returns—except our count takes weeks.

Also, I review possible committee assignments for trustees. In the past two years, I have brought several new members onto the board. And some of our wealthiest trustees have served on boards before. Consequently, they may not take their role as seriously as the younger and less-established members. Also, able people are in great demand; they become exorbitantly busy. We cannot call upon our most helpful people too often.

At noon, Doug Lewis, president of the Wesley Theological Seminary, meets me at my office and we walk to the faculty dining room for lunch. Located adjacent to AU, the seminary is independent from us but both institutions were founded by the Methodist church and have parallel heritages. Like AU, Wesley has no tradition of major financial support. A Methodist bishop jokingly once told me: "Fundraising from Methodists will be hard. This is the religion for the common man. When a Methodist becomes wealthy, he converts to being an Episcopalian."

As we enter the dining room, some faculty members go out of their way to say hello; others pretend not to notice me. Doug and I go down the cafeteria line and find a quiet table. Many professors smile and wave across the room, while others stop to say how excited they are about the new term.

Even though Wesley and AU are different—Wesley being far smaller and offering only graduate-level theological studies—Doug and I have enough in common that we understand each other instantly. An experienced academician once observed that the only people with whom a university president can converse fully are other university presidents. Only they fully understand the yarn about a university president who died and went to hell. His students were not surprised, his faculty had predicted it, and his trustees had arranged it. Worst, he was there a term before he realized he was not on campus.

A university president has great responsibility with relatively little authority. Many people in higher education want other people's authority but not their responsibility. On a campus, personnel matters involve elaborate safeguards; budget decisions require concensus-building. And a university president must defend his actions before an army of critics.

A university president has scant professional privacy. An unlisted home phone is the extent of mine. My staff consists of Joan Leach and Roberta Goldstein, a part-time typist. There are no executive assistants, speech writers, or advisors, which is how I like it. Fortunately, Joan devotes the time and effort of two people. Such devotion is as helpful as it is rare. Still, that is the extent of my office.

Petite Joan ably screens callers and appointment-makers. But persistent people can reach me. As Doug and I walk from the dining room to my office, two professors and three students stop us. Two of them had wanted to see me in my office but Joan, correctly, had referred them elsewhere. They were determined to see me and they did.

I enjoy my luncheon with Doug. We understand each other's jobs and I do not have to be on guard with him. When presidents of two competitive universities meet, the polite non-speak is deafening. Cordial to a fault, each praises the other while quietly boasting about how well things are going on his own campus. In July 1982, as our enrollment projections fell, I asked other university heads about their trends. "Fine," they replied. Come September 1982, AU's enrollment was down almost 5 percent. I wondered why we were alone. Then national data emerged: many private universities were down 3 to 6 percent.

After lunch, I confront the classic problem: how to be several places simultaneously. A few days ago, a student urged me to be visible on campus. At lunch today a professor said, "I hope we'll be able to talk to you often this year." Now I am supposed to speak in Washington and New Jersey on the same day. A TV show invites me for the same time I have a faculty lunch. The best dates for board committee meetings conflict with luncheons with donors.

Gail calls. Natasha has just returned from her first paying job: She delivered four hundred *Northwest Current* newspapers to dorms and offices. In order to follow university regulations about distributing publications, she spoke to officials who gave her permission, showed her a map, and suggested a route. She comes home today, Gail tells me, covered with news print and pride.

I hang up and rush to a reception for Carmen Neuberger. Born in the Philippines, she obtained her doctorate in the U.S. She is married, has six daughters, and looks ten years younger than she is. Now she holds the responsible position of dean of students. Today's fete is to honor her on recently earning a law degree. She's a superb role model for students. I arrive at the reception as vice-provost for student life, Bruce Poynter, proposes a toast. Upon seeing me, he stops and asks if I would like to make a speech, which brings forth a chorus of boos.

Next on my schedule is a reception to honor black students. AU is one of the most pluralistic universities in America, with students from the District of Columbia, all 50 states, and more than 130 nations. Our student body comprises every major ethnic and religious group. And we have a higher percentage of minority students than any other private university in this part of the U.S.

I am proud of this diversity. Any institution with a name as presumptuous as ours—The American University—should reflect the character of America itself. But we're concerned that the number of black students entering AU may decline. As the cost of education has risen faster than the Consumer Price Index, lower-income students have been unable to matriculate at private universities. On a per capita basis, we award more financial aid to black students than to white. Still, our scholarship funds are limited.

Because this is the first time we have held such a meeting, I wonder how it will go. Will the students be angry? Will they accuse us of not trying hard enough to recruit blacks?

Initially, they eye me nervously, but their mood is warm. As I move about the room, I am struck by how much they appreciate this event. Gail and Natasha join me at the reception. One of our black professors arrives with his thirteen-year-old daughter. When I introduce the two girls, they almost hug each other, they are so delighted to find someone their own age. Meanwhile, Gail tries to talk with every student individually. Soon the room buzzes with conversation and laughter. This is a joyous occasion and I am delighted we held it.

By 7:30 P.M., Gail and I are to be at the Wolf Trap Park Farm for the Performing Arts in suburban Virginia for the annual end-of-the-season gala. Gail looks stunning in a daring, off-the-shoulder evening gown. Normally, she is reluctant to wear it; a university president's wife ought to look demure. Tonight, however, she is convinced that it will pass the censors.

Some months ago, Wolf Trap's main facility burned to the ground. Now it is being rebuilt, and tonight's function will be held under a large, elaborately decorated tent. As one of the major art centers in the Washington area, Wolf Trap attracts cultural, political, and civic leaders. The cachet of the arts is so great that almost everyone wants to be involved. Gail and I are friends of Kay Shouse, the founder of Wolf Trap. So we attend tonight out of respect for Kay, now eighty-nine years old.

As we enter the reception area, I remind myself to go through the Washington ritual of cheek kissing. I never understand if it should be one cheek or two; I do know to make it the right cheek first. When I started attending such functions, I forgot the latter and accidentally pecked women on the nose or chin. Are such matters discussed in Emily Post? Or in *The Joy Of Sex*? Of the first seven women I meet tonight, two are one-sided kissers, three are two-sided kissers, one wants to shake hands, and one is an air kisser—that is, she kisses the air just behind my right ear. I have no idea why this constitutes a refined way to greet one another. But as I look around the crowded tent, dozens of other couples are going through the same ritual.

As we make our way to Kay Shouse's table, I hear a robust "Hi, Dick," coming from Bob Schieffer, the CBS newscaster. He has lost so much weight that I scarcely recognize him. "Have you been on Mike Deaver's diet?" I ask.

"No," Bob replies. "I'm using Jane Fonda's."

He can lie on the floor with legwarmers all he wants, but he will never look like her.

Tonight's seating arrangement does not comply with normal Washington protocol: wives and husbands are placed at the same table and even beside one another. The customary boy-girl rotation remains nonetheless. Gail is seated next to Alex Trowbridge, head of the National Association of Manufacturers. We have not met before and I am impressed by him. Distinguished and dapper, he is remarkably informative. Furthermore, I discover that his father used to be a professor at AU. We shall invite the Trowbridges to our home and Gail will ask Mrs. Trowbridge to one of her functions.

A few years ago Gail made a simple yet profound discovery: in

Washington there are extraordinarily powerful women, some known in their own right and others known by virtue of their husbands. She has striven to nurture this women's network. This is but one way to try to bond AU with Washington.

A university should stimulate the intellectual and cultural life of its community; conversely, it should draw upon talent in its community. AU's community is one of the most exceptional in the world— the capital city of the United States. Gail and I attempt to link AU with Washington so that it can take full advantage of the city's resources. And the greatest of those is the people.

What attracted me to AU initially was that it could become what it had been founded to be—a great national university that would use fully the opportunities of the capital. We work constantly to make that happen. I attempt to interest leaders in Washington and elsewhere in joining our advisory boards. I attempt to bring prominent speakers to campus and to provide entree for our students and faculty to influential people in their fields.

But to do so, Gail and I must seek out influential people and bring them into the university's widening circle of friends. To do that requires dramatically more social life than either of us had expected or wanted. Yet, it is part of the job—in Washington, a vital part.

And Gail attempts to bring AU to the attention of key people by having professors speak at our home to Washington groups. The professors come from diverse fields, such as Allan Lichtman in history, James Fyfe in justice, and Doris Hadary in chemistry. Also, Gail brings non-Washingtonians into the mix, with such varied speakers as Page Rense, the editor-in-chief of *Architectural Digest,* and Ann Landers, the columnist.

This is just one way that Gail is invaluable to me. When I became president, she was a curriculum coordinator at Georgetown Day School, where Natasha attends. On her own, Gail decided to resign so she could help me and the university. Since then she has arranged countless receptions and is involved in numerous support activities. For example, she chaired a committee that awards scholarships to promising poets. She has obtained job contacts for students. And she introduced a professor to the U.S. chief of protocol, who was so impressed by his research that she took him to the White House.

Someone once remarked: "Every speech is too long and every dance floor is too small." Unfortunately, that's true tonight. The theme for the evening is New Orleans. And as the band strikes up

"The Saints Go Marching In," we go slipping out. After we dash home and change into casual clothes, we attend another student dance. It is loud, but we enjoy it.

SATURDAY, SEPTEMBER 10

Crisis has hit the Berendzen household: Natasha's chameleon is sick. Or so she claims. With a chameleon, how can you tell? It does seem sluggish, but maybe it is hungry. So we crawl about the backyard searching for insects. The yard is visible from a dorm, and I wonder if students are watching us and taking bets on what the president is up to now. I ask Natasha why she cannot get a vegetarian lizard or one that eats from the table. "Really, Daddy," she replies. "Don't you know anything about reptiles?" The truth is that I don't. I understand people pretty well, but the rest baffles me. Sometimes people do, too.

This evening I attend a reception at the home of Bob Cleary, dean of the College of Public and International Affairs. He has been here for years—as dean, provost, and, briefly, as acting president. An able administrator, his institutional memory is without peer.

Bob's reception honors Rita Simon, the new dean of our School of Justice, who comes with impressive credentials. Over punch, a professor tells me with satisfaction that he has sold twenty thousand copies of his book. "See how much visibility I've given AU," he boasts. As I congratulate him, a secretary tugs at my sleeve. "I hear the fall enrollments look good. When do I get my raise and how big will it be?"

Last winter, as we struggled with our finances, we decided not to give a traditional salary increase on July 1. Instead, we would decide if a pay hike were feasible after registration in the fall. The way universities set budgets is illogical. In the spring, they announce salary increases and issue contracts starting in mid-summer; yet they are dependent on tuition, so they do not know their income until they know fall enrollments in October. Thus they commit dollars they do not yet have.

The employees understood why we delayed the increase, but that did not help pay their bills. We promised last spring that if our enrollments were up this fall, we would give a 4 percent raise in January 1984. But most employees have forgotten that if the enrollments are not up this September, there will be no increase. The secretary assumes it will occur. Repeatedly, she asks: "When will I know how large the raise will be?" A professor and another staff member ask the same thing. Academics may be less concerned with money than some people, but they, too, live in the real world.

At ten o'clock I return to my office and work for an hour or so before walking the campus. I chat with several students, all of whom are ebullient on this balmy Saturday night. All, that is, except one. He looks so forlorn that I ask, "How're you doing?"

"OK, I guess."

"No better than that?"

"Everybody's very nice but . . . I don't know . . . I just feel sort of . . ."

"Homesick?"

"No, just . . . well, maybe it's being homesick . . . I've never really been on my own before."

"What you're feeling is absolutely natural. Everyone feels it sometime. Don't worry, though; it'll pass."

I go on: "Have you gotten to know many other students yet?"

"A few, but it takes me awhile."

"There's nothing wrong with that," I point out. "Just give it a few more days."

"I guess. Anyway, thanks for your interest."

"Not at all. If you've got a minute more, I'll tell you about my first day as an undergrad at MIT."

As we sit together on a park bench by Bender Library, I wonder if my little story will perk him up. Last year, I told it at Freshman Day in the amphitheater. This year, I forgot it.

"When I arrived at MIT," I begin, "I found myself surrounded by students from top prep schools and by professors of international renown. I was from a fairly humble background in East Dallas. While the more cosmopolitan students carried green book-bags and wore jeans, I had a vinyl briefcase and a polyester suit; I resembled an awning salesman. Nonetheless, I was determined not to be intimidated or to let my nervousness show.

"As I wandered the labyrinthian corridors, I became totally disoriented. Ultimately, I came to the end of a long hallway filled with professors and other awesome-looking persons. It seemed they all were staring at me. Determined to display self-confidence, I chose an important-looking door with no name on it, knocked, and entered—and found I was in a janitor's closet!

"As I shut the door, I was sure I heard at least a thousand people bursting with laughter. There I stood in the closet—humiliated—in semidarkness, surrounded by buckets, mops, and brooms. I tried to think what a young Jefferson or Einstein would have done under the circumstances, but I concluded that a young Jefferson or Einstein or anyone else sensible wouldn't have gotten himself into such a ridiculous situation. I just stood there for what seemed like weeks, hoping I could escape in private, when a terrifying thought struck me: 'What if I wait in the closet too long and they come to see if I'm okay or if I've committed suicide?' After all, a well-balanced person wouldn't spend his day in a janitor's closet.

"Finally, I decided to rejoin the world outside. But I resolved to do so with dignity. I opened the door confidently; I surveyed the pails, the soap, the rags; and I gave the entire scene a wise, knowing nod. As I turned around, a dozen people were staring at me, uncertain whether I was a well-groomed custodian, a lost student, or a weird prodigy. I figured I'd leave them guessing, so I said to no one in particular: 'All's well here. You may continue now.'

"In that brief afternoon, I taught myself modesty, resourcefulness, and never to enter an unmarked door."

The young man, who has stared at me wide-eyed, laughs loudly.

SUNDAY, SEPTEMBER 11
Our guests—the university's administrators, key staff members, and faculty leaders—arrive for an eleven o'clock brunch. For many, this will be the first time to get together since spring. Most disperse through the house, talking with each other and inspecting our artifacts.

Since I was a graduate student, Gail and I have collected an eclectic assortment of things, primarily from the Middle East and the Orient. They include a nineteenth-century dragon chair from China, a number of Oriental wall hangings and rugs, and a dark, heavily carved antique desk from Japan. No one reacts neutrally to the desk; people love it or hate it. Gail's mother says that if we have a fire, the first thing to remove is Natasha and the last thing is the desk.

When I lived in Boston, I became intrigued with Oriental rugs. Aside from their durability and worth, they are genuine art objects. They encapsulate myths and legends; they are keys to understanding the Middle East. They constitute frozen time.

From my astronomical background, I have an obsession with the concept of time—the most baffling, profound idea ever embraced. We make time, take time, use time, waste time, spend time, discuss time, but never understand time. Only Asians genuinely try. Japanese silk-screens and Chinese prints, for example, freeze time in their symbolic metaphors. To weave a silk rug with hundreds of knots per square centimeter requires an enormous investment of time. The theme of our belongings is not so much diversity as it is encapsulation of time and respect for tranquility.

In a hectic, workaday world, what I wish at home is peace. And that is what I have—from my family and from my surroundings. In our entrance hall, a Burmese Buddha greets visitors and exudes peace. The two ends of the dining room are flanked by statues of a Buddhist monk and the Chinese goddess Qua Lin.

While our guests wander about staring at the objects, telling others how much they admire them, they probably think to themselves: "What junk!" Unfortunately, most do not know what they are seeing. One small object is overlooked by all. Approximately one hundred years old, it is a wooden book made in an accordian style on the island of Sumatra. It contains a witch doctor's magic incantations. If students become too restive, I will have it translated.

On our mantlepiece sits an inconspicuous stone that goes unnoticed by almost everyone, but its hidden secrets enchant the mind. Eons ago, young molten earth errupted in volcanic explosions, spewing forth water and gas. Some of that material solidified into bubbles, trapped forever inside rocks. Rough and ugly, they scarcely catch your eye—that is, until one is carefully planed by a minerologist, ultimately leaving a thin, transparent piece of the stone through which you can see the liquid inside. With our stone, you hold in your hand some of the early liquid and atmosphere of the planet—an artifact against which even Greek antiquities pale.

And the carpets contain wondrous tales for those who know how to read them. My own study of these rugs has led me into strange circumstances. In the late 1970s, I traveled to Iran frequently. On one visit, I toured the famous rug shops on Ferdouzi Avenue in Tehran. Casually, I mentioned the cosmological symbolism in a rug's motif to a merchant there. He was so fascinated that he called out to several of his friends. Within minutes, dozens of rug dealers assembled, coming from blocks away, to hear this American expound on their nation's most famous handicraft. The crowd grew so large that I had to climb to the top of a mound of rugs to be seen and heard. Never have I been less comfortable before an audience; this group knew infinitely more about the rugs than I did. But they knew little about the astronomical myths woven into the patterns. When I finished, they applauded enthusiastically, even though most of them probably did not understand a word. Humble merchants, they largely spoke only Farsi.

Some months later, the press said that Ayatollah Khomeini's most vigorous support came from the bazaar. Could it be that the simple men I met that day were among his zealots?

Of the items in our home, two attract the attention of all first-time guests: Gail's spectacular aquarium and my medieval suit of armor. The aquarium fascinates everyone because it is large and its fish are rare. And the suit of armor, looming at the end of the entrance hall, is the fulfillment of one of my childhood fantasies. We secured it from Spain years ago, and now it is a member of our family. As an infant, Natasha named it Tin Man after the character in *The Wizard of Oz*. That is what we still call him.

In 1974, I came to AU as dean of the College of Arts and Sciences. Wanting to create a major national university overnight, I attempted to raise standards and expectations for the faculty. After I had turned down several promotions and applications for tenure, the faculty in one department grumbled and said they wanted to meet the brash young dean. I agreed to meet them in a conference room. Most had never seen me before. Before the meeting began, my assistant said: "The dean will join you and attempt to defend himself." Then I lumbered through the door wearing my suit of armor. Fortunately, the startled professors took my prank with humor. What they did not know was that I had put on the sixty-pound suit too early. To wait, I had sat down in my office chair, a recliner. In an instant I found myself staring at the ceiling, calling frantically for help, my voice echoing inside the steel helmet.

Having toured the house, the guests gather for brunch. Gail and I don aprons and I wear a tall chef's hat, undoubtedly looking foolish, as I cook blintzes. The symbolism of our serving, however, is lost on no one. And they even seem to enjoy the food.

This evening we notice that a nearby fraternity is having a barbecue. So we decide to attend. AU has only three frat houses. But in the past they often have been in trouble because of neighbors' complaints about noise. As my family and I walk into the barbecue area, all conversation stops. Like explorers from alien planets meeting for the first time, they gawk at me, wondering if I am there to chastise them. Instead, I ask the female guests if the fraternity brothers are good cooks. They grin and relax. We wish them well and leave.

Although Greek life does not appeal to me, I realize how important it is. Many benefit from it and a number of our Greek organizations provide valuable community service. And the last thing an adolescent wants to hear is: "When I was your age . . . ," so I refrain from saying it. I cannot help but think it. When I was their age, I worked twenty hours a week to support myself and my daughter, Deborah, while majoring in physics. There was no time to party and scarcely time to sleep.

Our dinner tonight is the annual gala for the Weizmann Institute of Science in Israel, one of the world's great research centers. It deserves support. Trustee Stuart Bernstein seats us across from the son of the host, Albert Abramson. A highly successful developer, Abramson is a philanthropist, too. Moreover, I discover he is an astronomy afficionado, and I hope to interest him in becoming a trustee.

Tonight, I am barraged with questions. Politics to archaeology, monetary policy to chamber music, quantum physics to existentialist philosophy—all presumably lie within my compass. A university president supposedly knows everything about his institution. Indeed, he supposedly knows everything. Proper credentials for someone who wants to improve a university quickly are not so much scholarly publications or teaching awards as social graces and general knowledge. Am I up on world affairs? Can I speak French? Am I a gourmet? How is my tennis? Can I dance well—ballroom or disco? What do I know about museums in London and Madrid? I have scores of conversations like this. A potential benefactor may dismiss me and therefore the university if I cannot maintain an informed discussion on whatever his favorite subject may be. But how can I possibly be up on such things? Constantly, I feel like a student the day before exams.

This constitutes a splendid stimulus for lifelong learning. And it reminds me that the beginning of wisdom comes not in knowing the answers, but in recognizing the questions. However much we learn, we always have more to discover. I also realize that the primary role of an educator is to educate; the university president should be first among peers. Certainly, my unrelenting responsibility is to raise money and increase institutional visibility. But at heart, it is to educate. Like all teachers, I must study and I must teach. The difference is that my students are not in a classroom; instead, they include faculty and staff, trustees and dinner companions, and, of course, myself.

MONDAY, SEPTEMBER 12

Double tragedy strikes: this is Natasha's first day of school and her chameleon has died. She rushes out to bury it in a L'eggs container and then heads to school.

I have breakfast with Rudy Maxa, a reporter with the *Washingtonian,* who is preparing a story about computers. I tell him that through direct and indirect signals our society tells girls that math, science, and computers are not for them. Subtly, we say: "Boys, study computers and math. You can do it. Girls, you don't really care about that." The female image from TV, movies, magazines: soft, gentle, subjective. The male image: precise, sharp, analytical. The female writes the poems or sings the songs; the male figures out new technology. The result of this mind set: Half our nation is losing opportunities for worthwhile, high-tech careers.

Obligingly, Gail and I took Natasha to see *WarGames,* in which a high school boy breaks into a secret military computer and almost starts World War III. Although an underachiever, he is a genius, far smarter than most of the adults in the film. The main female role is a girl who is baffled by computers. She is just his companion. That is one of the signals I mean.

Even with computer games, boys are dominant—except in our household. Recently, Natasha challenged me to a video game. I accepted, tried my best, and achieved a score of 940. Her score was 117,000. That's humiliating! She gave me a handicap, but still beat me. I had her play lefthanded, but she still beat me. Like me, she is nearsighted—so I made her play without glasses. I know that is cruel, but the world is cruel. Where better to learn that than at home? Even using her left hand and without glasses, she trounced me. Clearly, no one over twenty-five should play anyone under fifteen on one of these games.

Back at my office, I make calls, dictate letters, and read mail: an angry letter from an AU parent, an encouraging one from a corporation about a proposal, a cheery note from a trustee, and thirty-one other items. I then deal with two legal cases and outline a forthcoming speech before rushing downtown to the historic F Street Club. After Reagan had been elected but before he was inaugurated, he invited

two dozen Washingtonians to a dinner there. Gail and I were surprised and honored to be included. Some of the guests were Democrats who thought the invitation was a mistake. But it was not. The
charming evening was planned with extraordinary taste. Had the
president-elect chosen the ballroom of a major hotel, he could have
invited five hundred couples; instead, he selected this small, informal
room with only four tables. I talked with Reagan about education,
and he told me briefly but clearly that the federal government should
not intrude into education. He was a newcomer to Washington, he
added, and he wanted to be accepted by our town. He had a real
twinkle in his eye and even partisan Democrats were moved.

Today my schedule will let me stop only briefly at the F Street
Club to wish Ursula Meese a happy birthday. Jim Barrett, a vice-
president of Mutual of Omaha and one of our trustees, has arranged
a luncheon in her behalf. She asked that only a dozen people be
invited. Gail and I are pleased to be among them, along with her
husband, Ed. Here I stand talking to the counselor to the president,
and he seems genuinely interested in my perspectives. His information about the Soviet's downing of the Korean airliner far exceeds
mine; nonetheless, he asks my views and shares his own. Warm and
outgoing, Ursula smiles broadly as she unwraps the AU T-shirt we
have given her. Then I dart to National Airport to catch the shuttle
to New York.

As I cross 57th Street at the Avenue of the Americas, an attractive
young woman does a double take as she passes me. So many people
in Washington whom I do not know by name—students, faculty,
alums—recognize me that I have developed a sappy cordiality towards strangers. At receptions, people will say, "How good to see you
again." And I will reply, "Yes, and how has your summer been?" As
we depart, Gail will ask, "Who was that?" And I will tell the truth:
"I haven't the slightest idea." So when the young woman glances my
way twice and smiles, I say, "Good to see you again."

She frowns: "Have we met before?"

Embarrassed and standing in the middle of the street, I stammer:
"Well, I thought we had."

"Don't leave yet, honey," she says. "Wouldn't you like company?"

Heavens, she is a streetwalker! Well-dressed and professional
looking, she could have been a student or an alumna. Then a second
shock occurs: perhaps she *is* a student somewhere. Well, I reason,

tuition *has* gone up lately. I thank her for her interest, assuming that it is not my money she seeks but my irresistible charm. Before I make it to the curb, she is talking to another "old friend."

Back at my hotel, I call Natasha to find out how her first day at school has gone. She gives it a seven on a scale of ten, which is pretty good. My first days were sheer trauma. I started school in the second grade after being bedridden for three years with asthma and rheumatic fever. The doctors told my parents that if I were to survive, they had to move from Portland, Oregon, to a dry, hot climate. In a splendid example of parental love, they sold their home and business and moved to Dallas, where I improved rapidly and ultimately started school in the second grade. But for years I was convinced the other children were substantially ahead of me; it took me until high school to learn that I could compete. I would have given my first day in seventh grade a two.

TUESDAY, SEPTEMBER 13
At 7:30 this morning I am interviewed over the "Ralph and Ryan Show" on WMCA–AM. The topic is how best to achieve educational excellence. Then I catch a cab to the World Trade Center to tape an interview on CNN–TV. Back in midtown again, I stop at a custom-tie tailor. Few people have heard of custom ties. But they exist and cost no more than a standard tie. Most of all, I enjoy the tailor, a distinguished craftsman from Saville Row. In his eighty years he has become an authority on his trade. In his quiet tenth-story workroom, he is overjoyed to have a visitor and starts to explain about fabrics. But even though I enjoy learning such interesting yet useless information, I have no time. I must catch the shuttle to Washington.

Back at my office, fourteen telephone messages await me, five marked "urgent." After the crisis calls, I return one from Charles Wick, director of the U.S. Information Agency. He explains that his daughter in Australia is interested in our graduate business program, and I agree to mail application material to her.

Then I have several phone conversations with professors—one about a grant, another about the professor's new book, two about ways to improve our curricula. These I deeply enjoy, for the faculty are the heart of the university and teaching and scholarship are why we are here.

As I shave at my desk, Joan fills me in on the calls that came while I was on the other line. A prominent Washingtonian wants to get his son into our law school. I call him back. He hints that if his son gets in, he will give a large donation to AU. Unfortunately, he is vague and the amount sounds low. After all, I have principles! Actually, I refer such inquiries to the law school's faculty admissions committee—without pressure.

Tonight, Milt and I make an unannounced visit to the AU Tavern. Usually, the tavern is quiet while the library is jammed. But, by custom, it is popular late on Tuesday nights. After talking with several students, all of whom are proud about the size and the quality of our freshmen class, Milt and I chat alone for an hour on our building's backsteps.

With a Brooklyn childhood and a University of Wisconsin Ph.D., Milt gracefully blends New York with the Midwest. An astoundingly genial man, he is always upbeat. Over any small incident, he bursts into laughter. In fact, during some somber meetings in my office, waves of laughter cascade through the ceiling from his office directly above. I buzz him on the intercom and say: "Knock it off!" This, of course, elicits more laughter.

The position of provost, as I know from my own experience, is vital at AU. The president is the chief executive officer; the provost is the chief academic officer. An authority on civil liberties, Milt coauthored the highly popular *American Political Dictionary.* At AU, he oversees the academic sector while I oversee it all, with special emphasis on finances, physical plant, fundraising, the trustees, and the university's contacts with the outside community. As next in line to the president, the provost is central to the institution. In Milt, I have a good colleague and friend.

WEDNESDAY, SEPTEMBER 14
I plunge into a two-hour session with Milt, the vice-presidents, the general counsel, and three members of our "self-study" committee. At least once every ten years, universities must be reviewed for academic accreditation by a team of external peers. AU's last evaluation was a decade ago. Since then, we have made enormous progress: SAT scores have come up more than 130 points, a new library has been built, and the student course load has increased by 25 percent. AU remains a private university of about 11,500 students, with undergraduate, graduate, and professional programs that particularly stress Washington-related fields. But qualitatively, AU scarcely resembles its former self. Accreditation should be a breeze; nonethe-

less, we must expect the unexpected. We take the exercise seriously. Our accreditation body—the Middle States Association—will send a team here in January 1984. A key document for its review will be our own appraisal of AU. What should this study include and what should it omit? It should be informative and factual. But how critical? Should we highlight our own weaknesses? Would it be disingenuous if the study were only positive? And how much should we discuss intangibles—happiness, pride, satisfaction. As important as they are, you cannot measure them. On almost every campus, some people say: "My morale is low." It may be, but what would make it higher? How do you calibrate it? How does this affect the institution's ability to reach its objectives?

Some months ago, Milt and I asked Don Dennis, the university librarian, to chair the committee preparing this report, which has produced a voluminous document. Two weeks ago, I distributed it to key administrators and asked them to review it. Back and forth the conversation jumps this morning, with almost every suggestion canceling ones before it. Dennis and his aides take notes to hammer out the final draft.

Greenberg, Myers, Triezenberg, and I then meet privately. "I know final data aren't in, but do we or don't we have a budget surplus?" I ask.

Triezenberg replies, "According to registration data, we should end up with a surplus of a few million dollars."

Myers shakes his head and says, "The controller's figures don't support that. Unexpectedly high expenditures—such as for air conditioning—will nullify much of the increase. The surplus may be modest. We just don't know yet."

Employees, I remind them, want to know about salary increases. "Yes," Triezenberg says, "and the news media do too. What should we say?" We agree to meet on this issue next Tuesday, when the data will be more reliable. With each passing day, the error margin narrows.

At noon I go downtown for a luncheon with Gilbert Grosvenor, president of the National Geographic Society. A receptionist greets me in the lobby, gives me a badge, and ushers me past the guard. As I enter the executive office suite, I am struck by the secretaries' desks: Each has a world globe. Where else would you see that? The walls are covered with photographs from the magazine and the hallway contains archaeological artifacts. The offices themselves are dignified, paneled, and quiet. Everyone is an adult and everyone wears business clothes. What a contrast to a campus.

Although professors' tastes in clothes vary, most seem to prefer studied casualness. While some professors wear suits, many will wear an L. L. Bean shirt, Levis, and hiking boots. And polyester or wool ties abound. In his most famous photographs, Einstein never wore a suit or tie. Somehow the visual image of the intellectual being casual, if not sloppy, has become so inculcated that it is now assumed. To be an academic, you should look the part: Your desk should be cluttered, your room should be stacked with books, your clothes should be clean but not stylish. You should appear so preoccupied with things of the mind that you overlook things of the body.

Gil joins me and we have lunch in his private dining room. Although we discuss cooperation between AU and the Geographic and the possibility of his joining our National Advisory Board (NAB), neither of us has a particular agenda today. Not long ago it dawned on me that I spend most of my life either with students who are younger than my older daughter or with donors who are my father's age. Rarely do I spend time with a contemporary. That is one reason this luncheon is fun.

I rush back to my office, entering just as Joan tells me: "WGST–AM in Atlanta is on the phone. Hurry." For the next twenty minutes I am bombarded with questions about merit pay and the politics of education. The interviewer has read an article I wrote several months ago. It is a special treat to be questioned by someone who is prepared.

After returning my afternoon calls, I walk home for dinner. Natasha is not feeling well, but as a family we enjoy looking through a magnificent new book, *People and Places of the Past*, which Gil gave me at lunch. With clear text and remarkable pictures, it summarizes world history and anthropology. Natasha is entranced. I intend to show her how to use it, then leave her alone with it for a week. After that I shall ask casual questions about particular diagrams and photos. In due course, she will have to go back to the book to find the answers. Then we shall discuss them together.

At 9:30 P.M. I return to my office for another hour before heading home by way of the university library. More than any other structure, the library epitomizes a university. When I was in my teens, I worked at the Dallas Public Library, shelving books in the history and philosophy sections. The books' feel and smell enthralled me then and enthralls me now. As a graduate student, I spent days in the stacks of Widener Library at Harvard. And when I worked on my Ph.D. dissertation, I spent weeks in the Library of Congress. The largest library in the world, it is also one of the wonders of civilization. How humbling to consider the effort its volumes represent, to realize that you can never master more than a fraction of the knowledge they contain.

As I walk through the stacks tonight, a startled student puts down his pen and we talk quietly. A junior who transferred to AU last year, he says, "I love it here. Some of the other students would appreciate AU more if they had been somewhere else first." He has a point. The innocence of youth gives students expectations but not experience.

As I climb the steps to the top floor—one of my few forms of exercise—a professor says, "Oh, hello, Mr. President." I greet him and ask if his classes are going well. "Indeed they are," he replies. "My students this year are the most challenging I've ever had. I'd really like to congratulate everyone responsible for recruiting the new crop. They are outstanding." As we go our separate ways, I am reminded of how much all people want to be proud of their institutions.

When I was interviewed for the deanship of the College of Arts and Sciences, I said that AU needed many things. But what it needed most was pride. Not a pride based on boast or hyperbole but one based on accomplishment. And as our improvements demonstrably have increased in the last few years, our institutional pride now has reached an all-time high.

I walk briskly from the library to our home in a residential neighborhood adjacent to AU. Gail and I review routine family matters—Natasha's upcoming visit to the doctor, Gail's recent telephone conversation with Deborah, and stacks of bills.

THURSDAY, SEPTEMBER 15
Because I go to bed late, I get up as late as possible—at about 8 A.M. In my morning rush, I do not have a normal breakfast. I grab a high-protein bar as I run out the door and eat it as I drive. It tastes bland, but the astronauts survived on them so I figure I can, too.

This morning I attend an editorial breakfast at WRC–TV. The paneled room is attractive and the food looks tasty, but I have no time to try it as I am flooded with questions. As soon as I answer one, another is shot my way. For an hour and a half, we play this verbal ping-pong; the questions are pointed and thorough; the discussion is remarkably comprehensive. Exactly how this will benefit WRC or AU remains unclear. They make no tapes and take no notes. But they seem genuinely interested and I learned long ago that you never know where such things may lead.

When I arrive at my office, I find that I remain popular with my fans. A man in Walnut Creek, California, writes to let me know that what I said recently on his "TV 56 was very interesting." I have no idea what he's talking about, but it hardly matters for he proposes "a foolproof solution" to our energy problem—a perpetual motion machine. Why do my talks on astronomy bring forth such people? I need a better caliber of groupies.

Late this afternoon, I meet with Greenberg and Myers. Don says he has good and bad news. He gives us the good news first: All offices now confirm the same budget data—it will be a bonanza year. Even though the size of the surplus is unclear, we know now that the pay raises can go through.

Then Don gives the bad news: He has picked up rumors that our custodial employees may go on strike against the contract firm for whom they work. Even though they would not be striking AU, their picket lines would circle our campus and the TV cameras would train on us. Moreover, if these workers strike, then our only other union —the food service employees—may join them.

"But there is a no-strike clause in their contract," I point out.

"The law and good sense should be on our side," Don replies. "But that does not ensure that reason will prevail, especially with emotions stirred by the media."

We decide that we should use informal, third-party contacts to urge the cleaning firm and the union to resolve their differences. We agree that the custodial employees must be treated with dignity and compensated fairly. But the institution must not capitulate to unreasonable demands. I do not understand why such discord is necessary. Reasonable people can avoid it; the problems are not intractable. They arise when the participants have hidden agendas or when they distrust each other.

This yin-yang discussion of good and bad news typifies much in education today. In almost everything he does the university president encounters: "Yes, but . . . ." "Enrollments are up, but admission standards are down." "We can give the salary increase, but our pay rates remain below the competition." "The energy conservation program is working, but hot weather is driving up our energy costs." "We devote more financial aid per capita to minority students than to white students, but our percentage enrollment of minorities is going down." The roller coaster metaphor fits. The question is whether you can control it or you are on just for the ride.

While I shave, Natasha tells me about her day at school. Then we look through her math book, at the end of which is an introduction to algebra. Obviously, she is proud to be studying such material even though she claims, "I'll never be able to understand all that." Together, to her amazement, we calculate the volume of a cone. She follows my derivation of the equation and its application. Then we work on one of the simpler problems. When she finds it is not too hard, she shrugs and shows me tomorrow's homework.

Gail and I say goodnight, leave Natasha with the housekeeper, and head downtown to the Organization of American States building, the site tonight of the farewell reception of the ambassador of Saudi Arabia and his wife, Nouha. As we arrive, Lalo Valdez, the chief of protocol under President Carter and a trustee at AU, and his wife, Margarita, are leaving. Lalo's is an outstanding personal success story: having come from a sharecropper family near San Antonio, he went on to obtain a Harvard law degree. They rush to their next function as we join the most remarkable receiving line I have ever seen. The Alhegelans are on the second floor and the line stretches down the long marble staircase and winds in a serpentine fashion back and forth four times across the width of the large OAS hall.

As we wait in line, we see many friends. Pam Jacovides, wife of the ambassador of Cyprus, yells, "Hi, Gail," as she leaves. Her husband is a member of our International Advisory Board (IAB). The tall, dignified ambassador of Japan says hello. A refined gentleman, he can be warm and even grandfatherly. Two years ago his photograph appeared in the *Washington Dossier* watching Natasha play her flute at our home. His look—and hers—had caught the photographer's eye.

Chuck Percy enters and discovers the extraordinary crowd. As chairman of the Senate Foreign Relations Committee, he wants to pay respects to this important diplomatic couple, but he does not want to wait in such a line. If he goes around the line, someone is bound to complain. I wonder how he will solve this dilemma. Soon I find out. An aide leads him around the line, shaking hands with friends, and they ascend another staircase with no one but me noticing.

Finally, we reach the top of the stairs and sadly say farewell to the Alhegelans. Inside the great second floor hall, a hand darts out of the crowd to grab my arm and a voice says, "Hi, Boss." It is John Wallach, foreign affairs editor for the Hearst newspapers. His greeting refers to a seminar he is teaching this term, which grew out of a dinner a year ago. Every few weeks, I host a dinner for about a dozen professors and media people. Each dinner focuses on a current concern: Central America, the economy, violent crime. The media guests are drawn from the Washington press corps. John attended a dinner last year when the topic was the Middle East. The next day, he sent me a note asking if I would be interested in his teaching a seminar to which he would bring such guests as Zbigniew Brezinski, Henry Kissinger, and Hodding Carter III. I told him yes and asked Milt to take it from there. John is giving the course now and our students are listening to speakers they could not hear anywhere but in Washington.

FRIDAY, SEPTEMBER 16

In a changing world, how reassuring it is to know that some things remain constant. The *Washington Post* lives up to its reputation today. Reporter Lois Romano's piece about the Alhegelan's reception begins: "Even by Washington's very social standards, it was easily one of the largest collections of names and egos assembled under one roof since the last inauguration."

To the *Post* reporter's mind, it is insufficient to say that an event was attended by a large number of prominent people. Instead, it is cuter to refer to "egos." The second sentence claims that the Alhegelans "threw themselves a farewell cocktail party." In truth, they held the party for people whom they had known for many years. It was their farewell tribute to colleagues and friends. All ambassadors give receptions when they leave. Would Romano have preferred for the Alhegelans to leave without saying goodbye?

Someday I want to write a parody of a *Post* reporter interviewing Santa Claus. It would begin:

"Mr. Claus, I'm with the *Washington Post* and I want to ask you a few questions."

"I would like to help you, but tonight is Christmas Eve and I have a lot to do. Could we talk in a few days?"

"Mr. Claus, perhaps you don't understand. I am with the *Washington Post.*"

"No doubt you have a fine paper, but I really am busy now."

"Many people say they are busy, Mr. Claus. But I hope you will cooperate. If not, I shall have to print what I have gathered from other sources. For example, your elves tell me that they are not unionized. Is that true?"

"The elves are not unionized? Well, I never thought about that, and they never mentioned it to me."

"Also, Mr. Claus, is it true that you fly a sleigh around the world in one night with only a team of small reindeer?"

"Yes, it is, but the reindeer look forward to the trip all year and they . . ."

"As you can see, Mr. Claus, we have much to discuss."

And so the interview would go with Santa giving his replies and the reporter jotting down what he wanted to hear. The result:

There is concern in some quarters about the anti-Semitic implications of Mr. Claus's flying only on Christmas Eve . . . . Mr. Claus said he has no explanation for why the toys he leaves for boys are more intellectually challenging than the ones he leaves for girls. He claimed, nonetheless, that he is not sexist . . . . The toy manufacturers contacted by the *Post* insisted they were not providing kickbacks to Mr. Claus. Still, all of their offices contained conspicuous photographs of him.

With my mind on the media, I arrive at my office to discover a remarkable phenomenon: an objective issue of our student newspaper. In the past, the *Eagle* sometimes paced the nation in malicious journalism. This year, however, it has a new editor and many new writers. In addition, the news here is good. Today's headlines trumpet that message. How refreshing that student reporters get the facts straight. One article, for example, notes that our tuition increase this year equals the average of those at competitive schools. We said the same thing a year ago. Then we were met with derisive shouts: "So what? If other universities act like fools, must we as well?"

Buoyed by the *Eagle*, I go into a meeting of the trustee task force on the sports and convocation center. Chairperson Sondra Bender is gentle but unrelenting, pressing for real action. For her, statements of hope are not sufficient, nor are suggestions that we "put this off." Sondra's voice is the mildest in the room, but everyone listens when she speaks. She has something to say and she does not waiver. That is the stuff of leadership.

This afternoon two trustees—Mike Masin and Barrett Prettyman—meet with Triezenberg, Joe Conrad, and me to discuss our development program for this year. Masin and Prettyman, both attorneys, are not philanthropists or business executives, yet they have keen insights into finances and they are strongly committed to the university. The towering (six feet six) Joe is our director of development.

How many children ever say, "When I grow up, I want to be a fundraiser"? Deborah wanted to be a rodent exterminator or a school teacher; Natasha has wanted to be a department store detective or a birds'-nest watcher. Neither has ever wanted to be a fundraiser. To the best of my knowledge, no university offers a degree in fundraising. So how do people get into that field? And why? As I ponder this, I think not about Joe but about myself.

The development meeting goes well. As I walk back into Joan's office, she has a barrage of questions: "Richard, are you willing to be interviewed by the *Eagle* on Monday? Do you know David Lane who called to set up an appointment? He said he was a personal friend. The School of International Service wants to know if you'll give your talk a day earlier in February."

My answers are: "Yes." "I've never heard of Lane. Refer him to someone else." And: "I will if I'm free that day."

Yesterday, a chain-smoking visitor pleaded that he be permitted to smoke in my office. Despite the sign on my desk—THANK YOU FOR NOT SMOKING—I told him it was all right. After he left, I could barely breathe. So I raised my window. The fresh air was wonderful, but the window would not shut. So earlier today, I asked Joan to have someone from Physical Plant fix it. Two repairmen showed up. "Oh, no, it won't bother me if you hammer while I talk on the phone," I said. "It's good to see you here; please shut the window." They sprayed it with a lubricant.

When I return from meeting with the trustees, the window is shut and locked. But the spray, containing silicone, has made the air unbreathable. Finally, I raise the window, leave the room, and wait for fresh air.

Later, Gail calls to tell me that our Volvo is ready at last. Since we bought it a few weeks ago, we have taken it to the repair shop every several days. None of the problems has been serious—just minor things such as a defective warning light and the manufacturer forgetting to install the cruise control lever. And another defective light. And a loose door panel. And a window that breaks inside the door. Naturally, each item requires three visits to the shop: the first to report the problem; the second to return when the missing part is available; and the third to come back a week later to get the missing part put in properly.

Such inconveniences are omnipresent. I am convinced that God intended to create the world in three days—not seven—but the parts arrived late. And I am sure that when I die, the morticians will cram my six-foot frame into a four-foot casket. All of which brings to mind the classic response of one of our astronauts when ground control asked him how he felt just before lift-off. "How would you feel," he replied, "if you were sitting on top of the most powerful rocket in the world, knowing that it was assembled by the contractor who submitted the lowest bid?"

And I think back to when I was an undergraduate. A rigorous professor gave my class a complex assignment that required three specific books. It was a morning class, so I decided to go to the MIT library immediately after lunch, before the other students. But when I arrived, all copies had been checked out already. Through sleet, I made my way to the Boston Public Library, only to find that the books were checked out there, too. Desperate, I rushed to the Harvard library. It had the books but I could not check them out because I was not a Harvard student. I scurried about looking for a Harvard student to check them out for me. Finally, I found one and we went back to the library. But by then it was closed.

The next day my paper was due. Given that I had tried valiantly, I was certain the professor would commend me. Instead of the assignment, I turned in a saga about my effort. At the next class he gave it back, marked *F*. Trembling with rage, I told him the assignment was unreasonable. Then he replied: "The books weren't in our library because more enterprising students went to the library first, then ate. They weren't in the Boston library because other students got there before you. You've told me your problem; now tell me your solution."

I will remember that incident always. Education can come in unexpected ways.

After we pick up the Volvo and I express my displeasure to the service manager, Gail heads home and I stop by my office. "For heaven's sake," Gail says, "don't get bogged down in your work. We have to be in Potomac by 7:30." I rush into my office with one objective in mind—to shut my window, an elementary task.

But then I discover the lock has to be undone, not only to raise the window but also to shut it. Any child could accomplish such a trivial chore. It takes me twenty minutes. And now the window is stuck at "up." All we need to do is call Physical Plant and tell them to come again on Monday; three men will arrive between nine in the morning and two in the afternoon; they will take out my window frame and fill the room with more silicone spray. All this just because one man wanted to smoke.

I refuse to be defeated by anything as simple as a wooden window. Mustering my strength, I start to yank it down when I discover that what works best is gentleness. I shut the window and arrive home at 7:25. "Yes, I know, Gail, it's almost 7:30 and I've not shaved or dressed. But there was this problem with my window."

As it turns out, we arrive just as another couple does—Roger and E. J. Mudd. We know the Mudds well enough that our greeting can be a smile or handshake without air kisses. It is appropriate that we arrive with them, for we first met our host tonight at one of the Mudd's spring picnics. In the huge yard beside their northern Virginia home, the Mudds hold family gatherings. This one featured a volleyball game with dozens of players on each side. Roger and I were on one team and Natasha was on the other. The man next to her showed her how to serve. Later I told her who he was: John Glenn, former astronaut, current senator, and would-be president. Tonight John and his wife, Annie, are our hosts.

They greet us warmly at the door and I am struck by their informality. Annie is wearing casual clothes and John has a white shirt and tie but no jacket. I show him a copy of today's *Eagle* with a picture of President Reagan holding an AU T-shirt in front of him. "To be fair," I say, "we'd like you and Annie to have these," as I give them both T-shirts. John laughs heartly as he places his on the mantlepiece and calls everyone's attention to it.

The other guests are three Democratic senators—Howell Heflin, James Sasser, and Paul Tsongas—and their wives. Soon the final guest arrives—Vernon Jordan, former head of the Urban League. In the den, the classic separation occurs: the men congregate on one side and the women on the other. Suddenly, from the female side, shouts ring out as a wasp flies overhead. It makes the mistake of landing on the wall. Annie climbs up on a chair, takes careful aim, and smashes it with her shoe. We applaud and several voices say, "John, you should make her secretary of defense."

Annie tells each of us where to sit. The table setting is attractive but far from grand with mismatched chairs filling with the regular set. Jordan sits across from me on what appears to be a child's chair. When Annie asks if he would like a larger one, he replies, "No. This is fine." To which Sasser quips: "If I were sitting in that chair, the top of my head would be under the table." As it is, the massive Jordan looks me straight in the eye.

John bows his head to say grace, at the end of which comes a chorus of "Amens." Then, scintillating conversation. In marked contrast with stuffy Washington dinners, this one sparkles. John and I discuss education today. His views are brilliant, which is to say that they agree with mine. He laughs as he interrupts one of my harrangues to say, "That is almost verbatim from one of my speeches." Clearly, he has been briefed on the issues; he has developed a coherent, thoughtful program; and he presents his case convincingly. Even though he is not a spellbinding orator, in our talk tonight, his ideas glisten.

His father, I discover, worked in a plumbing store in Ohio. Mine worked in a hardware store in Texas. As we compare notes on threading pipe and the importance of a work ethic, I wonder, "Will he make it?" Whether he does or not, he is intelligent and compassionate; he would make a responsible and decent president, and parents could say to their children: "Grow up to be like him."

Suddenly, Roger Mudd asks, "Senator Heflin, where are all the nude beaches in Alabama?" Heflin gives a wonderfully Southern non-reply: "A fellow down my way once was asked to witness in church about what religion had done for him. The other parishioners dutifully told how much the church had improved their lives. Finally, this fellow rose and said, 'What has improved my morals the most has not been church but old age.'"

Gail, in an unusually feisty mood tonight, says, "You got out of that one well, Senator. But I'll let all of you decide if you believe my husband's story about Tiki Tiki." I think to myself, "Oh, Lord, why did she have to mention that?" But everyone insists that I tell the story.

"A few years ago," I begin, "we received our monthly credit card bill, which Gail always pays. In skimming over where we had made purchases, one name caught her eye: Tiki Tiki Massage Parlor.

" 'Richard, there is an entry I would like to discuss with you.'

"I looked at the listing and was baffled, for I had never been there. When I explained that, she said, 'Well, I haven't been, so who's using our card?' We wrote to the credit card company and asked them to send a copy of the signed slip. In due course it arrived bearing my unmistakable signature.

" 'Richard, you really could tell me about this.'

" 'Darling, I would if I knew anything about it. But I honestly don't. That looks like my signature, but I haven't been to Tiki Tiki. I don't know anyone who has. I don't even know where Tiki Tiki is.'

"Feeling like Dreyfus, I decided I'd get to the heart of the matter. I looked up Tiki Tiki and called the number. Someone there referred me to another office and that person referred me to yet another office. Finally, the story became clear. A barber shop was owned by the same people who owned the massage parlor. Apparently, when I paid for a haircut, the barber used the wrong card machine. And that is how an innocent man, merely getting his hair cut, came to be so wronged."

"Likely story," the guests howl. "You should sell used cars. No wonder education is in trouble."

By this time everyone is making a loud comment about something to someone else. Everyone except John Glenn. With a grin, he takes it all in and says nothing. Several times during the evening as delicate topics have come up, he has said, "I'm going to keep away from that one." Clearly, that is his intent about this repartee. Then, from the far end of the table, Mudd booms: "John, if word of this conversation got out, you could shed your Boy Scout image." We laugh heartily, John more than anyone else.

After dinner, I have a lengthy conversation with him about training programs for blue-collar workers, science and research initiatives, and the magnet schools he helped found in Ohio. On issue after issue, he has solid ideas. I am impressed. And what impresses me most is that he does not appear to be attempting to impress me. At 11:30 we say goodnight. As Gail and I drive down the dark streets of this suburban neighborhood, we wonder if we just dined with the next president.

SATURDAY, SEPTEMBER 17

The day is filled with the bric-a-brac of ordinary life—getting a haircut, washing the car, the three of us riding our bikes around campus.

At dusk we walk to the AU track to view the plaque commemorating the 1963 speech by President Kennedy when he announced the nuclear test-ban treaty. Historians view that address as being among the most significant of his career. We want to be sure the plaque and the grounds around it are in good shape because a TV crew will be here Monday to film a documentary that will air on the twentieth anniversary of JFK's death.

Sure enough, high grass surrounds the plaque. I call our grounds director, Scott Jenkins, at his home. After I apologize for disturbing him on a Saturday night, I explain the circumstances. He says a team will spruce up the area before the TV crew arrives.

SUNDAY, SEPTEMBER 18
This afternoon, Scott calls to say that he could not wait until Monday to clean up the plaque area. He will do it today. I thank him and hang up, admiring such personal responsibility.

Quietly, Gail asks: "What do you think of Jody Powell, Carter's press secretary?"

"Why?"

"Well, I saw him yesterday at the gas station. I introduced myself and asked if he'd speak to our students. He agreed."

Overwhelmed by her aggressiveness, I tell her that I am delighted. But had she met him before? "No," she replies. "But if you can ask Volcker out of the blue, I can ask Powell."

MONDAY, SEPTEMBER 19
A TV crew arrives to film a show about John F. Kennedy's impact on youth and his form of leadership, and I ride with them to our athletic field where several joggers are working out. As my makeup cakes, a bee flies about my face, the wind blows my hair straight up, my shirt sogs with perspiration, my voice dries from the heat, and the TV crew encounters technical obstacles—AU's fifty-thousand-watt radio station interferes with their sound, the president's helicopter flies overhead, the bells chime at Wesley Seminary. The crew is undeterred.

We move to the Quad to get background. I look into the camera and say, "John Kennedy challenged youth then and even today. He asked us to give more of ourselves than many of us thought we could. He asked us to give to the nation that had given us so much. He was bold, handsome, witty, articulate, and dynamic. The resonant way he said 'vigah' still echoes in my mind. The nation still could use his vigor."

The sight of cameras, a slate board reading "Scene 4, Take 2," and men holding large reflectors to light my face is too much for students to resist. One runs up and shouts, "Hey, what's this all about?" We stop, tell him, and start the shooting again. Then another student walks behind the interviewer, smiles at me, and jumps around. My eyes dart back and forth between the interviewer and the student. The TV viewer at home will have no idea anyone was distracting me. I will simply appear to have a nervous twitch.

Due to the taping delays, I get back to my office thirty minutes late. From there, I dash to a luncheon at the Georgetown Club, hosted by trustee Wallace Holladay. As I enter the second floor dining room, expecting to find my host and perhaps four guests, I discover a banquet table with Wally at one end and twenty high-level business executives seated all around.

Three years ago, we started asking trustees to host luncheons to which they would invite their friends and business associates in order to hear me describe AU's history, programs, and hopes. Nowadays we hold such functions once a month. Through this process, we have expanded our circle of contacts. Two guests at these luncheons ultimately became trustees; others have become financial supporters; and the rest are informal ambassadors of goodwill for us.

Today's luncheon covers a substantial amount of ground. After my informal remarks, the guests fire questions. If nothing else, I hope they leave with increased respect for AU. If so, our graduates may find jobs that would not have existed before.

Late this afternoon, I talk with Don Triezenberg who has just met with a self-appointed student task force on the sports and convocation center. They want to know *precisely* when it will be built. They offer extensive advice on fundraising with the implication that we are not trying or that we do not know what to do. Finally, Don tells them: "What we need is not your advice but your money. I have neither the time nor the interest to listen to anyone tell me how to raise funds. What I will pay attention to is your cash. Will you graduating seniors sign a statement now pledging to give one hundred dollars a year for the next five years?"

We dislike being pushed to such a position, but some students' arrogance is almost intolerable. Basically they say, "I want it, so provide it. *Now.*" Facts and realities are irrelevant. I receive at least one such student comment per day about the sports center; today I got two blistering ones.

I rush home, shave, discuss Natasha's homework with her, and start to leave with Gail to attend a reception at the World Bank for the financial sponsors of the Ambassadors' Ball, which Gail chaired last year. As we head to the door, Natasha says, "Do you *really* have to go tonight?"

"Yes," we try to explain, "We do. We were with you yesterday, remember?"

"That was then. What about tonight . . . or tomorrow night? Will you be here then?"

"No, Sweetheart, we won't. We just can't be."

"How about on Wednesday night?"

"Natasha, I'll be out every night this week until Saturday, and Mommy probably will be, too."

"Other kids' folks are busy, yet they stay home in the evening," she says, tears welling up in her eyes. "Why can't you?"

"Natasha," my voice cracks. "We'll be with you. . . ." Then Gail intercedes with a motherly hug. "How will it be if we try to get home before you go to sleep?"

"Okay . . . I guess."

At nine o'clock, we rush home to discover that Natasha has just gone to sleep. With my throat raw from a virus, I wonder why I still have not eaten, why I did not spend the evening with Natasha, and why I went to the reception. The answer, I know, is to aid AU. But there are moments when I feel like saying "To hell with it," and this is one of them.

TUESDAY, SEPTEMBER 20
My sore throat has turned into laryngitis. So during my first meeting this morning—with Greenberg, Myers, Triezenberg, and their respective budget officers—I listen more than I speak, which is not a bad thing.

Even though data still are incomplete, they suggest a substantial budget surplus this year. Two high priorities must be met simultaneously: to increase the university's financial reserves and to give employees a pay increase on January 1. Milt wants us in the future to go back to the conventional calendar and give raises on July 1, but the others argue against that because it exposes the institution before revenues arrive in the fall. I agree. We must not make commitments until we are sure to obtain the funds.

As the debate continues, I excuse myself to catch a train to Philadelphia. At the 30th Street Station there, I am met by a professor from the University of Pennsylvania who drives me to the Annenberg Center where this afternoon's symposium—on excellence in education—is being held. The audience fills the room, the spotlights flood the stage, and the moderator begins. He asks us to speak in alphabetical order; my last name puts me first. I open by saying, "The United States is so apathetic about education that during the past twenty-four hours there hasn't been a single national study released condemning our educational system." The audience smiles and I proceed to hammer on several of my favorite themes:

"Teachers should be expected to teach well, but they should not be expected to do the other things now thrust upon them." There is loud applause. "Let us abolish social promotions. Some people say it is cruel and inhumane to hold back a fourth grader. I say it is cruel and inhumane to promote a fourth grader if you know that person is unqualified to do fifth grade work and ultimately will become a twelfth grade functional illiterate."

Despite the ovation, I doubt if today's discussion will contribute to improving educational quality. How could it? Each panelist spoke for only five minutes; the time for panel discussion was about fifteen minutes. We glossed over the main issues. Perhaps that is all we could do. But I leave the meeting feeling disappointed. Will a single child benefit in a tangible way?

Back in Washington, I drive with Gail to the annual Ambassadors' Ball. As we dance, we see many friends and people we are trying to interest in the university. Naturally, the affair is studded with diplomats. The courtly French ambassador kisses Gail's hand and I thank him again for speaking to our students last year. Then I say hello to the Egyptian ambassador who arranged for Mrs. Mubarak, the head of state's wife, to speak at AU a year ago.

At the head table I am seated across from Ed Meese who sits between Selwa Roosevelt, the chief of protocol, and Obie Shultz, wife of the secretary of state. Gail is next to Steve Bell of ABC–TV's "Good Morning, America," who is tonight's emcee. Bell is charming, and George Shultz gives a gracious toast to the diplomatic corps. Then Bell calls upon the evening's special guest, Dame Margot Fonteyn, the famous ballerina, who lives in Panama and who came here especially for this event. She talks touchingly about her husband's illness and his service in the diplomatic corps. She speaks as artfully as she once danced.

Gail and I exchange glances, each knowing what the other has in mind. The only question is which of us will do it, or should we do it together. Without talking, we decide across the long table that she will be the one. So Gail says to Dame Margot: "No doubt your schedule is tight, but we would enjoy it if you could come to campus to talk to our students. Could you?"

"My itinerary is already filled," Dame Margot replies, "but I would be delighted to do it on my next visit. Let us plan to do that."

Soon I plead with Gail to leave. My throat is raw and I have several hours of work to do.

WEDNESDAY, SEPTEMBER 21
Nursing my laryngitis, I chair a morning meeting with Greenberg, Myers, and Triezenberg. Even though our data still are not final, we are confident enough to make firm decisions: We shall add at least $1 million to the university's reserves (our savings account); we shall restore funds deleted last year from high-priority areas; we shall hold sufficient funds to enter the next fiscal year on a sound footing; and we shall ask the trustees to approve a salary hike for employees on January 1.

Today, Milt and I host a faculty luncheon. For the last two years, he has joined me in these, and both of us find them a productive way to spur informal exchange. I start the discussion today by reviewing AU's recent history, noting the good parts and the bad. I attempt to put the story in a national perspective. Then I recite the litany of our accomplishments this fall: Our freshmen enrollment is up substantially, the yield on our endowment now is the highest of any private university, our admissions standards are the toughest in AU's history. Then I mention the pay hike. All I see are smiles.

THURSDAY, SEPTEMBER 22
In Philadelphia this morning, I attend a meeting on accreditation visits sponsored by the Middle States Association. Given the importance of accreditation, it seems worth my while. Soon, however, I discover that it is not. The speakers are articulate, but everything they have to say already has been summarized in documents. Part of the difficulty, I know, is my high impatience level. Most meetings bore me

because they seem so tedious. Almost without exception, the useful information could be condensed into a document or a brief oral statement. Fortunately, the cost of today's trip is covered by the Middle States Association and I do learn a few things.

As I cross the lobby to leave the hotel, loud rock music bursts forth and several scantily clad young women pirouette toward me. When one of them asks, "Would you like a kiss?" the offer becomes clear. The establishment's name is the Hershey Pennsylvania Hotel and the "kiss" comes wrapped in silver foil. The young women, it turns out, are cheerleaders for the Philadelphia Eagles. Cheerleaders have always presented a problem for me going back to the eighth grade.

The most beautiful female on earth, I was convinced then, was a cheerleader named Carol. From September to spring, I stared in rapture at wonderful Carol while she—oblivious of me—talked with her girlfriends. As the end of the school year neared, desperation set in; I had to act decisively.

I decided to approach her before school, and I would look as dashing as a fourteen-year-old could. My outfit was masculine enough: a red flannel shirt with sleeves rolled up and the two top buttons undone, revealing a skin-tight white T-shirt. Naturally, I hid my glasses. If I squinted just right, I could overcome some of my nearsightedness. I convinced myself that squinting actually made me look pensive or in pain. Girls liked men who seemed to be suffering.

Patiently, I waited until a morning when no one else was around. With number-two Mogol pencils in place at thirty degree angles behind each ear and Clearasil applied, I strolled up and said, "Hi, I'm Richard Berendzen." She turned and smiled, looking somewhat puzzled. I went on: "For several weeks I have noticed you. . . ."

Suddenly, an enormous dog, appearing from nowhere, decided my left leg was a female of his species in heat. As I shoved him away, Carol said: "Really, why do you do that with your dog?"

"But he isn't my dog."

"Well, then, why do you do it with someone else's dog?"

"I don't. I've never seen this dog before."

"Well, he certainly seems to know you. Why don't you do such things in private? Why do you do them at all? This is disgusting."

I was frantic. The dog was large enough to bite off my hand with one chomp. Nonetheless, I banged him on the head. Everything I did only increased his ardor. Carol changed from pink to red to scarlet.

As she wheeled to go, she shouted, "This is perverted. Don't talk to me again. You're sick."

In tears, I tried to explain. But she was gone. At least I could take revenge on the dog. But when I looked, he too had vanished as quickly as he had appeared.

With this eighth grade vignette on my mind, I grab a taxi for the Philadelphia airport. My flight is to Oklahoma City where I am to address 350 of the state's top businessmen. Enroute, I read the TWA magazine, which has an amusing story about elevators. It quips that "the odds of getting stuck in one are about fifty-thousand to one—or about the same as being invited to Brooke Shields' birthday party." I save it to send to Bob Shaheen, aide to Adnan Khashoggi, who is a new AU trustee. He will understand why.

Khashoggi has become an almost legendary figure. Born in 1935 in Mecca, Saudi Arabia, he studied in Egypt and California. Through real estate and business, he quickly parlayed his modest funds into a sizable fortune. But what brought him to the public's eye was his grand lifestyle and his business dealings in the 1970s.

Frank Church chaired a Senate committee that investigated allegations that many prominent Europeans and Middle Easterners, including Khashoggi, had been paid illegal commissions to secure contracts for U.S. corporations with Middle Eastern countries, especially Saudi Arabia. In fact, the practices were not illegal then, although they were questionable. Despite his vindication, Khashoggi became known as a wheeler-dealer and "an Arab arms merchant." The "arms" were military supplies that the president of the United States had asked to be sold to Saudi Arabia. Congress had approved the sales, and major U.S. corporations had made them. Khashoggi was the middle man.

Today such arms deals involve a minuscule portion of his business. His investments in the U.S. are diversified: real estate, technology, and energy. In Salt Lake City, Utah, he and his brothers are building an international center and a $600 million urban complex. His ventures range from agriculture in Kenya to resorts on the Mediterranean, from property in Houston to companies in Europe. And he is a major philanthropist. Although estimates vary, his wealth is pegged at a minimum of several billion dollars. Clearly, he is one of the world's richest men.

Is he too controversial for a university? Perhaps. But his business activities nowadays are respected, even deeply admired. Corporate executives and heads of state more than accept him now; they seek him out. And consider prototypes of wealth in the past: John D. Rockefeller, Andrew Carnegie, Cecil Rhodes (of the Rhodes Scholarships), and even Alfred Nobel (of the Nobel Prize). They, too, were controversial, but look what they gave the world.

Last spring Gail and I held a dinner for Khashoggi to introduce him to prominent Washingtonians. It was to be an elaborate affair in the back courtyard of our home. In case of rain, the area was covered by a large yellow-and-white tent. But then the rains came—the heaviest in Washington's history. Natasha, who had been playing under the tent, ran inside and shouted, "Come quickly. The tent's collapsing." Gail and I rushed outside, and shoved here, bailed there, like Mickey Mouse in *Fantasia*. But it was to no avail. The guywires gave way and the tent collapsed.

What to do? By then it was 11:00 A.M.; guests were to arrive at 7:00 P.M. I found a conference room on campus and asked our staff to help move everything—tables, chairs, decorations, flowers, food, wine— there. Cleaners tidied up. I arranged the tables and Gail rented transportation to take our guests through the downpour from our house to the campus. At 6:45, we put the last things in the place and I threw on my tux.

Fifteen minutes later, the limousines arrived, delivering, among others: Alejandro Orfila, secretary general of the Organization of American States, and his Austrian wife, Helga; former secretary of treasury G. William Miller and his wife, Ariadna; the Charles Wicks; Senator and Mrs. Henry Jackson; the former vice-presidential candidate Edmund Muskie and his wife, Jane; the Ed Meeses; the ambassadors of Germany and Spain with their wives; trustee Stuart Bernstein and his wife, Wilma; Cy Ansary, chairman of our board of trustees, and his wife, Jan; publisher Austin Kiplinger and his wife, Gogo; Selwa Roosevelt, the chief of protocol, and her husband, Archie; General David Jones, former chairman of the Joint Chiefs of Staff, and his wife, Lois.

After everyone had assembled at our home for cocktails, I announced: "In Washington you must have an alternative plan. Due to the rain, we shall go to Plan B. Don't worry; all will be well. This will be a different evening, but trust me. Please go out the front door to transportation, which will take you to dinner."

Shielding themselves from the rain, wives and husbands stepped aboard a yellow school bus. I rode standing by the driver. As we started this odd trek, I told the passengers: "No rowdiness on this bus, no rocking it or throwing things. However, you may sing camp songs." Fred Fielding, the White House counsel, replied with the quip of the night: "This whole thing is odd because Ed Meese objects to forced busing."

When we arrived, the room looked charming—largely because it was too dark in the candlelight to see anything well. After dinner, I gave a toast to Khashoggi. Then we sprang another surprise: members of our Performing Arts Department entered the room in turn-of-the-century costumes, singing songs from the 1920s and 1930s. The finale was a surprise as well. As they began the last piece, virtually no one recognized the beginning stanzas. But then came the stirring theme: "God Bless America." Mary Jane Wick jumped to her feet and clapped. Ursula Meese squeezed my hand. It was a show stopper. And Adnan beamed.

By then the group *did* trust us. Next we took them under umbrellas to the AU library where on the top floor we had an exhibit on loan from the National Geographic Society and the Smithsonian. Entitled *Symbols of Faith,* it told the story—through words, pictures, and artifacts—of the three great monotheistic religions: Judaism, Christianity, and Islam. Two elevators were available. Gail, Adnan, and others got in the left one. I chose the one on the right. The odds may be fifty thousand to one, but mine stuck.

Several people said, "Okay, Dick, this is a cute way to raise funds. I'll give, I promise. Now open the door." I pushed every button. Nothing happened. We giggled nervously. With Scoop Jackson, Fred Fielding, and Ed Muskie behind me and Bob Shaheen in front of me, I pushed the buttons more frantically. Again, no response. Jokes flowed, especially from Fielding, a truly funny man. The women trapped with us men said they would claim either that wild things had happened or that nothing had—whichever would get the door open faster. Outside, we could hear people working to free us. What started as amusing turned more serious as the crowded space became hot. Still, everyone remained calm. A few minutes later, the door opened. Our waiting friends applauded and a few students looked puzzled, wondering why these sweating people in gowns and tuxes were getting out of their library elevator.

When I arrive in Oklahoma City, I return a call to a *Post* reporter who interviews me about AU's enrollment and finances. Then I go to the businessmen's dinner. Something far back in my memory tells me

I have returned to my roots. I was born in Oklahoma, but left before I was two. These men resemble my father except they are more prosperous. I listen to their banter and learn about the many charities they support. Politically, they are Reagan people. More broadly, they represent America's heartland—hard-working, deeply religious, decent folk. None of Manhattan's sophistication here; none of Washington's political clout. I could never live here; I like the East Coast too much. But there is a fundamental goodness about these people that I admire deeply.

FRIDAY, SEPTEMBER 23

Before boarding my flight back to Washington, I call Gail to find out what the *Post* had to say about AU. She reads it over the phone. Basically, it is accurate, although the article fails to note that we shall increase our reserves by more than $1 million and states that more than 90 percent of our revenue comes from tuition. In fact, less than 70 percent flows from that source; the remainder comes from dorms, the bookstore, food service, the endowment, gifts, and grants.

With only minutes to go, I make the flight and settle back for a quiet interlude without meetings or calls. I have read somewhere that commercial aircraft soon may have telephones. What a dreadful idea. My time on planes is precious. It provides a unique opportunity to read and think.

The driver meets me at Washington's National Airport, but not in my "chauffeured Cadillac stretch limousine with glass partition." Versions of that description have floated about campus for years. Truth is, it is an Olds, not a Cadillac; a standard model, not a limo; and it has no glass partition. The "uniformed chauffeur" is a student who works part-time in the campus security office. His attire is jeans and jogging shoes.

As we ride to campus, I read a thick folder of mail that Joan has sent. On top is today's issue of the *Eagle*. The lead headline announces that the student government president has resigned to devote more time to his courses. The story goes on to say that someone broke the university's computer code and found that this student is on probation. Commendably, the *Eagle* handles the story fairly, even compassionately. I am proud of the *Eagle's* restraint and of the student's courage in deciding to resign. I hope he will devote himself to his studies and will have a successful career.

My desk is stacked with phone messages. My first calls are to the outgoing student president and to Paul Schroeder, the vice-president who now becomes president automatically. A remarkable young man, Paul visited me this summer. I was impressed by his array of interests, his composure, his self-confidence. At the end of our meeting, I showed him to the door. As I pointed him toward his next destination, he assured me that he could make it on his own. And he did, without a cane or dog, even though he is totally blind. On the telephone, I tell him that he can count on my full support. He thanks me and says he hopes to be worthy of our trust.

I rush home to shave and put on a sober suit. At 4:30 P.M., Gail and I arrive at the southwest gate of the White House. The guard checks our driver's licenses against names on his list and looks us over carefully before permitting us into the Rose Garden. A group of us are there to receive the president's thanks for our help with refurbishing the National Aquarium. As Gail and I walk toward the South Portico, Charles Wick arrives and thanks me for sending his daughter information about our business school. We climb the stairway into the Entrance Hall and enter the State Dining Room. There we see several friends including two trustees, Climis Lascaris and Luther Hodges. Lascaris and I talk about his forthcoming trip to the Middle East. In preparation for it, I have written a letter explaining why we want to build the sports and convocation center and how a donor could benefit from supporting it. We have translated the letter into Arabic and have appended my business card in Arabic. Lascaris will hand-deliver these to the royal families of Saudi Arabia, Kuwait, and Bahrain.

Gail talks with the wives of several cabinet members—Mrs. Malcolm Baldridge, Mrs. William French Smith, Mrs. John Block. Secret Service agents usher us away from one of the doors. Moments later it opens and President Reagan enters the room. Looking vibrant, he smiles widely and begins shaking hands. Briefly, he huddles with Smith and Wick for what looks like serious conversation. Could it be about Secretary of the Interior James Watt's latest gaffe? Then he smiles again and walks our way. Among other things, he tells us about a pond on his California ranch. He wanted to stock it with goldfish, permitting them to grow to larger than normal size. But soon the original dozen had multiplied to a few thousand and several hundred had died. He says this rate of expansion astounded him. A military aide taps him on the elbow: "Mr. President, it is time for your next meeting." He looks genuinely distressed. He shakes hands with us again, looking each of us squarely in the eye. I joke about his fish story and, with a twinkle, he smiles and laughs, head back.

Voice strong and handshake firm, how can a man my father's age look so fit? I am struck, too, by the casualness of his conversation. He is irresistably charming.

As Reagan spoke this afternoon, he stood beneath a large portrait of Lincoln in contemplation. Lincoln not only resided in this house, he anguished here as the nation nearly tore itself apart. There is a majesty and mystique about the White House; I hope I am inspired by it always.

But now I must come back to reality. This will be a difficult evening: Natasha's first dance class for 1983–84. For a twelve-year-old, that is sheer trauma. She maintains that she "despises, detests, loathes, and hates" the dance class. But when we ask, "Do you truly not want to go?" she replies, "Well, I suppose I will." When you are twelve, it is obligatory to say you do not like it; you go only because your parents force you.

Tonight will be more painful than usual. To expedite transportation, Gail has agreed to drive a boy to the dance class. Fortunately, he is outnumbered. Natasha's friend, Cynthia, will accompany her. With two girls along, no one could conclude that Natasha and the boy are arriving together. He is simply a passenger, like a rider on a bus.

Before dance class begins, we eat pizza for dinner. As I wipe cheese off my chin, I reflect that an hour ago I was talking to the president in the White House; now I am sitting in Jerry's Sub Shop. Only in America. . . .

Gail drops me at home and drives off to pick up Eliot Dam, son of the deputy secretary of state. When she returns with him, he is quiet, which makes good sense when you are in a stranger's house confronted by two girls who pretend not to see you. Neither Natasha nor Cynthia says a word to him. He knows the rules and says nothing to them. As the three mutes climb into the Volvo, I walk to my office and attempt to find my desk underneath the paperwork.

SATURDAY, SEPTEMBER 24

In the distance I hear a bell. No, it is the phone. I should answer it.

"Isn't it something?" Cynthia's mother asks.

"Isn't what something?"

"The girls' reaction to dance class."

What dance class? What girls? Oh, yes. Miss Ostermann's. And Cynthia and Natasha. "Hang on. I'll get Gail."

To prepubescent Washington, Miss Ostermann's dance class is a blend of boot camp and finishing school. The youngsters are expected to come properly dressed—nowhere else in the Western world are there more boys in blue blazers—and they are taught "proper" etiquette: the boys seat the girls, they thank each other for a dance, and the boys offer to bring punch to the girls.

Natasha is a liberated, modern girl who fully intends to be a professional. Nonetheless, ballroom dancing and social graces are worth learning early. Usually, the dances are ones the parents like but the youngsters only tolerate. There have been exceptions, however, and last night was one of them. Room lights dimmed, strobes flashing, and rock music blaring, staid Miss Ostermann's exploded with noise. "Simply awesome," the kids agreed. Natasha says it was "Neato."

How odd to think she is entering the rock generation now. When Deborah was fourteen, we lived in Boston and gave her the ultimate Christmas gift: New Year's Eve at the Boston Tea Party, then *the* in place on the East Coast. She was ecstatic. Gail and I would take her but with one caveat: I could plug my ears to muffle the noise. "Sure. Great. What a wonderful dad I have."

From a block away, the thudding sound was audible. As we entered the building, I stuffed large wads of cotton in each ear. So Deborah wouldn't feel left out standing by the wall, I asked her to dance. When the ultraviolet light hit my cotton, it shone purple. With large, fuzzy, violet ears, I must have been a sight. Deborah winced and said, "Oh, Daddy, I don't want to be seen near you looking like that."

But then a young man with flowing hair and love beads approached me. "Hey, man, where did you get those weird ears? Far out." After I explained, he disappeared. Minutes later he returned with a box of cotton. Soon everyone had purple ears and Deborah was burstingly proud of her pacesetting dad.

Due to a cancellation, our day is blessedly free. I spend the afternoon running errands and the evening reading. Yesterday's *Eagle* is upbeat. How long can this go on? It is like springtime in January. The headline over an op-ed article reads: "Feeling Good About AU." Ironically, that is the same slogan students adopted two years ago. Six months later, their affection turned to wrath as we announced an 18 percent tuition increase, the highest in AU's history. Then a parade of campus problems plagued us until recently. Yet I am the same president as two years ago. The administration's attitudes and goals remain the same. What has changed is that AU's finances went from satisfactory to extremely bad to good; student leaders' attitudes evolved from apathy to near revolution to moderation again. In short, students' feelings correlate with AU's financial health. When the freshman class declines by 150 students, administrators become beasts; when it gains 150 students, we become respectable. The students' reflexes mirror those of sports fans. Yesterday's enemies are today's friends; today's friends can become tomorrow's enemies. Campus opinion depends not upon my vision or accomplishments but upon images and what shapes them—money, press, outside conditions, and chance. On this, Kipling said it well: "Meet with Triumph and Disaster and treat those two imposters just the same."

SUNDAY, SEPTEMBER 25

As I read the newspaper, I glance at TV. A woman is explaining how an evangelist cured her cancer. I change channels. Another evangelist is explaining that it is blessed to give, as his name and address flash on the screen. I change channels again. A Marx brothers comedy is on and I leave it on.

After a family lunch, Natasha and I work on her "Wordly Wise" assignment. She is to give the prefix-root meaning of such words as *lithograph.* Her dictionary does not supply this information, so we go to the magnum opus, the *Oxford English Dictionary.* Squinting through a magnifying glass, we find not only the root meaning but also the word's origin in Greek and its first recorded usage. For an hour, we look up obscure words neither of us has seen before. When we finish, two questions come to mind: How is a child to complete this assignment without an unabridged dictionary; and, if all seventh graders went to schools like Natasha's, what would the nation's educational status be?

I walk briskly to my office, not so much to save time as to exercise. On this lovely fall afternoon, the campus feels vibrant. Three students sit on a park bench holding an animated conversation over a textbook. Others sit across the Quad, reading quietly. A couple tosses a frisbee, while a boy turns a girl upside down and shakes her vigorously. This is either a mating ritual or an unusual mugging.

AU's founders selected a superb location for the campus. Its eighty acres in far northwest Washington convey the ambience of a

New England college, yet AU is only fifteen minutes from the White House. Its rolling hills and stately trees belong in a park. Although I wish the campus had more uniformity, we are trying to impose some standardization now. Without knowing why, a student or visitor will gain a sense of the institution from its appearance. Looks can be deceiving, but they can be instructive, too.

After several hours in my office, I stroll the campus en route home. My first stop is the Mary Graydon Center, once a women's dorm and now the home for our student center, food service, computers, and much more. Tonight every computer terminal is taken and not a single student seems distracted from work. Next stop is the university library. Inside, I can barely believe what I see this late on Sunday, this early in the term: At least three quarters of the seats are occupied. Dozens of other students huddle around the card catalogs and the reference desk. As I leave, I ask the guard, "How's it going?" Not recognizing me, he replies, "Crazy as hell. Where'd they all come from?"

MONDAY, SEPTEMBER 26
This morning I have a long talk by phone with a friend and colleague whom I have known for nearly twenty years. Late on a Sunday afternoon in the fall of 1962, several graduate students and I were leaving the Harvard Astronomy Department when we noticed a shabby car in our parking lot. A young man with tousled hair, scuffed shoes, and a turtleneck emerged from the car, looked around as if he were lost, and entered our building. The newcomer was the youngest member of the faculty. Because he was new and I was head of the graduate students, someone decided I should be his teaching assistant. He had never taught the course and I had never taken it. What a dynamic duo! Clearly, we should meet. So I went to his office to introduce myself. He grinned, shook hands, and said, "Delighted to see you. I'm Carl Sagan."

The graduate students wanted me to determine if this interloper *really* knew science. Quickly, I concluded that he not only knew science but had an uncanny ability to communicate it. "He knows his stuff, is impressively articulate, and is quite witty," I reported. "The only negative is his odd pronunciation. He can make a two-syllable word sound like it has five. And you should hear the way he says *billions.*"

Today, Carl is the best-known astronomer of this century and I am delighted over his rise to fame. Through his writings and his remarkable TV series, he has awakened more interest in arcane science than any other person. As part of the inaugural ceremony when I became president of AU, we held the world premiere of Carl's "Cosmos" at the National Academy of Sciences building downtown. Some of the scientific elite did not like the show's special effects, but it was obvious to all that the series would mesmerize the public, which it did. Presently, Carl is studying the long-term effects of a nuclear war. Exactly what would happen to our atmosphere, water supplies, and weather? He says he will release preliminary findings at a conference in Washington next month. I offer to invite U.S. officials as well as representatives from other nuclear nations. The topic should concern us all.

Late this afternoon, Milt and I walk to the law college where the dean and faculty are holding a reception for us. As we near the Quad, I point out the "Gerald Ford Memorial Wisteria Tree." A few years ago, former President Ford spoke on campus. As we walked to the lecture hall, he turned to speak to us at the rear—unaware that he was walking directly toward a wisteria tree. "My God," I thought. I had read stories about him hitting people with golf balls or bumping himself on airplanes; however, with this branch, he could impale his own head.

What should I do? Clearly, the Secret Service agents were wondering the same thing. One said, "Mr. President, watch out." Ford kept on walking. Again, the agent said, "Mr. President, *watch out!*" Ford still did not hear. One agent glanced at the other and then yanked the branch upward just as Ford walked underneath, his head barely missing it. This little vignette took less than ten seconds. Yet I was bemused to note that Ford had not realized there was either a problem or a solution.

When we arrive at the law college, I scarcely recognize the second floor, which has been renovated extensively. Law colleges are odd places, populated by bright professionals who demand near-total autonomy from the rest of the institution. Our law college ranks quite high in recent surveys and its admissions standards compare favorably with the top schools nationally. The college's faculty are prolific and the students tell me they are good teachers as well. I begin by saying, "I hear frequently how truly outstanding this law college is —usually from the faculty." They laugh heartily. And I continue: "Your new facilities are extremely handsome and I look forward to visiting next year, because I know that next summer you will want to change it again." This time the laughter turns to groans.

As I drive to my next function—a reception for the president of Finland—I wonder if I should take the time to go. Such affairs pertain primarily to diplomats, not educators. I'm somewhat out of place at them. Still, the Finnish ambassador belongs to the IAB and a reception for a head of state draws government officials and business executives—good people for a university president to meet.

Floodlights illuminate the receiving line while cameras record the scene for Finnish TV. Soon the crush becomes intense. Flashbulbs pop and Secret Service agents shove as the president of Finland makes his way through the crowd. I think I see the back of his head. No, that is one of the agents, unless the president wears an earphone with a cord under his coat. Anyway, I am tired and hungry, and feel bad. I leave early.

Over dinner at the kitchen table, Natasha pridefully tells me, "Guess what? I got check double pluses in Spanish and on my Wordly Wise." I do not know what a "check double plus" is but it sounds good. I ask how the other children did on the Wordly Wise. She says five could not do it because they did not have unabridged dictionaries at home. When I was her age, I doubt if a single family in my school owned an unabridged dictionary.

At nine o'clock, Myers arrives at our front door for a late meeting. He is available any hour. And even this late, he is impeccable, attaché case in hand. Trustees often tell me: "Be careful with that fellow. I'd hire him if I didn't know it would hurt AU." Although not widely known on campus, his contributions have been substantial, from improvement of our food service to upgrading of our physical plant. His forte, however, is real estate and finance. If he had been around centuries ago, he would have bought Manhattan for ten dollars and added Long Island for good measure. Still in his thirties, trim, and businesslike, he is the acme of the young professional.

After he departs, I feel guilty for leaving the Finnish reception so quickly. I had taken the time to drive there and park. It was filled with people worth seeing. Couldn't I have stuck it out for another hour?

TUESDAY, SEPTEMBER 27

This morning I meet with the deans, the university librarian, Greenberg, Myers, and Triezenberg. Before addressing the principal item on our agenda—enrollment strategies for the future—I suggest we go around the table and review areas within our individual domains that might be of interest to everyone else. I start by summarizing AU's financial status and the recommendations that the trustee finance committee will give to the full board.

Bill Peters, the new dean of our business college, has generally good news but reports that his overall enrollment is down slightly. This is a change from the recent past. Tom Buergenthal, dean of our law college, says there was fierce competition among the regional law schools to secure the very best students. AU held its own, but he worries that applications may drop in the future. For the next two hours we discuss recruitment strategies, the geographic areas we should pursue most vigorously, and the role deans and senior administrators have in the process. My role today is to ask questions, not to answer them—to remind the deans and administrators that recruitment of well-qualified students will remain a high priority for an institution like ours. As the number of eighteen-year-olds declines over the next decade, this will become an even more difficult task.

After the meeting, I return phone calls and then dash to my doctor's office a few blocks away. He says I will survive my virus, writes a prescription, and encourages me to continue the self-imposed diet I began several months ago. Nothing complex about the scheme. I try to eat smaller portions and avoid snacks. Already, in three weeks, I have lost eight pounds. Now the challenge will be to keep it off. As I leave the prescription to be filled at a neighborhood drug store, the young man behind the counter says, "Hello, President Berendzen." No doubt he is a student. And I remember once again that anywhere near the campus my family and I have little privacy. If we have an intimate purchase to make, we had best do so on the other side of town.

Back in my office, I meet privately with Milt to discuss our nursing dean's impending retirement. Unlike our other teaching units, the School of Nursing does not have a compelling rationale. We do not have a medical school. And when I am asked, "What fields does your university stress?" I reply, "Those in which Washington itself has great strength—government, public affairs, international affairs, economics, communications, law, humanities, the arts." Nursing does not fit that mold. Still, a strong university should offer good programs in many fields, and AU does in areas that are not so strongly Washington-related. For us, nursing remains an enigma.

Milt and I discuss options: to select a new dean; to appoint one as acting from within; to merge the unit with the College of Arts and Sciences; to abolish the school entirely. I considered the latter possibility in the late seventies because the nursing school's enrollments then were dropping badly. But the school subsequently improved its cost efficiency, and problems would arise if we decided to close the unit. Tenure is not in a single teaching unit but rather in the university. Might we be required, therefore, to shift the nursing school's faculty to biology? Or psychology? Some of our endowment was earmarked for the nursing school. If we closed the school, could those funds be transferred to allied areas? How long a notice should we give students if we decide to end the program? Besides, the school's quality is high. So what is the best plan?

This evening I go to a TV studio for a taping. The topic is the D.C. Special Olympics, a program modeled after the famous sports event but designed specifically for mentally and physically handicapped persons. It will be held October 15 on the AU track. Again this year our students volunteered to assist this worthwhile program. The interviewer asks me, "Why is participation in the Special Olympics important for students?"

"Because it engages them in concerns beyond themselves," I reply. "The inflation of the seventies and the recession of the eighties pressed economic concerns so forcefully upon our youth that many of them began to come to higher education not to learn but to earn; not for education but for certification. This produced an inward-looking, money-oriented attitude. But young people need to realize that education should be for more than making a living; it should be for leading a life."

"But why do you suppose students perform such services?"

"Not because they have to," I answer. "Not because it is required in a course. Not because anyone in authority expects it of them. Rather, because they want to. Perhaps because some of them realize the maxim is true that you get back more than you give. What they are obtaining through this experience will endure; it will last far longer than any quick monetary gain."

In a time of overwhelming material concerns, it is heartening to know that altruism lives.

WEDNESDAY, SEPTEMBER 28
The phone rings as I drag myself from bed. A major donor wants the son of his friend to start at AU next week. Next week? We have

received no papers about the young man and classes have been under way for a month. He must apply and even if he is admitted, he cannot start until next term. Never mind. The family has decided that he should go to college *now*. We shall do only what is appropriate—despite the donor's intercession. Such lobbying arises frequently and we try to handle it sensitively.

My first meeting this morning is with my cabinet. The issues are routine. The Middle States study is on track. No repercussions have come from the resignation of the student government president. All is quiet with faculty and students. Library and computer usage are up. But the trustee committees need to be revised and we must activate our board members.

Back in my study, I spend the next several minutes on a delightful task. Government agencies send grant proposals to authorities for evaluation. When I was active in research, I received them frequently. I do not receive many proposals anymore. But yesterday I got one and last night I read it. Today I write my recommendation.

The proposal—on stellar energy—brings to mind the time I have spent in research on the history of astronomy. Original research is so intense and personal that it shuts the researcher off from the rest of the world. For hours on end, I used to dig through yellowed manuscripts in forgotten archives. Some were in libraries such as Princeton, Harvard, and the Huntington. But many were uncatalogued and stored in old file cabinets or cartons, often in such inhospitable places as the attic of the Mount Wilson Observatory.

Sometimes I would know precisely what I sought as I dug through thousands of old papers. More often, however, I would know only the general area. When I started using original archival materials for the study of early twentieth-century astronomy, almost no one else had done so. And most relevant documents had yet to be compiled, organized or preserved. In my pursuit of such original documents—from Lund, Sweden, to Pasadena, California—I encountered remarkable situations. The files I sought at the Lick Observatory near San Jose were in the basement, under the telescope, by the coffin of James Lick. His body was interred there at the end of the last century. As I sat alone in the basement at three o'clock in the morning reading yellowed, dusty letters written in the 1890s, I delighted at the pursuit of knowledge but wondered at the seeming pointlessness of it. Fundamental research, whether in history of science or modern electronics, does not always appear pertinent. But it has value. It forms the basis of all we know. What distressed me most, though, was that after months of toil, I would publish an article that would be read by no more than twenty people worldwide.

About ten years ago, for reasons such as these, I began to shift my attention from teaching and research to administration. In the process I gave up some of my personal thrill in pursuing problems that interested me. Instead, I had to work on issues significant to the institution: lawsuits, snow removal, broken steam lines, and staff disputes. It is the same as a writer becoming an editor; a doctor, a hospital director. For me, it has not been easy. Analysis of AU's budget or the nation's educational problems, for example, constitutes my current research. And rather than publish results in a scholarly journal replete with footnotes, I now give talks at conferences or appear on TV.

In the early 1970s, when I was an astronomy professor at Boston University, Bob Cohen, the chair of BU's Physics Department, recommended me to be one of the founding editors of the *Journal of College Science Teaching*. That in turn led to my meeting the new publication's editor-in-chief, Leo Schubert, who was the chair of AU's Chemistry Department. A bright, outspoken man, dedicated to high standards, Leo soon became my friend and unofficial mentor. I admired him deeply.

In the fall of 1973, he called me: "Dick, I'm chairing the search committee for AU's dean of arts and sciences. You're perfect for the post. Will you be a candidate?"

Stunned . . . and flattered . . . I stammered that I would think about it and call him back. For some time my fascination with Washington had been growing, as I discovered a metropolis in renaissance. And I was consumed with the dream of a great national university in the capital city. After discussing Leo's call with Gail and agonizing over the matter, I called him back: "I'm comfortable in Boston with many friends and a good career. But, *yes*, I'd be honored to be considered."

No sooner had I stopped teaching, however, than I discovered I missed it. Professors need to profess; lectures were welling up within me. One day I was in Garfinckel's department store. As the elevator door shut on the first floor, a strong compulsion overcame me. I turned to my fellow passengers and asked, "What would you like to know about the sun?"

There are two rules of etiquette on an elevator: face the front and never talk to strangers. I was violating both. By the time we reached the third floor, mothers were putting themselves between me and their children. But I continued, "The sun is a nuclear inferno that converts millions of tones of hydrogen into helium every . . . ." Finally, we reached the top floor. The door opened and my last passenger-student, a white-haired lady, started to leave. "Young man," she said, "this is the most interesting elevator ride I've ever had."

"It's just a service we provide in competition with other stores," I replied.

Sometimes I wonder if she ever returned with a friend. "He's in this one, Priscilla. A nice young man, he'll tell us about the sun."

Tonight we drive to the National Portrait Gallery. In its long, vaulted halls, we are to attend a function honoring the bicentennial of the Treaty of Paris. Although that treaty is obscure to most Americans, it began the United States. The Declaration of Independence on 4 July 1776 indicated what we hoped to do; the Treaty of Paris on 2 September 1783 celebrated what we had done. The British had accepted our independence and other nations had recognized us as well.

Joan Challinor, a tall, imposing woman, is the driving force behind this observance. After having four children, she returned to The American University and obtained her Ph.D. two years ago. Tonight she chairs the event.

I shake hands with Senator Charles Mathias, who frequently addresses AU's Washington Semester Program, and with Elliot Richardson, former secretary-of-everything. Sol Linowitz walks by, a sensitive man who provided wise counsel during the Camp David accords and whose brother, Bob Linowes, is an AU trustee. O. B. Hardison, director of the Folger Shakespeare Library, is on the other side of the room, as is former diplomat Ellsworth Bunker, whose wife, Carol Laise, used to be an AU trustee.

Over a dinner of John Adams mountain trout, I reflect on the provocative concept of time. We are here tonight to celebrate an event of two centuries ago. And we are holding the celebration in this special room where Lincoln received the guests at his inaugural ball. Out the window, past the speakers, I hear horns and see distant airplane lights. None of that was there at Lincoln's ball. Could he have imagined our presence tonight? Can we imagine what other group will sit in this room a century from now? Will AU have its sports center by then? Will it be a national university? Will these issues be of significance to anyone? They consume my life now, but will they have permanence over time?

While the other guests' eyes lock on the speaker, mine roam the room, stopping on a statue far up one wall. How perfect that it should be there: it is of Benjamin Franklin who made possible the signing of the Treaty of Paris. I come back to the speaker, Joan Challinor, who is saying that the title of the current exhibit at the National Portrait Gallery sums it up well: "Blessed are the peacemakers." That is what the Treaty of Paris was about, and that is what education should be about. We should be preparing the peacemakers of tomorrow. It is useful to do a task. But it is also useful to know what the task is that you need to do.

THURSDAY, SEPTEMBER 29

My morning meeting with the provost, vice-presidents, and vice-provosts has two agenda items: the accreditation review and affirmative action. I tell the group about the Philadelphia meeting and we attempt to anticipate any weak spots that an accreditation team might find. Overall, we feel confident that we are prepared for their visit. But I point out that in at least one area, results have not met our goals. Only a handful of our faculty are black; none of our administrators is; and the number of our black applicants is declining. With respect to faculty, we are doing little hiring; in fact, we are attempting to reduce the number of full-time professors. When we do hire, it is usually in fields in which there are small numbers of qualified black professionals, such as law or computer science. Similarly, we have had few black applicants for the administrative posts that have come open in the past few years.

The answers and rationales are valid. But that does not remove the potential for criticism nor lessen our own desire for improvement. We conclude that Milt should contact his counterpart at Howard University to see if we can establish joint faculty appointments. Triezenberg will ask the admissions and financial aid offices to search harder for black students. And when the new director of staff personnel services arrives on Monday, we shall ask her to seek black applicants diligently.

Milt and I go to Mary Graydon Center to host a luncheon for distinguished scholars. Leaving the function, I bump into Gail in the hallway. She is coming from a meeting with an Egyptian student, Luby Ismail, who is planning a diplomatic night. Luby wants to invite cultural attachés from the embassies. Gail is advising her on protocol and will assist in contacting key attachés. "I think Luby will be able to go with me tomorrow to the tea at Blair House for Mrs. Mubarak," Gail continues. "She's pretty excited." Yes, I imagine she is. Gail is good about including students in such functions. She also tells me that one of her friends, Mary Ann Lundgren, public relations director of the Washington Neiman-Marcus, knows a prominent ninety-year-old Texan who lives in Washington. The woman would like to write her memoirs. Could Gail find a student to assist?

Several years ago, my father decided to write stories about his own childhood for Deborah and Natasha. The world has changed so dramatically since the beginning of this century, the youngsters would scarcely believe that he rode a horse to school and met with Apache chiefs. He wrote his narrative and Gail edited it into a saga of turn-of-the-century America. Both girls have enjoyed my father's stories just as they have mine. Why do children have such a fascination over their parents' childhoods? I have told them a thousand times about when I was a youngster and made my own Fourth of July fireworks. The gunpowder I brewed was exceptionally explosive. One summer evening I poured a massive amount of it onto my parents' front sidewalk. It ignited in a blinding fireball, sending a smoke cloud skyward. Moments later, a police car sped by. For the next half hour, we heard sirens throughout the neighborhood as emergency vehicles drove up one street and down the other. Then my father strolled out in the yard. "Boys, have you heard the news? People have called to report a plane crash or a UFO landing. What do you think of that?" The next morning he said, "I wonder why our sidewalk is busted." Like Brer Rabbit, I laid low.

And both Deborah and Natasha have asked repeatedly about my boyhood adventure with a homemade rocket. After weeks of construction, I launched it from my backyard. It rose dramatically for a hundred feet and then fell back to earth—on our neighbor's roof. It ignited the brittle shingles. Panicked, I turned on the back faucet and rushed to the neighbor's house with our garden hose. It would not reach. So I aimed the water in a high arc, attempting to reach the roof. Instead, it cascaded through the neighbor's bedroom window. In moments the furious neighbor, who had had other experiences with the odd boy next door, screamed: "What are you doing? There's water all over my room."

"Well, sir," I stammered. "I'm just trying to put out the fire on your roof." That perfectly rational explanation did not mollify him. He was always difficult.

Similarly, I enjoyed my mother's story of how her Scotch-Irish father rode in the Oklahoma landrush of 1889. With other settlers, he positioned his wagon at the starting line. When the gun was fired, the homesteaders sped across the prairie to stake their claims. My grandfather hoped to acquire fertile land. Decades later, oil was found on adjacent farms, but none on my grandfather's. He had selected the Israel of Oklahoma.

When I return to my office, Joan says that Myers has asked to have an emergency meeting at four o'clock. If it is that important, we must have it. I can guess the subject. The group assembles in my office. "I have had further communication with the union leaders," Myers begins, "and they hint that the custodial employees may strike and the food service employees may have a sympathy strike. For weeks I have offered to negotiate, but the union has yet to tell me what they have in mind. They know we have a contract with the cleaning firm. And they know that the custodians work for the cleaning firm, not AU. Nonetheless, they insist that the custodians' salaries must be increased substantially. The cleaning firm says it doesn't have the funds. We're at an impasse."

How can the food service employees strike when their contract says that they will not? Are the union's demands reasonable? If we comply with them, what will they demand next? What would be the overall cost to students and employees? Are we on sound footing, legally and morally? How will the campus react to union activities? And on the questions go.

Triezenberg notes: "Irrespective of the rightness of our position, how much are we willing to pay in time and effort to see this through? Once a strike starts, it could become ugly and last for weeks or months."

"Certain basic premises are inviolate," I reply. "We shall not commit unfair labor practices; we shall not infringe upon the rights of workers. Nor shall we capitulate to unreasonable demands. This confrontation need not happen. Our contract with the cleaning firm is fair and they're paying the market wage. We have attempted to be good employers. When any of you speak to union leaders about this, quote me. We will not bend on principles."

From that low point, I return to a joyous high. WRC–radio called this morning and asked me to be on this afternoon to discuss astronomy. To bone up, I rummage through my old papers on astronomy. I have not seen some of them since the early sixties when I was a teaching assistant at Harvard. There, written on the back of a note about measuring the molecular weight of the upper atmosphere, I find something I have not seen for twenty years—a poem Gail wrote me shortly after we met. Misty-eyed, I read it this afternoon and then reread. Beneath the poem Gail had written, "When you're forty-five, I wonder what kind of notebook I shall be sneaking corny poetry into. And will you love me enough to put up with it then?" I call to answer the question she asked twenty years ago: a resounding *yes.*

"Let's skip our function tonight," she replies, her voice quivering. "Why don't you come home—and bring the poem with you."

FRIDAY, SEPTEMBER 30
After having lunch with an assistant secretary in the U.S. Department of Health and Human Services, I return to hear from Milt about the latest proposal to restructure campus governance. As regularly as the change of foliage, some group devises a new scheme to revise the university's decision-making into a "more efficient and democratic process." Each of these grand approaches is touted to last forever. Remarkable amounts of time are spent arguing their merits and liabilities. Someone once said: "Passions run so high in academic life only because the issues are so shallow." Despite the sarcasm, there is some truth in that.

As I flip through today's *Eagle,* an article catches my eye. It is about the sports and convocation center. "Students Push Administration on Sports Center Plans," the headline declares. "University Remains 'Mum' on Possible Starting Dates." The article goes on to say that the student task force on the center is going to raise funds. One project will be to sell T-shirts. Another will be to host a concert in the Tavern featuring "Steve Smith and the Nakeds." Why hadn't I thought to have Steve Smith and the Nakeds? *Who are* Steve Smith and the Nakeds?

SATURDAY, OCTOBER 1
Dinner tonight is simple and delightful. Over fried chicken at our kitchen table, Gail, Natasha, and I discuss Natasha's school study of hypothesis and deduction. That leads into one of my favorite games. We call it Sherlock Holmes. I give Natasha a small amount of data and from that she—like Holmes—is to deduce as much as possible.

Tonight I say she is a detective who has to find out as much as possible about the family in this house by studying only one object and the things around it—the chopping block assembly. As we eat our chicken, she starts deducing: The family must be middle income to afford the assembly; an amateur drawing on it means that a child may be in the family; of the three saucepans, the largest has scarcely been used, which suggests a family size of under four.

"What else do you see?" I ask. "How can you prove that? Are you being consistent? Is that the only plausible interpretation?" It is like first-year law school, except more fun.

After dinner we play with Sparky, Natasha's black puppy, who is talkative tonight. Standing on his hind legs, he wails plaintively about his need for more food—that is our hypothesis. We try to test his intelligence. He loves cookies. We let him watch as we place one under a tall, overturned plastic juice container. If he pushes at the bottom, the container will slide but not fall; if he pushes at the top, it will fall and the cookie will be his. Can he understand this? He goes directly toward the cookie at the base. But often the best route to a goal is not the most obvious. How can we teach him that?

He tries and fails. Over and over again, he fails. Then he gives up and barks. He is determined but confused. Finally, the teacher in me comes forth as I get on all fours and push the container with my head. When I do it his way, I fail; the right way, and I succeed. Can he learn? Not fast, apparently. We try again, but to no avail. Natasha is disappointed, but I point out that the experiment is worth continuing and that all animals require time. "Work with Sparky," I say. "Give him clues. Learning doesn't come easily or quickly. He needs help and time."

SUNDAY, OCTOBER 2

This evening, Gail and I drive to the Leisure World Retirement Community in suburban Maryland where I am to talk about astronomy. Along the way, we come upon an auto accident. One of the damaged cars has New York plates. Instinctively, we check the bumper for an AU student sticker. Sure enough, there it is. I stop and go back to the wreck. "You've arrived at just the right time, Dr. Berendzen," a young man exclaims. AU people are everywhere.

The driver recognizes me as I ask, "How do you feel?"

"Shaken. And my neck hurts," he replies. I tell him to go to Sibley Hospital as soon as he finishes with the police report.

Is My Armor Straight?

Care and concern about students is one of the most significant responsibilities we have. Usually, it is a joyful task. But there are exceptions. A few years ago, someone called after midnight to inform me that a student had just fallen to his death in an air-conditioning well. A freshman, he had been playing with a frisbee in front of a dorm. It had rolled under a ledge into a dark, out of the way place. He went to get it but never came back. Somehow, he had fallen past a grate into the well.

When I arrived, the area was surrounded by police. They asked me to climb into the well to identify the body. As I came up, the young man's girlfriend arrived, learned what had happened, and fainted. I carried her to her room and her friends offered to stay with her. But then I faced a painful, obligatory task: to notify the parents. For several minutes I stared at the phone. Finally, I called. When I explained what had happened, there was silence on the other end. Then sobbing. What could I say?

That was the first accidental death in AU's history. Our physical plant is safe, with guard rails and lights. Yet at any moment one of our thousands of charges may be in danger. The students demand freedom and independence while they need protection and care.

MONDAY, OCTOBER 3

Every major city has expensive neighborhoods. Among Washington's are Kalorama Circle, Foxhall Road, Spring Valley, Chevy Chase, Potomac, Great Falls, Georgetown, and Old Town. But one small stretch is special, not only for Washington but the nation as well. It extends for a mile or two on the Virginia side of the Potomac River starting at Chain Bridge. There, standing amidst high foliage, scarcely visible from the road, sits a promenade of mansions owned by extremely influential people. One of them, Merrywood, has had a rich heritage. Jacqueline Kennedy Onassis and Lee Radziwill grew up there, and that is where then Senator John F. Kennedy wrote his *Profiles in Courage.* Now it is the home of Nancy Dickerson, the striking TV personality. For the past several months, she has labored over a show commemorating the twentieth anniversary of JFK's death. She and her associates have viewed and edited hundreds of hours of TV tape. She narrates the film and acts as hostess for this premiere.

We arrive late—just as Kennedy and Nixon go at it in their famous TV debate. When I watched that live, Kennedy looked young while Nixon seemed relatively mature. Seeing it again, they both look young. Kennedy in the film is roughly my age today. And Nixon looks untrustworthy; his eyes dart, his answers evade. Kennedy is handsome, urbane, witty, self-confident. Despite his accent, his eloquence stimulates anew. The phrases flow, the ideas sparkle, the challenge comes back. He had style. And grace.

The film ends with his death and Nancy wisely permits the camera to linger, showing tears on a black woman's face and hurt on a young man's face as they realize they have lost their leader. That is when the nation began to lose its innocence. It lost Camelot and gained experience.

After the film, Nancy ushers us to a reception area before we have dinner. With a string quartet playing in the background, I talk with Bill Webster, the highly regarded director of the FBI. His schedule must be outrageous, yet he promises to attend the next meeting of our National Advisory Board. Lucy Sirica says hello as she looks in the throng for her husband John, who, as a judge, played a critical role in the Watergate case. It was at the Sirica's some years ago that I first met Nancy Dickerson and later asked her to join our board of trustees.

WEDNESDAY, OCTOBER 5   .

In my office today, there is the usual deluge of phone messages, some of them slightly absurd. Yesterday, when the temperature was seventy-four degrees, a student screamed at Joan that the dorm air conditioning had to be turned on immediately. Joan explained that this is Indian summer: One day is warm; the next, cool. In our large and complex system, either the air conditioning is on or the heat is. Last week students insisted that the heat should be. Physical Plant complied and cannot turn back to air conditioning for just one day. But that did not satisfy the caller.

A student sends a blistering letter claiming that he was denied the opportunity to register. We check and find that the financial office stopped his file because his payments were months in arrears. I wonder what he has experienced with charge accounts and credit cards.

Another student calls, demanding to see me at once so he can tell me how the curriculum should be changed. We refer him to the appropriate people. None of them will do, not even the provost. Only the president will do, and he must be available *now*. As politely as possible, we tell him no.

Such situations are delicate, for I do not wish to offend our students. It falls to the university to be surrogate parents, even for headstrong youth. Fortunately, the fraction of ours who fit that category is small. But when you have as many students as we have, that can leave some who think only about themselves.

THURSDAY, OCTOBER 6

As I walk to my office this crisp fall morning, I jot down things I want Physical Plant to change. Last summer I spent hours walking the campus, filling yellow legal pads with lists of shrubs to be removed, signs to be repainted, and curbs to be fixed. Almost all those changes are in place today.

Few people on campus realize the hundreds of changes we made. Even when something as large as a dead tree is removed, remarkably few notice. The overall effect, however, has been magnificent. "I don't know why it is," many have remarked to me, "but the campus looks better this fall." That is just what we wanted.

Because I was out of town earlier this week, many people must touch base with me. After eleven phone calls, I am ready for lunch. At noon I shake hands with Martin Agronsky, a friend and member of our NAB. In the faculty-staff dining room, we discuss everything from the federal deficit to the role of TV. Martin concurs with my assessment of the decline of academic rigor in the schools; he agrees that the home and family must shoulder much of the responsibility. As we walk back to my office, we talk about students' problems these days. And I tell him a story.

"Students are accustomed to seeing my lights on late in the evening. So after midnight several years ago, my office phone rang. 'Dr. Berendzen, several of us must see you. It is an emergency.'

"Minutes later, five young men were in my office, looking exceedingly glum. One of them began, 'As you know, staff can give out perquisites. Well, one person who makes such decisions for us is a woman'—she was several years their senior.

" 'Yes, I know that. But what's the point?'

" 'The point, sir, is that . . . well . . . she won't give these favors unless we're willing to sleep with her.'

"Was this a joke? Were they serious? 'Are you complaining that we don't have enough such staff members?' I asked flippantly. This was clearly a mistake.

" 'Oh, not at all,' they solemnly replied. 'The problem is that she doesn't respect our minds—just our bodies.'

" 'You don't understand how degrading all this is,' snapped another young man. 'We don't want to be exploited just for her pleasure.'

"Surely, I thought, this has to be a put-on. If they get me to believe their story, will they be admitted into a fraternity? Despite my doubts, this curious conversation went on for almost an hour, with each young man seemingly more earnest than the one before. If they were joking, they were doing it convincingly. Finally, I assured them that we would not permit them to be exploited; that they were people, not objects; and that we would look into the matter soon."

Martin laughs heartily, wondering if he attended college during the wrong era.

Then to our executive committee meeting. I open by noting AU's status, which is good, and turn to Triezenberg, who summarizes the fall enrollment data. This is obviously a special occasion, for Don wears his only dark suit. Spiffy dressing is not his forte, but precise thinking and excellent staff work are. He has prepared his numbers carefully and presents them well.

Milt reviews proposed faculty personnel actions, which the executive committee approves. Then intense discussion arises over complex business items. In his customary fashion, Myers has discussed these items individually with almost everyone. All of these opportunities bode well for AU. But one jolts us: whether to accept a confidential offer to sell one of our buildings, Nebraska Hall, so that it can be used for a chancery. A foreign nation wants it badly—enough to offer us a multimillion-dollar profit in cash. What a temptation.

After lengthy discussion, the committee votes in favor of my suggestion to make the sale. Still, the decision bothers me. We must not sell our heritage, irrespective of instant gain. On the other hand, think what those millions would mean for the sports center campaign. We could announce ground-breaking.

Later, I go to the student radio station where I am to be interviewed. I enjoy the interviewers tonight, both of whom are courteous and well prepared. I cannot say the same, though, about all of the student callers, some of whom drip sarcasm.

"*Exactly* when will the sports and convocation center be built?" demands one.

"As soon as we secure the money or have a high likelihood of obtaining it. If you want to speed the process, write checks and encourage others to do so. Rhetoric gets us nowhere; money talks."

"Why aren't there students on the board of trustees? If there were, you administrators couldn't keep raising our tuition."

"Our bylaws prohibit AU students or employees from being trustees. This is to avoid conflict of interest and almost all private universities follow like practices."

After the interview I return home. Finding our cupboard bare, I drive to Roy Rogers, where I bump into three more students. Back home later, Gail and I try to figure out how to console Natasha. She ran for the position of class representative but was defeated today. In my view, keeping out of school politics will give her more time for study and leisure. But that is not how she sees it. What do we tell her?

FRIDAY, OCTOBER 7

As I shave, I anguish over yesterday's decision to sell Nebraska Hall. The decision is not final because the committee only recommended it for board action later this month. The board likely will agree. But does that make the decision correct?

At 9:30 A.M. Milt, the two Dons, and I have our weekly meeting. Apparently, they have been sharing my anxieties. "Yesterday, the executive committee made many important decisions," I begin. "The trustees were helpful and Don Myers prepared the materials well. But one issue haunts me—the proposed sale of Nebraska Hall. Myers has indicated his reservations to me. Because he has handled the negotiations, I'd like him to speak now."

Don acknowledges the temptation of providing this cash-thin institution with a sudden infusion of several million dollars. But he ticks off a litany of possible problems. How would the neighbors react? Where would we move our existing facilities in Nebraska Hall until another structure was available? Is this the *only* way the university can raise such funds?

And then I voice a concern that was raised yesterday; it has bothered me since. "What happens if the buyer decides to sell in a year or two? Zoning would prohibit commercial development and AU might be unable to meet the asking price. In that case, a different country—a Libya or a South Africa—might buy the building and we would have no control. Then our campus could be exposed to demonstrations or even violence."

Even Triezenberg, the fundraiser, speaks against the sale. Milt agrees, noting that only two years ago we announced that we had no choice but to purchase Nebraska Hall because it likely was the last adjacent land this institution could ever acquire. We should not backtrack now.

This conclusion is useful, but what are we to do? Largely at our request, the executive committee has endorsed the sale and it will recommend it to the board. "That may be," I say, "but we should change the decision rather than proceed with a bad one." We agree that we shall call the trustees and explain why we have decided against the sale. I am confident they will understand and support us.

We turn from this to other issues, yet Nebraska Hall echoes in my mind. The infusion of cash could launch the sports center. I would be a hero. But if our predecessors could have known the future, would the Indians have sold Manhattan? Would Russia have sold Alaska? I am convinced. Our decision may or may not be right for today, but it definitely will be right for posterity. And one of our responsibilities is to ensure the future. I shall ask the board to rescind the recommendation of the executive committee.

This evening I go to the Folger Shakespeare Library on Capitol Hill for its annual reception. As one of the world's premiere humanities centers, the Folger is a vital force in academic life. I am asked to speak. The Folger's long, medieval-style hallway reverberates with laughter and talk of scholars from numerous universities—so much so that the first speakers can scarcely be heard. How odd that professors accustomed to lecturing are oblivious when someone else tries to speak.

After quoting a few lines from *As You Like It,* I say, "Shakespeare caught the rhythms of his time and they continue today. But it is neither his wit nor style that concern me; nor is it literature from three centuries ago. Rather, it is literature of today, not published in England but just a few blocks from here; not the work of poets but that of educators; not written by quill pen but by the U.S. Government Printing Office. I refer to *A Nation at Risk.* This blistering indictment of the U.S. educational system is incontrovertably correct. Its prose is not Shakespearean, but its message is clear. By any reasonable measure, the academic achievement of our schools has declined for the past two decades. And two factors related to that decline are germane here today.

"One of them is the all-consuming quest for money. Spurred by inflation and then recession, many people have sought money before all else. Some cynic once claimed that the only value of a classic brain is that it enables you to despise the wealth it prevents you from obtaining. Regrettably, too many people have forgotten that the bedrock of knowledge lies with the humanities. Jobs may not abound there, but the foundation of civilization does. And that is what the Folger epitomizes.

"A second problem has been the demise of our language. Our facility with words has shrunk from elegant poetry to mundane prose to technical jargon to sloppy cliches. Insofar as language reflects the mind, this deterioration may suggest a growing imprecision of thought. And if we do not think clearly, we cannot write clearly. Here, too, the Folger is a beacon. In our modern electronic world, the microchip may dominate, but the well-chosen word has no peer. The Folger, therefore, is not merely a library of arcane materials from three centuries ago. It stands as living testament to the timelessness of the written word, the grace of the spoken word. It symbolizes from the past what is needed in the present: a renaissance of the intellect, the spirit, the nation."

Back on campus again, I meet Milt so we can be on hand for the beginning of the students' Muscular Dystrophy Dance-a-thon. By now it is nine o'clock and I have not eaten. I do not feel like dancing. But then I see Natasha. I ask if she would like to dance with me, but she is nervous in front of these "big kids." Her excuse is, "This music is by a really old-timey group." It is the Beatles! Life is a matter of perspective.

SUNDAY, OCTOBER 9

Our efforts at a family bike ride this afternoon are thwarted because my rear tire—which was fixed last week—is flat again. It has been fixed four times in six months. Also, the cruise control on our Volvo does not work; it has been fixed twice. I feel I am getting overly heated about these issues when I realize that the house itself is hot. The furnace is on and will not go off. We adjust every thermostat, but to no avail. Finally, flashlight in hand, I crawl in the boiler room and find the magic switch. Given that it is a warm day, I assume that even with the boiler off, there will be enough hot water in the pipes for a quick shower. There is. But the drain is clogged and the water backs up to my ankles. We will get that fixed tomorrow, too.

As I walk to my office, I think about an old movie I saw on TV late last night—*Fail Safe*. It told a hair-raising story about the accidental outbreak of nuclear war between the U.S. and the Soviet Union. Either man or machine had failed; it made no difference. If my tire is flat, my Volvo broken, my heat on, and my drain clogged, why do I assume that larger things always work? But what is the alternative?

MONDAY, OCTOBER 10
Even though AU does not observe Columbus Day as a holiday, today is remarkably calm: no mail, few phone calls, no interruptions. When the office is hectic, I pray for solitude; when it becomes quiet, I long for activity. Nonetheless, today has its virtues, because I am able to plan for the next several months.

The campus mood this term is congenial, even euphoric. But it could become negative again. On a gray day in January 1982, we added the budget numbers for at least the tenth time; recounting would not change them. We had to face the cold facts. A year earlier, we had implemented a relatively modest tuition increase and had given employees a relatively high salary hike. In fact, in three years, our employees' average salary rose more than 35 percent and, with merit, some went up almost 45 percent. When we presented this generous budget, we were confident that we had sufficient funds. But by winter '82, the weather numbed and so did our financial posture. The nation was in a recession and AU was "cash-thin."

Only too late did I learn that the budget officers had not done their jobs well. And they had not wanted to rock the boat. Apparently, they had hoped for a miracle. So there we were in January coming up with budget guidelines for September. They were jolting: a relatively modest salary increase coupled with the largest tuition increase in AU's history. We tried to obtain budgetary information from other schools. Georgetown University's tuition increase would be larger than ours and George Washington's would be even larger than that. But to our students, that made no difference.

At a university senate meeting, Milt made the first disclosure of the budget figures we would propose. To say the reaction to his announcement was explosive would be to understate. The *Eagle* blasted the budget and condemned the administration. The faculty—not being treated generously but at least less severely affected than the students—remained restive but quiet.

The winter of 1982 was exceptionally long and bitter, gray day after gray day. That pall alone would have made for gloom. In addition, the Reagan administration was proposing to cut student financial aid. And so it was that by February 1982 there was a campus chorus of protest. Such frustration needs a vent. The students could not meet with Reagan, so some other authority figure would have to suffice. At AU, I became a convenient target.

The board of trustees ultimately approves the budget. The students knew that and decided that their best strategy would be first to challenge me and then take on the board. In mid-February, student government leaders said they were going to hold a rally to protest the tuition hike. I was in Denver, Colorado, to speak to a business group. When I called the office, Milt said, "Richard, I don't know what the students have in mind, but they're planning a large rally and they want to know if we'll attend." Whereupon I called the student confederation office and agreed to speak.

As chance would have it, the exceptionally bitter winter broke for the day of the rally. Bright sunshine replaced the pall and springlike warmth brought out sweaters instead of overcoats. The students' disdain for authority figures was self-evident. I wore my oldest corduroy jacket and a turtleneck sweater. Nowhere are images more important than at a university, where, presumably, ideas reign.

When we reached Mary Graydon Center at the heart of the Quad, we found several thousand students in a festive mood. The protest leaders were extremely courteous to me—until they started speaking publicly. Then it was their chance to shine. With ringing demagoguery, they twisted facts and denounced AU, me, and the Reagan administration, all in one vast sweep. Truth made no difference; only firebrand oratory counted, adroitly designed to elicit applause at regular intervals.

The podium was surrounded by news media representatives—print, radio, TV. Quite aware of Reagan's budget cuts, they were curious about the impact on universities. I had agreed to appear in whatever way would be most appropriate. After students gave a couple of blistering introductory speeches, the organizers called upon me. Confronting a wave of catcalls, I stood silently before the mike. Then I spoke in a soft voice. The catcalls were replaced by shouts of "We can't hear you." I continued with my soft delivery until there was silence. Only then did I speak loudly into the mike. I pointed out that our proposed increase was in line with comparable universities. That brought forth: "So what? Who gives a damn what the others charge?"

One young man jumped up and down throughout my entire delivery, his face red, his hands clenched. I had not seen such passion since the 1960s.

I looked at the eyes. Some screamed hatred; many were passive; others had a twinkle, relishing the spectacle. Later, students would say that they attended the rally not so much to protest the tuition hike as to see what such an event was like. Their older brothers and sisters had attended rallies years ago. But they had never attended one. They were curious.

The issues were numerous and complex. Some students genuinely anguished over their ability to pay bills. Others wanted to embarrass the administration. A few wanted to lash out at anyone representing authority. Some, perhaps the majority, felt the tuition increase was high but were willing to accept it if we would explain why it was necessary. A distinct minority just wanted to raise hell.

Without notes, I simply addressed what I perceived to be their anxieties. "I understand your concern," I said. "I sympathize with it. The national economy is troubled and may get worse. AU is strained fiscally as well. We'll do everything we can to keep tuition down. I have no objection to your protesting rising costs. Far from it. I commend you for caring so deeply about your education. But I urge you not to do anything you'll regret. Remember that we're a community; don't rupture those fragile bonds. We'll come through these dark days together."

As I walked back to my office, several students accompanied me. Some remained angry, but most were polite and asked good questions about the budget. One, who had shouted throughout my remarks, approached me and said, "This is the first time I've been to a protest rally and I got carried away. If my parents had seen me, they would have been embarrassed. Please forgive me." I smiled, swallowed hard, and said, "It's okay. Object if you must, but please don't harm yourself or your university."

The protesters' next target was the board, which was scheduled to meet in March 1982. The students reasoned that if they could lobby individual trustees and make impassioned pleas, then the board would hold down the tuition hike and might even fire the administrators. They also reasoned that external pressures could be effective, so they sent a form letter to parents of AU students. It decried the proposed tuition increase and complained about "rodents" in the dorms.

A few days later, an irate mother called me from the Midwest. "You heartless monster," she began. "How dare you permit killer rats to roam my daughter's dorm? Why don't you and that son-of-a-bitch Reagan go sit in a country club and leave us working people alone?" After twenty minutes, she concluded that she should talk to our financial aid office, that AU was where she wanted her daughter to go, and that we had no "killer rats."

Within the next two weeks, I received four dozen phone calls and 110 letters from AU parents. Most of them, expressing anguish over the rising costs of education, were truly touching. Some asked for financial aid. A few attacked me, AU, the Reagan administration, "big business," or universities in general. I wrote individual letters to each family. I reassured them of my own concern about their financial plight. I told them the university was seeking additional student aid funds and I expressed the hope that through some combination— financial aid, loans, part-time jobs—their children would be able to continue at AU.

The board meeting began and the experienced trustees steeled themselves for an explosive session. Students ringed the building handing petitions to trustees. The president of the student confederation gave an impassioned speech, pleading that the trustees defer making any decision about the tuition increase. After lengthy discussion, the motion to approve the increase was called. The board voted unanimously in favor of the 18 percent hike.

With that crisis past, in the spring of 1982, I went on a three-day fund-raising trip to California. On one of my daily calls to the office, Joan read the latest enrollment projection. As I listened, I sank into my hotel chair feeling sick. The summer enrollments were bad and the fall projections were worse. I hung up and called Milt. "Who's doing what about the sagging enrollments?" I asked.

"The admissions office is doing all it can and summer sessions is beating the bushes. But we're hearing from other schools that their summer enrollments are looking bad, too. And we can't get reliable information for next fall from other institutions; they may be down."

"That they're down will prove this is part of a larger trend," I suggested. "But that won't help pay our bills in September. Please ready your people. I'm coming back."

I called Triezenberg next. "Don, we have an emergency. Get details from Milt. And work with him to assemble everyone for crash meetings about revenues. Ask Myers if he can come up with ways to cut costs or raise money. I want a meeting tomorrow afternoon."

We met; we planned; we advertised. The summer enrollments sank below budget projections and September approached with the number of freshman applications down. In June, I directed that the budget should be cut before the fiscal year began on July 1. In August, with enrollment projections still looking poor, we decided that the budget should be cut again.

Then came September. Students are required to make non-refundable deposits for tuition and dorms. To our dismay, dozens did not show up—thereby forfeiting deposits. We called other private universities; they were experiencing the same phenomenon. Then we called community colleges; their enrollments were skyrocketing. During the darkest days of the recession, numerous families had decided that higher education was exorbitantly expensive; the financial outlook was so gloomy that they would move from private universities to less expensive community colleges. And so it was that in September 1982, higher education experienced a major enrollment shift. Enrollments at many private colleges and universities dropped while those at most state-supported schools rose.

When we published our data, we became the first private university in the region to reveal that enrollments and revenues were down. In October 1982, our projections indicated that we would end the fiscal year at least $3 million in the red. The university's officers met repeatedly to determine a priority list of possible cuts. We did not want to harm programs, worsen morale, or create a defeatist attitude. On a campus, image can become reality; attitude can become fact. If our students believed AU was in financial crisis, the prophecy would become self-fulfilling. And this was not paranoia on our part. Several parents called to ask: "Will AU remain open long enough to give my son his degree? We have put a lot into AU, and I'd hate to have it close before he graduates."

I assured the callers that rumors of AU's death, like those of Mark Twain's, were premature. Indeed, AU remained a strong and vital institution. Its endowment was growing; its gifts were increasing; its admissions standards were the highest in its history; its academic programs were not suffering. And, I assured the callers, we would come through stronger than ever.

But first we had to weather the storm. Where could we find more money? We could not increase student fees and we could not cut faculty salaries. Aside from supplies and travel, the only place to trim costs was in personnel. So we closed fifty staff positions, virtually all of which then were unoccupied.

Staff reductions brought us into another crisis later that winter. Myers, whom I had recently appointed as vice-president for finance, proceeded apace on an idea Milt had proposed at least nine months earlier—to replace our custodial service with a contract firm. At that time, AU had more than ninety custodians, all employees. In discussions with several contract cleaning firms, Myers found that for the scale of our operation, only sixty custodians were required and that AU was paying more per hour than the going rate. After discussing this with contract cleaning authorities and labor attorneys, he selected a particular contract cleaning firm. Shortly before the winter break in December 1982, he met with me to discuss the dilemma we faced.

The savings to be achieved through shifting to the contract firm would amount to several hundred thousand dollars per year. For substantially less money, the new service would be at least as good and possibly better. The large contract firms had extensive experience and were efficient. But we would have to fire our custodians. Some—but not all—would be rehired by the contract firm. Moreover, all were minorities. The contract firm that Myers recommended was also minority-run. That helped, but the anguish of the situation remained. On a cold December day, all the university officers recommended to me that we make the change. I agreed with them.

Then the first explosion occurred. Employees received their dismissal letters and the news media descended upon campus. From Christmas through New Year's is usually a slow news time. Congress is in recess; the president leaves town; breaking news disappears. And so developments such as the firing of AU's custodians receive more attention than they would normally. The *Post* ran an article sympathetic to the workers, with a touching photograph of one of them. The campus itself, however, remained calm.

Then the second explosion occurred. Our dismissed workers did not have collective bargaining nor had they requested it; nonetheless, a union sprang to their defense. This we had not anticipated, nor had we fully expected the response of students and faculty when they returned. Professors, students, some staff members, and a handful of alumni—angered by the news stories—called my office and demanded that we rehire the custodians. We attempted to explain the enormous savings that would benefit students and employees alike.

We tried to show that we were concerned about the plight of the workers. But that did not stop the charges. Because the displaced custodians were black, we were accused of racism, even though the new custodians were black themselves. The union claimed we fired them because they wanted to unionize, even though they had never attempted to do so. Students and faculty asserted that we dismissed them during the winter break so as to avoid the wrath of the campus. In fact, we chose that time to minimize disruption of service.

The protest had just begun. Union organizers manipulated the campus community, an easily malleable group during such an emotion-laden time. They met with students and faculty members to mount an attack upon the administration. They organized demonstrations on the Quad, around my office building, and around my home. For these marches, they brought back several displaced custodians who waved signs demanding their jobs back. The marchers were joined by some students and one or two professors. But, more importantly, the union worked hard to have the news media cover the demonstrations. To us, it seemed that the union was trying to provoke arrest.

Demonstrators appeared—sometimes announced, sometimes not —circling my office building or home. We shut the shades, locked the doors, and carried on as usual. Union leaders pounded on the doors; demonstrators sang "We Shall Overcome." How ironic this was, for I had joined in civil rights activities and had sung that song myself many times. Meanwhile, professors—many of them close friends— signed petitions condemning the firings and insisting upon the reinstitution of "collegial democracy." A spate of proposals came from both faculty and students. We should hold referenda to decide matters such as this. We should establish a committee composed of professors, students, staff members, and administrators to determine how best to rehire the custodians and make policy decisions as a group.

I met with campus leaders. And Myers and labor lawyers met with the union. Soon it was evident that with only minor accomodations, the university, the contract firm, and the union would reach accord. But some people on campus saw a larger ethical issue. Almost out of nowhere, faculty members appeared whose names I did not recognize; in fact, students and professors within their own teaching unit knew little about them. Yet, suddenly, here they were, center stage, passionately condemning the administration. The law college became particularly active, which puzzled everyone. Normally, our law students—like most law students—are so pressured by their courses that they disassociate themselves from campus life.

But while all these public events took place, there were private ones, too. Gail and I received dozens of harassing and obscene calls on our unlisted home phone. On one occasion union organizers shoved Joan out of the office doorway, almost knocking her down. They declared that they were staying in the building until they saw me, knowing full well that lawyers had instructed me to say nothing about the matter to them. When we informed them that if they did not leave the building they would be arrested without the news media seeing them, they left immediately.

Eventually, the university agreed to provide a transitional subsidy for some displaced workers and the contract firm agreed to rehire more of them. All sides declared this a victory—in part because it was a victory for all sides and in part because by then everyone wanted peace. Once the accord was struck between the university and the union, all sides went back to normal pursuits. In a matter of weeks, the longtime bonds of friendship, trust, and respect held mutually between the administration and the faculty began to mend. By April, all but the most impassioned critics were part of the same team.

In December, I had asked for our employees to be treated as humanely as possible. That, I discovered later, did not happen in every case. Once we learned what could and should be done, we did it. But in the interim, some workers suffered. And that I deeply regret. The decision to change our custodial services unquestionably was right. The financial savings are dramatic, and they will benefit students and employees for decades. The service we receive today is at least as good as it was a year ago. But the custodial matter has been the saddest issue in my administrative life.

TUESDAY, OCTOBER 11
After a breakfast meeting with a donor, I spend the morning talking to Triezenberg about fund-raising. We must obtain more scholarships. The cost of higher education burdens many families, and if we are to remain competitive, we must assist them. Also, we face the continuing struggle of obtaining the most difficult dollars to raise—those for the operational budget. Donors like to give for a specific cause. Whether it be for the arts program or students from India, they have individual goals. When we request operational funds, we ask them to provide for the general university budget. They cannot attach

their names specifically to their gifts. In the past few years, our unrestricted giving has almost tripled. But the task of raising it is burdensome indeed. I spend the rest of the morning making a list of people I can approach this year. And if I do, will they return my call next year?

Lunch is with the staff of a TV station. They want to know how they should be covering the new, explosive issue of education. "Don't overemphasize or underemphasize education," I urge them. "Don't treat it as a fad. It's enduring and will remain vital to the nation so long as we have anyone who wishes to learn. Don't make education the new herpes. That ailment has afflicted humankind for millennia, yet there was silence about it until a few months ago when it suddenly commanded media attention. Now there is virtually nothing about it in the news. There has been no cure. But the media have fallen silent. All too often, that's the media's response: silence, lots of attention, and then silence again. Education and the nation deserve better than that."

THURSDAY, OCTOBER 13
I confront the usual welter of letters and phone messages. Deborah Szekely, the vivacious founder of the Golden Door in California, has sent us a check to support a project AU is starting. To assist freshmen congressmen, AU will produce a resource guide on government. Congressmen will advise us on what they would have found most helpful when they arrived. As the proprietress of one of the nation's most famous health spas, Szekely knows many major political and financial leaders.

While I munch on fried chicken at my desk, the three offices that separately monitor the university's budget present their monthly review. They are increasingly concerned that we may be unable to collect several hundred thousand dollars in tuition from Mexico. Even during Mexico's economic travails, its embassy here has assisted us in collecting funds. With its continued help, we may be able to collect some of what is owed us now.

One of the risks involved with international students is cash. When a nation experiences a civil war or depression, it may become incapable of meeting debt obligations. Its students suddenly can be stranded on U.S. campuses without money for tuition or living expenses. AU has had this happen with students from several nations.

The most significant problem came from Iran. When the

Khomeini government took over, several hundred of our Iranian students had their financial resources cut off. The simple approach would have been to dismiss them. But we had a moral obligation to extend credit for a while. After all, we had accepted the students and even had recruited them when we thought their finances were sound. So through our campus ministries and our financial aid office, we provided temporary assistance. But if Iranian students did not pay full costs, someone would have to subsidize them. So we extended this credit only temporarily.

Many U.S. citizens, understandably outraged over the holding of our hostages, didn't understand the Iranian students' trauma. In the late seventies, before he was deposed, the shah was scheduled to visit Washington. Notice came to one of our Iranian students, here on a government scholarship, telling her to be at the White House grounds to show her support. This communication went on to say that the government "has ways" of knowing whether or not she had gone. If she did not, her funds would be cut off; her family in Tehran would be charged for the cost of her U.S. education; and she would be ordered back to Iran.

The student read this message as she walked from the mail box to her room. As she unlocked her door, the phone rang. She answered it and a voice said, "We supporters of the Ayatollah know your whereabouts all the time. We know you just entered your room. And you're considering going to the White House to support the shah. Do not do it. If you go, we'll know."

The young woman's solution to the dilemma was brilliant: She was "sick" on the day of the White House demonstration and went to the infirmary.

Wisdom often comes in retrospect. If I had been adequately perspicacious, I could have forecast the shah's downfall. On my first visit to the Tehran Hilton, I was impressed by a huge portrait in the lobby of the shah and his wife and son. On subsequent visits, I noticed that the original portrait had been replaced by smaller ones. On my final trip, the changes fascinated me. This time there was only a small head-and-shoulders photo of the shah.

After the others leave, I ask Myers to stay. "How're things going with the union?" I inquire. "The process is slow," Don replies, "but we're making progress. Things could go wrong, but I doubt if there'll be a strike."

Buoyed, I return to my office and find more good news. Several of our professors recently have published articles in significant journals; several have given talks at major professional and scholarly meetings; others have received important grants. I am delighted and proud. A frustrating aspect of being president is that I cannot interact with faculty as much as I would like. If my discussions with them become truly substantive, there is a serious risk that the chain of command will break. If a professor believes I will approve a budget denied by the department chair, the dean, or the provost, then all the administrative procedures will collapse. In addition, I can be drawn into campus debates that are someone else's purview and take time that I should spend trying to advance the university. But I refuse to disassociate myself entirely from day-to-day faculty life. How to maintain proper balance on this is a challenge facing every university head.

FRIDAY, OCTOBER 14

Triezenberg and I meet this morning to plan for this afternoon's first formal meeting of NAB and IAB members who live in the U.S. About a year and a half ago, I established the two advisory boards. I asked individuals I knew personally to join, and trustee Henry Dormann helped with his contacts. Today, the two groups consist of more than 110 members. Remarkably diverse and distinguished, the members are scattered around the globe and excel in many fields—for example, Walter Cronkite (CBS–TV), Shirley Hufstedler (Carter's secretary of education), Paul Laxalt (U.S. senator), Josh Logan (playwright and director), Sam Nunn (U.S. senator), Frank Press (president of the National Academy of Sciences and Carter's science advisor), Jack Valenti (president of the Motion Picture Association), Bill Webster (director of the FBI), Harry Woolf (director of the Institute for Advanced Study), Christiaan Barnard (surgeon), Gunter Eser (head of Lufthansa), Bob McNamara (former president of the World Bank), Mike Sandberg (head of the Hong Kong and Shanghai Bank), and His Holiness, the Dalai Lama of Tibet.

Lunch is with Ed Pfeiffer, station manager of the CBS–TV affiliate in Washington, D.C. As we ride to the Metropolitan Club downtown, we discover we have many things in common. He worked for several years in Dallas, where I grew up, and we both lived in New England for a long time. He tells me about his student job of chauffering a wealthy dowager. And I tell him about the fateful night, shortly after Gail and I were married, when the phone rang in our shabby apartment located a half block from the Cambridge city dump. A woman who knew Gail had recommended us as being a "nice, reliable young couple" who might be interested in house-sitting for a wealthy family in Chestnut Hill. We hardly could believe what was proposed to us: Not only would we live in a mansion while the owners were in Palm Beach, but we'd be paid for doing so. We accepted at once. And as soon as we hung up, we drove across town to see our winter home. It was spectacular. Our entire apartment, including the parking space, would fit inside its library.

For several years while I was a graduate student, we house-sat during the winter. But in due course the owners ended our pay, and the omnipresent responsibility of the house hung heavily over us. We were reluctant to go out to dinner, much less a movie, for fear the house might be burglarized while we were away. Equally frightening was the thought that it might be burglarized while we were there. And there were many burglaries in that neighborhood. When the house-sitting arrangement ended, we were ready to leave.

Over lunch, Pfeiffer asks me if I would be interested in making two-minute capsule statements about education that would air on the evening news. They would start with the Washington affiliate, and if all went well, the spots might become a regular feature here and elsewhere. The idea intrigues me, for it is what a national university in Washington, D.C., should be doing today.

Back at my office, the NAB and IAB members assemble. Briefly, I tell them about the founding dream of The American University. Several of the nation's founders thought that the capital city of the U.S. should have a national university. Not a novel idea, this mimicked what already existed in some world capitals. Yet the dream here went unfulfilled. And so in 1893, a new university was chartered by act of Congress and given a presumptuous name. My hope is that AU can be precisely what it was founded to be and what its name implies.

Then I discuss a number of ways in which advisory board members can help. To my delight, they seem genuinely interested, asking many questions and offering useful ideas. The ambassador of Kuwait wants to know the fields in which most foreign students study at AU. The ambassador of Algeria says his staff will meet with ours to determine if specific training programs can be established for Algerian students here. Bill Bolger, postmaster general, offers to arrange internships for our students. Mike Forman, president of Pacific

Theatres in California, is interested in our film program. Father Theodore Hesburgh, president of Notre Dame University, already has responded to my request that we link our universities through the Washington Semester Program, by which students from other institutions come to AU for study in Washington. Barbara Thomas, a commissioner on the Securities and Exchange Commission, offers to help us in Hong Kong, where she is moving soon. Marta Istomin, artistic director of the Kennedy Center, agrees to try to arrange opportunities for students at the center.

While this highly productive meeting of advisory board members takes place, Gail holds a meeting in our house for wives of male members of these boards. I rush home to pick her up, and with Ted Hesburgh, we head across Chain Bridge to the McLean, Virginia, home of Carol and Climis Lascaris.

Potomac House, as it is called, is one of the most spectacular residences in this region. The facade is Williamsburg, but the interior is Lascaris. Experts in design, they have made their home into a remarkable showcase. Our hundred guests, a worldly and prestigious group, do not hide their amazement.

After cocktails, we assemble in what the Lascarises modestly call the basement, an area suitable for a sit-down dinner for 250. Gail's friend, Mary Ann Lundgren, has arranged the evening, and the room is stunning. The Lascarises graciously permit us to use their home and provide the dinner while they are in China. Carol Lascaris's sister and brother-in-law and Congressman Bill Nelson and his wife serve as surrogate hosts.

Bill Nelson gets everyone's attention before dinner. Then he turns to me, and I say, "Some of you may not yet be thoroughly familiar with AU, and some of you have children attending other universities. I would like to point out that this building is one of AU's off-campus dorms." More soberly, I call upon Jim Mathews, former chair of our board of trustees and a bishop of the Methodist Church, for the invocation.

After dinner, I thank our hosts for their hospitality and the board members for their support. Then I call upon the board chairman, Cy Ansary, who makes witty and touching remarks. As the group leaves, I get a genuinely good feeling from everyone. Whether people can help now or not, I am delighted by their enthusiasm and goodwill.

As Gail and I drive Hesburgh back to his hotel, we enjoy his many stories. A man of multiple talents, he's received more honorary degrees than any other person in history. And his interests range from theology to aviation to civil rights to education. And they include the scientific search for extraterrestrial intelligence, the pursuit that brought Ted and me together years ago.

SATURDAY, OCTOBER 15

If the leaves were only slightly more golden, this would be a perfect autumn day. Bright sunshine, slight breeze, crispness in the air, it is a joy; and so, too, are its events. The first is the opening of the D.C. Special Olympics, to be held on the AU track. When we arrive, the athletes are assembling, balloons are flying, and our students are serving as volunteer hosts. My post brings numerous obligatory tasks that I carry out begrudgingly, but it also brings joyful opportunities. And being the honorary chairman of today's event is one. The master of ceremonies announces that the athletes will start the parade. Around the track come dozens of Special Olympians. With a John Philip Sousa march blasting behind me, I clap and then choke up as I watch their beaming faces pass before me. Several Olympians wave at the crowd, reminding me of politicians in parades. We are not waving to the athletes; they are waving to us. Today, for these few moments, they are stars. Every human being needs to feel accomplishment, and these games give these special people that special feeling.

The last athlete to pass can barely walk. His body is so twisted that he can only move one foot at a time, inch by inch, even assisted by his coach. Yet, move he does. For him, this walk of a few hundred feet equals any marathon. And the fact that he tries it, much less makes it, is testimony to the human spirit.

In my opening remarks, I say how proud I am of our students and of the athletes. Win or lose, they win. We win.

This afternoon is one of my favorite times on the university calendar. It is Parents' Weekend, and at four o'clock I address the parents. Some of them have heard me speak many times, so I cannot use old material. I start by telling them about John Punnet Peters.

In the summer of 1888, he dug at the mound of Niffar, fifty miles north of the ancient city of Uruk. Peters, an archaeologist from the University of Pennsylvania, discovered some forty thousand tablet fragments. After they were translated from Old Persian, they told an epic poem about Gilgamesh, the fifth King of Uruk. In length, the poem was comparable to Homer's *Iliad,* the work that influenced so much of Western thought and writing. But this poem predated the

Iliad by more than two thousand years. It is the oldest written story we have ever found.

From that, I jump five millennia to John Kennedy's speech on the AU track. And then I attempt to pull things together. The stories are about two different leaders, in different countries, at different epochs. What they have in common is that both touched time. And from that, I lament that of the national educational woes of the last two decades, the most serious have not been those that have been widely trumpeted —in science and math, in computers and foreign languages. Rather, they have been in two basic areas, literature and history. Understandably, in this highly professionalized world, parents and students worry about employment opportunities. But we must teach our youth the power of language and the meaning of history.

Later, we hold a reception on the Quad. On this glorious day, family after family come up to say: "We're so delighted with this university." "Everyone has treated us extremely well." "My son's thrilled with his professors and says he feels he's really preparing for life." "My daughter's matured so much since she came here, and I want to thank you for it."

SUNDAY, OCTOBER 16
Tonight, Gail and I go to the Kennedy Center for the premiere of *The Right Stuff*, Tom Wolfe's saga of NASA's early days. The film interests me because of its relationship to my own field.

The long hallway from the front of the center to the entrance of the Eisenhower Theater is flanked with TV cameras and photographers. As the Mercury astronauts and the stars of the movie walk down the hall, cameras roll and bulbs flash. As Gail and I start to enter the theater, one photographer takes several dozen photos. He follows me, irrespective of the crowd's wandering course. Although I am fascinated to know who he thinks I am, I do not ask. The answer might be deflating.

Once inside, we see many Washington friends, including the Roger Mudds, who sit behind us. Next to Roger is Helen Cronkite, Walter's mother. At ninety-one, she is a delight. Bright, vivacious, and attractive, she neither looks nor acts within decades of her age.

A few years ago, Walter was coming to campus for a special event. Helen had arrived but he had not, and our starting time was drawing near. I said, "I hope he makes it on time." And she replied, "Don't worry. I told him just yesterday: 'Walter, this is important. Don't be late.' " She said this to the white-haired man that polls rank as the most believed person in America! Well, he is still her son.

Last summer, Gail and I attended Helen's ninetieth birthday party, held at the Edgartown Yacht Club on Martha's Vineyard. The crowd had the largest collection I have ever seen of green pants with pink whales. When we arrived, we saw Helen sitting in a wheelchair, wearing a long gown. I said to her, "What happened to you? You're injured and I'd hoped we could dance."

"Oh, Richard, I broke my leg and they have it in a long cast. Here, feel for yourself."

I felt as she instructed me, but instead of a cast, I touched her knee. Pulling back my hand, I said, "I'm sorry. Apparently the cast is in two parts."

"No, I tricked you. I just wanted you to feel my knee."

Walter asked everyone to be quiet as I gave Helen our birthday gift and Art Buchwald snapped photos. We gave her an AU T-shirt and a certificate providing her free tuition for a course at AU. I told her, "I hope you'll enjoy the certificate, but it comes with one restriction: You'll have to pay a fee if you take karate." She broke into giggles, but not nearly so much as I did when her son retorted: "Knowing my mother, she'll probably sign up for sex education."

Before the film begins, Walter comes on stage to serve as master of ceremonies and to introduce astronauts in the audience. Conspicuously absent is John Glenn. The night we dined with him, he said he planned not to attend. He thought that if he did, it might appear he was trying to exploit the film for political gain. In the movie, he comes across as a hero, almost bigger than life.

The movie itself, however, is long and dull. During some protracted footage of the astronaut training program, my mind wanders back to the early 1960s when I worked in the summer at an aerospace firm. It had flight simulators for test pilots and astronauts. But my work there had nothing to do with aviation. I was studying the development of sunspots. To do so, my assistant, who was an undergraduate student, and I wanted to observe films of solar activity. We needed a room we could darken and in which we could leave materials for several days. As elementary as that requirement seemed, we could not find such a space. My assistant and I wandered the maze of corridors, searching for an appropriate place. Finally, we came upon one that was even more than we desired.

Although the light switch in the room did not work, light coming through the doorway showed the room to be empty. We plugged our movie projector into a wall socket and used the wall as a screen. That was all the light we needed, and we sat on the floor to study the films.

When I asked my assistant to shut the door, he mumbled something about there being two of them. I thought nothing of it. After awhile, we decided to take a break. As I pointed the movie projector his way, using its beam like a flashlight, he tried to open the door. He turned the knob, but nothing happened. He said it was locked. How could that be? I tried, and it *was* locked. Then we noticed a small sign: "Sensory Deprivation Room." I had heard of such rooms where test pilots and astronauts were placed for psychological study. Soundproof and dark, they would give the subject the feeling of complete isolation.

Being bright young men, we pounded on the door and shouted for help. After a few minutes, it occurred to us that if this were a soundproof room, shouting would be of little help. We laughed at ourselves and our predicament. But our laughter faded when we realized it was four o'clock on Friday. Everyone would leave by five. And, considering the dirt on the floor, no custodian cleaned this room. Consequently, no one would come to find us and we could be trapped for the weekend. Already, the air was stale and we realized we were in serious trouble.

Frantically, we searched for an escape. We had examined the walls so carefully using the projector like a flashlight that we had not noticed a small hole in the floor. Putting my eye to it, I recognized that we were above an airplane assembly line. A gargantuan room, the space below held several planes in stages of being built. Some of the equipment was extremely loud and the ceiling was high enough to accommodate the tail of a large aircraft. The cement floor separating us from the assembly area appeared to be at least two feet thick. And the hole was no more than the size of a pencil in diameter. Still, we had to try. So my assistant put his mouth close to the hole and shouted. A hundred feet below, men in hard hats were welding and hammering. What sound came out of that hole must have been inaudible.

Then we had a brilliant idea: We unlaced our shoes and tied the four laces into one long string. Carefully, we lowered it down the hole. Our reasoning was that at least some of it would dangle past the ceiling. If we could bob it up and down, someone might see it. So there we sat, bobbing our lace, trying to remember the S.O.S. code. Now

Is My Armor Straight?

I wonder what a workman would have thought if he had looked up and seen a few inches of shoelace bobbing up and down through the ceiling far above his head.

Eventually, we concluded that technique was ineffective. My assistant persisted in urging a plan he had proposed earlier: we should disrobe. I'm locked in a soundproof room with little air and everyone about to leave the building, I thought, and this fellow wants us to undress. I don't need this.

But he explained that we should stack our clothes against a wall and set fire to them with his cigarette lighter. The wisdom of this did not leap out at me. So he further explained: "Our clothes will set the wall on fire, burning a hole through it. And then we can escape through the hole." I was not sure which aspect of the plan I disliked most: that the room would fill with smoke and we would suffocate, or that the wall would burn and we would emerge, seminude, through the burning hole into a secretarial pool.

We scanned the room again with the movie projector, this time examining the ceiling, too. We discovered a fire sprinkler. But the ceiling was too high for us to reach. Still, if my assistant were to stand on my shoulders, he might be able to hold his lighter under the sprinkler. We were not circus acrobats, and I had visions of the room filling with water long before the firefighters would find us in this obscure location. So we scrapped that idea.

Finally, in a corner, we found a lead brick. We tried pounding on the door with it, but to no avail. Then we reasoned that perhaps we could make a battering ram with it. Just then, the door opened and in walked a company official and some military officers on a tour. They were startled to find anyone in the room and stared at us incredulously as we left clutching our projector and one long shoelace.

Everyone else in the Eisenhower Theater soberly worries about the astronauts' safety, as I chuckle to myself over my youthful folly.

MONDAY, OCTOBER 17
Upon leaving the distinguished post of president of the University of California at Berkeley, Clark Kerr said, "From my lengthy experience in education, I have learned that all educational concerns come down to three things: sports for the alumni, parking for the faculty, and sex for the students."

Fact is, creature comforts do mean a lot, on a campus as well as elsewhere. And so when I became provost, I said I wanted our food service improved. Students routinely complain about standardized college food. But our food then was widely criticized by everyone, from students to professors to me.

At least our students did not go to the lengths that some have elsewhere. A few years ago, as I sat down to eat at the University of Colorado, I noticed the grill's name. I asked nearby students, "Where did the name come from?"

"We named it," they replied. "We students voted on it." And so it was that they had named their dining hall the Alferd Packer Grill after the first man in the U.S. to be convicted of cannibalism. He ate his companions during a trip across the Rockies in the nineteenth century.

Certainly our dining service was never that bad. But in the late seventies, I was convinced it should be changed. A campus committee evaluated several food companies. Finally, they recommended and I approved the selection of the Marriott Corporation. Today, my guest for lunch is Bill Marriott, company president.

We stroll through our two fast-food restaurants, chatting with students and food servers. And then we go downstairs to the large student dining room. "Bill," I ask, "Do you have the nerve to join me if I ask a tableful of students how they like lunch?"

"Sure, if you do."

We pick a table at random and walk up to six young men. "Excuse me, fellows. This is Mr. Marriott and he wonders how you're enjoying lunch."

"It's really good."

Gratified by the response, I am also relieved. To ask a leading question to male undergrads can be risky.

We go through this routine at several tables, and the students give similar replies. We do notice differences, however: whereas the males' plates are heaped with meat and potatoes, the females' have dainty portions of salad and fruit. If you are what you eat, what does this mean?

Before my next appointment, I walk the campus. This gives me an opportunity to chat informally with students, professors, and staff. No appointments have been set; no agenda exists. They do not even know I am coming. Similarly, from time to time I stroll through staff offices and dorms. That can be especially interesting. By now, students are accustomed to my drop-in dorm visits. And their student security guards at the dorm desks know me on sight. Even so, the routine remains.

"Pardon me, sir. Do you live in this dorm?"

"No. I don't."

"Well, then, do you have a student I.D. with you?"

"No. I don't have a student I.D."

This exchange goes on for another minute or so. The motive behind it, I assume, is to dazzle me with the effectiveness of their security while someone calls upstairs, "He's coming!"

Whatever their tactics, all I know is that when I get to a dorm floor, bedroom doors are shut, stereos are muted, and students are laboring over Hegel and Kant.

On this afternoon's brief stroll, I encounter: a professor who has just published a research article, a student who is delighted with AU, one who is annoyed because he could not find a parking space, and a lost cab driver. Also, I encounter a student who says, jokingly I hope, "I know about the new university policy requiring all dogs on campus to be on leashes. But would that apply if I had another pet, like an ocelot?"

What does he expect me to say? "Oh, no, ocelots can run free"? As much as I am tempted to say that, I know students well enough to realize that they may show up with an ocelot. So, I give a boring, straight answer: "Our policy applies to all animals." Knowing how precise a budding scholar can be, I worry that he will ask if my definition of *animals* includes birds and fish. Instead, he asks: "Well, what are you going to do about Vice-President Bush? I understand his dog recently ran with him without a leash while he jogged our track."

That is true. Before Bush became vice-president, he lived near AU and frequently jogged our track. Now he lives in the vice-president's mansion, only a short drive away. And he still jogs our track. I assure the young man that we will enforce the rules for everyone.

TUESDAY, OCTOBER 18

Lunch today is the biweekly meeting of the consortium of universities of the Washington area. Most people, including most educators, do not realize that the U.S. city with the largest number of universities is not New York or Boston but Washington, D.C. In part, this startling statistic arises from definitions. I refer only to universities, not to colleges, and only to the city *per se,* not to surrounding towns.

Nonetheless, Washington has more universities than any other U.S. city.

A popular Washington canard is that the area is devoid of a great university. This assertion, invariably forwarded by graduates of elite universities elsewhere, contains characteristics of any cliché; i.e., it is partially true and partially untrue. Washington has yet to develop a major research university, but it has high quality undergraduate programs and distinguished graduate professional programs. And Washington uniquely provides an education that blends the theory of the classroom with the practicality of the world's most action-oriented city.

The consortium holds biweekly meetings of the presidents, a talented group whom I enjoy and from whom I learn. This year is my turn to chair the group, a task made simple by the executive director, Father John Whalen. Today is no exception. I call the meeting to order and turn it over to Whalen. He brings us up to date on numerous issues, such as our joint effort to obtain authorization to offer tax-exempt bonds. After two years, we are now on the verge of having this in place. He speaks with such authority about arbitrages, puts and calls, and contingent liabilities that I wonder what he studied in seminary.

After lunch, I return to my office. Two people have called with the same query: "Have you seen this week's *U.S. News & World Report*?" I have not, but the phone messages say I should. I pick up a copy.

Last summer, I met Marvin Stone, editor of *U.S. News.* Along the way, our conversation turned to the status of education. And he made such generous remarks about my analysis that a few days later I wrote to him, expanding on what I had said at dinner. I assumed that later I might ask him to speak to students and Gail would invite his wife to one of her functions. Perhaps, eventually, Stone would join our NAB. But beyond that, I expected nothing. To my surprise, his editorial this week is based on that casual letter. And his introductory statement flatters me and AU.

Family dinner tonight is at a neighborhood Mexican restaurant. While we munch on tacos, Natasha explains why she got a *C* on a paper. "The teachers are really tough," she says. "They're almost mean. They're doing what you keep saying they should do, Daddy." When did I say teachers should be mean? And why is her teacher giving my daughter a *C*?

WEDNESDAY, OCTOBER 19

My 8:55 A.M. flight to Newark, New Jersey, is delayed two hours by weather. Eventually, I land in Newark and am met by a representative from the Perth Amboy public schools. Most large public school systems hold in-service days in which they bring together all their teachers, counselors, and principals to hear speakers in a program arranged by the superintendent. I have been asked to give the keynote speech for such a day in Perth Amboy.

New Jersey is home for many AU undergrads. In the past few years, the university's image there has improved markedly, and now we receive applications from more academically gifted students than in the past. When I speak at an in-service event, I do not talk directly about AU; no school system would invite an outside speaker to do that. But AU is mentioned many times throughout the day and by local newspapers.

Perth Amboy will not be a prime recruiting area for AU. As a private institution, our tuition is at about the sixtieth percentile level nationwide. Perth Amboy is not affluent. I knew that when I was invited. Still, we may attract a few students from there; the superintendents across New Jersey know one another and this talk may lead to an invitation elsewhere; and, irrespective of attracting students to AU, I believe what I say about school reform. I am glad to speak in this economically troubled yet courageous community.

Last year, Perth Amboy celebrated its three-hundredth anniversary. Now about 75 percent of the schools' population is Hispanic. Many industries have left, and although it is not so distressed as some urban areas, Perth Amboy faces significant challenges.

After I am shown the public housing units, fire department, city hospital, and junkyard, I am taken to a bar for lunch. It has a dark interior decorated with miniature Christmas lights and dusty, crooked photographs. The head of a trucking company, who is also the school board president, joins me for a hamburger.

Next, we go to the high school. Again, I am given a tour: of shops for woodworking, metalworking, and auto repair; of a kitchenlike facility for home economics and an area for sewing classes. Roughly half the graduates go on to higher education, often to two-year colleges; the other half go directly to work.

This is the living and learning environment of many American youth. Some of them are preparing for careers that will not exist. In the recent past, the nation has undergone the most profound transition since the industrial revolution. Smokestack industries have closed that will never reopen. And youngsters who learn skills related to them will be unemployed in the future just as their parents are now.

But there is more here; I sense it everywhere. My guide is especially proud of the library and learning-resource center. And the counseling and job-referral offices are attractive. I notice an almost complete absence of graffiti. The students respect their school.

And then I meet the heart of it all—the teachers themselves. Upbeat, smiling, affectionate with one another, they enter the auditorium enthusiastically. In some schools, teachers attend such days reluctantly; they come only because the superintendent demands it. But this group is cheerful and high-spirited.

"There's something peculiar about a society that doesn't appreciate the obligations falling on teachers," I tell them. "No one expects a surgeon to stop disorder in a hospital. A librarian doesn't prevent violence in the stacks; a museum curator isn't a hall monitor. Yet those professionals are supported by taxes, too. Why are only teachers expected to do it all?"

The applause thunders. I go on. It thunders again. And again. They clap even when I say, "Many teachers are poorly prepared and teacher's colleges are weak." The eyes are not just with me; they dance and sparkle. When I finish, the applause swells. I acknowledge it and walk to my seat. But it continues. The master of ceremonies invites me back to the rostrum. And then come the people. "You said just what I've thought for years." My guide ushers me into the cafeteria, but it does not stop there. Teacher after teacher puts down coffee and comes up to say, "I care deeply about teaching. I'm doing everything I can to have excellence in my classroom."

Finally, my host extricates me and we drive back to the Newark airport. While waiting to depart, I people-watch. One distinguished-looking man after another circles a corner of the waiting room. Then I see why: an enticing young woman who is five years Deborah's junior.

When we board the plane, I find that this beautiful woman is, in fact, a flight attendant. How different reality is from image. At the terminal, she had looked like a New York model on her way to a White House dinner. Now, up close, she is as alluring as before but I see that her shoes are scuffed, nails chipped, hose torn. And it is easy to understand why. She and her fellow attendants serve 150 passengers, some of whom are demanding. "Put in more soda." "I don't want coffee. Get me tea." Her cart stops beside my seat. The plane tosses. She balances herself. With her hands flying, she opens bottles, scoops ice, pours drinks. It must be tiring, yet she smiles constantly. She has a quiet dignity.

Neither she nor the Perth Amboy teachers might understand it, but they exemplify the work ethic I am calling for. They may have modest incomes, but they have zest for their professions.

Over spaghetti at the kitchen table, Gail asks Natasha about GDS Curriculum Night. She fills us in, and Gail and I head to her school.

The parent turnout tonight is so great that we cannot fit into the lobby. Although the families have a common concern for education, they have a diversity of incomes and represent numerous ethnic groups.

Naturally, the children use computers extensively. In addition, they interview one another with video-tape cameras to practice both interviewing and being interviewed. In music, they are studying opera and will attend a Kennedy Center performance. In Spanish class, they will tour the Organization of American States building. A father says the students should meet with desk officers at the State Department. And Gail volunteers to ask Latin American ambassadors if the class could visit their embassies.

What remarkable opportunities Natasha has. Will it be surprising if her SATs are higher than those of a typical Perth Amboy student? Will it be surprising if she's admitted to a selective university while the Perth Amboy student goes to a community college or into a blue-collar job? If I am a good educator, why can I not think of ways to educate not only Natasha but also the children of Perth Amboy?

But before I feel sorry for them, I remember the dignity of their school and their teachers. And the lack of graffiti. And the pride.

THURSDAY, OCTOBER 20

"Given declining demographics," a *Chicago Tribune* reporter says to me this morning, "I assume your freshman class is down."

"No," I reply. "In fact it's up 14 percent. And admission standards are up, too."

"That's close to miraculous. To what do you attribute it?"

"We've done many things. Deans and professors have joined the admissions staff and me in talking to prospective students and their parents. Even our current students and our trustees have helped."

"And in the face of the greatest challenges higher education has encountered, AU resolved not to lower standards, but to raise them. Rather than drive students away, this has attracted more."

Originally, I was to host a luncheon meeting in Mary Graydon Center for campus volunteers who will assist our United Way drive. But after thanking them for coming, I have to dash to the Kay Spiritual Life Center to meet Senator Gary Hart. One of his principal aides, a freshman last year, took a leave from AU to work in his campaign. A few days ago, he called Andy Sherman, head of the student lecture series, to say that Hart could speak on campus today. The Residence Hall Association cosponsored the event, and I approved it.

Hart enters the lounge and we shake hands. Floodlights shine; TV cameras roll. We have never met before, so our greeting is formal.

"Senator, welcome to The American University."

"I'm delighted to be here, Mr. President."

With that opening, I cannot resist: "Of course, you prefer my title to yours." He smiles broadly. As we chat, I notice his tie: maroon with small white eagles. "Your tie resembles our AU tie," I tell him. "We'll have to get you the right one." Lightning fast, he retorts, "The 'right one' is okay. I'm grateful you didn't say the 'right stuff.' "

I slip away to give students an opportunity to talk with Hart. And I ask Andy to go to my office to pick up an AU tie. He will introduce Hart to the crowded audience. I tell Andy, "When you present this, be sure to use the line, 'the right one.' "

As Hart leaves for the auditorium, we shake hands again. "As soon as you're inaugurated," I tell him, "we want you back wearing an AU tie." He replies instantly, "I have to wait that long?"

The auditorium overflows. I have declined to participate: This should be purely a student function. They have arranged it; they should get to run it. Paul Schroeder begins with an inside joke the students enjoy. Josh Ederheimer welcomes the group on behalf of the RHA. And then Andy goes to the rostrum, introduces Hart, and presents the tie. Hart's opening line refers to "the right stuff." The audience roars while the press takes notes.

I return to my office for an afternoon of calls, letters, and dictation. When I arrive home tonight, Gail is too busy to cook. So I volunteer. No hamburger or chicken; this clearly is a steak evening. It is easy to prepare. Gail and Natasha are not impressed by my culinary talent, but one household member is: Sparky. A stubborn beast, he is so accustomed to table scraps that he refuses dog food. At least *he* respects my cooking.

As I shave, I hear Gail and Natasha talking about what Natasha will wear tonight. The talking grows louder. It becomes excited. It borders on shouting. For this quiet twosome, such an exchange is remarkable. But it is happening more frequently these days, as Natasha approaches the trying age of thirteen.

Once, while talking to a National Security Council member's wife, I said that when Natasha reaches her teens, "We're going to place her in a boarding school in New Zealand." The woman replied, "We put ours in Japan. Why did you select New Zealand?" Stammering, I explained I was only joking. But she was dead serious. We have not reached such a state nor shall we. But these flare-ups about Natasha's clothes are becoming more passionate.

Somehow the two of them resolve their differences. And the three of us go to Leonard Hall. This is International Week on campus, and a student committee has planned daily events—film festival, food fair, fashion show, art show, and lecture series. Tonight they hold a reception for cultural attachés from the embassies, some three dozen of whom attend.

Leonard Hall is an exceptional dorm, composed half of U.S. students interested in international affairs and half of foreign students. We are greeted by dark-suited young men; well-dressed young women take our raincoats and show us to the reception. Students have decorated the room and have prepared the buffet. Polite student hosts abound, many in native costume. If Hollywood were to film here tonight, a snide reviewer would assert that no student group looks this good. One attaché after another tells me how pleased he is to have come and how he wants to assist the students.

Then several students approach me. "Dr. Berendzen, we plan to hold a "serf auction." People volunteer to be auctioned, and students bid for them. Funds will go to a soup kitchen in Washington. Are you willing to be an auctioned serf?"

Eyes rivet on me as I consider what I should do. Because my reply is slow, a young man adds, "Don't worry. A serf doesn't have to do anything that he or she feels is immoral, illegal, or degrading."

That is reassuring. But I am concerned how I will fit this into my schedule. Still, so many students want me to do it that I weaken. I agree, with the caveat that my serfdom can be no more than an hour. They squeal and literally jump up and down. I have been many things before, but never a serf.

FRIDAY, OCTOBER 21

In the morning mail, I receive a letter from someone proposing to do consulting for us. He states, "As a highly respected consultant, I can provide guidance your university desperately needs." He will do this even though he has never visited the campus. Someone once said a consultant is a normal person who is just a long way from home. In my experience, a consultant is someone who is unemployed.

Then he says, "I will call your office next week to arrange our appointment." No, he will not arrange such a meeting.

I have lunch in the faculty–staff dining room with Jill Dutt, this year's remarkably competent *Eagle* editor. Aside from running the student paper, she is an able student academically. And she is active in the women's movement; neither shrill nor strident, she is concerned about equality for everyone. She tells me that mail intended for others comes to the *Eagle* office; any envelope with "eagle" on it may end up on her desk. I tell her about misplaced mail I receive. If an envelope contains three key words—president, American, Washington—it may come to me. Sometimes I get letters intended for President Reagan. I wonder if he receives my mail? If so, I hope he is handling it: a professor late for class, a shower with a dripping faucet.

My afternoon mail includes a six-page, handwritten letter from a student in Ethiopia who heard me over the Voice of America. He wants to study in the U.S. but does not have enough money. He almost screams for help. I wish I could assist him. I shall write him and give suggestions. But advice is easy; help is harder.

My next meeting is with the well-prepared Andy Sherman. In the summer, he told me he would like to have a session in spring on education. I suggested that he arrange a panel composed of a representative from the Department of Education and the education advisors for the Democratic presidential candidates. He is here today to discuss this.

"Andy, to attract the speakers, we must put ourselves in their place. How will this forum help the candidate? How might it harm him?" Andy replies, "We can assure them this won't be an ugly confrontation. Each speaker can explain his candidate's philosophy. Then we'll take questions from the floor. The discussion may be lively but it shouldn't embarrass anyone."

If Mondale's office agrees to come, Glenn's will, or vice versa. If both agree, then other Democratic contenders will. The Republicans could say no under any circumstance, but if we secure a representative for them, then the Democrats will come. Where to begin? "Would you like me to call Mondale's camp?" I ask. "I may be able to get a yes or no there quickly." "Sure," he says. "Meanwhile, we'll contact the Department of Education and Glenn's office." As he is leaving, Andy adds, "I love this university. I hope that whatever press this panel brings will help AU. Can we get the AU seal on the rostrum so TV cameras will show it?" I assure him we can.

I then meet Ravi Tikkoo, a native of the Kashmir state of India. He grew up in the mountains but his career has been on the seas. He owns the world's two largest tankers, one so vast that the Empire State Building placed on its side could fit inside it. These massive ships, plus half-a-dozen smaller ones, comprise Tikkoo's fleet, which transports oil from the Arab states to Japan.

A tall, dignified man, his slightly graying hair complements his Hermes tie and diamond tie tack. As an IAB member, he funded a scholarship for international students last year. We have met over lunch in New York, but he has never been to our campus before. He is impressed by the fall foliage, the rolling hills, and the academic atmosphere.

As we walk the campus, he tells me about his childhood. He's intensely proud of mountain people—of their pacificity and their strong work ethic. He admires their "discipline," the marshaling of their time and effort. When we return to my study, his eyes focus immediately on my astronomical photographs.

"If we could see the Milky Way Galaxy from outside, where would the sun be on the spiral arm?"

Startled at his knowledge, I start to answer when he notices a photograph of a cluster of galaxies. "How far apart are these binary galaxies? And do you believe there are black holes at the center of them?" We have a phenomenal conversation, touching upon cosmology, field theory, general relativity, and quantum mechanics. How, I ask, does he know such things? After all, he is in shipping, not astrophysics. "Math underlies everything," he says. "Mathematical discipline and precision are what many youth today are missing."

While I have dinner at home, Natasha returns from dance class almost in tears. Where has the jubilation of last time gone?

"Tonight's class was dumb. My partner just moped like a zombie. The other kids learned the Pretzel, but the dummy I was with wouldn't do it. Next time, they'll know it, but I won't. And it's not my fault."

MONDAY, OCTOBER 24

CNN–TV calls me in my New York City hotel room to say that my early morning interview must be postponed due to the tragic killing of U.S. Marines in Beirut. Can I appear at their studio in the World Trade Building at eleven o'clock? With some rearrangement, I can.

After making several business calls, I try to check out. Standing in line is always annoying, but especially so when you are there to pay a bill. Cleverly, I assume the line with only one man will be fast. But he must be the same fellow who gets in front of me at the post office. He is shepherding dozens of Japanese tourists. As they snap pictures of everything in sight, he settles their account. Then it is my turn. The flustered attendant glances at my sheet and says, "Are these your charges, Dr. Berend Richard?"

My name has come out many ways before, but never like this. For such a simple, three-syllable Dutch name, "Berendzen" has generated substantial confusion. One of my teachers called me "Benzedrene." And the name has become "Bergason," "Bearingson," and "Beringdz." If a last name starts with *B* and has more than one syllable, I answer to it.

Last spring, while I was waiting in the green room of a Hollywood TV studio, a technician entered and said, "Is Dr. Richard here?" For a moment, that threw me. But I reasoned correctly that he had given up on the last name. When I returned to the green room, I settled into a bout of people-watching. An excellent person to watch entered— tall, slightly pretty, and well dressed, this woman was not ordinary. But then a Hollywood TV studio is not ordinary.

The technician reentered the room and said, "Dr. Richards." I stood up and so did the unusual woman. I hesitated, staring at her, as she walked out behind the technician. The host then introduced his next guest—Dr. Renee Richards, the former male tennis star who had undergone a sex-change operation. What was I to do then with half-a-dozen people staring at me? I slipped into calisthenics, as if my soul compelled me to stretch and do aerobics. After jogging in place for a few seconds, I sat down. Later, they could tell friends about the odd person they saw at the studio, and they would not be referring to Dr. Renee Richards.

Eventually, the hotel attendant handles my bill, although he has charged me for the wrong room. He explains, naturally, that the computer malfunctioned. What did people blame before computers? Did a nineteenth-century Chinese say, "My abacus is off today?" Murphy had something when he coined his rule that if something can go wrong, it will. The ultimate proof of that came in 1895. There were only two automobiles in all of Ohio, and they ran into each other. "Hey, George, look what I've got." "Me too, Bill." Smash!

The cab drops me at the World Trade Center in time to tape an interview about quality in education. Those of us in the backwaters of Washington, D.C., do not have cable TV, while most of the nation does. So I shall hear nothing from my Washington friends about this interview.

Back in midtown, I have lunch in the office of Henry Dormann. Some years ago, I happened to see an exceptional magazine, *Leaders*. From its stunning cover through its articles by world-renowned figures to its full-page color ads, it is the ultimate upscale publication. The authors comprise a *Who's Who* of the powerful and prestigious —corporate giants, prime ministers, presidents, kings, and even popes. Not for sale to anyone, the magazine is distributed free to world leaders. The *crème de la crème* talk to the *crème de la crème*.

Anyone who has achieved this should be interesting and could be helpful to the university, so I called the office of the magazine's president and editor-in-chief, Henry Dormann, and asked to take him to lunch. And so began one of my most unusual and enjoyable friendships.

When I arrived at Henry's office on the third floor of an inconspicuous Manhattan building, I expected to find a routine publishing facility—a few people, sleeves rolled up, typing, while others interviewed someone. Instead, I found walls lined with pictures of Henry with virtually every major leader of our time; display cases of his medals and medallions; and his inner sanctuary, which is more a museum than a study. And his staff, far from Lou Grant in appearance, resembled their boss: crisp, the acme of efficiency.

Aside from his silver mane and rosy cheeks, I first noticed his clothes: with each piece custom-made by Lanvin of Paris, he makes

James Bond look shabby. But more mysteriously, on him nothing wrinkles. With pants creased like knives, it is as if he never sat. And who else in the U.S. wears a homburg?

I was fascinated by him. Over the months, we met several times and I grew to admire him. Always smiling, charming, and thinking, he is a joy and a challenge. On one of his visits to Washington, I arranged for him to meet several trustees. They, too, were amazed. After trustee Stuart Bernstein met Henry, he said, "What's with this guy? Everything about him is perfect. And he knows everyone, although he's not a name dropper. I almost feel tacky around him." That was quite a statement coming from Washington's most impeccable man.

I was delighted when Henry joined our board, and he has been a loyal trustee. From his contacts, he has provided excellent entree. This already has benefited AU, and I think he enjoys doing it.

My next meeting is with an executive at a major investment firm. At parents' weekend, a father told me I should meet him. Joe Conrad, our director of development, did background research and I was glad when the executive agreed to the appointment. As I understand it, he is anxious to talk to me and has been highly philanthropic with other universities. Could today bring a windfall?

I am ushered in and we exchange pleasantries. Then we stare at each other. Five seconds go by. Ten. Fifteen. Finding the silence deafening, I break it, "Have you been to our campus?" "I don't know much about AU," he replies. "But I'm deeply involved with Brown University."

"Brown is a fine school," I concede, "and we're trying to do good things in Washington. We hope to build a sports and . . ."

"At Brown, we're trying to build a number of things, too. That's where my interests lie."

This is great for Brown. But why am I here? He does not seem to know. And I do not. Yet I wonder if the person who urged me to meet him had something more in mind. What is the right approach? I try a dozen twists in conversation, all of which lead back to Brown. Perhaps patience is the way—just stick it out and see what happens. What happens is silence, then more conversation that leads to Brown. Finally, I excuse myself.

In the Eastern shuttle boarding area, I scan the passengers. On almost all shuttle flights I see at least one person I know. Today, however, I see no one, except I note a perfectly polished shoe beneath a crisp trouser leg. Could it be? It is.

"Hi, Stuart. What a coincidence to see you here."

TUESDAY, OCTOBER 25

My meeting with the deans begins with new formats for the university's internal newsletter. Our publics are so varied that we must use several publications to reach them all. Whereas we have specialized ones for alumni and parents, we have tried to reach all of our campus community—undergraduate students, graduate students, part-time students, faculty members, staff, and administrators—with the same publication. It will not work.

I propose that we print two publications. One will contain job listings and official notices. The other, in tabloid format with photos, will contain general news. I ask for people to be emphasized—faculty research, student internships, alumni achievements. People like to read about people, and reading about successful ones in our own organization will help promote pride.

The next agenda item is summer enrollments. They have declined for the past three years as increasing numbers of students have found it necessary to stay home and work. Many have continued to take summer courses, but at nearby community colleges. I urge that we talk with our students about next summer and that we recruit aggressively. Milt will report back to me on this in a few weeks.

My luncheon meeting today is unusual. Gail is a member of the Capital Speakers' Club, an organization of Washington women who would like to improve their public-speaking ability. Now that they are in Washington, they suddenly have found themselves behind a microphone. They benefit from this club by giving talks to one another and by receiving criticism on their presentations. Today, I am their guest.

The after-lunch program consists of four women speaking on education. Not educators themselves, they have been assigned the topic. During the reception, I sense their nervousness. After lunch, Gail thanks the women for coming and introduces the speakers. Composed, informed, and articulate, they give more insights into education than I have heard by professional educators and journalists. After they conclude, a woman calls upon me to respond. I begin by noting that, "This has been an exceptional luncheon for me. For once, I've listened, not talked. And that's such a good thing that I'd like to found a new club—not the Capital Speakers' Club, but the Capital Listeners' Club. In this town, thousands should sign up."

My brief remarks about education may interest the audience. Their primary concern, however, is not what I say but how I say it. An unusually attentive group, they hang on every word and inflection.

At home this evening, I look for Natasha. To find her is not difficult. With rock music coming from her radio, she lies on her stomach on the floor doing algebra.

"Natasha, how can you think with that music on?"

Her succinct response: "Huh?"

What should I do? The educator in me impels me to turn off her radio. I remember my parents' admonition: "When you play, we don't ask you to study; when you study, don't play." But Gail gives me an all-knowing look: "Stay out of it." I say publicly that parents should have the conviction to change the TV channel or turn off the set. Doesn't this apply to radios? Preteens are a special breed, however, sometimes best permitted to have their way for a while. So I leave Natasha to her algebra and rock. After all, I remember Harvard graduate students studying astrophysics to Mozart.

Such parental dilemmas will have to wait, for Gail and I are late for a dinner hosted by the president of the Counsel of Ministers of Bangladesh in honor of Vice-President Bush. But Bush has gone to Beirut. In an unusual protocol substitution, the honoree tonight has become Chief Justice Warren Burger.

The room is abuzz. Yesterday, the subject was Beirut; tonight, it is Grenada. Senator Ed Zorinsky, an NAB member, and I discuss both topics, while Kurt Waldheim, former secretary general of the United Nations, Chuck Percy, and several others talk elsewhere in the room. Because of the change in the evening's plans, the after-dinner toasts are brief. We leave by ten o'clock.

As I open the back door at home, the phone rings. It is my dad.

"Richard, the silliest thing happened a few weeks ago, and it illustrates what an addle-brained father you've got. My phone bill had a thirteen-dollar call from Dallas to Alaska. When I saw it, I thought, 'Well shoot, did I call the wrong number? I don't know anybody in Alaska.' Then I noticed the number was the same as yours, except the area code was different. Apparently, when I'd meant to call you, I'd gotten Alaska."

A few years ago, my father lost 99 percent of his hearing. With the remaining 1 percent, he attempts to communicate. Despite my loudest shouts, though, he hears nothing but scrambled murmur; yet, he keeps trying. And so he tried to call us but reached an unsuspecting person in Alaska instead. Given the thirteen-dollar charge, they must have had quite a conversation.

"Hello, Richard," he would start.

And the other person would reply: "You have the wrong number. There's no Richard here."

But my father would go on: "How are things at the university?"

"Look, mister, there's no Richard here and I don't know about a university."

My dad must have kept on going: "Your mother and I were wondering how you are."

By then, the person in Alaska must have been frantic: "Didn't you hear me? Are you deaf or something?"

And on my father would have gone: "You'd better slow down, son. Don't burn yourself out."

Our Alaskan friend by then would have been confused or fascinated. But it would not have mattered to my dad: "How's Sweetpea? At twelve, she must be really big."

My dad laughs and laughs. I offer to call the person in Alaska to explain what happened. But then—with the quick wit I had when I tried shouting in a soundproof room—I realize that my dad cannot hear me. Anyway, by now the person in Alaska must have devised elaborate explanations for the bizarre call.

WEDNESDAY, OCTOBER 26

Milt and I walk together on this crisp morning to Kay Chapel where we jointly chair the fall faculty meeting. He calls the group together, thanks them for coming, and turns the mike to me. Professors are too jaded to enjoy a formal speech, especially in this city of unending political harangue. But they do want up-to-date, reliable information about their institution. Each of us can become so preoccupied with his own area that he fails to see the whole. Part of my role is to paint the total picture and provide information not otherwise available.

After reviewing trends in higher education for 1981–82, I remind the faculty of the difficulties we faced in 1982–83. I try to place us in a national context. Then I tell them about our current status and our projections for next year. Like many realistic stories, this one is a balance of good things and bad, a "best of times, worst of times" saga.

Our freshmen enrollments are up; next year they could go down. Our admission standards are higher than ever; they should be higher still. Our endowment is the highest in our history; it is still too low. Our library is packed; we need more books.

On balance, though: "We've faced disaster and won. With your help, despite external economic difficulties, we're now, by any normal measure, in better shape than ever before."

My informal remarks run too long—almost thirty minutes. Milt speaks briefly about the upcoming accreditation visit and our newly launched program review. Last year, national rankings came out for Ph.D. programs. Neither AU nor any other D.C. university excelled. Milt and I mandated a thorough review of our doctoral programs, to strengthen good ones and improve, change, or abolish weak ones. Most people applaud such an initiative until they have to sort weak programs from strong ones and act decisively.

If eyes are telling, the faculty follow our every word. And after our talks, they ask good questions. No academic legislation is formulated in this informal meeting; that is handled by the university senate. But this forum provides a convenient way for faculty and administration to communicate. Whether or not today's session is useful for faculty, it is for me.

THURSDAY, OCTOBER 27

When I enter the TV studio for a live interview this morning, I find the other guests are leaders of the D.C. public schools—superintendent, teachers' union president, and school board head. I had been asked to discuss education, but I did not know until I arrived what the specific topic would be. The interviewer asks questions, then takes them from callers, one of whom says, "You have praised the D.C. public schools' recent progress. But test scores remain well behind those in Northern Virginia and surburban Maryland. Why?"

The other guests provide lengthy answers, defending D.C. schools. Given that they are the schools' main leaders, I do not intrude. But during a commercial break, I point out that the caller failed to note that he was comparing unlike things. Test scores often—but not always—correlate with parental income, education level, and family involvement. Some low income people and their supporters argue as if test scores correlate perfectly with family income. Although there is a relationship, it is imperfect. Cal Tech and MIT students have among the highest SAT scores, yet they do not necessarily come from affluent families. Nor does a high parental education level necessarily ensure a student's academic performance. Nonetheless, parents' characteristics and their children's test scores are related. On average, higher income students outperform lower income ones. But another parental ingredient—close involvement—can transcend income levels. Respect for learning and reading and thinking—such home attributes profoundly mold a young person's desire to learn and ability to succeed. Therefore, rather than compare public schools in urban Washington with those in affluent suburbs, compare them with those in Baltimore or Philadelphia or with schools in suburbs where the population is similar to that of the District.

While I was at lunch downtown, a welcome telephone message arrived: Khashoggi *will* attend tomorrow's board meeting and he accepts my luncheon invitation. I am delighted. And I am even more pleased when I read the full roster of trustees who will attend.

But then comes disquieting news: a student group has decided the sports center will be built immediately if they tell trustees how badly they want it. They plan to demonstrate outside the board's meeting room. We face the prospect that our volunteer trustees, several coming for their first meeting, will encounter a group demanding, "Build the sports center *now!*"

FRIDAY, OCTOBER 28

Yellow and orange leaves, autumn crispness, dazzling sunshine—if weather can set a mood, this should be quite a day.

At 10:30 A.M., Bob Shaheen calls: "The chief, Patricia, and I are on our way. We'll be at your office for lunch by noon." The "chief" is Adnan and Patricia is Bob's attractive, cosmopolitan wife. The crackling sound indicates he is calling from a mobile unit.

Slightly before noon, the peripatetic trio arrives. Bob and Patricia have been here many times, but this is Adnan's first visit. He is intrigued by the astronomical photographs in my study. With the provocation of an even slightly interested audience, I go into a mini-lecture. He seems fascinated, asking numerous questions. Especially intrigued by black holes, he asks what would happen to a traveler who passed near one. And he asks how scientific findings jibe with theological teachings.

By now it is 12:30 P.M. and I worry about our time. So I remind him that last spring I offered to give an astronomical slide-show sometime in his New York home. He says he remembers and would like to arrange it soon.

The four of us pick up Gail, and we go to the Jockey Club for lunch. With reservations in my name, we are seated in a back corner. From my perspective, this is ideal; we can talk privately. If I had given Adnan's name, no doubt we would have been seated at the front.

Over lively lunchtime conversation, Gail and I reestablish ties with these friends whom we have not seen in two months. As we leave the restaurant, Adnan says, "We arrived from Riyadh at four this morning and we return to Europe in three days. This is short notice, but could you give an astronomy talk in New York tomorrow night?" "Sure," I reply, as I try to remember what I shall have to get out of.

As trustees arrive, dozens of students and a few faculty stand on the Quad and stare. The student demonstration is restrained and mature. As Adnan and I ascend the steps, Henry Dormann alights from his limo, impeccably attired, homburg in place. Mike Masin arrives with John Coleman, owner of the Washington and New York Ritz hotels. Jim Barrett, of Mutual of Omaha, squeezes my shoulder and says, "Hi, Prez."

The first hour and a half of the meeting, held in executive session, focuses on fundraising and financial matters. The heart of this session is one subject—progress on the sports and convocation center campaign. Sondra Bender summarizes our need for the center and our progress in obtaining funds. Her delivery is smooth, her message clear. The construction of this center is AU's highest priority now, and we need the trustees' strong financial support. She does not mince words. And best of all, she speaks from authority as well as conviction —she and her husband already have pledged at least $1 million.

A lively discussion ensues, with many people participating—Dormann, Bernstein, Ansary. And I chime in, doing what all the others are—ostensibly speaking to the full board while actually talking to Adnan. Last spring I asked him to join the board and this is his first meeting.

To build this center, we need one large benefactor to contribute, say, $5 million. With such a lead gift, everything else would follow, from other gifts to campus morale, from alumni participation to enhanced enrollments. In the past, AU has had trustees with loyalty but little money. Now we have several with substantial funds, but they are new to the board. Their support of AU is real but not yet sufficiently strong to warrant a multimillion-dollar pledge. Certainly, his wealth is sufficient for the lead gift if not to buy an entire university. But how quickly will he become adequately committed?

At 3:30 P.M. the executive session ends, the board takes a brief break, numerous campus representatives enter, and the ambience changes totally. From a free-flowing confidential discussion among trustees, the meeting now turns to classic campus concerns.

As so often occurs in social settings, two groups—in this case, trustees and campus representatives—eye each other warily, as they pretend to be absorbed in conversation with their peers. Trustees and administrators at one end of the room, students and professors at the other—such separation suggests campus dichotomy. One of my responsibilities, I believe, is to bring together disparate peoples. My new trustees and advisory board members, for instance, include liberals and conservatives, Republicans and Democrats, young people and old, women as well as men, Christians and Jews and Muslims and Buddhists and Hindus. For a university that wants to be national, this is as it should be. And at any university, the building of bridges remains vital.

The students' uneasiness, when I walk up to shake hands, probably reflects their discomfort in this setting. Even though campus representatives assert that they must attend board meetings, they seem to feel awkward when they arrive. I urge them to come to the other end of the room and meet the trustees. Board members greet them warmly. After some initial hesitancy, everyone seems to enjoy each other.

Chairman Ansary calls for the meeting to resume. The first order of business is to hear from campus representatives. Paul Schroeder, our blind undergraduate student president, speaks first. With a broad grin, he begins: "A cliché has it that an effective public speaker is not awed by the audience and understands their interests and sensitivities best by pretending that he can see them in their underwear. In my case, I can't do that."

The trustees laugh.

"So I'll ask you to do it for me. Please just imagine yourself in your underwear." The board laughs louder.

And Paul continues, "Even better, look at each other, and pretend you can see one another that clearly. I'd appreciate your help." The board roars and applauds. What a smashing beginning for this remarkable young man.

Then he elaborates on a written statement he gives out. Some of his suggestions, in my view, are undesirable if not naive. And most of them should be presented not to the board, but to the university senate or the provost; if the board were to adopt them, it would undermine the campus's deliberative process. Paul likely does not realize this; nonetheless, he presents his ideas so positively that he charms the board. At the end of his remarks, the trustees applaud heartily.

The head of the graduate students, Susan Jablow, is equally upbeat. Graciously, she thanks trustee Bill Moss for establishing generous graduate scholarships last year. Professor Ruth Landman, chair of the university senate, arrives with a box full of books authored by AU faculty. She urges trustees to review them as samples of our professors' scholarly work, wryly noting that they can be purchased at the campus bookstore. The last campus speaker, Bonnie Muir, represents staff. Politely, she asks the board to approve the pay increase scheduled for January 1. Like the preceding speakers, she speaks glowingly about the university.

Barrett Prettyman, the chair of the board's finance committee, compliments the campus representatives, noting that, "None of them asked for pay raises beyond what we've contemplated in the budget. Their restraint is admirable and responsible."

And I tell the board, with the campus contingent listening, how deeply proud I am of the AU community. Our students are impressive; the faculty, productive; and the staff, hard working and underpaid, yet strongly loyal to the university.

This was the best AU board meeting I have attended. The mood at the end reinforces that conclusion, as everyone—from freshman to board chairman—exudes warmth and pride.

It's happening, I think to myself. And this is deeper and will be more lasting than just the result of a good fall enrollment. The university now has more able people involved with it—from students to trustees—than ever before. And, consciously or unconsciously, they themselves know that. Most of all, institutional pride is building apace.

I escort several trustees to the door, including Adnan. The ever-efficient Shaheens are waiting with his car. They and Gail have spent the afternoon downtown.

Adnan, wrapping his arm around my waist, says quietly, "I really enjoyed this. The meeting was more fun than I'd expected. I'm impressed by what you're doing and by your people. Also, I'd like to know more about the sports and convocation center."

The last sentence thunders. A sonic boom, a nuclear blast could be no louder. But I do not flinch: "I'll get information to you at once."

Back in my office, I read the mail and reflect on the meeting. Then the phone rings. "The chief wonders if you can give your talk tomorrow night," Bob Shaheen says.

"Yes, I've checked my calendar and I can."

"Great. And of course you should bring Gail. How about bringing Cy Ansary, Nancy Dickerson, and some other trustees? You could include other Washington people, too."

"I don't know how many we can get on such short notice, but we'll try."

"Fine. Of course, we'll send a plane for you and we'll make reservations for everyone at the Helmsley Palace. Just give me the names."

As soon as he hangs up, I start calling. Cy Ansary's wife is ill so they cannot go. Several trustees do not answer. But others can come —the Benders, the Bernsteins, Dickerson, Moss, the Prettymans, and Lalo Valdez.

Gail and I discuss arrangements for Natasha. She can stay at a girlfriend's home. Then we ponder the next question: How many Washington people other than trustees should we invite? We agree upon some names and Gail and I start calling.

SATURDAY, OCTOBER 29
By noon, I am able to tell Bob our group. It will be the trustees, Gail and me, Secretary of Agriculture and Mrs. John Block, and Carolyn Deaver. Mike Deaver, Reagan's assistant, said he would like to go but this past week hit him hard. Other people Gail called were chagrined they could not accept due to conflicts.

Bob gave no guidelines on how many to invite, so I am nervous that we may have asked too many for the plane. "How many will it seat?" I ask. He replies, "About thirty-three, and there are three in the cockpit."

Such a large crew reassures me, for I do not enjoy small planes. And the thirty-three seats implies a far larger craft than I had imagined.

This evening, Gail and I pick up Carolyn Deaver. The three of us discuss our daughters, who used to play together in the summer, as we drive to Butler Aviation at National Airport. Having never been there before, I am uncertain where it is and I see no sign at the airport entrance listing it. I assume, therefore, that it is a small commuter line. In due course, we find Butler and are able to park in front. Its lobby is neat but empty. I ask a man behind the counter if our plane is ready. Puzzled, he says he does not know what flight I mean. Feeling nervous as I look at the group we have assembled, I wonder if Bob or I made a mistake. Still, he is always efficient and I am sure I got his instructions straight.

Then three sharply dressed flight attendants enter and ask, "Is Dr. Berendzen here? We'll take you to New York." I identify myself and our intrepid band follows the attendants from the terminal to the runway. Amidst a sea of expensive private planes, I see it. By now I should not be surprised. Yet I am. When will I learn?

There before us sits our thirty-three passenger plane—one of Adnan's personal Boeing 727 jets. Specifically outfitted for him, it seats only thirty-three because half of it resembles a hotel lobby with sofas. And the other half contains private drawing rooms, a bedroom with movie projection facilities, and even a shower. As Valdez notes, "It puts Air Force One to shame." In fact, it is possibly the most tastefully elegant aircraft in the world. Its key rivals would be other members of Adnan's fleet—his other 727, his helicopter, or his DC8. Tucked in the corner of the largest lounge is a guest book. Inconspicuously buried in pages of accolades to Adnan from a world *Who's Who* is Jimmy Carter's inscription.

We land smoothly and as we descend the plane's rear steps, four stretch limos and their chauffeurs await us. This strange armada glides across the runway and along the highway from Newark towards Manhattan. On this clear and crisp night, the Statue of Liberty's beacon shines. And even though it is 9:30 P.M. on a Saturday, lights glisten jewel-like in the World Trade towers and the Empire State Building. Through the tunnel and across West Side Manhattan, we pass Madison Square Garden and the porno shops of Eighth Avenue. Then through the theater district, past Rockefeller Center, on to Adnan's home: two floors of a premier Fifth Avenue tower, occupying the space of sixteen standard apartments.

Bob and Patricia greet us as we come out of the elevator, and Lamia, Adnan's wife, does too. Her dark hair highly coiffed tonight, she wears a tailored European original appropriate for this statuesque Italian beauty. At the door, beaming, stands the man himself.

The group with me stares unabashedly, as I did upon entering his home the first time, glancing past the Picasso, the Kandinsky, the Léger, and the interior garden, through the massive windows, to the city below. The panorama sweeps from the Citicorp Building, past the AT&T Tower, to the Empire State Building, Saint Patrick's Cathedral, and the Helmsley Building. With possibly the grandest view in this city of grand views, the sights outside could engross me for hours. But the main story tonight will be within.

The first time I was in Adnan's home was for Lamia's birthday. One of New York's heaviest blizzards forced the party to be postponed. We rescheduled our flight and Natasha's sitter. Finally, the date was reset, yet the snow remained high. No cab was available that Sunday afternoon at LaGuardia. And it took us six hours to rent a car and make our way to midtown. Repeatedly, we asked ourselves if it would be worth it. I still wonder that about much of what I do. Such questions crowded my mind that first evening as Gail and I stood in a corner of Adnan's living room and surveyed dozens of strangers. No doubt many of them could help AU, but no one wants to meet another guest at a Manhattan party who says, "Hi, I'm president of a university. Let me tell you about my school. Wouldn't you like to help us?"

That first night I met several international business executives and numerous movie stars. As much as anyone else, I enjoyed meeting Cheryl Tiegs, Farrah Fawcett, and Christopher Reeve. But they had no burning desire to talk to a university president in Washington, and neither Gail nor I had the courage to invite them to campus. So we concluded that one benefit of attending such a function as a couple is that, if all else fails, you can have animated conversation with each other. And that we did. Finally, I told Gail that we were wasting a good opportunity. So we picked someone at random to meet. Quiet and unassuming, she stood alone at the room's edge. Feeling slightly sorry for her, I assumed that she, too, felt somewhat out of place.

"Hi, I'm Richard Berendzen and this is my wife, Gail."

"Hello, I'm Koo Stark."

My mental computers whirred; I knew I had heard the name. But where? In what context? Innocently, I asked her, "Well, what is your profession?" "Oh, I'm an actress," she replied. Then I felt them—Gail's two fingers, an inch into my side. When she wants my attention, she taps my side; when it is more serious, she pokes half an inch; when I have committed a major faux pas, I get the inch treatment. This was an inch incident, as I had forgotten the flap over Prince Andrew's controversial friend.

Tonight there are no movie stars, but there are international businessmen, magazine publishers, fashion designers, and several others whose names and professions I do not learn. I am introduced to one man with care and deference: His Royal Highness, Prince Nawaf bin Abdul Aziz, brother of the king of Saudi Arabia. He is a member of one of the world's most influential and wealthy royal families, and his brother is Adnan's sovereign.

Although the prince and I have never met, I know his son, Mohammed, who was an AU student in the 1970s. In fact, I attended his wedding reception in Riyadh. By chance, I was going to be in Cairo, making arrangements for an AU program in Egypt and Israel. It was easy to fly from Cairo to Riyadh, and I was honored to be invited.

That being my first visit to Riyadh, I was struck by almost everything—the surrounding desert, the proliferation of tall cranes, the remarkable private palaces. After seeing perhaps twenty abandoned cars along the road, I asked my guide why they were there. He explained that parts and labor were scarce in Saudi Arabia, so people simply abandoned cars and bought new ones.

The night of the wedding reception, I was picked up at my hotel by two men wearing traditional Saudi attire. When we arrived at the hall, my black suit was a piece of pepper in a sea of salt. Apparently, I was the only Westerner. Mohammed greeted me warmly and gave me a place of honor. And that indeed was a distinction. Rows of sofas and chairs faced the stage where top musicians of the Arab world performed. Everyone was male. The most intriguing thing to me was not the show but the interaction of the guests. A new arrival would approach Mohammed, shake hands and bow. Then the same ritual would occur between the new arrival and dozens of other princes. Miraculously, two princes would separate for the new arrival to be seated. The next arrival would go through the same process, but he might be seated closer or further away from Mohammed. Fascinated, I asked the man next to me what was happening. He explained that the young men knew one another; many of them, in fact, were distant relatives. They seated themselves in the order of their age. How could they know each other's relative ages with dozens of people present? They simply had memorized them.

More than that, I was struck—almost awed—by the grace and poise of these young men. Not one was over thirty, most were in their early twenties, and many were teenagers. Yet they exuded a maturity and composure that few Americans have at forty. They smiled and joked like any other people. But from erect postures to serious conversations, they were obviously the products of fine private schools and close family guidance.

The day after Mohammed's reception, I visited the bazaar, where I wandered through numerous displays. Nestled next to rug stalls and brass works were tiny gold shops. Not content with our concept of quality, their gold was twenty-four karat. What stunned me most was the sheer quantity of the gold. One small shop contained more of it than all the jewelry stores in Washington combined.

After overcoming my amazement at that, I was startled to note the shopkeepers—two boys no older than fifteen. There was no adult present. No TV cameras. No evidence of an alarm system. Just a ten-foot by ten-foot shop, laden with massive gold necklaces, tended by two young teens. Cautiously, I asked if I could look at a large necklace, stressing that I could not afford its clasp, much less all of it. It sold for $150,000. As I examined the workmanship closely and wondered how a woman would like such weight around her neck, I heard the calling of prayer from a nearby mosque. So frequently do you hear prayer there that I paid no attention.

Looking up from the necklace in which I had become so absorbed, I could find neither young salesman. In fact, I found no one. Where had everyone gone? The shop was tiny with no back room. I looked into the market. Again, no one. There I stood, alone, surrounded by millions of dollars worth of gold.

The Saudi criminal code may or may not contain the punishments reported in the Western press. But I had no intention of finding out. Nervously, I stood in the center of the room hoping someone would return quickly and all the gold would be in place. Shortly, the two young shopkeepers did return, as did life in the market. I asked where they had gone. "To prayer." Amazing! If all shopkeepers were to leave a U.S. store untended and unlocked for fifteen minutes, nothing would be left from merchandise to mannequins.

On my last day in Riyadh, our car passed a European designer boutique, its windows filled with the latest Parisian fashions. What, I asked, were such dresses doing here? After all, few women appeared in public. And when they did, they dressed from head to toe in black. My guide smiled and asked, "What do you suppose they wear under those black robes?

I had not the slightest idea, nor did I want to find out. I knew about their modesty. "In our society," the guide explained, "some women wear Western fashions, but they do so under black robes in public and go without robes only at home or in the company of other women. In your society, women wear such fashions on the street. We believe women should make themselves beautiful when they are with other women, their family, or their husbands. Your women dress for everyone. There is an old saying, 'For whom does the blind man's wife paint herself?' "

I tell the prince at Adnan's dinner how much I enjoyed attending his son's reception and how much I learned while there. Also, I ask him to have Mohammed contact me when he is in Washington and I extend a similar invitation to the father.

At about 11:30 P.M., Bob Shaheen ushers us to the dining room. Adnan quickly determines the evening's protocol and directs each of us to a seat accordingly. He places Sue Block to his right, John Block to Lamia's left, and the prince to her right. The Benders and I are at Adnan's table, providing us with a unique opportunity to watch this exceptional man.

At Lamia's birthday party, I was charmed to watch him, in black tie, crawl on the floor with his young son. He even permitted the boy to climb on his pair of bronze pumas by sculptor William Zorach. The man liked the art; the father loved the son. Now his eyes dance as the conversation jumps from Europe to California, from skiing to jokes. Despite Bob's masterful stewardship, Adnan himself checks the food and takes guests to the buffet table.

Earlier tonight, when I told Adnan I should set up my slide projector, he took me to the projection room. Together, we set up the equipment. After dinner, the group assembles and Adnan says, "Professor, it's all yours."

A challenging audience under difficult circumstances I have faced many times before. But this one is unique—a mixture of Washingtonians, New Yorkers, Europeans, and Middle Easterners. And it is one o'clock in the morning. For the next half hour, my challenge will be not only to inform but even to awaken.

Despite my initial trepidation, the eyes are with me. Adnan and Lamia ask several questions. From my speaker's perspective, that is great. And a guest asks if astronomy and theology conflict. I reply by paraphrasing the priest-astronomer who originally proposed the big bang theory of the universe: "These two great areas of thought, dogma, and belief—science and religion—need not conflict. Science deals with *how, when, where,* and *what.* Religion deals with *why* and *who.*"

By two o'clock I am finished; the group is weary, but alert. I round up the Washington contingent and we thank the Khashoggis and Shaheens. As Adnan shows us to the elevator, I hand him a notebook about the center. He smiles and says, "I'll read this, Professor." I think as we depart that he has as much charm as money. All of us agree: we will remember this adventure forever.

SUNDAY, OCTOBER 30

Back in Washington, reality returns as we drop off Carolyn, pick up Natasha, feed Sparky, and prepare for an afternoon reception honoring people who have donated $500 to $999 to AU during the past year. For many of them, this was a genuine sacrifice. We want to thank them.

How many minutes of a 727's flying time would $500 buy? If I had such wealth, what would I do with it? Would I build a sports and convocation center at a university I had seen only twice? How would I respond to hundreds of pursuing charities, hopeful inventors, aspiring playwrights? Or to the president of AU?

MONDAY, OCTOBER 31

Darth Vadar, a skeleton, Wonder Woman—they are all here. The human crayon is the most innovative costume, but the two-foot-tall Superman is the most endearing. Tykes from our Child Development Center—which provides daytime child-care facilities for working parents—are making their annual trick-or-treat visit to my office. They have no notion of who I am; they like to swing in my big leather desk chair.

Certain people always get ready entree to my office—my family, trustees, major benefactors, my cabinet, key reporters, or the CDC children. Especially the last. In the midst of a meeting, Joan will buzz, "They're here. And their patience isn't long." The meeting stops and in troops a swarm of wide-eyed three-year-olds. As the last Princess Leia leaves, I receive an urgent call from an alumnus.

"About that change of grade, I've gotten all the necessary signatures except the department chairman's. And he was on vacation. How was I to find him?"

I try to break in to find out who is calling and why. But the man is not listening. "I wrote to the dean in 1952 about this. I can't find his letter back to me, but you probably have a copy. Anyway, he told me . . ."

And so it goes for ten minutes while I try to interject. Finally, I succeed. He wants a grade change for a course in 1948. He should have contacted the registrar or a dean; however, like hundreds of others, he uses the maxim "start at the top." I have heard acquaintances counsel their children to do that. So a new generation thinks the only way—not just the last-resort way—to achieve anything is to go to the top. If an item from a store is damaged, do not take it to the complaint department, the salesperson, or the floor manager; take it to the president. Of course, the president will refer the matter to where it should have begun.

Joan shields me, but some callers use subtle ploys. The number of "close personal friends" who have called me exceeds the number of persons whose names I know. The number who call me because I "asked them to" exceeds the number I have asked to do anything. The caller today is one of the manipulators.

Lunch today is with Georgie Anne Geyer, a widely syndicated columnist and a trustee. We met years ago in an odd way. During a torrential rain, several hundred people packed into the Greek Embassy for an important reception. Getting in was easy; getting out took an hour. The problem arose with retrieving your raincoat and umbrella from the cloak room. As I inched towards my prized possessions, the woman in front of me and I began to talk. Never had I met a more widely traveled or broadly experienced individual. The more we talked, the more intrigued I became. I asked the questions that night.

"With whom have you had some of your most interesting interviews?"

"Arafat, Castro, Begin, and certainly Sadat. Oh, then there was . . ."

Why did I not know her work? Because it was in the "other" paper, not the *Post*. And it was in more than a hundred other papers worldwide. I asked her to send me clippings. She did. Impressed, I asked for a luncheon meeting. Before it was over, I had concluded that she would make an excellent trustee. With her worldwide contacts, her speaking ability, and her accomplishments as a female professional, she would be an excellent role model for our students. Ultimately, she agreed to join.

She has spoken to several AU groups. And today we discuss a Chicago luncheon that she will host for me so I can meet two dozen of her newspaper and business friends. Originally her home, Chicago could be an important city for us, and she has excellent contacts there.

After an afternoon of reading mail, writing letters, and making calls, I rush home early. Soon we shall receive several dozen trick-or-treaters. These, however, will be twice the height of my morning visitors. They will be AU students. While Gail prepares the house, I drive Natasha to a friend's home from which she and two classmates will go trick-or-treating by themselves. Loosening apron strings is fine, but how much and when? On past Halloweens, Gail has given out things at home while I have taken Natasha trick-or-treating. Last year Natasha said I could accompany her with the caveat that I stay one hundred feet away. This year she is pushing for a twenty-block separation.

How different this is from five years ago when we took her door to door in our large apartment building. One year we went before the other children. Dressed like a giant tube of Crest, Natasha pressed a bell. The wife of a diplomat new to the U.S. cautiously opened the door. Before her an oversized toothpaste tube held a bag and shrieked, "Trick-or-Treat!" In badly broken English, the woman replied, "I'll be right back." We waited several minutes, wondering if we should leave. Then she reappeared—with a dozen cans of vegetables and a roast. As she started placing it all in Natasha's bag, my understanding, sympathetic daughter blurted, "Wow!" I shouted, "Oh, no. That's entirely too much. Just an apple will do." The woman looked as baffled when I took food out of the bag as she did when she answered the door. Americans are hard to predict or understand. I would give a lot to hear her tell friends at home about her first encounter with Halloween: "These crazy Americans send their children, dressed like toothpaste, to beg for food."

When Natasha has returned home safely and the last trick-or-treater has gone, I return to my office. Only Jermaine, the cleaning woman, and I are here. After several hours, she tells me, "Oh, sir, you really should go home. It's awfully late." It is? Indeed: 3:45 A.M. Maybe that is why I feel so tired.

The night is chilly and the dorms are dark as I walk home.

TUESDAY, NOVEMBER 1

Following an afternoon of calls and mail, Gail and I attend a reception downtown in honor of a man who aids families of cult victims. Fortunately, AU has almost no students in cults today. But it has in the past, and the threat still hangs over many American families. From there we drive to Capitol Hill to attend a reception for the United Negro College Fund. The predominately black attendees include U.S. Department of Education officials and local TV celebrities. Back in my office before midnight, I prepare written remarks for this Friday's luncheon. Speaking ad lib is fine, but I am to give the invocation at a banquet honoring women in the U.S. Olympics. The head table will include Sally Ride, Billie Jean King, and me.

What to say? I wonder if I can find an appropriate quotation in the Bible. So I look up "sport" in the concordance. It has a listing. With anticipation, I turn to Genesis 26:8: "Abimelech, King of the Philistines, looked out a window and saw . . . Isaac . . . sporting with Rebekah, his wife."

I shall try a different approach.

WEDNESDAY, NOVEMBER 2

My first meeting, with the vice-presidents and vice-provosts, is devoted to items I jotted down last night. The fourteen topics range from new formats for publications to improvement in international recruiting; from redesign of campus maps to improvement in affirmative action. On the latter, I understand that departments face real problems in recruiting well-qualified, full-time black members, especially in some professional areas. But we can obtain outstanding black adjunct faculty. Numerous black professionals work in Washington; some of them can teach part-time at AU. On this, I end by saying, "I want action. No excuses, just results." And I ask Nina Roscher, dean of faculty affairs, to so inform the faculty.

Originally, I had planned to dash immediately from that meeting to catch the shuttle to New York. But my desk is covered with mail and "urgent" phone messages. The *Eagle* asks about the accreditation review. The Council of Governments of Metropolitan Washington invites me to speak at its annual meeting. A student wants to interview me for a class. A parent of an AU student who heard me on the radio would like to discuss education. Among the calls is one from Gail.

"Hi, Bunny? You called?"

"Richard, Natasha's play is important to her. She's upset you'll be in New York tonight."

Slumping into my chair, I say, "I discussed that with her, and she seemed okay. How upset is she?"

"She wishes you could be there. She looked droopy when I took her to school."

Feeling negligent, I search for a way out: "Is the play put on only once?"

"No, and that's why I called. At one o'clock this afternoon, Natasha's class will perform it for the lower school. Could you attend then?"

To do so, I shall have to rearrange my schedule in New York. But that is better than not attending or canceling the dinner I have agreed to attend.

So I reply, "Okay. I'll be there."

At five after one, I enter the Big Room at GDS, where a hundred lower-school children watch seventeen seventh-graders put on a montage of plays based on foreign myths, with each child having a speaking part. Being twelve years old, Natasha's communications with Gail and me are becoming painful and uninformative. All she told us about the play was, "It's neato. You've gotta see it." Not a word about her part. To my amazement, I watch her make faces at the audience while the kindergarten children roar. And she does a somersault, something I have never seen her do before. Why do I have to come to a public place to learn what she can do?

I would feel fatherly warmth except my leg is asleep from sitting on a Lilliputian chair: half my bottom hangs off and my knee is at my chin. Finally, when I can stand, I approach Natasha to tell her how good she was and to hug her before heading for the airport. But her radar sends an unmistakable message: "You liked the play. That's nice. Bye." Translation: "Don't be maudlin with my friends watching."

She and her classmates look appropriately morose, as if the nation is at war, their families are bankrupt, or they have cancer. At twelve, it is obligatory to suffer—or at least to look distressed. I wave goodbye to this unhappy group, feeling proud of them and hoping the hormonal changes will end soon.

Senator Mathias stops at my seat on the shuttle and we shake hands. He has been an enthusiastic supporter of AU's Washington

Semester program. Behind him comes John Wallach, international affairs editor of Hearst publications. Now working on a book, he also makes TV tapes and gives radio commentaries for the BBC.

From my hotel, I call Joan. "Anything special happening?"

"A *Post* reporter called," she replies. "He wants to know about Bernstein, Moss, Dickerson, and other trustees. Sounds like it's related to Khashoggi's dinner last Saturday. I said only you could give details."

I take down the number but am too rushed to call because I am due at a reception at "21." As I walk from my hotel to the restaurant, I wonder what the *Post* has in store. Saturday's adventure was too intriguing, too out of the ordinary, for the press to ignore. I have told no one about it, yet rumors run fast in Washington.

Tonight's dinner is in preparation for tomorrow's meeting. Some months ago, I agreed to be on a commission that was organized by the U.S. Chamber of Commerce, dealing with a free and responsible press. The other commissioners include distinguished media authorities and business executives. Among them: John Wallach. Even though we are friends, we rarely have an opportunity for private conversation. Tonight he offers to help AU and I ask if he will join the NAB. He accepts on the spot.

Delighted, I still must call the *Post.* So I do so from a pay phone. The *Post* already has the facts. The reporter wants to corroborate them and get details. He is pleasant and I enjoy the interview. If it had been up to me, there would have been no publicity about the Khashoggi event. But that option is gone. Now may it be handled sensitively and well.

THURSDAY, NOVEMBER 3

At an eight o'clock breakfast meeting, commission members hear several brief talks; afterwards, the formal hearings begin. My definition of a good conference is one in which I leave with at least one new idea that I can use. Today's discussion consists of inside talk by media people about pressures, subtle or otherwise, within the profession. As fascinating as this is, it is a long way from my concerns back home.

Shortly before noon I slip out and start searching for a cab. It is raining. One hour later, I find one. The driver insists upon picking up another fare. I would object, except the other fare looks as bedraggled as I do and he, too, wants to get to the airport. I tell him I have been waiting for an hour. He says he has been waiting an hour and a half. Where do New York cabs go in the rain?

Tonight Gail and I attend a reception in the Mary Graydon Center to honor persons who gave AU from $100 to $499 last year. We give a certificate to each one, along with an AU tie or scarf. I end my remarks by saying, "Wear your tie or scarf with pride—pride in this institution, pride in your support of it. When you see someone wearing a similar garment, know that person is a backer like you. Go up and say, 'Hello, I too support AU.' And then pass on the secret information . . . ." The crowd looks baffled. I pause before adding, "Didn't we teach you the secret handshake and other information?"

"Oh, I'm sorry. We only do that with the people at the next gift level. So when you become one of the $500 to $999 givers, we'll let you in on it." My fears that they might be offended by such a ploy evaporate as they applaud enthusiastically and ask about the secrets. Of course, there are none. But if donors are interested, we shall invent some.

Back in my office, I finish my invocation for tomorrow. I ask Jermaine to be a critic. She looks stern as I read it to her. Then she smiles and says, "Oh, that's good, sir."

"But will women athletes like it?"

"I think so. You say good things without offending any religious group." As she goes back to dusting, she adds, "I'd go with it."

I will.

FRIDAY, NOVEMBER 4

Recently, a *New York Times* reporter called to request an "interview" because "President Berendzen is an interesting person whom we'd like to know better." My mother may think I am interesting, but this sounded odd coming from the *Times.* When I see the reporter this morning, I know he has other things in mind. He is impeccably dressed. Normally, male reporters arrive crumpled, with brown shoes and a stained tie. They cannot get a Pulitzer without brown shoes. No notebook or tape recorder is in sight, which arouses my suspicions more. Then he says: "A development officer at another university told me I should see you because you're such a dynamic educational leader." No, he is not writing a story; he is selling himself. He wants a job. I refer him to the appropriate office.

The normally tranquil cabinet meeting that follows becomes tense as Myers and Triezenberg tell Milt that he is overseeing their budgets too closely. They need more autonomy. And more funds. In John Glenn's words, "I'll keep away from this one." If the debate becomes intractable, I shall adjudicate; otherwise, I will leave it to them.

At eleven o'clock this morning, I meet my owner: Fahimeh Mortazvi, the raven-haired resident-director of Leonard Hall, our international dorm. At the serf auction held last weekend, she purchased me for seventy-eight dollars. The auction raised twelve hundred dollars for a D.C. soup kitchen.

Iranian by birth, Fahimeh has close affinity with international students, and she's an excellent dorm director. I am surprised she made the purchase, but maybe she wanted to save my feelings. It would have been embarrassing if no one had bid for the president. Anyway, she is here to give me my serf assignment: write to her wealthy friend in Germany who has donated funds to AU. She thinks he would like to hear directly from me. Of course, I will write, but what do I do as serf? "That's it," she says. What a civilized auction. Neither my fears nor fantasies come true. I write the letter before lunch.

And then I am off to the Capital Hilton. Security precautions cause long lines, as the crowd inches into the ballroom. I go directly to the head table where I am to sit. While I am having delightful conversations with Sally Ride, whose education parallels my own, Billie Jean King, and Bill Simon, former treasury secretary who now heads the Olympics, a woman runs up shouting: "Vice-president Bush is coming and we can't find the invocation guy."

"Hey, I'm the invocation guy," I say. Her look is one of relief mixed with pity. In this crush of athletes, my flabby frame, exercised only by occasional brisk walks, seems conspicuous even under my suit. Medal winners abound, one of whom asks me, "What's your best sport?" Does memo writing or committee chairing count? Quickly, my memory rushes to my high school days: "Oh, I used to run track. And I got an award for an unusual sport. . . ." Let her conjure up bareback riding in the Pampas, bear wrestling in Russia, cliff diving in Mexico. Truth is, it was horseshoe throwing. When Gail and I were dating, college girls wore sweaters festooned with boyfriends' athletic laurels. So I gave her my high school horseshoe-throwing ribbon. It did not help when I claimed that in Texas we threw the shoe with the horse attached. Even New Englanders were not that gullible.

Bill Simon calls the room to order and asks me to give the invocation. I walk confidently to the rostrum, knowing my prayer has received quadruple approval: from Gail, Natasha, Joan, and Jermaine. Then fate hits: My baritone voice turns into a teenager's squawk as a frog gets in my throat. What was to be ringing oratory turns into crackling gurgle. Finally, I close with an "amen" sounding like "ahnnh."

Bush, the principal speaker, has no frog in his throat. And he has a good joke. In an alleged conversation with John Glenn, Glenn asked him, "Do you think the nation is ready for an astronaut to be president?"

"Sure," Bush replies. "But is Sally Ride ready to run?"

The predominantly female audience thunders its applause.

When I return to my office, a caller wants to know, "How much do I have to give in order to name the sports center?" I tell him. He just says, "Too much," and hangs up.

In the past, remarkable donations have led to naming gifts. In 1718, Cotton Mather wrote wealthy businessmen that a newly founded school in Connecticut would be named after them if they made a substantial donation. One responded with goods later sold for 562 pounds sterling: Elihu Yale. Whence came Yale University. After the revolutionary war, Rhode Island College advertised that it would change its name if anyone donated as much as $6,000. A Providence merchant bid $5,000—Nicholas Brown.

Today, however, universities face sterner realities of contracts and debt financing. Although AU is willing to negotiate about name recognition, we must have enough money to proceed.

My next meeting is with Madeleine Green, the talented head of the Center for Leadership Development at the American Council on Education. She thanks me for agreeing to speak to a group of new university presidents in May, even though the last time I spoke to a group, I "terrified them," she says. "You hit them with hard realities about academic administration in the eighties," Madeleine explains. "And—if you remember—you said to do well in higher-education administration requires eighty hours per week; anyone working under sixty hours per week should be fired."

Yes, I said that and meant it. Madeleine goes on: "Afterwards, I mothered the group into some composure by noting that each administrator has a different style. One way is to delegate more responsibility." No doubt she is right; all management manuals say this. I *do* delegate—to Milt, the Dons, the deans. And I know it is conceited to think that I alone can handle certain tasks. When I am away, my office runs; yet that does not lessen my responsibility.

A professor in my freshman year said: "Success is 1 percent inspiration, 99 percent perspiration." And, as a teenager, I visited the Hall of Fame, isolated in space and time in far northwest New York City. Only my parents, guards, and I were there that day. Our steps echoed; even our muffled voices seemed to intrude. The honored's busts lay in dust; no one cared any longer about such sentimentality. Yet all people, especially youth, need role models. Maybe that is why my parents took me there. I was anxious to get on to Yankee Stadium. What did I care about Horace Mann or Eli Whitney? Still, a familiar poem, chiseled beside Henry Wadsworth Longfellow's bust, impressed me then, echoed during my college days, and lingers even today:

> The heights by great men reached and kept
> Were not attained by sudden flight,
> But they, while their companions slept,
> Were toiling upward in the night.

SATURDAY, NOVEMBER 5

After a family meeting, we divide chores. Natasha has the choice of going grocery shopping with Gail or on errands with me. She picks errands. Our first stop is Bruce's Variety Store, a wondrous place from another era. With narrow aisles and high shelves laden with goods, it does not belong in this high-tech age. Natasha loves it, as do I. We come for a piece of felt but spend an hour rumaging through buttons and pans and toys.

From there, we go to another of our favorite places—Strosnider's. Not a conventional hardware store, it sells everything from household items to heavy commercial tools. Last summer, I took Natasha and Gail through it, aisle by aisle, as we examined plumbers' bobs, cement-drill bits, and copper tubing. What more practical, vital information could a person learn?

Our trip today is brief. But I smile as I remember the traumatizing afternoon when four-year-old Natasha discovered the industrial tools. Amazed, she looked at chain cutters and professional wrenches. Then, discovering a giant screwdriver almost as long as she was tall, she shouted across ten aisles: "Daddy! Daddy! Wouldn't Mommy be thrilled if you came home with a driver this big?" As the smirking customers looked about for the father, I hid behind the car-wax case and asked, "Whose little girl is that, anyway?"

MONDAY, NOVEMBER 7

A stack of forms awaits my signature. A cover note from Nina Roscher instructs me to "sign at the paper clips." Okay, but why? Nina and others have scrutinized pages of technical jargon. With her assurance, I shall fulfill my CEO's responsibility and sign—all two dozen times. But I feel like the colonel in "M*A*S*H."

Next I face an intriguing challenge: to write a convincing letter in support of a student's Rhodes Scholarship application. Selection committees expect university presidents to stand behind their students. I genuinely believe in this young man. After starting the letter half-a-dozen times, I remember my own whimsical maxim: "When in doubt, tell the truth." So I say directly what I think about the student, neither understanding nor overstating anything. He compares well with the best students I have known. He deserves the scholarship.

The morning mail brings a journal article by Harold Durfee, one of our senior scholars. Its title alone reminds me that I am at a university: "Ultimate Meaning and Presuppositionless Philosophy." Any paper with such a title must be read. I shall do so this weekend.

Tonight we call Deborah to make Christmas plans. When she was small, her Christmas visits were not just special; they were my fall's raison d'être. Then it took months of savings to pay for her airfare between Dallas and Boston. But every cent was worth it; each of those few days in late December became a month. Feverishly, in early December, I would complete my work so there would be no diversion when she arrived.

Two decades ago, Gail, only in her twenties, seemed an unlikely stepmother. But in that young woman lay remarkable grace. Knowing instinctively that biological bonds are unique, she nonetheless embraced Deborah as her own. And the three of us had a special relationship. For weeks before Deborah's arrival, Gail and I would map a program that defied the laws of physics. In our ten days together, we would cram in more sights, adventures, laughter, and learning than normal home life would have allowed in ten months. The Boston Public Library and the Isabella Stewart Gardner Museum, Chinatown and Harvard Yard, the Boston Common and Back Bay—we compressed it all into days. We caroled with Beacon Hill bell-ringers on Christmas Eve; had midnight picnics beside Nahant Lighthouse;

explored art shops on Newbury Street; skied in New Hampshire.

This year, adult Deborah will arrive without wide-eyed wonder but with the same warmth. Families should not be apart too long; phones are fine but personal contact is better. The two sisters need to rediscover one another. Almost the same height now, they are becoming increasingly close in many ways.

How extraordinary children are. Not merely other human beings, they continue yourself. Individuals in their own right, they nonetheless embody your beliefs and biology, values and genes. They extend time. What a unique responsibility they are; as someone admonished: "Give them roots and let them soar."

TUESDAY, NOVEMBER 8

Betsy Hostetler, a member of our staff development office, stops to ask what activities or programs I think would benefit the staff. Whether here or elsewhere, I do not understand workshops on "interpersonal dynamics" or "mentoring." But there are several steps we could take that might benefit staff.

One would be to have an intensive orientation program, perhaps prepared in multimedia. It is not a novel idea, but AU has yet to do this on a systematic, large-scale basis. For employees to work well in the present and build for the future, they should understand the institution's past. With audio-visual aids, we could explain AU's founding, architecture, and plans. Betsy says she and her colleagues hope to implement such a program soon.

Also, I urge that staff members should understand the responsibilities of their colleagues across the university. Recently, a veteran professor asked me about a dorm. I replied, "You should see Phil Henry." "Who's he?" asked the professor. For more than a decade, Henry has ably handled the dorms, yet this professor did not even know his name. Such parochialism is common at most institutions. But we should reduce it.

Finally, I like for individual staff members to be highlighted, perhaps in an internal university publication. Again, not a novel idea. But we have not done it enough. Profiles of talented staff could be uplifting for everyone.

"One of the biggest problems is job mobility," Betsy points out. "Staff positions often offer little opportunity for career advancement." Everyone needs a sense of hope and dignity. She and I discuss means for improving this situation.

Is My Armor Straight?

Over dinner at home, we have a family discussion about current events. Such times are among my favorite interludes. Spirited conversation, lots of laughter, a sense of family closeness—such discussions are both informative and nurturing.

After dinner, I sort my astronomical slides. At nine o'clock I have to be on campus, where I am to speak to a meeting hosted by several student groups. I relish looking into the students' eyes, especially those encountering truly extraordinary, challenging ideas. Who knows, these students someday may explain the phenomena about which tonight I can only say: "We don't yet know the answer, but we're fairly sure of the question."

WEDNESDAY, NOVEMBER 9

The business-suited crowd of middle-aged men greet one another as longtime friends. After cocktails, we are seated at the International Club in downtown Washington. The emcee asks each member to identify himself. Their titles: director, Washington representative, vice-president, executive vice-president. And their organizations: electronics firms, high-tech manufacturers, energy exploration companies, financial analysts. The Washington Industrial Roundtable brings together several dozen corporate leaders, and I am pleased to be today's luncheon speaker. My topic: "Education and National Politics."

Their concerns are mine; their remedies are mine. We agree that the work ethic has deteriorated; that parental nurturance has declined; that there should be enhanced partnership between industry and public education. I argue that if schools have trouble obtaining well-qualified engineers, scientists, and mathematicians to teach, then local industry should provide these people on a limited basis.

"Won't the teachers' unions object?" someone from the audience asks.

"In the past, many of them have. They weren't convinced that industrialists knew how to teach and they wanted to protect teachers' jobs. Given the nation's mood today, however, they might be more receptive."

"Even so, these are but short-term measures for a long-term problem. We must attract high-quality students to the teaching profession. For that to happen, society will have to assume responsibilities that lately have been shunted to schools. Schools should exist to teach. It's not their job to prevent violence, inculcate a desire to learn, or develop rigorous home-study habits."

With respect to my talk's title, I outline the educational positions of each major candidate, concluding that, on balance, President Reagan may be the net beneficiary of the current discussion on education. After all, it has been during his administration that these problems have been highlighted and genuine progress has been made.

But in the eyes of many, Reagan is best known for his talk of abolishing the Department of Education and for his support of merit pay, prayer in school, and tuition tax credits. Whether he has been in Washington or California, many have viewed him as an enemy of education. In part, they reached this conclusion because of symbolism —because he believes that education is not so much the responsibility of the government as it is of the individual. Reagan would argue that education "is a right, not a privilege." And he would justify his reductions in student financial aid by noting the large number of students who have defaulted on federally subsidized loans and the number of people who have received federal educational assistance without demonstrating financial hardship. But the Reagan administration's reductions now have gone far enough. Further reductions would hurt middle- and lower middle-income families. If private universities become too expensive for many of our youth, then those persons will be forced to seek jobs for which they are not prepared or to enroll at community colleges, thereby increasing the taxpayer's burden at the state level.

"What do you think of bilingual education?" I am asked.

"Although I sympathize with many Hispanic families, youth should be placed as quickly as possible into rigorous English programs. The fundamental language of our land, English, now has become even more than that: insofar as there is an international language, English is it. To do well in business, science, economics, or a host of other fields, a student must understand English. And this can be achieved even for a youngster from a non-English-speaking home. We just must try. We all have the same goal."

Then I am asked: "Politically, what should Reagan do or not do now about education?"

"He should not propose abolishing the Department of Education. His right wing can be placated in other ways. And how unfortunate it was last April, when the National Commission report damned quality in public education, that the president replied that we need prayer in schools. He missed the point. We didn't need so much to pray *in* the schools as to pray *for* the schools.

"Also, he should stop touting merit pay. An interesting idea that's appropriate for our time, it nonetheless can't bring magical results, transforming mediocre teachers into outstanding ones. Nor can it raise teachers' salaries enough. That can be done only by society's placing higher priority on public education.

"Many vital reforms can be achieved at no expense—teachers can assign more homework, grade more rigorously, teach more material in each course, grade on grammar as well as content, and promote increased use of the school library. But it would be naive for the administration to assume that all the reforms it suggests and that our nation needs can be achieved without federal expenditures.

"Most of all, we need stronger bonds—between schools and universities, between industry and education, between teachers and parents, between the government and the schools, and between the educational community and the American public. The president should stress all this."

Back at my office, the Sports and Convocation Center task force meets. Sondra smiles warmly but speaks sternly: "I deeply appreciate the support we've heard from trustees and others. But we need money. Everyone likes to talk; no one likes to give. It's time we moved this enterprise." Bill Moss, a Dallas oilman, leans forward, takes off his glasses, and, in his soft drawl, says, "I agree with you totally. If the board's going to move this thing, it has to put its shoulder to it. We should have 100 percent participation by trustees. And those who can afford more should state for all to see that they gave $100,000 or whatever." Lascaris and Bernstein echo this theme.

I step out to call New York. I had hoped to hear something by now about Khashoggi's deliberations. But no one has called me. Now word comes from New York that Adnan is considering a $5 million gift. He will try to let me know within two weeks.

My initial response is euphoria. But what if the answer is no? Then the door would be shut permanently. "But," I think to myself, "if he wanted to say no, he could do so now. Perhaps he needs time to structure the financing." Many people assume that whatever is important to them will be what I shall consider first. I should not make the same mistake with Adnan.

When I relate the news to members of the task force, they are jubilant. Prudently, they decide to continue as if there had been no such revelation. If he does support us, great! If he does not, we must be prepared for alternative financing. The meeting ends as it began with Sondra saying, in effect, "Put up or shut up." All at the meeting agree.

While I write the inscription, Gail gets the wrapping paper. Our gift will be a copy of the National Geographic's, *People and Places of the Past.* He has been everywhere, studied everything from the big bang to the small amoeba. Astronomy is his field; social sciences are his obsession. Yes, we conclude, this will be a good birthday present for Carl Sagan.

At seven o'clock, we arrive at the Watergate apartment of Frank and Billie Press. Holiday spirit abounds, with birthday balloons and Halloween pumpkins. The other guests will be Al and Tipper Gore. Annie, Carl's wife, helped arrange this surprise party. And I enjoy seeing Carl look baffled upon entering.

The Presses have planned an intimate evening for just a few friends. What a delightful contrast to the crushing receptions we so often attend. As a former MIT department head, coauthor of one of the largest selling textbooks, former science adviser to President Carter, and current president of the National Academy of Sciences, Frank is the most influential science policy person in the world. Slight in build and soft of voice, he is the intellectual's intellectual. Scholar and administrator, he now advises the nation as he once advised the president—cautiously and prudently.

Al, a ruddy-faced congressman from Tennessee, is running for the Senate in 1984 and is attracting national attention. Tonight he speaks with authority on a remarkable number of topics—the nuclear freeze, AT&T divestiture, elementary particle physics. He would be an exceptional senator.

And, of course, Carl is the most widely heralded scientist of our time. No other professor has been seen or heard by so many people; the stimulation he has given to scientific understanding is without peer.

Quiet, blond Tipper is her husband's best campaign aide. Billie, an education specialist, is first lady of the NAS, a post she fills with dignity but irreverence. With a twinkle in her eye, she'll say the least expected thing, disarming and charming everyone. And Annie, a writer, brings from forty-nine-year-old Carl the adoring, almost sappy look of a freshman in love. Their thinking is uncannily similar; her support for him is boundless.

I ask Annie, "How's Carl feeling now?"

"For a while, we didn't think he'd make it last spring. He was very ill, so this birthday is special. For a time, I thought there'd be no more birthdays for him."

All of us want to hear about Carl's latest work—his scientific predictions of the consequences of a major nuclear war. The result, he projects, would be devastation of the planet. Innumerable species would end, possibly including humankind, a dreadful scenario he has dubbed "the nuclear winter."

As a lively discussion starts over dinner, Al's pocket beeper squawks. "Excuse me," he says, "but two hundred thousand folks in my district will be disappointed if I don't vote. I'll be right back." He runs to his car and races to Capitol Hill. When he returns, Carl and I ask him: "Why can't congressmen vote by phone?"

"Presumably because we should hear the debates. The debates actually are worth hearing. But we can't be there for all of them, so we use beepers."

The conversation leaps from standards in our schools to the nuclear freeze to obscure old movies. Everyone is a raconteur. As I look past the glass doors to the Kennedy Center and watch planes land over the Potomac, I think back to a similar evening a few years ago. Its setting was radically different. But the brain power and articulation were comparable.

Hosted by my friend Moshe Davis, head of the Institute for Contemporary Jewry, it was held in his unpretentious home in Jerusalem. For this Orthodox Friday dinner, no mechanical devices were used. Even electric lights were not turned on manually; automatic timers did it. The elevator was off—to press its button would constitute work, forbidden on the Sabbath. And so we walked to his upper floor and, in customary fashion, gave our hosts a bouquet.

We were joined by many of Moshe's intellectual friends. And over dinner, lasting some four hours, I was questioned more closely about astronomy and the history of science than at any time since my graduate days. Conversely, I probed and inquired about their respective fields. The conversation did not jump; it bounded.

Best of all, two young boys, both under fourteen, sat quietly at the table through it all. Eyes glistening, darting from one speaker to another, they took it all in. How much they understood I do not know, for I only understood a portion myself. But one thing was clear: they knew ideas were important and could be exciting. If they learned even a fraction of that discussion, it would have been more than many American youngsters obtain in a year of college. That is the true nature of education. And I am glad I told the Industrial Roundtable today about Moshe's dinner. Merit pay for teachers will help. But it cannot substitute for home conversations.

A study once was made, I have heard, of National Merit scholars to determine what characteristics they shared. Their race, creed, gender, and national heritage were not the same, but one factor was: all the scholars regularly had evening family dinners.

Shortly after eleven o'clock we say goodnight. As we pack into the elevator, I note that Annie's pinstripe coat closely resembles Carl's pinstripe suit. For someone else that would not be exceptional. But this is my old friend Carl. "What's happened to your turtleneck?" I ask. "Oh, I don't know," he replies. "I wear this kind of thing sometimes." Softly, Annie says, "I think his pinstripe suit is my influence." I think so, too. It is charming to see how he has remained himself while becoming part of her.

THURSDAY, NOVEMBER 10

At noon, Washington's Leonardo comes to visit, grandson at his side. For a quarter of a century, this city has been dazzled and enriched by the remarkable talents of its resident artist, connoisseur, collector, musician, and business executive: David Lloyd Kreeger. Past president of GEICO Insurance, he is best known in Washington not for his acumen and wealth, which are substantial, but for his devotion to the arts and philanthropy. His Foxhall Road home, across from the Belgian Embassy, is an architectural masterpiece designed to be a museum. David's art collection is ranked among the top ten private collections in the nation. And that says nothing about his Stradivarius, which he plays with concert perfection, or his authoritative knowledge about Shakespeare.

His grandson is college-shopping, and David, trustee emeritus at AU, has brought the young man here for a tour and interview. The grandson says that of the universities he has visited so far, AU has impressed him the most. Clearly, he has inherited his grandfather's good taste.

Minutes later, Bill Moss and Ursula Meese meet me at my office and we drive in Ursula's small car through torrential rain to the Mary Graydon Center. Dropping us by a loading dock, she insists upon parking the car herself. Bill and I make it through the labyrinth of the kitchen to a private room where he will host a luncheon for Moss Scholarship awardees. Shortly, Ursula arrives and the lunch begins. At dinner tonight, she will be with the head of state of a foreign power and the president of the United States. But whether with students at lunch or a royal family at dinner, she treats everyone warmly. Perhaps the most unpretentious person I know, she can "walk with kings nor lose the common touch."

Over dinner at home, Natasha wants to know about El Salvador for a report. Gail and I tell her as much as we can. Then I rush back to my office to meet with Myers, Josh Ederheimer, head of the students' Resident Hall Association, and others. A few times each term, I tour the dorms unannounced. And tonight, this entourage wishes to join me. As we troop into the first dorm, the students stare in wonder. Why are these men here? What do they want? Who are they?

We pick floors at random and stroll from one end to another, stopping to talk with students, looking in rooms when invited, checking lounges, and inspecting bathrooms. Overall, the dorms are in fine condition. Josh takes me into a room he thinks is especially impressive. Two roommates have worked hard to make it as creative as possible. As we are leaving, one of them says, "Dr. Berendzen, will you autograph it?" "Autograph what?" Then I see it: my photograph pinned to the wall next to two senators. Surprised and flattered, I sign my name. Then a student from across the hall asks if I will autograph his photo as well. Could they be related to the students at the campus rally eighteen months ago?

I get back to my office at 9:30 P.M. It is too late and I am too tired to attend a function at the National Portrait Gallery. "How about our cancelling tonight?" I ask Gail over the phone. "Oh, I'm so glad," she replies. So I clear my desk, walk home at midnight, and talk with Gail until 2:00.

FRIDAY, NOVEMBER 11

A student calls to ask if Khashoggi will lend his 727 to fly a group to a Denver conference. A Georgia farmer calls, asking for Adnan to pay his mortgage. A trustee asked me yesterday if I could help him get a contract with Adnan. A pastor wondered if Adnan would replace the roof on his church. A staff member proposed that Adnan give each employee a Christmas bonus. And several trustees have suggested, only half in jest, that he fly the entire board to Monte Carlo so they can hold their next meeting on his yacht.

All of this resulted from the *Post* article about the trip to New York for my astronomy talk. Immediately, scores of people hope to benefit. Even though this is understandable, it illustrates the predicament of the ultrarich. Publicity attracts people who seek funds, all with the belief that "my request is exceptionally worthy and he has so much money he wouldn't even notice the difference." No surprise, then, that the wealthy become wary.

Tonight will be unique: Natasha's first dance—not a class but a real dance. What is more, it is for the seventh and eighth grades together. Natasha is nervous about the "big kids," the eighth graders. Most of all, she is concerned about her clothes—nothing she owns will do. "Really! How could you even think it would?" she asks.

So she and Gail explore trendsetting Georgetown stores for the acne set. To call it fad is to understate. What is *in* this week is *out* the next; it is imperative either to be *in* or to be disdainful of being *in*. Gail returns looking like the famous photograph of Carter after jogging. Natasha beams, but spends an hour preparing before she will let me see her: black-and-white plaid shirt, striped slacks, black shoes. That is it. Yet we must discuss and admire each item.

Foolishly, Gail asks, "What'll happen at the dance?" "Unuhh," Natasha explains. "Well," I persist, "will the girls go with specific boys?" Natasha is consistent: "Unuhh." She is more expansive on one issue: "Be there at 10:45—not one minute early. Mommy, please watch him."

"Oh, Natasha, I won't embarrass you," I promise her. "Just have fun and be careful. We'll be there at 10:45 sharp."

After dropping her at the dance, Gail and I go to the Lascarises' for a dinner in honor of George Paraskevaides, the Greek-Cypriot builder who has helped transform deserts into modern cities almost overnight and who has sixty thousand employees in thirteen nations around the globe. Prince Bandar, the new Saudi ambassador, lives next door. And he, too, has a function tonight. Both driveways are lined with Mercedes and Rolls.

The Lascarises' evening fits their style—beautiful appointments, tasteful table settings, exquisite food (including baby veal in artichoke), and lively conversation. The guest-list sparkles—with Clare Booth Luce, Secretary of Commerce Baldridge, and numerous Capitol Hill officials.

Before the dinner, Climis gets everyone's attention and says, "It's our custom to say grace before dining. Senator Paul Trible will give the prayer." Trible eloquently calls for peace between Jews and Arabs, Greeks and Turks, Americans and Russians.

Seated next to Paraskevaides, Gail gets to know him well. He is a delightful, mischievous man who has built much and given away much. His influence, wealth, and generosity are legendary. We hope he will join our IAB.

Gail and I leave early in order to be at the dance on time. The GDS parking lot fills with station wagons, BMWs, and Audis, as other well-instructed parents arrive. Then out come the grinning mutes. Their expressions indicate the evening's success. But that is all the information we are going to get. The girls tell us *nothing*.

Such are the rites of passage. My seventh grade dance came in the spring. The boys stood on one side of the room, eyeing the girls, with such subtle evaluations as, "Nancy's a goose." "Betty's okay if you like them skinny." "Jeanie's a dog but I might do her a favor and dance with her." Mustering my courage, I crossed the continent-size gym and approached a target. "Hi. Would you like to dance?" She did not hear me, being absorbed in drinking a Coke. I repeated what I had said, adding, "I hope you will." This time, she heard: "No. I don't wanna dance." So I sauntered back with an air that dancing bored me and all I had just asked the girl was if she knew the time. The humiliations, the joy, the awkwardness, the growth.

SATURDAY, NOVEMBER 12

A quiet day of errands. My barber, Chung, fits me into her crowded schedule. In these unisex days, she cuts hair for Carmen Neuberger, our dean of students, and Don Myers as well as for me. More than her substantial styling abilities, I admire her drive. Alone, she has built a thriving salon; she sells cosmetics, runs seminars on hair styling and dabbles in small business ventures. All this by a pert, five-foot-tall Korean with children to care for.

Gail, Natasha, and I go downtown to see the new James Bond film. As Bond fans, we have seen all the others. But we are wearing out on them. Gimmicks, maniacal villains, unbelievable plots —we have seen too many. So for us the best parts of this film are the shots of Adnan's fabled 270-foot yacht. Sleek, elegant, expensive— it fits Bond and Khashoggi. The film's end credits note that funds for using the yacht went to the Grace Kelly Foundation, adding: "Thanks A.K."

MONDAY, NOVEMBER 14

Someone once said: "If you don't know where you want to go, it's unlikely you'll get there." Conversely, "You'll end up somewhere irrespective of what you do; the question is whether it'll be where you want to be." In short, planning is essential.

In the early 1970s, I had some experience with NASA's planning for longterm astronomical missions. The process alone was instructive to me. When I arrived at AU, I found that it, like many other universities, did not have a detailed, codified plan. Lofty goals are unhelpful. Hundreds of schools "seek excellence," yet few achieve it; none espouses mediocrity, yet many achieve it.

As an outgrowth of AU's Middle States evaluation in 1973, a serious concern for planning emerged. When I became provost in 1976, I urged the university to develop a written, fairly detailed outline of its strengths and aspirations with objectives and target dates. In the late 1970s, we started a wide-scale concensus-building review involving faculty, students, staff, administrators, alums, and trustees. What emerged was a written understanding of what we wanted to be. Given that our planning ended in 1979 and the goals were set about five years hence, the plan might have been called "AU 1984," except that would have been too Orwellian. So we extended the deadline, and I dubbed it "AU85."

The planning document itself, the process leading to it, and its implementation have attracted attention from educators and journalists. Although multiple-year planning is hardly unique to AU, such a comprehensive, precise process is rare in academia. This morning a group of American Council on Education fellows meets on campus to hear several speakers, one being me on AU85. Despite the differences among universities, the procedure we used and the external conditions we considered are generic.

My next meeting is potentially confrontational but turns out to be cordial. A dean wants to know why funds from his college's alums cannot go exclusively to his college. Why must they benefit the university as a whole? Every year the same issues reappear: faculty want higher salaries, students want minimal tuition increases, and deans want more funds. At times, a university appears to be not so much a cohesive family as a confederation of feuding baronies.

Tonight Gail and I have a professional/social evening of the most exhausting kind: four separate events. The first, in honor of a new book on the university presidency, is attended exclusively by educators. Jim Fisher, president of the Council for the Advancement and Support of Education, wrote the book based on his experience as a university president and his observation of other presidents. Always ebullient, Jim inscribes my copy to "a charismatic president." No doubt that is a good thing to be, but I am uncertain whether I deserve the accolade. As we leave, my eye catches an admonition on page twelve: "Enjoy the presidency." Not a bad idea, but I cannot right now. We are in a rush.

Our next stop is at the Mexican Embassy for a reception in honor of Bernardo de Sepulveda, Mexico's secretary of foreign affairs. Suave and darkly handsome, he was ambassador to the U.S. before assuming his current post. Gail and I knew him and his family then. The other guests are from the diplomatic community—the ambassadors of Sri Lanka and Greece, the U.S. chief of protocol. Aside from our being friends of the de Sepulvedas, I hope AU can develop new programs with Mexico and obtain full payment for the program we run today.

Our next stop is at the Foxhall Apartments, a distinguished address only a block from campus. This function, held in honor of Taco, who sings, "Putting on the Ritz," is decidedly more lively than the usual Washington affair. Show business brings pizazz. Natasha asked me to have Taco autograph her record so she can give it to Gail for Christmas. A clever if not original ploy, the record will revert to her; it is her current favorite. At Natasha's age, Deborah used to give Gail stuffed animals and me games that we subsequently gave to her. Children that age are either clever or genuinely believe that adults want what they want.

Taco autographs the record, and I tell his producer that we would be glad to arrange for him to speak to students and meet Washingtonians. He seems interested, not only for Taco but also for his other performers. The producer and I exchange cards and agree to keep in touch.

Gail and I rush from there to the handsome apartment of former treasury secretary G. William Miller and his wife, Ariadna, who are holding a farewell dinner for the ambassador of Yugoslavia. Although I know the ambassador slightly and his daughter attended AU, we attend primarily because we like the Millers so much. Their dinner guests are eclectic Washington—Paul Volcker, Senator Mark Hatfield, the ambassador of Algeria, David Lloyd Kreeger, Undersecretary of State Lawrence Eagleberger, sociologist Amitai Etzioni. We have a grand time.

TUESDAY, NOVEMBER 15

What I thought would be a routine meeting turns tense as Myers challenges Greenberg over several budget issues. At first, I consider the matter insignificant. "You guys can punch each other out later. My schedule is wild today. What do I personally need to know about the budget?"

Soon, I discover the key issue today is not the budget, but conflicts between my chief officers. It is somewhat like the classic tension between the secretary of state and the national security advisor. The jurisdictional boundaries can become hazy. Once I am aware of the real agenda today, I end the meeting, perhaps implying that I am unconcerned. To the contrary, I am not yet ready to step in. The key to holding ultimate authority is to use it sparingly. If necessary, I will cut this Gordian knot. But I hope they can do so first.

After the meeting, Myers asks to see me privately. More agitated than I have seen him before, he explains his concerns. I listen without comment, assuring him only that I appreciate his work and that we shall resolve the difficulties. Then I meet privately with Milt. I ask him to talk individually with Myers and Triezenberg, and then I call Myers and ask him to talk with Milt, just as a judge urges litigants to settle out of court. Ironically, the tensions here arise not so much over quests for power as over intense desires to do an outstanding job. If the officers did not care so much, there would be no problem.

I meet briefly with Joan to go over last-minute details before I leave for a week. As always, she is on top of everything. She knows where to route the mail, has my phone numbers in case of emergencies, and will keep the president's office operating single-handedly while I am away. Although understated and demure, she is a loyal, one-person efficiency operation.

After attending several meetings downtown, I make my way through tangled traffic to National Airport. The TWA terminal is so packed and my departure is so imminent that I have to check my suitcase at the gate. Then the plane sits for two hours as we wait for rainy weather to clear. Arriving at JFK in New York, I have but twenty-five minutes in which to get from the domestic terminal to the international terminal. But my suitcase, checked late, is misplaced.

Ultimately, I track it down and run through the rain carrying two heavy bags, arriving just as the Rome flight leaves the gate. Not to worry, as I am put on a Milan flight an hour later.

While the other passengers doze, I read. The wise thing would be to sleep, but an eastward trip is hard for me. My usual bedtime is close to the arrival time for a European flight. Consequently, I cannot sleep on such flights. Because the flight arrives late in Milan, I miss the connecting flight to Rome. The long delay in Milan proves useful, however, as I find my errant suitcase, which has been lost again.

When I arrive in Rome, I have not slept for thirty hours. Caffeine from a Tab has kept me going, but it is wearing out. Soon, I discover Roman caffeine: taxi drivers. As I lumber out of customs, a man snatches my heavy suitcases, saying, "Taxi to Rome."

"Wait!" I shout. "Are you an authorized cab?" He walks rapidly with my bags. I trot behind, shouting again: "Are you authorized?" But he keeps going.

"Do you speak English?"

As he keeps walking he says, "Yes."

"Then tell me, are you authorized?" Saying nothing, he keeps going. I conclude he must be one of the renegade drivers who prey on unsuspecting visitors. But if he is determined to carry my bags, that is fine with me. When we arrive at his unmarked car, I snatch the bags back. "I'm going *only* in an authorized taxi." In impeccable English he replies, "My usual rate is sixty thousand lire; for you, fifty thousand." As a legitimate cabby takes my baggage, the first man gives us several descriptive hand signals and criticizes my mother whom I did not know he had met. By now, I am reasonably awake but I assume I can doze during the long drive to Rome. My smiling driver, however, stays three feet behind the car in front at sixty miles per hour.

Bug-eyed, I arrive at the hotel feeling as if I have downed a case of Tab. In my room, I look out at tile roofs and cupolas and listen to pealing church bells. Ancient and romantic, Rome's legend lives, the city where talent tamed time.

THURSDAY, NOVEMBER 17

As I dress, I wonder as I always do in Europe: why is the towel the size of a blanket, the soap the size of an acorn? And is it American chauvanism that makes me miss a smoke detector, door peephole, and bolt lock? Conversely, why is Rome so charming?

The American University has the only master's in business administration program in Italy and one of the few in Europe. Ours is given in conjunction with IRI, the colossal Italian business combine. I last visited our Rome MBA program two years ago. This afternoon, I return to talk with faculty, staff, and students. A dedicated group, the students come from Italy, the U.S., North Africa, South America, and Asia. When I enter the room, they smile and stand. They seem pleased to see me and ask about Washington. Despite the distance from Rome to Washington, most of them want to identify with the home base.

FRIDAY, NOVEMBER 18

At six o'clock this morning, I get up, for I am to give the opening address at the annual conference of the European Council of International Schools. So at seven, I set out by taxi from the Spanish Steps.

As hair-raising as Roman driving is, it is child's play compared with Third World nations. In Cairo, anything—cart, donkey, camel—may cross your path. In Bangkok, three-wheel vehicles, quaintly called putt putts, careen in every direction. But the ultimate of vehicular madness is Tehran, Iran. Twentieth-century high-powered vehicles are maneuvered by nomadic goat herders, and the results are bizarre. Once while I was being chauffeured through Tehran, my driver cut down an alley at about fifty miles an hour. Cowardly huddled in the back-seat well, I braced my neck to avoid whiplash, for I knew a wreck was unavoidable. I pleaded with him to slow down, but either he did not understand or thought it amusing that I sat on the back-seat floor. He continued breakneck until the inevitable happened: another car, racing at similar speed through a perpendicular alley, crashed into us. Both automobiles were destroyed, although—miraculously—all passengers were safe. My driver got out of the car, surveyed the wreck, and left. I sat in the back seat, badly shaken, wondering what to do. Already late for my meeting, I felt I should rush. But how? Several dozen people appeared from nowhere to stare at the wreck and the odd American who still sat in the back seat. After waiting for fifteen minutes, I was starting to leave when my driver reappeared in a Mercedes identical to the one he had wrecked. He motioned for me to get in, which I did. We set off down the alley at the same breackneck speed we'd maintained before. The wrecked cars remained where they were.

Finally, I reached my destination and asked an English-speaking person what had transpired with the driver and the new Mercedes. He explained: "There are so many accidents in Tehran that some government agencies have Mercedes stationed every few blocks. After he wrecked the first one, he got a replacement."

The next day, intrigued by the accidents I had seen, I decided to count every wreck I witnessed or arrived at within moments after it occurred. In a full year in Washington, I may see one or two accidents. In a ten-hour stretch in Tehran, I saw seventeen. Back at the Hilton Hotel, I went out on the balcony. Still amazed by seventeen accidents, I looked down at the parking lot. Smash! There was number eighteen.

My Roman taxi, careening as it takes me past incomparable art and history, deposits me at the conference site. The audience pours into the auditorium. I am introduced. And for forty-five minutes I talk about international education and how it can be viewed uniquely with an astronomical perspective.

While I am waiting to be seated for lunch, I feel a tap on my shoulder. It is Francis Clivaz, superintendent of the Collége dû Léman in Geneva. A few years ago I gave the commencement address at his school, one of the distinguished private schools beside Lake Geneva. Gail and Natasha were with me then. And on our last day, as we were packing, the desk clerk called: "We have some chocolate for you."

"Fine," I said. "Please bring it up."

"To your room? All of it?"

What an odd question, I thought. "Yes, of course." A friend must have sent it as a farewell gift. Shortly, the doorbell rang and in came three hotel attendants with cases of chocolate, so many that they stacked from floor to ceiling several times over. "What's this?" I asked. They shrugged and left. There was no note, no explanation. My Geneva friends might send us a single box but no one would send us a chocolate store. I called the desk. They had no idea who sent it. Our plane was to leave that afternoon, and we faced the odd problem of what to do with scores of boxes of expensive chocolate.

At a farewell luncheon, Clivaz remarked, "I hope our going-away present reached you."

"Did you send chocolate?"

"Yes," he replied.

"How much did you send?" I asked, knowing how rude a question that was. But these were not normal circumstances.

He frowned and said, "Three kilos. Is something wrong?" When I explained, he, too, was baffled. And then it dawned on us that the person taking his order over the phone had written down 103 kilos instead of 3. With that cleared up, the problem still remained of what to do with 100 kilos of chocolate.

I explained to the owner of the chocolate store what had happened. In Swiss style, he said: "It was our error. Please keep the chocolate and enjoy it." For a moment, we were tempted to do so, although we had no idea how we would transport it. But someone—the chocolate company or the hapless clerk who took the order—would have to absorb the cost. So I kept but three kilos. Clivaz and I chortle about these memories over lunch.

SATURDAY, NOVEMBER 19
Shortly after the flight from Rome reaches Geneva, I arrive at my hotel. A unique friend of mine who is my host here calls and says he will meet me at six o'clock. His dashing, twenty-four-year-old son accompanies him. With brown eyes as arresting as Paul Newman's blue ones, the young man seems more a movie star than a budding world businessman. Yet he helps direct the family's far-flung enterprises.

Immediately, my host asks, "Is Khashoggi on your board now?" Rumors spread fast among the very rich, and I assume my Geneva friends get the *Washington Post*. "Yes, and he recently attended his first meeting." Without a second's hesitation, my host asks, "How much has he given?"

That triggers an electric conversation about board members' responsibilities. In my host's view, they must give to the annual budget of the university. What a refreshing point of view. Few donors want to contribute to the annual fund, yet it remains our most critical need. My friend not only understands this but also stresses that board members should solicit their friends. Then he lists his friends and the amounts he could ask from them. The total: hundreds of thousands of dollars per year. Could this materialize?

Over dinner in the posh Hotel Richemond, this conversation continues. Never have I seen my friend more intent. And never have we discussed anything more frankly and thoroughly. He is as inconspicuous as Khashoggi is flamboyant, yet his wealth approaches Adnan's. And the rich calibrate themselves against their peers. After all, most of us do so in our own way. I presume the few at the financial top do so not just out of ego but out of competition; greyhounds pacing one another.

A string quartet plays a haunting rumba beside our table, stopping conversation. During the interlude, I scan the red velvet walls, the room full of Cartier and Bulgari jewelry, and realize I am sitting next to one of the world's wealthiest men in a room that has served European aristocracy for decades. What is this fellow from East Dallas doing here? What has this got to do with physics? Or the birth of the universe? I stop wondering as the music ends and our conversation resumes. I must be prepared to discuss Middle Eastern policy, the Reagan administration, Democratic presidential contenders, Grenada, the federal deficit, the latest Geneva watch creation, and J.F.K.'s role as president—or anything else that interests him.

SUNDAY, NOVEMBER 20

Shortly before noon, I meet my host and his wife in the lobby. With their car and driver following, they have walked miles to my hotel. He wears a sweater and carries a walking stick; she sports sneakers, jeans, a Hermes scarf, and a lynx jacket. Lunch today is in their home, a family affair including their children. After lunch, my host and I have a lengthy conversation. Both he and his son back AU. For seven years, I have known them and tried to bring this about. I have attempted to be helpful, just as they have been extremely kind to me. And I have kept in mind the great power of time: In a world of haste, patience can be a virtue. Now, at last, this seems to be coming to bear.

A complex Middle Easterner, my host is like no one else I have known. One moment he is silent, the next effervescent. I respect his intelligence and insight, for both are amazing. In little more than a decade, he has amassed a fortune. A remarkably quick study of people, he nonetheless likes to ponder them for months and even years. His instincts are keen. I try to learn from him while thrilling at the prospects ahead for AU.

MONDAY, NOVEMBER 21

At eight o'clock, a driver takes me from my hotel to my host's home, where I meet the head of a major bank and his son. The young man, who has just completed an international baccalaureate, would like to enroll in January. Given that I had not expected this meeting, I have no application materials. But I review his folder and advise him on steps he should take. Also, I assure him that our international admis-

sions people will contact him soon. To put his mind at ease, I give him
Triezenberg's number. I do not enjoy being told, "Don't call us; we'll
call you." Others must feel the same way.

Another businessman, the head of a major import/export company, has a son now studying in the U.S. who would like to apply to
another university. The father wonders if I would write a letter of
reference for his son. Except for a one-hour telephone conversation
last summer, I have never met the young man, so I reply that in
principle I will help but I cannot write without knowing him. The
father suggests that his son should meet me in Washington. I agree.

At London's Heathrow Airport, I hear my name called over the
PA. It is the London representative of my Geneva friend. A car and
driver are at my disposal but my shrewd Geneva friend has arranged
for me to use his "unusual" vehicle. So I am chauffeured about in
what appears to be a London taxi. The interior, however, is appointed
like a Rolls. There is no meter or For Hire sign. This is a specially
designed automobile for those who want anonymity. How ironic it is
that the nouveau riche seek status symbols while some truly wealthy
people downplay the appearance of wealth.

Even before unpacking at my hotel, I call Joan, who reassures me
that all is well. The tension among my senior officers torments me. So
I try to reach Triezenberg, but he is in New York. I ask his assistant
to have someone call the student I spoke to this morning. No admissions decision can be made until I'm back in Washington with the
student's file. But, as I tell her, I would like to "dazzle them with our
efficiency." Rather than try trans-Atlantic peacemaking, I decide not
to call Myers or Greenberg.

Tonight, Ziad Idilby and his wife, Sirene, host a dinner to introduce me to twenty of their Arab friends who now reside in London.
A round-faced man in his forties, Ziad graduated from AU at the very
ceremony during which John F. Kennedy delivered his famous commencement address. And his wife is special. With high cheekbones
and flawless complexion, Sirene does indeed look serene. In an odd
way, she and Ziad resemble Wilma and Stuart Bernstein; in fact,
much of tonight resembles an evening at the Bernsteins. The guests
are in their forties or early fifties; all are self-made; most are in construction, engineering, or land development; and all are impeccably
groomed and impressively courteous.

"Have you ever tried Middle Eastern food?" I am asked repeatedly. "Yes," I assure my questioners. "I have, many times, and I like

it." Even so, they watch to see if I enjoy the meal. Indeed I do, for it is a feast of Middle Eastern delicacies. At the end of it, Ziad says how proud he is to be an AU alum and welcomes me to London. He notes AU has been mentioned frequently during the past week over British television because of the twentieth anniversary of Kennedy's death.

Now it is my turn. I thank the Idilbys for their graciousness and then elaborate on the heritage and hopes of AU. Many of the guests have graduated from The American University—not in Washington, but in Beirut. Despite their identical names, the two institutions are totally unrelated. I tell them about the recent rapid increase in the number of our foreign students and about the Middle Eastern and Islamic programs we have under way. I stress that "we have not only Middle Eastern students but also Middle Eastern leaders. We were perhaps the first university in the United States to have an Arab on its board of trustees—an Arab woman at that. And now we have a second Arab on our board and others on our International Advisory Board. We strive to be pluralistic, recognizing talents and concerns of diverse peoples." I close by observing that all of them have come from somewhere else; none is a London native. Yet now they embrace London as home. So, too, may they embrace Washington, D.C. as their surrogate home. In that context, I hope they will consider The American University in Washington to be their second alma mater.

As I am about to leave, I notice a small photograph on the hall table. It appears to be Charlie Chaplin, but on closer examination, I realize it is the beautiful Sirene in a Chaplin costume.

TUESDAY, NOVEMBER 22

London may have the highest concentration of high-quality small shops in the world. Anyway, it has more than I can see in a morning. I dash along Piccadilly and through the Burlington Arcade, quickly selecting gifts for family and friends.

Lunch is in Knightsbridge with a couple I met at Khashoggi's last month. The man is developing a transportation system between Hong Kong and Macao and the woman, recently divorced from another man, is busy raising her children. She enters the dining room, fur coat billowing, shoulder-length hair flowing. Resembling the model Christy Brinkley, she attracts everyone's attention. I ask her where they met Adnan. "St. Moritz." Naturally.

The three of us are joined by one of their friends. I ask in passing what her husband is doing today. "Oh, he's playing polo." Gnashing my teeth as the words slip past my lips, I blurt out: "Polo is a boring sport. Don't you agree?"

"Absolutely not!" both women shout back at me. The woman with the polo-playing husband goes on, "Perhaps you've only watched poor games. If you see a top-grade one, you'll see it's exciting." And the other woman adds, "From the thunder of the hooves to the dash of the men, it's earthy, requiring talent and practice."

And money, I think to myself. Normally, I am more cautious than to render a negative judgment that might prove offensive. But this time I slipped. I learn that the husband who is playing polo owns more than twenty horses. That is a substantial investment; obviously, he does not consider it boring. And whether I do or not, I should keep it to myself.

After lunch, I rejoin my driver and inch through traffic to the city. There, close to Fleet Street, next to Samuel Johnson's home, is the London Broadcasting Corporation. No sooner am I seated than the interviewer fires off a barrage of questions: "What did John Kennedy mean to Americans?" "What do Americans think of Margaret Thatcher?" "Is America ready for a female president?" "Do Americans view England as America's poodle, as some here have claimed?" "What is the effect of TV on American youth?" "How do Americans respond to deployment of cruise missiles in Europe?" "How do computers effect U.S. teaching?"

Although the interviewer is gracious, I am dissatisfied with my performance. I cannot find the right words. As I leave and rejoin my driver, he remarks, "Quite interesting, sir." What did he think of it? Not wanting to be too inquisitive, I ask, "You were able to pick it up okay?"

"Oh, yes. Just fine." That's all he says.

Is this British understatement or was I truly that bad?

We return to the hotel just in time for me to meet with Ramzi Dalloul, a business executive and AU donor who has two sons at AU. He says his boys enjoy the university, and I tell him about several of our programs. He seems quite interested, asking insightful questions. I like his attitude about his sons, wanting them to appreciate the value of money and the importance of self-reliance. He has made it on his own, and even though he will provide for them, he wants them to understand the struggle.

Later, the driver and I head northward, past Regent Park, to the residence of Geoffrey and Sylvia Leigh, whose son attends AU. Geoffrey is a prominent real estate executive and an IAB member. The outer brick wall, tall and dark, hides treasures within. The former residence of Sir Kenneth Clark, this magnificent Georgian home, now surrounded by spotlit statuary, is one of the oldest in the city. The Leighs greet me warmly and usher me into the library. Wood paneling, books galore, portraits—the trappings of an intellectual, prosperous British family. One picture in particular catches my eye—of Charlie Chaplin. An odd common bond between the Jewish household tonight and the Arab one last night. Is humor truly the universal language?

No time to ponder such matters now, as introductions go all around. The Leighs' guests are distinguished and delightful—the head of one of England's largest banking groups, an important member of the Thatcher government. The dinner exudes gentility with course after course served on fine English china; the chandeliers glow, frost forms on the window panes. The conversation scintilates; my head snaps from side to side, as if I were watching a tennis match.

At the end of the dinner, however, I realize I am about to be part of a dreadful British tradition. Cigars are offered to the men as the women exit to the drawing room. The door shuts to the dining room and most of the men light up. Now is when the heavy conversation begins.

My first experience with this came in the late 1960s, when I was a guest of the master of a college at Cambridge University. Everyone stood until we took our places at High Table, a table placed on a platform, making it a few inches higher than the others. When my host sat, everyone else did. When he raised his fork, everyone else followed suit. When he placed his knife and fork parallel, signifying the end of his meal, everyone else did too. Then the women left the room and the men smoked cigars and talked . . . and smoked and talked and smoked. With my acute aversion to smoke, that evening was branded in my brain. The conversation was enthralling, but I could not breathe.

With slight dread, I begin to feel the same tug tonight—enjoyment of the conversation coupled with a deep desire for air. Finally, I excuse myself, saying, "Forgive me, but I still must pack for an early flight tomorrow." As I ride back to my hotel, I make notes for follow-up letters. I dislike being the first to leave this lovely couple, but I must prepare for tomorrow's departure.

WEDNESDAY, NOVEMBER 23

As I wait in the departure lounge at Heathrow Airport, a beaming face and outstretched hand rush towards me. It is Leonard Marks, international lawyer and former head of the U.S. Information Agency. "Dick, is that really you?" He is returning to Washington from New Delhi. As chance would have it, Leonard and I are seated almost next to each other on the mammoth 747. He jokes about the *Post* article on the Khashoggi dinner. And we agree that our mutual friend Stuart Bernstein is a great asset to AU. The captain comes on the PA: "Folks, I'm afraid I have bad news. Due to fog, ground control is holding our departure for twenty minutes." That twenty minutes becomes three hours.

The man at my side, who'll fly on to Tampa from Washington, shrugs and says, "Oh, well. All that counts is that we get there safely. When I was young, I used to fret over delays. Now I take them in stride." I know what he means. Now I expect them. If there is nothing you can do to change a situation, you might as well relax and try to enjoy it. And so for eleven hours on this plane, I read seven newspapers and six magazines, write three letters, and watch a boring movie.

One of the papers—the *Wall Street Journal*—contains a blistering editorial about education. Its thrust is that universities lack courage and morality when it comes to free speech. Freedom of speech sometimes means that a speaker is free to say whatever he or she wishes—so long as it agrees with the prevailing dogma. Even though the *Journal*'s editorial is simplistic, it is close to true.

This reminds me of when I visited a repressive country a few years ago. My hosts boasted that their university had academic freedom just like in the U.S. "What would happen," I asked, "if a professor publicly denounced the head of state?"

"Oh, he'd keep tenure."

"Really?" I went on. "What *would* happen?"

"He'd be put in prison of course. But he would keep his tenure."

Finally at Dulles Airport, Gail and Natasha rush up to welcome me home. As I try to turn off a week's thinking about a speech in Rome, a supporter in Geneva, Anglo-American relations, and the *Journal*'s editorial, I am told about Natasha's two new hamsters. This is Thanksgiving eve, one of the busiest times at an airport. It takes us forty-five minutes to get out of the parking lot. But I do not mind as I watch the spotlit U.S. flag flap proudly on its high pole and listen to my family. I am home. Corny or not, Dorothy was right: there is no place like it.

After unpacking and giving Gail and Natasha their European gifts, I go to my office. Joan has shunted all but essential items to other people. Still, my desk is heaped high. Until my eyes grow bleary, I wade through papers. "AU Postal Workers Threaten to Strike if Demands Not Met," the *Eagle* headline declares. With a strike threat pounding in my mind, I start to drive home when I note a light in Myers's office. It is now ten o'clock on Thanksgiving eve, yet he is here. And when I arrived at my office an hour ago, I saw Nina Roscher. Similarly, I know Joan will work this weekend on material I have brought from Europe. Such are the people we have here.

Don jumps when I rap at his window, but when he sees who it is, he grins and lets me in. He says I should read the *Eagle*'s editorial. It says a strike would be ill-advised. Don's assessment of the campus mood jibes with the editorial; the would-be strikers have little campus support.

Quickly, we review a dozen other matters. I want to know how the senior officers are functioning as a team. His smile suggests that all is well. If he is aware of problems, he does not tell me. By now, dinner must be growing cold and I am truly exhausted. I leave Don, rejoin my family, and collapse in bed.

THURSDAY, NOVEMBER 24
This morning, we call Deborah to wish her happy Thanksgiving. She is thrilled with her new Honda and sounds excited about accompanying us to New York at Christmas. It has been a dozen years since she was there, but most of all I want the sisters together. A strange, almost indescribable feeling comes over me as I watch Natasha cuddle up with the phone and say, "Hi, Debbie. Let me tell you about my hamsters and my Christmas play. And what have you been doing?" So goes their conversation for more than an hour. What special thing is there in genes? These two, so widely separated by distance and age, seem drawn to one another. Sisters are supposed to care about each other, but these two have never lived together and rarely see one another. Still, the bond exists now and it's growing stronger. Whatever they are discussing, I am not to be party to it. If I get near, Natasha says, "Here he comes, and you know how he is . . . ."

This afternoon I drive to WRC for an hour radio call-in show. The subject is supposed to be the infrared astronomical satellite, which stopped functioning yesterday. This morning I read everything I could about it, as well as about next Monday's launch of Spacelab. Quickly, however, the conversation jumps to other subjects—the big bang, the evolution of heavy elements, the nature of time. Although the interviewer is excellent, the callers are appalling. The first one has a pet theory about the universe, three want to inject theology into science, and two are simply naive. Some call-in shows are challenging and encouraging, suggesting that the American public is curious and well informed. But today's is depressing. The producer thanks me for coming, but as I drive home through deserted streets I wonder if it was worthwhile.

Natasha plays maitre d', as we eat turkey by candlelight. Feebly, I try to remind her of the true meaning of Thanksgiving, but she explains that she already has discussed it at school.

SATURDAY, NOVEMBER 26
On this special day for me, I reminisce. One afternoon in April 1960, at the end of my junior year at MIT, I walked home from class, entered the apartment, and said, "Hi." There was no reply. Stepping into the bedroom, I spotted a note from my wife: "Dear Richard, I am leaving and taking Debbie with me. I'm sure you will do great things and will have a wonderful life. I wish you well. Barbara."

My heart almost stopped. During our four years of marriage, we had never fought. We *had* had differences, but I thought we had resolved them. Both of us had tried hard to provide the best for Debbie, who was just three. But we were young, with vast responsibilities. Suddenly, I was left totally alone. I missed them deeply; I cried until I gagged.

Barbara had flown home to Dallas with Debbie. I had almost no money; I could not afford an airline ticket. So I drove for the next three days. Barbara's parents would not tell me where she and Debbie were, but they said she definitely wanted a divorce.

With final exams coming in May, I drove back to Boston and threw myself into my work. Because I had spent so much of my time studying, I had few friends. In bouts of melancholy, I sat alone at Revere Beach and watched the sun rise. Soon we signed the divorce papers; Debbie remained in Dallas and I missed her terribly.

Growing up in Dallas myself, I had gone outside on clear nights, looked at the stars, and wondered: "Does space end? Did it begin? Has it always existed?" I had run inside to ask my parents, but they did not know. So I had dug books out from the library and tried to read about the universe. Then, years later at MIT, I studied high energy physics, which is allied to astronomy. One day I decided to visit the Harvard Astronomy Department a few blocks away. I entered it through a door at the base of a telescope dome. The dark room with stone walls contained display cases and photographs of nebulae, stars, and galaxies. Alone in this odd room, I examined them. Then I sauntered down the hall to the library. The books there explained things I had always wondered about: the birth of the universe, the origin of the elements, the death of stars, the end of time. This, I thought, is for me.

Largely because I had found what I wanted to do for the rest of my life, my life began to improve. In 1961 I received my bachelor's degree and entered Harvard for my master's and Ph.D. As the first person in my family to have a college degree, I was a curiosity. My parents did not understand why I was in Cambridge or why I was studying astronomy rather than something practical, like business. But they backed my choice. They were intensely proud of me, even if they did not exactly understand why.

In 1963, after a year of living in a "group" house, I got an apartment on Sherman Street in Cambridge for seventy dollars a month. Never mind that it was filthy or that it was next door to a bar—drunks would bang on my door at all hours. The apartment was *mine*. So I tidied it up, bought drapes at Zayre's, and decided to take myself to dinner to celebrate.

To my dismay, the Harvard graduate dining hall was closed. At least that is what the sign said. I looked about and found a number of young women inside. I was about to leave when I spotted a shapely blonde standing alone at the door. Normally, I am reticent; to this day I do not know what came over me, but I said, "Excuse me, can you tell me what's going on here?"

"It's a mixer."

"But you're not in it?"

"Well, I found it boring. I don't like mixers anyway."

Her name was Gail Edgar; she went to Wheelock College in Boston; and when I asked her if she would go out with me the following week, she hesitated but said, "Okay."

"Would you like to go dancing?"

"Great."

But I changed my mind. After taking her for dinner to a private room in the Harvard Faculty Club, I escorted her to my car. She seemed slightly nervous when she saw me pull on my tight leather driving gloves. But I did not think much about it. Then I started to drive—not to the dance hall but to the Harvard Observatory. There was only one problem: I forgot to tell her where we were going.

The four-lane highway gave way to a two-lane road; then to a one-lane road; to a gravel road; to no road at all. She was huddled next to her door holding the handle. For some reason, I started talking about horror movies. I had always liked them and I was telling her about a Dracula film I had just seen: "What do you think about vampire myths?"

Because she was looking increasingly anxious, I did finally think to tell her we were going to the Harvard Observatory. To her, however, that meant Cambridge; she had never heard of Harvard's facility twenty-five miles away in the country. I just assumed everyone knew about it. Then I turned off the lights and eased the car slowly into the woods. If I had been more thoughtful, I would have realized that a non-astronomer does not know that you always extinguish your headlights when you approach an observatory at night. But I had not warned her. No wonder she was trembling by the door.

Another thing the public does not realize is that, to avoid heat waves in front of the telescope, you don't heat an observatory. An astronomer keeps warm by wearing an electrical suit—a cumbersome, blanketlike garment with a cord protruding from its navel. We arrived at the observatory, I turned off the engine, and a tall colleague of mine wearing a huge electrical suit with a parka approached us from the dark. "Glad you've arrived, Berendzen," he growled in a deep bass voice.

At that point, Gail grew pale and silent. She must have thought that she had stepped into the clutches of doom. Once inside the building, however, her fears melted. We climbed to the observing platform and she looked back into time, staring at objects so distant that their light left them before the earth was born. An evening that had started dreadfully became enchanted. On the way home, we stopped by the old Concord Bridge, held hands in the moonlight, and decided that we wanted to have a second date.

She was exceptional: pleasant, smiling, and happy; attractive and sensitive; bright and challenging; and a bit shy. She was exactly right for me. By January 1964, our relationship had become serious; by April, we knew it was leading somewhere. Then, in September, Dr.

Is My Armor Straight?

Leo Goldberg, the director of the Harvard Observatory, invited me to a dinner for graduate students. Gail was with me when I called to RSVP. I told his secretary that I would like to take a friend with me.
"Your wife or your girlfriend?"
"No," I replied. "It will be my fiancée."
Gail blushed. "What did you call me?"
"Why don't we talk about that?" So I sat her down, knelt at her side, and asked her to marry me. We hugged and kissed and made plans for a future together. We held our engagement party at the Harvard Observatory and then, on Thanksgiving evening 1964, we were wed.

About three years into our marriage, we were lying in bed together one Sunday morning when Gail rolled over and said, "Well, I guess you're not him."
"Not who?"
"Not the Boston Strangler."
"What are you talking about?"
Then she told me how scared she had been on our first date. The strangler was still at large and he had claimed a number of victims. She did not really know me on that first date. When she saw the leather gloves, when I doused the lights and drove through the dark woods, she was convinced that I was the man the police had sought for months.

We chuckle about this tonight as we celebrate our nineteenth wedding anniversary.

MONDAY, NOVEMBER 28

Because this will be my first day back after the trip, I have held most of my calendar free. How good it will be to return calls and talk with my staff. But then comes a flood of new calls. My Geneva friend phones because his friend cannot reach his son who is studying in the U.S. Can I help? I call the boy's university. After being switched to three offices, I locate someone who knows him personally. He is sure the young man simply is away for the Thanksgiving weekend. Nonetheless, I ask him to look for the student and tell him to contact his father. Then I call Geneva to reassure my friend.

The morning mail, fifteen inches high, brings the welcome word that one of our doctoral programs has received reaccreditation as well as the unwelcome news that the dean with whom I met recently misunderstood my position about fundraising for his college. A student phones to tell me she has made it to round two in the selection process for a prestigious fellowship. I call Climis Lascaris to ask if he will write the daughter of one of my European friends because she is interested in a career in design. He in turn urges me to invite George Paraskevaides to join the IAB.

Lunch is a delightful break from the hectic routine. When I appeared on Carol Randolph's TV show, she and I agreed to get together soon. Viewers can see that she is charming and articulate, but not until today did I realize how impressive she is. As a youngster, she wanted to be a doctor. After obtaining a bachelor's degree in biology from Fisk, she went on to acquire a master's degree and a law degree. She might be interested in teaching a seminar at AU. And as a talented black female professional, she would bring special strengths to the class.

Back in my office, the calls start again. The U.S. Department of Education wants to know if I will chair a panel next week at the National Forum on Education. I agree to do so. Then I receive an invitation from *Encyclopaedia Britannica Yearbook* to write an essay about educational developments in 1983. How I will find time to do so between now and the deadline of December 12, I have no idea. Nonetheless, I accept. Then Patricia Shaheen calls. A member of the Saudi royal family would like to know when Spacelab will pass over Saudi Arabia so he can call it on a ham radio. I have no idea. Could I find out? Sure.

The first stop on my phone journey is NASA headquarters in Washington. They don't know the answer and refer me to Cape Canaveral. Two offices later, the Cape refers me to the Johnson Space Flight Center in Houston. There I talk with three engineers before reaching the right person. But he does not have the information at hand. He will call me back. Meanwhile, a producer of ABC's "Nightline" has called to ask if we can have lunch. Sure, if Joan can find a free time. Joe Conrad returns my call and I fill him in on my trip.

Now the man in Houston calls back. He gives me times for the Saudi overflight—on the ninety-first orbit—measured from moment of launch. And I jot down the frequencies Spacelab will use for transmitting and receiving ham radio signals. I call Patricia back and relay the information. Even though it is somewhat technical, she handles the data with ease. I am burning to know where we stand on the sports center but I am reluctant to ask. As we are about to hang up, she volunteers: "Bob's working hard for you. I am, too, but I'm more shy than he is."

Delighted, I ask, "Does it sound promising?"

"Bob wouldn't pursue it if it looked like a dead end. And he's known the chief a long time."

TUESDAY, NOVEMBER 29

Maury O'Connell, our new dean of admissions, joins our monthly deans' meeting to discuss recruitment for fall 1984. Given the inevitable decline in the number of eighteen-year-olds in the northeast during the next decade, AU must plan to have a smaller enrollment and to recruit vigorously elsewhere. While the college-bound population is declining in the frost belt, it is increasing in the sunshine belt. We discuss the feasibility of AU's making concerted drives in the South. To do so, however, would require diverting resources. What is the most effective way to spend our limited funds?

Today Gloria Lemos hosts a luncheon on my behalf attended by prominent Washingtonians. Only in her thirties, she is the youngest person and the first woman to be a corporate officer at Coca-Cola. She is also the second youngest member of AU's board of trustees. As dessert arrives, she introduces me. Briefly, I tell the AU story, stressing areas I think will interest this group. Some have given guest lectures at AU and most live near the campus. So they have a prior impression of the institution. My task is to give them up-to-date information and urge them to become our advocates.

After I speak, Bill Fulbright, the former senator, picks up on my remark that our public administration program recently was ranked fourth in the U.S. He asks, "Is anyone in your school studying alternative ways to structure government?" Before I can reply, the table erupts in crossfire conversation as this Washington crowd seizes on the theme. Finally, they return to AU. And I am pleased by the overall discussion; it has been so lively that they will long remember the affair.

Following an afternoon of calls, memos, and meetings, I dash home and drive with Gail to the West German embassy where Postmaster General Bill Bolger is to receive a citation. A fine public servant, Bill thoroughly deserves the accolade. As we enter the living room, former deputy secretary of state Walter Stoessel grins and says hello. A short man with gray hair and ready smile, he projects a calmness rarely seen among high-tension diplomats. When George

Shultz announced he was going to bring in his own deputy secretary, I asked Walter to come to AU. As the highest ranking career diplomat in recent U.S. history, he would be invaluable in the classroom. He has held the sensitive posts of U.S. envoy to Poland, West Germany, and the U.S.S.R. Walter did come to AU and teaches here now.

No cheek-pecking from the next guest I encounter; she gives me a big hug. Evelyn Hayes—professor emerita of music and wife of Patrick Hayes, founding director of the Washington Performing Arts Society—is a concert pianist as well as a teacher. Tonight she reminds me of the first time we met: at my interview for the deanship of the College of Arts and Sciences. She was on the search committee. For days I had prepared for the interview. When it came, I quizzed the committee as well as vice versa. One of my questions, wrapped in politeness, still came out bluntly: "Why should AU survive?" At least it sparked discussion! And somehow I got the job.

After dinner, the ambassador and Bolger exchange toasts. And then the floor opens for anyone to speak. The gregarious Pat Hayes cannot bear the silence. He rises to tell about his childhood job in the postal service, and he ends his brief remarks with characteristic wit and charm. Moments later, former defense secretary Melvin Laird pays tribute to Bolger. Then Dan Boorstin, librarian of Congress, follows suit. All these toasts are given with aplomb. Comics tweak Washington and cartoonists depict politicians as windbags. Some local gentry fit such images, but many do not.

WEDNESDAY, NOVEMBER 30
Lunch today, at Mel Krupin's restaurant, is hosted by Bob Wallach. The luncheon is Bob's Hanukkah/Christmas tribute to his friends. About twenty-five of us—including Bob Strauss and Charlie Wick—gather in a private room. Bob seats me between two of my trustees: Sondra Bender and Ursula Meese. When I ask Ursula where she and Ed are going to spend the holidays, she replies Palm Springs. That means only one place: the desert home of Walter Annenberg. I ask her to thank Annenberg for a contribution he made recently to AU.

For nearly three hours this afternoon, I meet with Myers. Today's date is propitious, for it was one year ago tomorrow that he and Triezenberg became vice-presidents. Aside from appointing them, I reorganized the upper administration, placing the two vice-presidents under the president rather than the provost. Today Myers comes to review what he has done since then and to outline what he proposes to do next. Aside from the host of positive things we discuss, he seems tense. I had hoped this was over, but it is not.

THURSDAY, DECEMBER I

At my regular meeting with the vice-presidents and vice-provosts, our otherwise upbeat discussion is clouded by what the federal government may have us do. Recently AU received a single grant for more than $1 million. When that happens, numerous government requirements spring into play. Investigators want extensive documentation, and they may require procedures that would reduce our efficiency and increase our costs. Just the process of responding to their inquiries will be expensive. But we have no choice.

Lunch will follow a working session at the OAS Building. Two years ago, at the invitation of Alejandro Orfila, secretary general of the OAS, the consortium focused on the possibility of creating an Inter-American Studies Center to be located in Washington and operated jointly by local universities and inter-American organizations. The concept seemed meritorious yet raised questions immediately: How would the center differ from existing ones? Would it conflict with universities? Who would pay for it? Who would control it? After two years of deliberation, today's meeting is to decide, once and for all, whether the center should be established.

Orfila, an Argentinian of broad smiles and warm bear-hugs, is one of the most prominent envoys in Washington. But he has announced his resignation, effective next March. In his opening remarks, he reaffirms his belief in the center, argues that it is more necessary than ever, and asks if we want to proceed. Clearly, he does, and he would like to see progress before he leaves his post.

After introductory remarks, the room of eighteen men falls to silence. Representatives from local universities are here, as are people from inter-American organizations, foundations, and corporations. But once the issue has been put before us, silence reigns. Five seconds go by, then ten. It seems an eternity. "Conceptually," I begin, "I support the center even more today—given recent events in Grenada —than two years ago. Before endorsing our proceeding, I'd just like to know a few final details."

The staff responds. Then there is more silence. I think to myself: "Hell, we've discussed this for two years. Let's defecate or abdicate." I break the silence, saying: "If it will get things moving, I move that we proceed. My university will pay its share."

More silence. Am I alone? I have not discussed the issue with the other presidents in months. Is my position out of step with theirs? For the next fifteen minutes, the discussion moves slowly with perfunctory questions and answers, as the eighteen of us eye one another around the large table. I wonder if my motion was premature. Are the others thinking to themselves, "Berendzen's impetuous"?

Suddenly, a president says: "I support Dick's motion. My university will be involved and will contribute financially." The head of an inter-American organization immediately pledges its backing. And another president says his university will follow suit. Once the flow starts, the cascade follows. Person after person springs to voice, each saying his organization will support the center. When the meeting ends, the group's mood is more than buoyant; it is expectant. Over lunch, a business representative asks how his corporation can be involved. And someone suggests that universities in Latin America might like to join. Now everyone speaks.

This afternoon I meet with Triezenberg. I assume that he wants to see me because of his one-year anniversary; instead, he unenthusiastically, almost despondently, asks my preference on several routine matters. I ask how he is feeling, and he says, "Frankly, pretty down." He looks as bad today as Myers did yesterday. "What's happening with my senior officers?" At first he has no answer. Finally, he says his conflict with Milt has worsened.

Ironically, it has taken a year before tensions reached this point. The reason for the long delay is that we are in the first budget cycle since the Dons took office. They and the provost, who formulates the overall budget, are having trouble determining their respective areas of authority.

Quietly, I listen to Don. I try to bolster his morale and thank him for his outstanding past year. After he leaves, I ask Milt to come to my office. He slumps. His voice is different and his usual smile has turned to a frown. Finally, it comes out: He has problems with Triezenberg and Myers. I tell Milt and then phone the two Dons: "At our meeting tomorrow, we're going to thrash through this matter." I have not wanted to enter their discord, but now I must.

FRIDAY, DECEMBER 2

After a restless night, my stomach gnaws as I approach the confrontational meeting. Before turning to the issue on all our minds, we discuss routine matters. Myers has two good-news items: our collection rate on student bills now is higher than in the past, and the Mexican government has informed us that it will pay almost all its debt.

That is fine, but I cannot postpone the inevitable. So I say, my voice cracking more than I had anticipated: "In the past few days I've heard complaints from each of you. I had hoped you'd resolve matters yourselves but you haven't. So now we're going to do so together."

In detail, I review the steps that led to last year's reorganization and I explain why this structure is wise. And I note: "Perhaps I don't say it often enough, so let me do so now. You're three of the best professionals I've ever known. I'm delighted you are my friends and my colleagues."

"What precisely," I ask, "is your difficulty?" Slowly at first, each of them begins to speak. Then the momentum builds, the passions flare. Aside from their conflicts, each is feeling pressure within his own unit. Each must contend with bickering staff, insufficient funds, exorbitant workloads, strident critics, and me.

After an hour and a half, almost all the problems seem settled. I ask them to meet among themselves to work out final details and report back to me. As I push away from the table to leave, Milt says, "I'm afraid we have one matter left to resolve." Triezenberg adds, "We sure do." The tranquility I have sought suddenly dissolves. Within moments, the acrimony becomes worse than ever. Finally, at 11:45, Joan buzzes to remind me that I have a noon luncheon downtown. By now, I'm exasperated anyway. As I walk to the door I bark, this time with no quiver in my voice: "Listen, you characters. What you're arguing about is who has the most sand in his end of the box. I'm disappointed with you. I truly am."

My lunch at Mel Krupin's with a producer of ABC's "Nightline" would be more enjoyable if I didn't have the morning meeting still in mind. Nonetheless, I enjoy my companion, a widely read and insightful man. He says he would like to teach a seminar. His impressive résumé reinforces my impression that he could bring vast experience to the classroom.

After returning afternoon calls and reading mail, I write letters of reference for students, send a handwritten note to parents of a student who died recently, read financial reports about two prospective trustees, study annual reports from several universities to get ideas for ours, and meet with Milt to select this year's winner of the Teacher-Scholar Award. Our most prestigious faculty accolade, it carries a two thousand dollar prize provided by the Methodist Church. The deans nominate faculty in their colleges, and Milt and I make the final, university-wide selection. This year we pick Kent Baker, a phenomenal young professor of business administration. Only in his thirties, he already has turned out impressive publications in addition to obtaining six degrees.

The way we left the morning meeting disturbs me, and my final caustic remark troubles me as much as it may bother the hearers. By nightfall I talk individually with Milt and Myers, both of whom sound their old selves again. Triezenberg and I miss phone calls. We will make contact on Monday. I am confident that by then he, too, will be in a good frame of mind.

The day has been draining, and the last thing I want to do is to get gussied-up for an ultraformal dinner-dance. But that is the agenda tonight. Of Washington's galas, the annual Symphony Ball is one of the grandest. Women bring out their finest jewelry, while men come in white tie. So tired, physically and emotionally, that I can scarcely walk, I don my tails, top hat, and red-lined cape. Natasha finds the outfit bemusing. "Daddy, you look like Dracula." Gail, however, is striking in a burgandy silk gown. She assures me she got it on sale and can use it for many functions. I'm too tired to care.

For three hours Gail and I circulate throughout the cavernous ballroom, talking with trustees and prospective trustees. Shortly before midnight, I ask Gail if she would like one dance before we leave. I have been so tired that we have not danced at all. And I have been a boring companion—scarcely speaking—at our table. She says she would love to dance. We make our way to the floor. But after only ten seconds, I ask "Would you mind if we left?" "Of course not," she replies. "Let's go."

So we turn and leave the floor—to great laughter from friends sitting nearby. John Hechinger, an AU trustee and head of the Hechinger hardware chain, and former Senator Frank Church both chide us: "That's the shortest dance on record. Are you getting old?" Maybe I am. Or maybe the morning affected me too much.

SUNDAY, DECEMBER 4

This evening, I turn to an assignment I accepted but now dread: writing a special report on education for the *Britannica Yearbook*. Given my forthcoming travel schedule, I must have a draft ready by tomorrow morning. So far, I have written not a word. But I have been pondering the essay and have it outlined in my head. Besides, I know when I write best—between 11:00 P.M. and 4:00 A.M. And so at 11:00 P.M. I start writing. Unfortunately, I do not finish until dawn.

MONDAY, DECEMBER 5

After I drag through morning meetings, I chat with Triezenberg. He seems okay and even jokingly parodies the old movies: "Thanks. I needed that."

This afternoon, Mel Eggers, the chancellor of Syracuse University, arrives. He will chair the Middle States accreditation team that will visit campus in late January. He is here today to be sure everything is ready for the visit. Nina Roscher shows him the rooms and documents we will provide the team. He says the preparations look excellent.

At five o'clock I tell Joan I must leave early because we are having about ninety students and alums to the house at six. As I drive down the hill from my office, a startling revelation comes to me. Traffic is backed up thirty-cars deep on our main campus road. They are attempting to exit onto Massachusetts Avenue. Never before have I seen such a lineup at our gate. As I drive in the opposite direction past the waiting cars, I glance at the drivers. They are professors, staff members, administrators, and a few students. Finally, the obvious occurs to me: all these people leave at 5:00 P.M. Like their counterparts worldwide, they are gone by 5:05. There is nothing wrong with that; it fits their pay schedules and contracts. And it makes for harmonious home life. Certainly, I have been aware that most people work on such a schedule. But not until this evening have I realized how many AU employees do.

Why haven't I noticed until now? The answer comes quickly: because this is one of the few times in the nine and a half years I have been at AU that I have left the office by 5:00 P.M. That may say more about my efficiency than my effort.

When I arrive home, Gail has everything ready. The preparations for such a large reception are substantial. Natasha and one of her friends will be in charge of guests' coats. And soon someone from our alumni office arrives with name tags. Tonight's event is intended to introduce students to successful alums. In theory, the alums will tell the students about professions and provide useful guidance.

From across the room, I watch Gail being the consummate hostess, greeting guests, introducing students to alums, showing groups through the house. All this she carries out quietly and effectively, not knowing I notice.

At the end of the evening, one student excitedly says she has obtained a job from an alum and two others say they have made good contacts. Everyone, in fact, seems to have had a good time.

TUESDAY, DECEMBER 6

I send my essay off to *Encyclopaedia Britannica*. Then I clear my phone log and desk. Early this afternoon, I make my way through the rain to National Airport and fly to Newark. A driver is supposed to be waiting for me, but no one is here. I am uncertain what to do, so I stand at the gate. The PA system finally calls my name and asks me to go to the nearest flight agent. A caller informs me that I should take a taxi from Newark to Princeton. As I enter the taxi, I ask what the fare will be. "Forty-two dollars." At least my Princeton host will reimburse me.

The stench of petroleum is annoying; the rumble of trucks, jarring. As we approach bucolic Princeton, however, the scene changes. Factories give way to Victorian homes, smokestacks to stone turrets, oil drums to leaded-glass windows.

I am here to attend a meeting on graduate education sponsored by the Carnegie Foundation for the Advancement of Teaching, the Institute for Advanced Study, and Princeton University. Presidents and graduate deans from several research universities are here, along with some professors and journalists. The first session rambles, without focus. But even the rambling is constructive, as each speaker provides thoughtful ideas wrapped in articulate prose. Ideas fly, with facts and logic balancing ideas and wit.

Someone observes that the same two things are always said about reviewing any graduate program: "It's too early to tell how worthy the program is. Or, it's now too late to evaluate it: The faculty have tenure, the students are recruited, the alumni are protective, and the advertising asserts the program will continue."

The group laments that the demographic decline yielding fewer undergraduates also will lead to fewer faculty openings and hence fewer job opportunities for graduate students. Ph.D. students, especially in arts and humanities, who turn to universities for employment will find an increasingly tight job market. But there is a bright side:

able young Ph.D.s are taking faculty positions today at teaching colleges. This could be good for such colleges and for the distribution of talent among the nation's schools.

The issues today are too broad for us to reach any conclusions. The meeting's main benefit comes in the opportunity it affords participants to chat among themselves. Several lament the deplorable preparation of current students—not at the high school level but at the undergraduate level. And many agree that all well-educated people no longer share a large common body of knowledge. Greek myths, Biblical allusions, and Shakespearean sonnets—these are no longer part of many students' experiences.

Dinner is at Prospect House, once the home of the president of Princeton. Woodrow Wilson lived here, and his presence seems real even now. From his large hall portrait to the rooms' decor, all is from his era. After dinner, William Bowen, the president of Princeton, introduces the speaker—Kingman Brewster, former president of Yale and former U.S. ambassador to Great Britain. A thoughtful speaker with a droll wit, Brewster starts by saying that Bowen intimidates him because he's an economist. And he adds, "If you tell an economist you've forgotten a phone number, he'll estimate it for you."

Afterwards, several of us walk back to the Nassau Inn and talk in the lobby. Most then retire to the bar or their rooms. For me, however, the night is young and I am anxious to see Princeton. It has been a decade since I was last here, and the Princeton campus is one of the most handsome in the nation. Moreover, I need a tube of toothpaste. The desk clerk tells me of a twenty-four hour grocery store with the wonderful name of WaWa Market. To reach it, I stroll through the campus, admiring the dignified architecture. On my way back, I join a few hundred students singing folk songs and carols in the Quad.

Back in my room, I try to sew a button back onto my suit. I dig out my sewing kit and thread the needle. Bifocals usually are annoying, but they are a godsend for this. I am proud of how well I do it, except a tailor would not sew his finger to the coat.

WEDNESDAY, DECEMBER 7
The drive from Princeton to the Philadelphia airport takes more than an hour. The flight from Philadelphia to Louisville gives me an opportunity to review papers about the National Forum on Education,

which I will attend this afternoon. The flight from Louisville to Indianapolis takes but twenty-five minutes.

Department of Education people meet me in the convention hall and show me where I am to speak. The other panelists and I greet one another, and I call the first session to order. Several people ask if I will ban smoking. I announce: "If you must smoke, please do so in the rear of the room only—and if possible, don't exhale."

Then we launch into a serious theme—whether or not the recommendations of the National Commission regarding basic curricula can be implemented without excluding the arts and vocational subjects. In my judgement, they all can fit. But to enable them to do so, schools must use their time better and must expand their time—the school day and school year. Most in the room do not want to do that. Many argue that their area—the arts, band, vocational education—is essential. Each person sees the value of his own field, only begrudgingly acknowledging that other areas are important, too. Each is unwilling to reduce the time devoted to his subject to make way for others.

Because I chair the session, I speak last. And I am direct: "In most discussions, everyone says his or her school system is fine, implying that the problems lie elsewhere. Well, the aggregate national data demonstrate that there are large-scale problems; to ignore them would be irresponsible.

"To solve the problems, we first must identify their causes."

And then I go through a litany dealing with teachers, TV, parents, the economy, and the national work ethic. In contrast with the preceding speakers, I assert: "It doesn't matter if the commission refers to five 'New Basics.' Perhaps the number should be five or something else. Perhaps they're new or not. Perhaps they're basic or perhaps they're not. Let's not quibble over words. Frankly, that's something we academics love to do—rather than reach a decision and implement action, we debate nuances. But the issues here are too vital for us to fritter away our time. The important issue is that children should receive a common body of knowledge."

The floor discussion becomes lively with far more hands going up than I can call upon. Afterwards, participants gather around each panelist; the interest level is boundless. Never have I seen more intensity about educational issues. The nation may have been at risk, largely from sleeping during a time of peril. But now the giant is awakening.

Before attending the evening reception, I call Joan who tells me about routine matters—a neighbor's complaint about our use of a building, a job application, several invitations, a request to write an article, and a stack of interoffice memos. Milt happens to pass by Joan's office and asks to speak to me.

"Richard, it's now 6:05 and I just returned from a university senate meeting that began at 1:30."

"What happened?" I ask.

"On a campus, you can never guess what will happen next. Today's meeting was supposed to focus on the budget. As you recall, the university senate finance committee recommended that the law school tuition should go up two percentage points more than the undergraduate tuition. Well, two hundred to three hundred law students marched into the meeting today, several carrying placards. And a TV crew came with them."

"I hadn't heard this was coming. Had you?"

"Absolutely not," Milt replies. "No one warned us. No one even indicated displeasure. They simply came en masse. It was quite a show."

"No doubt," I lament. "But how did it end?"

"With everyone exhausted and time running out, they passed a motion basically saying the central administration should put together a budget with as low a tuition increase as possible. That's it."

Ah, democracy. Such a sublime system. But, as someone once asked, who can think of a better one? Now the central administration will work out a detailed budget, including tuition, that meets our needs while not burdening any segment. Then we will explain to the campus why it makes sense. By March, the university will have a new budget.

THURSDAY, DECEMBER 8

Up at 5:30 A.M., I fly back to Philadelphia. From my hotel there, I try to handle numerous administrative matters by phone; Joan and I talk for an hour. Then I take a cab to the Cherry Hill Mall in New Jersey, where I am to be interviewed on the "Maxine Schnall Radio Show" on WCAU–AM. Maxine asks me about the National Forum, and I expound on our public schools' problems and on ways to solve them. All of Maxine's phone lines light and a throng gathers around the broadcast booth. During a commercial break, I glance at the crowd and beyond them to the stores—Florsheim, Parkland Hosiery,

Ups 'N Downs. Children ride the Santa train while parents in mackinaws stock up for the big day. At the end of our hour, several shoppers stop me for further discussion. Finally, I break away and hail a cab back to Philadelphia.

The driver, a thirty-six-year-old man, becomes the second person today to tell me I look and sound like Bill Moyers. Well, going from Dracula to Moyers is progress. The driver wants to know if it's practical to get a bachelor's degree in history. "Have you had any college?" I ask. "No, but I have a family, I'm deeply interested in history, and I'd like to get a degree someday."

"Don't put it off," I urge. "Many people do, only to discover that the clock's run out. As hard as it might be for you, try to take at least one course per term, perhaps in an extension program. As for your actual career choice, talk with counselors at the university. Your interest in education and in your career are deep; I hope you'll start soon. It may seem like a long struggle to the degree, but graduation day will be a celebration for you and your family."

"I'm sure it will be," he smiles. "And I'm determined. Can I write to you for advice?" As we shake hands I say, "I'll be glad to hear from you."

At my next interview—WTAF–TV—I join an educational consultant and the head of Philadelphia's teachers' union. The latter argues that we cannot solve educational problems without far more federal money. I challenge that assertion. I, too, would welcome more money from any source, but about 92 percent of public school funding comes from state and local revenues. That proportion has remained roughly the same for many years. Since the nation began, public schools have been under the purview of local communities; hence, they have provided the bulk of the funds.

It is appropriate to ask, "What should be the federal government's role in education?" In my view, it is to ensure equity among the states; to support special projects, such as Head Start, learning disability programs, and programs for the unusually talented; to provide student financial aid for worthy recipients who could not obtain it otherwise; and to serve as a catalyst for nationally desirable educational goals.

FRIDAY, DECEMBER 9

"Could this be?" I ask as I gaze at my reflection in the mirror this morning. Years ago, the hair on the sides of my forehead started to recede. Eventually, all my hairline will do so, following my father's pattern. But today, for the first time, I notice that the central peninsula is thinning. Why so soon?

I walk to the Franklin Plaza Hotel for the Middle States Association meeting. The session chairman calls the group to order and introduces me. "No doubt you're already familiar with our speaker. You may have read one of his articles or seen him on TV. It's an honor to present Dr. Richard . . . ." He has forgotten my name! And in the darkened room, he cannot read his notes. With a loud whisper, I remind him.

In my address, I discuss academic deterioration. The critical national reports about education focused on kindergarten through twelfth grade. But I ask: "What barrier holds back the rising tide of mediocrity from the shores of higher education? With school problems so severe, why do we suppose that universities have been immune?"

"Overall, higher education, too, has diminished in rigor," I argue. "Universities have accepted too many poorly prepared high school graduates, placed them in remedial programs, and then given them university-level credit. Like high schools, universities have given high grades, with the undergraduate class average often hovering at $B+$. This debased the coin of the academic realm. When everyone is honored, no one is.

"Institutions of higher learning face significant problems," I acknowledge. "Declining demographics, rising costs, diminishing public funds, rising public expectations—all introduce new pressures. But our purpose must be more than mere survival. We must also set goals for ourselves, ones that are bold and ennobling."

The American University has done so. I tell the group about AU85, noting, in conclusion, that, "Even though we're interested in what Middle States thinks of us, we're even more concerned about what we think of ourselves."

Preceding my talk, a distinguished educator argued that one way educational institutions and accreditation associations could measure excellence would be through "value-added." Conventionally, the way to do so is to monitor admission standards, the number of library volumes, faculty scholarship, faculty salaries, and other analytical parameters. But these may not correlate with the actual education. A better method, he suggested, would be to assess how much the institution improved a student's learning; that is, its "value-added."

I disagree. Although I acknowledge benefits of this approach, I note its dangers. An institution can become complacent through such a procedure, thinking it has succeeded just because its students know more when they graduate than when they enter. But what they know at graduation still may be mediocre.

In the question-and-answer session afterwards, someone says: "Higher education faces severe times. Can you recommend how to weather them?"

"Most universities, especially in industrialized states, must plan on enrollments shrinking," I begin. "And this may hit independent institutions more severely than state-supported ones. As enrollments shrink, tuition may rise even faster than it would otherwise. To offset this, universities must seek outside funds and cut expenditures." I conclude: "If there's a single prescription for success in higher education, it will be through quality. The consumers—as parents and students today can be viewed—will demand it."

The questions from the floor are excellent, the last one being the most arresting: "In the face of shrinking enrollments, how will universities be able to hire women and minority faculty members?"

After a pause, I try to respond: "Unfortunately, shrinking enrollments will force universities to forego most new faculty hiring; except for essential replacements, most will reduce overall faculty size. What new hiring does occur will be primarily in growth fields, areas in which women and minorities often don't hold advanced degrees, such as computer science.

"A partial solution to the role model problem," I go on, "will be for universities to hire women and minorities as adjunct faculty. But that has problems, too. Many universities will cut their number of adjuncts to save funds."

After my address, many from the audience come up to talk. And the man who introduced me apologizes for not knowing my name. "Don't worry," I tell him. "I was eighteen before I could remember it."

In the taxi to the train station, I think how underrated Philadelphia is. A New York or a Paris it is not; nor is it the city of W.C. Fields. With new buildings galore, it has maintained its heritage while revitalizing its downtown.

The train ride to Washington allows me to reflect. I cherished the hours at Princeton. My conversations there recharged me, and my stroll through the university's stately grounds reminded me of what my occupation is about. The Department of Education was right to hold the National Forum in Indiana. It should not have been in New York, Washington, or Los Angeles; it should have been in the heartland. The rich potpourri of people at the meetings in Indianapolis and Philadelphia reminds me of our national diversity. Every race and creed, dialect and persuasion abounds somewhere in the U.S. educational system. Our students sometimes compare poorly against the Japanese. But their society is far more homogeneous than ours and they have established—while we have no intention of establishing—a codified national education. Such is the warp and weave of our social tapestry.

As the Metroliner rumbles past Baltimore's rowhouses, I ponder the last question in Philadelphia. Educators can't resolve such issues; our influence and resources are inadequate. These matters belong to politicians, business leaders, news media—American society generally. This is not to shift responsibility but to face reality.

Gail and Natasha run up to greet me in Washington's Union Station. How good it is to see them again. It has been only four days, but I have missed them enormously. I covet my family time.

After dinner, I walk to my office. Despite Joan's routing things to other people, my desk is covered. From a lofty national perspective, I come back to earth: A fraternity claims AU Security violated its rights; a former employee threatens a lawsuit; three donors send end-of-year checks, but for less than I had expected.

I call a student who called me yesterday. Joan's note says: "He sounds upset." And he is, for he just lost out on a major graduate fellowship. I try to cheer him up, and he says he will try for another one.

Until 11:00 P.M., I read mail; then I decide it is time to go home and reintroduce myself to my wife. As I rise from my desk, my eye catches a letter in the stack.

"Richard, I'd like to send AU more money this year but this is all I can afford now. Best wishes."

The check is for less than 1 percent of what I had hoped from this donor. He gives no explanation, with no prior warning. And this despite what he has led me to believe. I slump in my chair. Halfheartedly, I sort through a few more letters when familiar handwriting catches my eye. Surely this cannot be. "Here's my contribution, which I wanted to get in before the end of the tax year. Hope it'll help." It will, but it is a pittance compared with this donor's potential.

Have I assumed unrealistically high figures for each donor? Perhaps, but this man told me that a substantial sum was coming. And he repeated it three times.

I turn off my desk lamp and sit in my darkened office. The old building creaks in the autumn wind. In the distance I hear a siren, perhaps an ambulance going to Sibley Hospital. Others have far greater problems than I. But here, in silence, I wonder, "What's the use?" I rush about the country and go to every event in town that might benefit AU. Gail pursues every lead that seems feasible. We try to bring everyone we can into the fold, whether in Washington, Geneva, New York, or London. We go at it seven days a week. And Milt, the Dons, the deans, many professors, the staff, and others do so as well. Successes do come, and they are rewarding. But sometimes the struggle hardly seems worth it.

Why are donors so cavalier? Many—maybe even most—mislead and deceive. They ask innumerable favors. Some state directly that they will contribute, citing the amount and the date. Then they do nothing. I remind them but they do not respond. I ask them to put it in writing, but they do not reply. I ask others to approach them, as my surrogates, but they, too, get no response. I ask again where the matter stands, but I am told, "Oh, I'm thinking about it." And so it goes—for weeks, months, years. It is frustrating as hell!

SATURDAY, DECEMBER 10
Esther Coopersmith—friend and dynamic Democratic lobbyist—called me Thursday. I return the call today. "Richard, a few years ago you tried to get President and Madame Sadat to AU, but he was killed before it could work out. Would you be interested if Madame Sadat were available to teach next year?"

"Of course. Could she give a seminar on the role of women, perhaps with people like Rosalyn Carter, Betty Ford, and Nancy Reagan as guests?"

I agree to write to Mrs. Sadat. And I call Milt to get his views. He is extremely enthusiastic. But, as Esther notes, we must treat the matter as confidential until we receive a reply from Mrs. Sadat.

SUNDAY, DECEMBER 11
This afternoon Gail and I take Natasha and her friend, Anna Hurwitz, to see an exhibit of Southeast Asian art. We admire the nineteenth-century Malay fabric and sixteenth-century Burmese Bud-

dhas. As we leave, Gail asks the girls what they would most like to have from what we have seen. Anna's reply: "The orchids at the entrance. They're really pretty." And Natasha's: "The building where the exhibit is held. It'd be fun to have an apartment there." So much for art appreciation.

Our next stop is the annual Lucia reception at the Swedish embassy. Ambassador Wilhelm Wachtmeister and his wife, Ulla, invite guests to bring children for a classical Swedish Christmas celebration. Anna and Natasha admire the lengthy banquet table covered with cookies, gingerbread houses, and innumerable delights. Ulla has transformed the embassy into a Scandinavian fairyland.

Soon after we arrive, Eliot Dam and his parents enter the dining room. Being a healthy twelve-year-old boy, he circles the table many times. To my surprise, Anna and Natasha do as well. Mike Deaver and his son arrive but soon join the group in the study where sturdy Redskins fans rivet on the battle of the archrivals: Dallas versus Washington. Attorney General William French Smith and Ed Meese chat in the living room while William Clark, former assistant to President Reagan for National Security Affairs, and Warren Burger talk in the hallway. The Weinbergers' rambunctious two-year-old grandson squeals as he blows out one candle, then another. Gail quips: "He's just like his grandfather—running around putting out fires," which causes Jane Weinberger to laugh heartily. Martin Agronsky, Roger Mudd, and others crowd into the living room as the ambassador suggests: "Have the little ones sit in the front so they can see."

Parents shush their children while in the distance we hear angelic voices. The volume increases. Then in the doorway appear the embassy children dressed in traditional Swedish Christmas attire—boys wearing long pointed hats and a girl with several lighted candles on her head. Their carols are in Swedish; the message is universal. And then one song is familiar to us all: "Silent Night." Traditions, holidays, families—when all is said, this is what life is for.

As we leave, the girls say how much they enjoyed it and how much they want to attend next year. We arrive home in time to watch the final quarter of the game. Washington wins decisively. Anna leaves early to study Hebrew, Natasha reads her school work, and the TV reports disquieting news: in international academic competition yesterday, American sixth graders placed last in math, scoring only half as well as the Japanese.

MONDAY, DECEMBER 12

The Eastern shuttle tosses in a heavy rainstorm. As always happens in a downpour, cabs are scarce. It takes nearly an hour to get one at LaGuardia and another hour to inch to midtown. After checking into my hotel, I find another cab and set out on the long ride to WNYC, the public radio station in New York. It is housed on the twenty-fifth floor of the Municipal Building, an architecturally striking structure —from the outside, at least. The studio itself is remarkably decrepit, reflecting the sorry state of many publicly supported facilities. Amidst peeling paint, collapsing furniture, and antiquated equipment, the station broadcasts to a loyal audience.

For nearly an hour, the interviewer and I discuss topics that range from preschool programs to recent astrophysical discoveries. For me, it is fun. But I did not come to this dreary place on this dreary day for enjoyment. I came, in part, to inform the public about education and, in part, to highlight AU. The interviewer does the latter nicely throughout the hour.

TUESDAY, DECEMBER 13

Early this morning, I walk from my hotel to WMCA–AM, where I am interviewed about educational standards. This live program is heard by many people as they start their day. Again, the interviewer's introduction gets AU's name across many times. This afternoon, I go to yet another studio—RKO near Times Square. This will be an important taping, I understand, because it will be broadcast over five hundred stations nationally. After spending a quarter hour searching for the correct floor, I wait another twenty minutes for the producer. Given the national character of the broadcast, I assume a seasoned professional will interview me. Instead, a young woman several years Deborah's junior appears. "Hi. Follow me." Obediently, I do so. She points a mike in my direction and asks for a voice level check. "Hello," I say. "Testing. One, Two, Three . . . " She interrupts, "Okay, you might as well start. What do you have to tell us about education?"

Did that go on the tape? Will it be edited? For that matter, is the tape running? I do not know the answer; still, I proceed. Finally, she says the tape is filled and thanks me for coming.

As I step over rubbish in the gutter and try to flag a cab, I think how different reality can be from illusion. If this program is broadcast nationally, as I am assured it will be, people in Spokane will hear my voice coming from glamorous Manhattan. They can conjure up a carefully scripted broadcast with a team of technicians running an elaborate studio situated amid towering skyscrapers. As with the flickering shadows in Plato's cave, can we discern reality from illusion?

WEDNESDAY, DECEMBER 14

I catch an early shuttle back to Washington and reach my office by 10:30 A.M. There an angry letter awaits me, claiming that a recent symposium on campus did not have enough conservative speakers. The next letter is equally angry—a recent alum, who does not yet have a job, obliquely threatens the university: it is AU's fault, he implies, that he has not been hired. The third item requires a change of gears: the Methodist Church wonders if it can borrow our portraits of past Methodist bishops for a display at a forthcoming convocation. My answer: "Of course. We'd be honored." One of the paintings—of John Fletcher Hurst, AU's founder—hangs in my office.

Further down in the stack is a plaintive letter from the Philippines.

> Dear Mr. Principal:
> I want to study in your school. I'm intelligent and work hard. If I come to your university, I will not be a bother. But I do not have enough money. If you give me a scholarship, you will do a kind thing for the world.

I ask our international admissions office to reply. By now, I must leave for a luncheon downtown. As I ride, I read the rest of my mail. A student asks, "Why do I have to take the math competency exam before I can graduate? My grades are fine. The only thing in my way in this damn exam. It's unfair."

When I was a student, I too considered some requirements to be unfair. But our math and English competency exams are reasonable. We instituted them in the late seventies, becoming perhaps the first major private university to do so. AU, like many other universities, was graduating seniors with good grades who wrote badly and had inadequate math skills—the evils of grade inflation. To guard against this, we instituted competency-based exams that must be passed before seniors can graduate. Substantial resources—courses, counselors, teaching aids—are available to assist them.

At the Mayflower Hotel, I am surrounded by local political leaders at this annual meeting of the Council of Governments of Metropolitan Washington. Marion Barry, mayor of Washington, shakes every hand in sight. Is a campaign on? Virginia senator John Warner enters the room less aggressively; it hardly matters because so many people rush up to shake hands. After an hour and a half of this group's patting each other on the back, literally and figuratively, the lunch ends.

Then I am introduced. I had been asked to speak for thirty minutes. But when I get to the rostrum, it is 1:42 P.M. and the meeting is to end at 2:00. So for eighteen minutes, I talk extemporaneously about public education, praising advances in the metropolitan area but noting what is left to be done. I suggest that nonacademic courses—such as driver education, sex education, cooking, preparation for life—be relegated to after school or Saturday. I tell this predominantly Democratic crowd that as helpful as federal funds are, primary responsibility for public education lies with state and local government. With this audience, the easiest approach would be to damn Reagan. But the problems are more complex than that; I would prefer to say what I believe even if they don't want to hear it. The audience, however, is extremely receptive.

Afterwards, Larry Feinberg, education writer for the *Post*, asks me about shifting nonacademic courses to after school hours. He pretends that he does not understand an issue when in truth he understands it thoroughly. And he probes with countless questions. I used to be put off by his approach. Now I enjoy it.

In my afternoon mail, a memo indicates that salaries in one staff area are too low. And a petition, signed by several dozen students, urges that a professor be awarded tenure. Students' views on such matters are important, but tenure is not awarded through a plebiscite. Also in the pile is Physical Plant's annual memo about snow emergencies.

When I moved from being provost to president, fewer benefits came than most people supposed. But one advantage loomed large, although no one but I knew it. The provost decides when the university is open. Normally, there's nothing to decide. But on those rare occasions when Washington receives snow, that changes dramatically.

After years in New England, I was baffled by Washingtonians' moisture paranoia. In a snowstorm, the capital city panics. People abandon cars. Others, apparently thinking snow should be polished, spin their wheels frantically. Even a forecast of snow will precipitate an avalanche of calls asking if classes are canceled, demanding that they be, or insisting that they not be.

As provost, I learned about the cost of salt versus sand, windchill factors, and the personnel policies of AU, local industries, and the government. I listened to the physical plant director tell me at dawn about weather conditions and our ability to dig out. Finally, like Harry Truman, I could pass the buck no further. While I talked to the man from Physical Plant, Gail listened to the radio for announcements of other closings. Never could I prove it, but I suspected that throughout Washington my counterparts were listening to radios. For within minutes of my announcing AU's plans, other universities, businesses, and school districts would announce theirs, invariably following suit. Perhaps it was just coincidence. But one frigid morning, I concluded that whoever gave the snow announcement first controlled the capital. Such power!

But mine was far from absolute. I had to face my daughter. One morning, while Physical Plant told me in one ear about the corrosive effects of salt, Natasha lobbied me from the other side. With her hands on her hips and frowning deeply, she fumed: "If you don't shut the university today and let the students play in the snow, I'll never speak to you again."

Late one night when I was provost, I emerged from my office to discover knee-deep snow, something I had never seen in the capital. At 2:00 A.M., the white meringue blanket smothered sounds and scattered light. As I dug out my car, I thought, "We're in trouble." And so we were. After managing to get home, I put on snow gear, loaded up with food, and returned to my office for the duration. Every news outlet screamed that this was the heaviest snow in Washington's history. I closed the university, except for "essential" services. Some staff were incensed not to be considered essential; others were angry to discover that they were. Our next task was to plow out. With three thousand dorm residents, I had to ensure safety. And the joy of playing in the snow would melt as quickly as the snow had fallen if food trucks could not enter. Night and day, crews plowed. The next day I had to shut the university again. We were far from clear.

For three days after the blizzard of '78, virtually every Washington institution was shut. Finally, I staggered home, unbathed, having slept on my sofa and eaten in my office for three nights. The phone rang.

"Dick, the university's been shut for days. When's it going to open?" a professor asked excitedly.

"I don't know yet."

"Don't be evasive," he screamed. "You've got to open it. You've got to."

Sensing that more was involved here than de-icers and snow chains, I asked, "What's the big deal? Why are you so passionate about our being open?"

"Damn it, Berendzen," he bellowed. "For three days AU has been shut. And I've been cooped up with my family. I can't stand it any longer."

At last, I understood his dilemma and the university's function— we are a refuge from families. What an ennobling thought. With glee today, I file the snow emergency memo and wonder if Milt is paid enough.

THURSDAY, DECEMBER 15

Greenberg, Triezenberg, and I meet to make final plans for the winter commencement. They seem to be working together well again, although both appear tired. The winter break will come none too soon.

The regular budget meeting jumps from this fiscal year, which continues to look good, to the next, which is less certain. We want our employees to have high morale. Good raises would help. But Myers has a list of urgent physical plant needs and Milt has a comparable one of essential academic needs. Triezenberg argues that he cannot do his task without an adequate budget. And Kevin Cornell, director of planning, urges us to assume an enrollment decline for next fall: the demographics remain real. Against this backdrop, we remember the students' plea about tuition. How do we balance the countervailing pressures?

Over lunch at the Georgetown Club, trustee Bill Moss explains how he would like to restructure the Moss Institute. A few years ago, our mutual friend, Nancy Dickerson, introduced Bill and me to one another. Immediately, I found him engaging and creative. Even though his business success enables him to live well, he has not forgotten the common man. He believes that the average American wants to know more about his own future. Bill aims to provide factual information so people can understand their destiny and control it better. To accomplish this, in 1982 he established the Moss Institute in affiliation with AU. Unlike think tanks, the institute is not designed to produce reports read only by authorities. It attempts to inform—even to instruct—the average citizen about critical future issues.

This afternoon, I drive to the WDVM–TV studio, where I am to tape brief statements about education. These pilots will be reviewed by WDVM and possibly by affiliate stations. This sounds promising, but I have no idea what we are to shoot today. There are no cue cards or scripts. We are going to wing it. The producer asks me, "Can you suggest what parents should ask school officials to ensure that their child's school is up to par?"

A dozen diagnostics cross my mind, most of which would be impractical for a parent to pursue. But a concerned parent can—and should—ask about the curriculum, homework, and grades. The producer says, "Fine," and the cameraman says, "Roll 'em." The taping takes only ten minutes. Naively, I ask, "Wouldn't it be better if we did two on each topic? Then you'd have a choice."

"Let's go with what we've got," the producer replies. "It'll show what these would be like." Perhaps, but I am glad I am not counting on this for a job.

Back in my office, I clear my desk, write letters, and return calls. Then I rush home to the latest crisis: Natasha has not been invited to a classmate's bar mitzvah. That she has been invited to others does not lessen the hurt; that several classmates were omitted from this one does not help. Maybe, I suggest, he just wanted his closest friends to attend. "Daddy, don't confuse me with logic. I was left out. And I want to be unhappy about it."

Having failed to solve this dilemma, Gail and I assure ourselves that Natasha is feeling okay. Then we head to prominent Washingtonians Bill and Buffy Cafritz's holiday dinner-dance. The hotel's private dining room resembles a winter's woods, with real trees and snowlike decorations. With large, expressive eyes and an estate necklace, Buffy looks like the perfect Washington hostess she is. Gail's dress pales in tonight's crowd. The dinner party we had expected for twenty people becomes one for a hundred: Mike Deaver, William French Smith, Bill Moss, Luther Hodges, Sandra Day O'Connor, John Warner, Nancy Dickerson, David Lloyd Kreeger, and many more. And a glamorous New York group augments the Washington crowd. While we are dancing, three couples stop to stare at someone who has just arrived. With this crowd, everyone would stop for the president, some would stop for the vice-president, but for whom would three couples stop? Then I see him: Canadian Prime Minister

Pierre Trudeau. He is in town as part of his effort to persuade the nuclear powers to hold disarmament talks.

FRIDAY, DECEMBER 16

Even though we are ending the term well, Milt and the Dons look exhausted. Although my cabinet meeting is upbeat, it lacks spark. Clearly, we are all tired. As the meeting concludes, I ask, "Is it true some people were upset by the administrative organization chart?"

Milt looks up gloomily and says, "I'm afraid it is true. We needed the chart for Middle States and it's probably useful anyway. But some people feel they weren't recognized properly." Genuinely baffled, I compare the recent chart with the old one. Some people troubled by the new one have not gone down in the chart one iota. Then I realize what bothers them: other people appear to have come up. This, surely, cannot be a problem beyond our ability to solve. I suggest ways to do so, one being to print several charts, expanding each operational area. "People then can complain about which chart they are on," Myers notes. "It'll be better to be on chart 1 than chart 5."

How petty. But then I realize the positive side. It gives meaning to the message. The disgruntled people are unhappy because they were not highlighted enough. They do not want to go elsewhere; they do not want to hide their involvement here. They feel they are doing something of worth and they want the world to know it. They are proud. And that is profoundly good.

As I come out of the meeting, Gail stops to see me. She is taking our excess food to SOME (So Others Might Eat), a Washington soup kitchen. But it is located in a rough area and I do not like her to go alone. Today, however, my schedule is impossibly crowded and the perishables cannot wait. She will have to go alone.

This afternoon, the trustees' investment committee discusses a pooled life-income fund and the purchase of an apartment building for university housing. It concludes ahead of schedule, giving me time to rush to the Christmas party of Triezenberg's staff. I have not met many of them because they are new at AU. How ironic it is that everything in the institution depends upon revenues, yet the front line for obtaining those monies in admissions and development is staffed by our youngest and newest employees.

Two of them ask me: "How was your Thanksgiving vacation in Paris?" What are they talking about? I have not broadcast where I have been, much less what I have been doing. So, from rumors, people construct images: not reflecting reality but projecting their own fantasies—a Rorschach test.

Also, many people believe that everyone at the top of an organization is inept or lazy, just as people at the top often hold the same view of those below them. This came home to me when I was promoted from dean to provost. A department head, who was a friend and colleague, said: "Dick, you're a good guy. But now you'll become a bum." Why?, I wanted to ask. My responsibilities will be larger. But I will be the same person.

Popular media reinforce these stereotypes. In numerous TV shows, people at the top are portrayed as callous or bumbling. Meant to be funny, this reflects Hollywood's disdain for authority and relish for mass appeal. If only each of us could view our compatriots from afar, we might find that others, wherever they stand in the hierarchy, are decent people trying to do responsible jobs.

MONDAY, DECEMBER 19
In this last week of exams, the campus becomes quiet. This morning I pass a frenzied student who tells me: "I'll be glad when exams are over. I've got two today, a paper tomorrow, and another exam on Wednesday. The pressure is too much, and it's been this way for a week."

"Someday," I reply, "you'll be able to live that way all year long, every year."

She couldn't look more shocked. "You mean late nights, early mornings, and deadlines all the time?"

"That's how it is for me," I tell her. "Maybe not for others. I don't know about them. Don't dread it. You'll do fine once you get the stride."

In my mail, three items stand out. One is a citation from a graduating student who thanks numerous professors, staff members, and administrators for assisting her. I don't remember what I did for her. Joan retrieves a letter the student wrote in 1980 requesting financial help. Apparently, I sent it to others who took care of the matter. Now she expresses her gratitude. In a world in which many complain but few say thanks, the certificate is touching.

An ardent Methodist writes to complain about student activities she considers to be immoral. With an intelligence-gathering system superior to mine, she informs me that students recently showed an X-rated film in a dorm at 1:30 A.M. She claims that the AU Tavern "encourages alcoholism among teenagers." And she complains that a fraternity has the annual spring rite of a nude streak at one o'clock in the morning.

I reply that although we are concerned about values, we do not attempt to set or regulate students' morals. To do so might be presumptuous; it certainly would be impossible. If we were to ban beer, students could obtain it elsewhere and bring it to campus. Our tavern does not sell to anyone who is under age or appears intoxicated. We do not condone the fraternity's annual brief streak, but if we were to stop it, new groups likely would decide to streak; a minor matter could blow up into a major confrontation.

And I note that among our diverse students we have some who consider things we take for granted as being hedonistic. Some complain about "impure" foods; others come from cultures in which women do not work, men and women do not take courses together, and short dresses are prohibited. At the other extreme, we have a few students who object to any regulations—true libertarians. This independent university, therefore, must strike a balance.

The third item is entitled "Italia Vogue Bambini." Blemishless skin, tousled brown hair, enormous moist eyes—the cover child on this Italian issue of *Vogue* is two-year-old Ali Adnan Khashoggi. The item in the mail—a reprint of the magazine article—is Adnan's unique Christmas card. The best part is the interview with mom and dad. "Children believe themselves big or small," Lamia Khashoggi says, "according to how their parents make them feel. And Ali feels very big."

And to the question, "What does it mean, in the truest meaning of the term, to educate a son?" Adnan replies: "The luxuries one gives to a son are a gratification to the parents rather than a pleasure for the child. However, one day there could be no more money. Then, all that is left is the education. Real wealth is in the intellect: this is the greatest legacy a parent can pass on to his children. The boy who is merely born rich is not lucky. The lucky boy is one whose parents help him to be himself to the best of his abilities."

Tonight, as Gail, Natasha, and I drive to a shopping center, Natasha says she is studying the phases of the moon in school. I tell her that I will give her a puzzle for her class. Whoever solves it will win a giant pizza. Galileo, I remind her, was the first person to observe celestial objects with a telescope. The year was 1609. In those days, anagrams—basically, one-line riddles—were used to establish priority of discovery without revealing exactly what had been found, thereby staking the claim for the writer while giving him time to do more research. In 1610, Galileo sent such a message: "Cynthia's figures are imitated by the Mother of Love." What does it mean?

Instantly, Natasha replies: "The Mother of Love was Aphrodite. But I don't get the rest of it." Startled that she got that far so fast, I remind her that Aphrodite was a Greek goddess. What was the Roman name of the same goddess? She does not know, so I tell her to look it up. Later tonight, after Natasha has gone to bed, I put the *Oxford English Dictionary* and a hint on the kitchen table. The hint: "Look up Aphrodite and Cynthia."

TUESDAY, DECEMBER 20

Before I get up, Natasha leaves me a note: "The anagram means that Venus has phases like the moon's." I write back on the sheet: "Good. But you've only got half of it. What does Venus's having phases mean? Why is it important?"

My first meeting fills my office—Milt, the Dons, the deans, and several people who deal with graduate affairs. Today's topic: graduate programs, specifically graduate recruitment. Many universities have a schizophrenic problem in determining whether they are fundamentally teaching or research institutions. They want to be both. In the real world, that is not easy. Research scholars often are more interested in their own studies and in graduate students than in freshmen. Research universities, therefore, attempt to obtain a mix of teaching and research faculty members and, ideally, professors who stand out at both. Conversely, institutions that stress teaching often find it difficult to recruit professors who excel at teaching and research. Reward systems are critical too. At a research university, the teaching load usually is light, whereas at a teaching institution it may be heavy —four courses per term. If a professor spends almost all his time on teaching and administration, he or she will have little left for research. Not surprisingly, institutions with such faculty do not receive much research funding and often are less visible. A prolific, creative scholar can generate publicity in academic circles and the public press. Such visibility implies that important things are happening at that university; corporations and parents alike are attracted to it. Sad to say, however, the professor whose research attracts headlines may not be an inspiring instructor.

What is needed is balance. A true university should create new knowledge and transmit existing knowledge. Research should not be separate from teaching; the two should intertwine. At the graduate level, research and teaching must fuse. And even at the undergraduate level, the methodologies of good research can be taught best by someone who participates in research. What most universities seek, therefore, is a "teacher-scholar."

Aside from this issue, we focus today on how to improve our recruitment of top quality graduate students. In a spirited discussion, everyone participates, ideas fly. At the end of the session, I say we should have another one like it in February and I ask them to return with specific suggestions.

After lunch at the consortium office, I dictate several letters, talk to two trustees by phone, start setting meetings for my January trips, and stop by three campus Christmas parties. Over dinner at home, Natasha says Galileo's riddle means that Venus is moving somehow like the moon. Outstanding! Still, she does not quite have it. So I take her to the living room to inspect two large reproductions on the wall from a medieval book on the Ptolemaic and Copernican universes. She has seen them for years; tonight we study them. She stares at the drawings, mumbling to herself. Then her eyes brighten: "Could it be that, with his telescope, Galileo was the first person to see phases on Venus, and that proved to him that it went around the sun rather than the earth?" She has got it.

As we step into the family room where Gail is reading, I hug Natasha and say, "Guess who won a giant pizza." Blushing and looking at the floor, her grin reveals her enormous pride. And she should be proud. The first time I asked someone to interpret that riddle was on a Harvard test. Not bad work for a seventh grader.

Better yet, it leads to a lively discussion among all of us about the Renaissance. Unfortunately, however, we cannot continue it—Natasha has homework and Gail and I are to join Ahmed and Judy Esphandiary at the Kennedy Center.

Gail asks Natasha what homework she has left. "Oh, just Worldly Wise, and that's easy." After Natasha leaves the room, Gail asks: "Have you seen the words they're studying?" We flip through her book. Typical words: boisterous, cudgel, emulate, irascible, precipitous. So that is where she has gotten the words she springs on me. I remark to Gail, "Is it surprising that a youngster with such an education someday will do better on verbal SATs than one who has not? Those exams depend upon vocabulary, and GDS has been building hers all along. That such students end up scoring better reflects years of preparation. The classes, homework, museum visits, and the like pay off. That underlies the skewing of test results from one community to another."

Tonight is delightful. What a pleasure to be with just one other couple, people we genuinely like. And what a pleasure just to enjoy Baryshnikov's staging of *Cinderella.* I even understand the plot. And although I do not fully appreciate ballet, I know it is difficult to stand on your toes for two hours.

THURSDAY, DECEMBER 22

It is time for my annual ritual: to be Santa Claus for our Child Development Center. Twenty-two three-year-olds excitedly await Santa's arrival. For days, their teachers and parents have told them that the jolly fellow will visit their class personally. The parents, I am told, appreciate my being Santa—not because I am good at it but because when I visit they do not have to take their children to shopping centers. Santa sees them personally in class.

Shortly after the CDC opened in the late seventies, its director asked if I would play the role. Sure, I said, if someone would give me a suit. Presto, a suit appeared in my office and I have been Santa every December since. And what experiences I have had. If I am going to the trouble of putting on the outfit and if I feel foolish walking to the CDC, I might as well take full advantage of the opportunity. So I stroll across the campus unannounced, popping into a startled dean's office, the library, the student dining room. Fortunately, the beard and hat mask my identity. And that in itself has led to intriguing experiences.

A few years ago, Physical Plant was holding its Christmas party when I arrived. Santa strode confidently into a room with wine flowing and rock music blaring. A woman approximately Santa's shape sidled up and purred: "Hey Santa, you wanta boogie?" I was not certain what she had in mind, but what the hell! Soon the too of us were on the dance floor, grinding and bumping. Yet another time, as Santa walked into the computer center, a staff member, with his feet on the desk, screamed: "My God, it's Santa Claus. No. It's the president!" With that, he crashed from his chair pulling his phone down on top of him.

Today, because it is starting to sleet, I visit only the CDC. Despite the cold outside, it exudes warmth. After the children take turns sitting on Santa's knee, they sing him several songs.

My experiences as Santa have not always been so tranquil. Twenty years ago this December, Deborah accompanied me as I donned a Santa suit to visit shut-in children. We explained that Deborah was Santa's helper. She took great pride in assisting dad. The problem came when we attempted to cross ice-covered Harvard Square. On that arctic night, the beard froze to my lips, my glasses fogged, and my pillows slipped from my shirt into my pants. Quick-witted scientist that I am, I had forgotten gravity. And, new at being Santa, I had not realized that I did not need two pillows and a towel for stuffing. In the middle of Harvard Square, it all dropped into my pants, shoving them to my knees, leaving me sliding on the ice, blinded by the fogged glasses, wearing long gray underwear.

Deborah tried to support me, but we both crashed to the ground. Every time we stood, I fell again. When I struggled to pull up my pants, the pillows were in the way. When I shoved them into the shirt, the pants fell around my ankles and I tripped again. Cars backed up, their horns blaring.

Despite my blind haze, I could hear sidewalk conversations: "Mommy, look! It's Santa, and his pants are falling off."

"Don't look at him, dear. That's not really Santa. He's disgusting. Can you imagine Santa getting drunk? And he even has a child with him."

SUNDAY, DECEMBER 25
On this special day, Gail and I drive to National Airport to meet Natasha, who is coming back after a few days in Massachusetts with Gail's parents, and Deborah, who is flying in from Dallas. Even the five-degree weather does not chill our family warmth. As we return home, we get reacquainted with one another. And then we have the epitome of a Christmas evening—roaring fire, candlelit dining room, succulent food, numerous gifts, and endless laughter. Gail and I delight in having Deborah and Natasha together, and the two of them enjoy each other.

To my surprise, Gail gives me a magnificent gift. Usually, she has gotten me odd or practical ones, the best one being a popcorn popper. But this year she fulfills one of my childhood fantasies. Since I was ten or so, I have wanted a peculiar assortment of things: a suit of armor, a large ivory chess set, a Chinese dragon chair. Tonight she gives me a magnificent globe, twenty inches in diameter, complete with floor stand and lamp.

Then, the moment of truth: booming from the family room comes Natasha's gift from her grandparents—Michael Jackson's "Thriller." Deborah, in tight jeans and baggy sweater, begins a pulsating dance. Who are these two strange but familiar people: an emerging adolescent and a remarkably grown young woman? For a moment, even through Michael Jackson, I swear I can hear *Fiddler on the Roof.* "Wasn't it yesterday when they were small? . . . sunrise, sunset . . . swiftly flow the days."

MONDAY, DECEMBER 26
We rush about the house, shutting shades, feeding Sparky, turning on the alarm—preparing to leave for four days in New York City. After we have waited patiently forty-five minutes, I growl: "These damn cabs. I told the dispatcher almost an hour ago to send a cab to . . . ." Even as I mumble the address, Gail replies: "But that isn't our number. You've combined your office's street number with our street name."

How could I be so stupid? In the pandemonium of leaving, that is exactly what I did. Deborah grins and asks, "Are you going to try a different company?" Tempting as that is, I reply, "No, that wouldn't be fair to some poor driver who's been searching for us. I'll call them back, even though I hate to think what the dispatcher will say."

"What's the matter with you, man?" he barks. "Don't you know where the hell you live? You've wasted my driver's gas. Go look at your house so you'll get the number right this time."

Shortly, the cab arrives, and, with a broad grin, the driver says: "I've been driving all over these parts. I'm glad to find you."

"It was my fault," I tell him. "I'm sorry."

Gail adds, "You must run into all kinds of situations."

"Lady, I sure do."

"Have you ever delivered a baby in your cab?" Gail asks.

"No. But one was born in my cab. The silly part was that the woman wouldn't let me stop at three different hospitals because they weren't related to her church. Once the baby was born, her husband refused to pay anything more than the regular meter. Usually, we charge extra for a birth."

"You mean the company has a fixed fee for births?"

"Well, sort of," he replies. "After all, we gotta have the cab fumigated afterwards."

Fumigated? By now we have arrived at National Airport, and I give the driver a handsome tip to compensate for my wasting his time. Startled, he beams: "You have a Happy New Year."

After checking into our New York hotel, the four of us push sophistication aside and gawk unashamedly at Manhattan's towers. As we go back to our hotel, Deborah tells us about her current apartment search in Dallas. With only limited finances, she is looking for a modest place.

Once the girls are in their room, Gail and I reminisce about our past living accommodations. For a year as a graduate student, I shared a dilapidated apartment with four friends. On one side of us, a car without wheels sat on brick columns as men met each evening, ostensibly to work on its engine. Actually, this was their means of fellowship. For the year I lived there, they worked almost every evening on the car; when I left, they still were laboring away.

On the other side of us was a playground where local urchins gathered every night, each with a radio blasting rock music. One warm evening, as their sounds vibrated our dishes, my roommates and I resolved to respond. Repeatedly, we had asked them to lower the volume, but to no avail. That night we counterattacked. My roommates had stereos with huge speakers. We raised our windows facing the playground, placed the speakers on the sills, and turned Bach on full volume. Startled, the kids lined up their radios as close to our apartment as possible. What a cacophony! Rock versus Bach. Who would give in? Five minutes went by . . . ten . . . twenty. We expected the Cambridge riot squad to arrive at any moment. People a block away must have thought it a protracted sonic boom or a nuclear test.

JFK recently had shown us the way in the Cuban missile crisis: he had looked the enemy squarely in the eye and the other fellow had blinked. Our situation was more important than missiles; it involved the sanctity of our slum apartment, which we had dubbed "The Dung Hill Arms." After half an hour, the enemy blinked. The radios clicked off; the kids left. My roommates and I declared victory.

A few days later, we noticed the kids hanging around our building. They said nothing and actually seemed pleasant. Perhaps Bach had civilized them—perhaps not, as we learned later. One night we found our front porch had collapsed. The kids had removed the bricks one by one. We Harvardites were ready for stereo warfare but not guerilla tactics.

There was a final struggle. I had brought home a device I had made for my undergrad physics thesis. It was so large, bulky, and heavy that I could barely move it. Festooned with wires, knobs, and dials, it looked like part of Frankenstein's lab. And because I liked the sign, I had pasted a notice on it: WARNING. RADIATION DANGER. Now I wanted to return the device to MIT.

After lugging it from the apartment to the curb, I had to get my car a block away. The device would be safe; after all, who would want it? But I had forgotten the local kids. By the time I returned with my car, they had carried it down the street. What to do? Outnumbered eight to one, I had few options. So I called out to them: "Have you had your shots?" Their responses ranged from silence to "Hunh?" to colorful obscenities. And they kept walking.

I went on: "Well, if you haven't had shots, I assume you've at least taken pills. Still, why aren't you using rubber gloves?"

With that, they slowed. Then stopped. "What shots? What pills?"

I strolled up to them and said: "The ones for radiation sickness. Read the sign there. I've had mine, so I assumed you'd had yours."

The cursing stopped; the insults ended. "Hey, man, what's this radiation crap?"

With feigned alarm, I said: "Haven't you heard about it? It can give you cancer or kill you—or even make your hair fall out! That's why I was trying to get this hazard off the street. What did you want to do with it? Maybe poison someone?"

Obviously worried by then, they said: "Naw. We just wanted to mess with it. We didn't mean no harm. Will this radiation hurt us?"

Victory was at hand, yet my conscience pained me. So I replied: "Help me get this thing into the trunk of my car so I can dispose of it. Then, let's see . . . you've only been exposed a few minutes. There's still time. But you'll really have to hurry. *Run* home—don't walk—and take a thorough bath. I'm sure you'll be fine then."

They trotted with the device to my car; then they dashed in all directions for home and a bath.

Aside from the neighborhood, we had difficulties with the landlord. Whenever the people above us flushed their toilet, we had only moments before refuse would leak through our ceiling, cascading down upon our toilet. So if you happened to be sitting there when you heard the toilet flush above, you had to move fast. We asked the landlord to fix the toilet and ceiling, but she refused. So we complained to Cambridge authorities. After repeated calls and a lengthy wait, an inspector finally appeared. He observed the scene and declared: "This isn't bad enough for official action." How comforting to know government is on your side.

The entrance hallway was equally deplorable. For months we pleaded with the landlord to paint it. One evening, as I entered the building, I found the floor freshly painted. Naturally, bristles were stuck in the paint and the coat did not fully cover the color before; the paint crew must have been the cheapest available. As I straightened the mat, I found the floor unpainted beneath it. The painters had just painted around it. Not to be deterred, we nailed the mat in place, crooked as it was.

And Gail and I had our share of peculiar apartments. Perhaps our strangest living arrangement arose when we moved out of an apartment but had a week's hiatus before we could move into our next one. Rather than spend our scant savings for a hotel, we hit upon a brilliant idea: we would live in my office.

As an aspiring assistant professor at Boston University, I virtually lived there anyway. Gail would join me after teaching in her school. We would have dinner at a Commonwealth Avenue greasy spoon and return to my office, where we both would work until midnight or beyond. So why not just spend the night? After all, I had a private office with a sofa. It was on the fifth floor of an office building, and on a lower floor there were showers. So we set our alarm for 5:30 A.M. I guarded the bathroom door while Gail took her shower; she did likewise while I took mine. This, we concluded, was an ideal arrangement: We imposed on no one; we had a secure place to live; and it cost us nothing.

By the third night, however, our downfall was imminent. To keep custodians away, I put a sign on my office door: "Do Not Enter." It kept them from entering but not from talking. The next day, an associate dean asked to see me.

"Berendzen," he began, "shut the door. I want this to be private." Then he came to the point. "I hear you've moved your entire family into your office."

"My entire family?"

"I don't know quite who," he replied, "but I gather it's your wife, kids, maybe your parents and brothers and sisters. How do all of you fit in there anyway?"

"Something has gotten distorted here," I tried to explain. "It's just my wife and me. How silly this is. My office is only large enough for a sofa and desk."

"You're missing the point, Berendzen," the dean growled. "So it's just you and your wife. My information may have been a little off. But I gather the two of you have, in fact, moved into your office. Is that true?"

"Well, we haven't exactly moved in. We're just staying there for a few days until . . . ."

"Look, Berendzen, the university provides you with salary, fringes, and an office. But it doesn't provide an apartment. And you can't make your office into one. Are you a professor or a gypsy?"

Sheepishly, I promised we would not sleep there anymore and retreated from his office.

Remembering those times tonight, Gail and I laugh so hard we almost become ill.

TUESDAY, DECEMBER 27

After I explain New York's simple grid street system to the girls, they set off together to shop while Gail and I go on our own. After-Christmas sales are in progress, and I take a pair of trousers into a dressing room to try them on. As I emerge, a man waiting to enter says unemotionally: "Hello, Dr. Berendzen." Who is he? I do not recall having seen him before. As he comes out of the dressing room, I ask: "How do I know you?" "Oh, I graduated from AU in the seventies. I recognized you from photos. We haven't met before." Is AU everywhere? Even in New York dressing rooms?

Reunited with the girls, we spend the day touring midtown. The sisters spend more time talking to each other than to Gail or me. And, back in the hotel, they insist upon privacy as they shut their door amidst giggles and chatter.

For dinner, I would like to take them to the stately University Club at 54th Street and Fifth Avenue. Its sooty facade hides a distinguished formal interior. Straight from a *New Yorker* cartoon, the paneled reading room contains heavy drapes, vaulted ceiling, and leather chairs. And the seventh-floor dining room exudes dignity, with walls two floors high, large oil portraits, and an ornate ceiling. My family will enjoy the experience but there is a significant drawback: it is a men's club.

Some years ago, while I was attending a meeting in Chicago, I was invited to a luncheon at an exclusive club. Not realizing that it was strictly for men, I took Gail and Deborah with me. We were stopped at the door and told that I could enter but they could not. Outraged, I said, "I will go no place my family can't go too." And I stalked out, to the dismay and chagrin of my hosts.

Later, when we moved to Washington, I was invited to join the Cosmos Club. It was, I knew, a prestigious institution whose members included distinguished scientists, educators, and writers, some who had won Pulitzer or Nobel prizes. I was delighted to be considered for membership and honored when accepted. Never did it occur to me that it was a men's club. Years earlier, it had not accepted black men for membership nor permitted women to enter through the front door, even as guests. Long before I joined, however, it started accepting black male members and its first-floor dining room welcomed female guests who entered through any door. But its membership remained open only to men.

A few years ago, some members decided to revise the club's bylaws to admit women. I assumed that this change would be ratified overwhelmingly. Instead, I found a rancorous debate. The opponents of change marshaled extensive arguments, pointing out that many professional clubs exist in Washington for women, several of which are exclusively for women. They also rattled off financial arguments against admitting women, a chief one being that expensive new toilet facilities would have to be installed. Eventually, the vote was taken. I voted for the change, but it was defeated resoundingly.

How silly, I thought, until I realized the different perceptions club members have. To me, a club is simply a convenient place for a business lunch. But other members—especially older ones—view the club differently. To them, it literally is a way of life; some of them, in fact, live there. They have bedrooms upstairs, take almost all meals there, meet longtime friends there, read in the library, attend lectures, doze in the lounge. For them, this is as it has been for decades. They do not want to change.

Tonight, my main concern is that my family not be embarrassed by the all-male University Club. When I inquire, however, I am assured that women are welcome.

The massive dining hall, almost empty tonight, is like a banquet room for four. With one waiter for each of us, we feel amply attended. Outside, the windchill factor is minus thirty degrees; inside, the family warmth is roasting. Deborah and Natasha instantly fall into the dinnertime games we've played since they were children. We start round-robin stories. One of us begins a story, stopping in midsentence for the next person to continue. The longer it continues, the more elaborate the tale becomes. Tonight I say: "Okay, everyone make up the most brilliant statement, the wisest aphorism in the world." In the hush of this dignified room, our roars of laughter seem out of place.

Unfortunately, artichokes listed on the menu are unavailable. Deborah enjoys them; Natasha's never had one, but now's a good time to learn. My first experience with artichokes came when I was in my early thirties. In search of archival astronomical materials related to a book I was writing, I visited Lick Observatory near Monterey, California. The great senior astronomer, C. D. Shane, invited me to his bucolic home for lunch. Little did I know that Monterey was the artichoke capital of the world. Before me at lunch sat a strange vegetable, one I had never eaten before and could not figure out how to eat. I waited nonchalantly, watching my hostess. Mrs. Shane pulled a leaf off the mysterious vegetable, dipped it in sauce, and placed it in her mouth. Easy enough, I thought, quickly following suit. But I had not watched her long enough to notice that she only scraped off the outer layer and discarded the rest. Boldly, I inserted the entire leaf into my mouth.

With a consistency like Neolite, the artichoke leaf sprang my jaws apart as I tried to clamp them down. Obviously, I thought, I am not chewing vigorously enough. With gusto, I chewed away, but my jaws kept bouncing open. I became so entranced in chewing I forgot the Shanes. When I glanced up, they were staring in wonder at their young guest. Mrs. Shane gently suggested: "We usually prefer eating just the leaf's outer part. Of course, if you enjoy it all, that's fine with us."

When we return to our hotel room, I read the *New York Times*. Fred Hechinger, a *Times* education writer, has an insightful article headlined, "After a Year of Criticism, Whither the Schools?" He claims that the prescriptions for improvement fall into two categories: to get tough and to find better ways of teaching, learning, and running the schools. He argues, correctly, that both have merit. Of the two, he seems more critical of the get-tough approach. Properly, he argues that minimum competency tests are usually set too low and that it is almost impossible to remove large numbers of incompetent teachers. He also notes, convincingly, that one of the reasons foreign-language enrollments have declined is that languages often have been taught poorly.

In the main, Hechinger's analysis is astute and his call for balance is correct. My only caveat is that he disparages "get-tough" too much. We can and should expect more of our schools, teachers, and students. As Benjamin E. Mays, the great black educator, observed years ago: "Not failure, but low aim is sin."

WEDNESDAY, DECEMBER 28

Through cold rain, we go separate ways: Gail and Natasha stereo shop; Deborah heads off to art galleries; and I have lunch with the publisher of the *Atlantic*. In the afternoon, we gather at the Metropolitan Museum of Art, one of civilization's jewels. From there, with only an hour left until closing, we rush to the Guggenheim Museum. The current exhibit is *Kandinsky: The Russian and Bauhaus Years*. Although Deborah genuinely enjoys it, the rest of us prefer paintings that are clearly rightside up.

THURSDAY, DECEMBER 29

The bus deposits us at Washington Square, where we begin our exploration of Greenwich Village and SoHo. The last time I was here was when Gail and I took Deborah to New York for New Year's Eve in Times Square when she was about Natasha's age. Always a center of the avant-garde, the Village then bordered on the bizzare. Today, SoHo boutiques abound with creativity, while a few Village shops retain the angry counterculture. As Natasha looks at Michael Jackson posters, I survey other items: a sign entitled Eat the Rich; another one showing a decapitated body, blood dripping from the severed head; an album cover showing a battered child.

In another Village store, Natasha discovers a wonderland of "neato" clothes. How different the same thing can appear to different observers. To her, the fashions are "far out"; to Gail and me, they are just old. Most are secondhand. While Natasha gleefully looks at garments, Gail and I observe customers. Clad in clothes like my father's rejects, these teenagers are breaking away, finding their identity, passing through adolescence. Natasha proudly proclaims: "Nowadays, you can wear almost anything, old or new. Things today aren't restricted like they used to be."

The protest posters, shaggy jackets, even drug apparatus in shop windows don't startle anyone anymore. And, to our relief, Natasha's biggest thrill this afternoon comes not from seeing the weird but from watching breakdancing. We return to midtown, where to Natasha's squeal and our eventual frustration, Gail and I buy her a real stereo, replacing her childish record player.

After dinner, Natasha says she is exhausted from the trek to the Village; she wants to go to sleep. Deborah, however, says that on this, our last night in New York, she would like to see the theater district again. How do we work this out? Like so many times before, Gail and I exchange silent glances, finding the answer: she takes Natasha to the hotel while I take Deborah to Times Square.

As we approach the theater district, I say, "At this moment Al Pacino probably is waiting to meet Debbie Berendzen." "Sure," she replies. As we approach the Booth Theatre, where Pacino is playing, I notice a crowd at the stage door. "Debbie, no joke. The play lets out now. I'll bet the crowd is waiting to see Pacino leave." Reluctantly, she follows me. But when she sees others holding Pacino posters, waiting for autographs, she concludes I must be right. In such cold, I would not wait long to watch William F. Buckley, Jr., mud-wrestle Dolly Parton. But this is special for Deborah, and in less than five minutes out Pacino comes. Best of all, he shakes her hand. Dazed, she mutters, "Why didn't I bring my camera?"

Friday, December 30

A surly taxi driver takes us to LaGuardia, where he collides his cab into another car. Even though we are far from the terminal, he shrugs and says he cannot go further. Only minutes remain until Deborah's flight, so we run the remaining blocks, with me carrying her heavy bag. The bigger burden, however, will be to say goodbye. When she was a child and visited us in Boston, I found the goodbyes almost unbearable. Now she is a woman on her own. Still, tears come to my eyes as I hug her goodbye.

Saturday, December 31

Even though we have just returned from an adventure, Natasha reminds us that before she is grown she would like another experience: to go skiing. As we have done for ten years, Gail and I promise to take her "before long."

Having grown up in New England, Gail is a moderately proficient skier; having grown up in Texas, I am completely incompetent. In the sixties, Gail and I took Deborah skiing in Vermont and New Hampshire. On skis, I found, I could neither stand nor see. Snow fell on my glasses, and when I exhaled, I fogged them. This, I assumed, must be a common problem, so I went to the ski shop. Naturally, the proprietor was six feet five and blond, with massive shoulders, steel jaw, and turtleneck sweater. Undoubtedly his name was Thor. Staring up his nostrils, I felt like a mortal before Zeus.

After I explained my problem, he suggested goggles. A sensible solution, I thought; yet, they painfully crushed my glasses into my nose and strained an elastic band around my head.

"Isn't there another solution?" I asked.

"Oh, ya," he boomed back. "Back in my country, we use da potato."

"What is 'da potato'?"

With a slight grin, he spoke more with his ham hands than his mouth. "You cut potato in half. Then rub it on glasses. It puts on film. Will keep them from fogging."

How quaint, I thought: folk medicine. But where to find a potato at a ski resort? My quick-witted young wife suggested the kitchen.

"Excuse me," I approached the cook. "Can I buy a potato?"

"Of course," he said, handing me an order of french fries.

"No. I just want a raw potato. And it should be cut in half."

He rolled his eyes and sold me one for two dollars. It was a rip-off, I knew. But it was cheaper than goggles, and where else could I buy a potato? Dutifully, I rubbed the potato over my lenses while the cook stared in amazement. With the expectation of Galileo peering through his telescope or Franklin flying his kite, I marched outside and put on my glasses. Sure enough, what I saw was just what you would expect: a blinding smudge of goo. Meanwhile, Thor no doubt was lifting his mug by the roaring fire, chortling to a bevy of admiring snow bunnies: "I got another one with da potato story."

For us, New Year's Eve normally is a quiet family affair. We decide to go to a movie tonight. Which one? Although I do not know much about it, I suggest *Terms of Endearment,* primarily because it may win Academy Awards and because it is a story of love between a mother and a daughter.

The movie tonight lives up to its plaudits; it *will* win Academy Awards. But it is too mature for Natasha and too somber for this special evening. The best part comes when we return home in infant 1984 and walk from our garage to the house. On this cold, crisp night, the sky's beauty transfixes us. Natasha sees it first: "Oh, look. Stars everywhere." Indeed, there are. We pause in our driveway and stare at Orion, birthplace of new stars. Just as our New Year begins, there new suns are beginning. And around some of them must be debris, some of which may form planets. Some of those planets may be similar to our own. And around some of them may be atmospheres, some of which may contain the same chemicals that existed in earth's early atmosphere. Some of those chemicals may be acted upon by their star's energy, converting them into biologically significant substances. And so life may spring forth on those distant worlds. It is a poignant moment—and an appropriate way to begin 1984.

SUNDAY, JANUARY 1

Normally, I find this season and this day depressing. The vacation hiatus surrounding Christmas and the New Year keeps expanding; now it fills almost a week and a half. The warmth of the holidays is undeniable, but the nation's productivity slowdown has become excessive.

Moreover, benchmark days—Christmas, New Year's, birthdays —always depress me. For then, like most people, I go through deep introspection. What have I done this past year? Have I achieved what I set out to do? How have I contributed? Most of my honest answers fall far short of my expectations a year ago. I resolve to try harder.

That much is not new for me at New Year's, but Gail's revelation is. "I've been thinking about something, and I'd like to discuss it with you," she begins. "Natasha is at a transition, moving into early adolescence. She'll continue to need my attention, but not so closely as in the past. A few years ago I quit my job to assist you and the university. Right after I quit my job, a man at a reception asked, 'Do you do something useful or just stay home?' That remark wasn't funny or appropriate but it was unforgettable. I am trying to determine, as a forty-year-old woman, where I am headed in life. Truth is, much of what I do centers on you and Natasha. I am totally happy about that; it is as rewarding and fulfilling a life as I can imagine. But I am also uncertain who I am.

"Certainly, I'm a mother and a wife. And I hope I am also my husband's helper and closest confidant."

At this point I interrupt, saying: "That you certainly are. If I fail to say so often enough, it is only my fault. Without your help, I couldn't be anything or achieve anything. Much of what I do I attribute to you . . . ."

"I am glad to hear you say that," she interrupts. "But my point is not to elicit such a response from you. I am simply trying to determine, as this new year begins, what I should do with my life. I live so much for you and Natasha, I sometimes wonder what would happen if I lost you."

Haltingly, she sobs: "If—and I hate to even say such a thing—you were to die, I really don't know what I would do. I would have lost everything—as a wife and even as a person." By this point, I am incapable of speaking, even if I had anything to say. And there are times when wisdom comes in listening, not speaking.

Gail goes on: "So, I've been wondering if I should get a job, perhaps with a public relations firm, and do the same type of thing I do now without pay for AU. Then, I'd do it with a salary and build a career. Or I wondered if I should go to AU for a master's degree. Or maybe the best thing is just for me to continue as I am. I really don't know.

"Don't answer now," she continues, "just help me think this over. After the spring term ends, I want to consider seriously what I should do. I am delighted with my life, but self-examination is appropriate."

Indeed, it is. I shall think about these things. And, most of all, I treasure that we will ponder them together.

FRIDAY, JANUARY 6
This morning I meet with Patrick Henry, religion department chairman at Swarthmore College. He and I have been asked to read the folders of finalists for Marshall Scholarships. Although they are less famous than the Rhodes, the Marshalls are possibly even more prestigious academically. A half dozen of us meet each January at the British embassy to select the finalists. In the meeting, chaired by Ambassador Oliver Wright of Great Britain, we review dozens of able candidates. The nation may be at risk educationally, but you could not prove it by these applicants. They have done everything from founding companies to publishing books. Finally, we agree on this year's winners.

Afterwards, the ambassador and his wife host lunch in the embassy's dining room. The stately surroundings resemble Windsor Castle, but the best part for me is the opportunity to sit next to Lady Wright. With accent and mannerisms more British than Christopher Morley's, she epitomizes English dignity—with a mischievous wit.

Noting the imperial ER imprinted on the back of her chair, I whisper to her: "This is shocking. If word gets out, it would become a diplomatic scandal. You *must* stop stealing chairs from the Embassy Row Hotel." Throwing her head back, she laughs loudly.

After lunch, I excuse myself before the rest of the group has disbanded. Drolly, Lady Wright says: "Oh, I see. You're trying to make us believe you have something terribly important to do now?" With equal sobriety, I reply: "I don't want to miss the soap operas." She gives me a ladylike squeeze and says: "Hug your wee wifey for me." Ah, may England last forever.

MONDAY, JANUARY 9

Many people write to me—students, professors, educators, government officials, lawyers. Some truly distinguished people write. But a letter today is in a category by itself. It is signed: "Sincerely yours, Jesus Christ II." It is sad while also somewhat amusing. As Milt joins me for a meeting, I tell him about the letter. His immediate response: "Quick. Get him to join the IAB."

Tonight, Gail, Natasha, and I attend an AU basketball game. Aside from enjoying the games, we know we should attend for visibility. We must support the team. Students know how crowded my schedule is, so they do not expect me to attend every game. But if I miss many, they grumble that I do not care about the team or them. Ironically, if I am not at a basketball game, it is probably because I am meeting with people who might benefit our sports center. Sometimes I wish I could send a double. Or just a balloon with my likeness on it. It does not matter whether I speak or think; I simply must be there.

WEDNESDAY, JANUARY 11

After doing a radio show yesterday and reviewing our fund raising this year, I fly to Pittsburgh today to do a TV show. The program host graciously introduces me as being from "an extremely important university—The American University." And he terms me a "national authority on education." The other guest, who gives a local perspective, is the Pittsburgh superintendent of schools. As I leave the set, the next guest, a psychologist, passes me. "Bill Murray," she says excitedly. "You look just like him—but everybody must tell you that." Actually, they do not. What kind of plastic face do I have, appearing like so many people?

This afternoon, I fly to Philadelphia, where I am to do a TV show tomorrow. My cab driver from the airport to the hotel has a thick Slavic accent. I ask him where he is from. "The Soviet Union."

"How interesting," I reply. "What have you found that's similar or different between the two countries?"

With stunning succinctness, he says: "In the U.S., the people run the government; in the USSR, the government runs the people." In one sentence, he encapsulates thousands of politicians' speeches and scores of scholars' books. Such pithiness is impressive. It reminds me of the sentence I heard that summarizes a year's worth of *Cosmopolitan:* "Men give love to get sex; women give sex to get love."

FRIDAY, JANUARY 13

This morning, a small group of us meet to determine next year's budget guidelines. We shall recommend them to the trustees' finance committee, which will forward its recommendations to the trustees' executive committee, which will do likewise to the full board. Then, on March 2, the board will consider the budget in detail. Despite the hurdles, the guidelines we set this morning likely will emerge as the budget.

So we approach the subject carefully, after weeks of preparation. I note that last year, when we felt the recession severely, the campus was traumatized. The ancient Chinese claimed: "One good scare is worth a thousand admonitions." For us, this could not have been more true. For five years I had warned that the national demographic decline was real and that AU's contingencies and reserves were too small. No one disbelieved me, but no one particularly heeded me. Everyone agreed that problems would come someday, but then they proceeded as usual. AU's budgets always have been austere; everyone always has felt the pinch. But last year we learned how much tighter the belt could be pulled. This year everyone concurs that our reserves and contingencies must increase and that our budget must be cautious. And so it will be.

Budget Director Harry Schuckel hands out three hypothetical budget models with tuition increases of 8.5, 8.9, and 10.2 percent. The 10.2 percent would give extra money we certainly could use. But I discount it immediately. I want to keep our increase under double digits and I am concerned about cumulative increases for '85 coupled with '84. On that we all agree. But we spend two hours discussing the other two models.

Three months of preparation already have solved most major

questions; today, we must fine-tune. Finally, Milt says: "Even at 8.5, we can increase student financial aid by redeploying existing funds." With that, the logjam is broken. We concur: the tuition increase will be 8.5 percent, which means about $600.

Our dilemma had been that Triezenberg wants more student financial aid monies because they assist with recruitment. The difficulty with increasing our financial aid budget through tuition is that we take from everyone to give to a few. That approach is appropriate and justified. But we have increased financial aid this way for four consecutive years. If we were to press this much further, tuition for everyone would become too high.

As I leave this critical meeting, a more mundane one awaits me. Jim Sampson, head of our campus store, has brought samples of our new class ring. Months ago, I sketched how I wanted the rings redesigned; today, I see the result. He says they are selling well.

Milt takes me aside. "Richard, we've gone over the Nursing School issue carefully. And we've concluded that it's doing okay and that we should appoint an acting dean for next year." I concur and ask him to proceed.

At four o'clock, the staff in the building—nine people—invite me upstairs for an anniversary celebration. Today marks my fourth year as president. I have told them not to make a fuss, and they do not.

When I reach the second floor, I wonder where the celebration is. Everything looks as usual. Then Bob Norris, a vice-provost, comes out with the cheapest champagne I have ever seen. Someone complains that our usual champagne glasses have been stolen. No great loss, however—they were plastic glasses with a stem. For substitutes, we use styrofoam cups. That is the extent of the refreshments. As I had said, make this unpretentious.

We stand bantering, with Norris pouring his cheap champagne, when a man comes up the steps. In a trench coat and floppy hat, puffing on a corncob pipe, he holds out a manila envelope. "I have a package for Dr. Berendzen." I rip it open, just as Norris and Greenberg shout: "Four more years!" The envelope contains a lawyer's letter threatening to sue the university on behalf of a student. What a way to begin my fifth year.

SATURDAY, JANUARY 14

I hug my family warmly, for I shall be gone a week. Poet Kahlil Gibran advised: "Let there be spaces in your togetherness." Maybe, but I shall miss them. And as I head to the airport, I wonder: will it be worth it?

I am met at the Newark airport and driven to Somerset, New Jersey, where I am to give the concluding talk at a meeting of the New Jersey State School Boards Association on means of implementing the national report's recommendations for achieving excellence in public schools. I am pleased to address this group because New Jersey is in the forefront of improving public education and because AU recruits heavily here. Despite sleet, the meeting is attended by several hundred volunteer school board members from across the state.

After a bad night's sleep, I feel dreadful today. Perhaps that is what makes me contentious. Whatever the reason, my remarks today bite. Unequivocally, I endorse the effort in New Jersey to permit people to become school teachers without taking traditional teacher training. How bizarre when a person can excel in history but be prohibited from teaching because he or she has not taken education courses. Yet someone who has had methods courses but scant preparation in history could be hired. That is wrong, and New Jersey may change the requirements.

Also, I boom that social promotions should be abolished everywhere, always. And I complain that too much of school bores students rather than educates them. We must increase the efficiency of school time. And then we must increase the *amount* of school time: from 180 days per school year to at least 220. Our current calendar was set during an agrarian society when parents wanted children's help during the summer harvest. To do so will cost in time and money. But education is not a purchase; it is an investment. And this investment is worth it. Most of all, I stress the need for parents to be involved, not by trying to be teachers but by being parents.

SUNDAY, JANUARY 15

My flight from Newark to San Francisco proceeds uneventfully, and I make my way on this chilly, drizzly Sunday afternoon to my hotel. After dinner in Chinatown, I stroll along Grant Avenue, looking in tourist shops. Incongruities abound. One quarter of the world's population is Chinese; the oldest continuous civilization is the Chinese. The Chinese, Japanese, Koreans, Vietnamese, and other Asians have faced colossal hardships. And, in this nation, the Asians have faced special problems; they truly have been aliens in a foreign land. Differing from Americans of European ancestry in appearance, language, customs, and religion, Asians in the U.S. were victims of discrimination for decades. Consider the detention of Japanese-Americans during World War II. Despite such obstacles, Asian-Americans today are the most financially successful minority group on the West Coast. How have they done it, especially facing such odds?

The answer, it seems to me, goes back to thousands of years of tradition, to respect of children for elders, to the benefits of close family ties, and to an unswerving work ethic. Americans who think our industry faces severe challenges from Asia should consider the educational challenge we face from the same region. Universities are reluctant to release data about student academic achievement broken down by ethnicity. But many universities know that their top academic ranks are filled disproportionately by Jewish and Asian students.

Still, if Asians are rising so rapidly, why does the U.S. continue to dominate the scientific and intellectual world? Why does the U.S. receive more Nobel Prizes than any other nation? If Asians truly are so brilliant, why do they not show it in achievement rather than test scores and class rank? Another incongruity.

Unless the U.S. improves its public schools, it no longer will maintain its preeminence in scholarship or professional achievement. The Nobel Prizes Americans win today are primarily for research conducted decades ago, often by immigrants who were educated elsewhere before coming to the U.S. The educational system of the nation is like a giant pyramid, with preschool and nursery school at the base and advanced postdoctoral studies at the pinnacle. For twenty years, the base has been deteriorating. So massive is the pile that the pinnacle has yet to feel the tremors. But it will. Before the edifice crumbles, we must build it up again, starting at the base.

Yesterday, following my address in New Jersey, someone in the audience asked: "I agree with your comments about families, but how are we going to get them more involved? Won't this be difficult in these relatively affluent times? How do you persuade children today that they need to work hard when they think success will be given to them?"

To that I replied: "You're touching on one of the anguishing issues of our time. Adversity seems to lead to strength, sometimes to genius. Historians have pondered but never answered why nations produce their greatest leaders during their most trying times. At no era did the U.S. need leadership more than at its beginning. And that is precisely when it had Jefferson, Franklin, and others of unparalleled talent. During the Civil War, the nation could have collapsed. But it survived and much credit should go to the extraordinary president at that critical time. Great Britain has had outstanding prime ministers, yet none better suited to his challenge than Winston Churchill. Bombs set London ablaze, but his voice gave his people courage and stole his enemy's victory."

Irrespective of the hardships many of our youth face, most middle-income youngsters nowadays do not encounter the adversities of the past. Perhaps things have become too soft. And so I suggested yesterday that we should overcome one of our nation's most difficult gaps, one even as bad as those of race, creed, and sex. Namely, we should endeavor to talk to each other over generations of time. I urged that children should talk more with their grandparents. If parents cannot instill personal challenge, perhaps grandparents who knew it well can. We all want the best for our children; ironically, though, it might be in their own best interest if they faced more challenges—like the ones their grandparents knew or their young Asian counterparts know today.

As I keep walking on Grant Street, I come to North Beach, once the hedonistic capital of the Barbary Coast. In the cold drizzle, it looks pathetic. Gawdy neon lights beckon, yet almost no one responds tonight. As I walk past the Condor Club, I notice a plaque similar to ones in the East on historic shrines. Another incongruity. But when I read the plaque, I discover this *is* a historical shrine: In 1963, this was the place that introduced topless dancing, followed in 1969 by bottomless. Millennia from now, an archaeologist, sifting through the rubble, may come across that plaque. Perhaps it will become our Stonehenge.

Back in my hotel, I stare across the city, watching the haze huddle about building tops. Under other conditions, this could be a romantic evening in a romantic city. Tonight, however, I am simply lonely and miss my family. I know I will do numerous radio and TV shows in San Francisco and Los Angeles and that I will meet many potential and current AU supporters. Still, why am I here? For that matter, why am I at AU?

I went to AU because I was attracted by the dream of a great national university in the capital city. And that is why I have stayed. But is the dream practical? Why devote my professional life to this singular pursuit? Is it that noble? Is it achievable?

Is My Armor Straight?

A thousand times before, these questions have gnawed at me, but never more painfully than tonight as I sit watching the rain so far from home. More than three quarters of AU's alums have graduated since 1960, so they are relatively new in their professional careers. Since AU's beginning, its endowment has been low. In the past three years, we have more than doubled it. But it still remains low. And, of course, we need a sports and convocation center, a performing arts facility, and more. Every institution has needs. But if I were president elsewhere, I would not have to build these basics.

And at a better known institution, I would benefit personally. Presidents of Ivy League universities automatically become important; presidents of major research universities routinely are invited onto corporate boards. They are worthy, even outstanding, or they would not hold those posts; nonetheless, they benefit from their title. Then, again, so do I. Perhaps I do not have the opportunities of some presidents, but I benefit from Washington.

Is it the haze or is my mind growing foggy tonight? I find it increasingly difficult to separate what is AU from what is me. There is nothing new in that; this ambiguity just has been increasing lately. Except for my family, I live for little else than the institution. No longer can I discern clearly my ambitions from the university's goals. No longer can I differentiate its success from my own, its shortcomings from my own. Somehow, at least in my own mind, the university and I are transforming into one another. Is that healthy?

I must maintain objective distance. I must know that the institution is bigger than I am and can survive with or without me. I must remember that it will go on for decades, centuries, after I am gone. And I must have a life beyond my job.

MONDAY, JANUARY 16
The haze has cleared; the temperature has risen. This evening, I am interviwed for an hour over KGO radio. One caller bitterly complains that although he has been a public school teacher for more than twenty years, his monthly income is only twenty-five hundred dollars. I assure him I understand his concern; salary scales for competent teachers should be raised to levels commensurate with other professions. But I also tell him that the discussion is returning to the wrong issue. For too long, most discussions of education centered on costs and benefits—the expenses born by taxpapers or students, the salaries

of instructors, and the job prospects for graduates. For too long, the cardinal concern was cost, not quality.

In March of 1983, the producer of the "Merv Griffin Show" invited me to be a guest. Then he asked, "What should we discuss?"

"Quality and standards," I said. "The nation's schools are falling apart."

"No," he replied. "Let's talk about costs. Who can afford an education?"

A month later, *A Nation at Risk* came out. Now, thank goodness, the emphasis has changed.

Later in the show tonight, another caller says that he considers a twenty-five hundred dollar per month salary to be attractive, especially when coupled with a lengthy summer break. Before school teachers can expect substantial pay increases, they must provide more convincing arguments than they have so far—not merely that their profession is poorly paid but also that if more money went into teachers' salaries, educational quality would rise. Intuitively, it seems it should. But the facts may not support this. For instance, the quality of instruction in many private schools is superior to that in public schools; yet, on average, private schools pay less.

TUESDAY, JANUARY 17

As I wait to do a morning TV show, I chat with the young Filipino producer. A proud mother, she boasts about how much her youngster already has learned and about how she and her husband have encouraged it. I tell her she is building the basis for lifelong education and there's no more vital time for doing so than in the preschool years. And I add: "Asians seem especially proficient in transmitting such education."

"Perhaps," she responds, "that's because we don't believe society owes us a living; whatever we have and achieve, we must make on our own. The way to do that is through education and work. We believe this as adults, and we teach it to our children."

The executive director of the Women's Sports Foundation meets me for lunch and we discuss ways her organization and my university can collaborate. I may be able to assist her with a major celebration in Washington to honor women. And after I tell her about our sports center effort, she asks, "Would you be interested in housing the Women's Sports Hall of Fame? We have the materials but no permanent home. Ideally, they should be displayed in Washington. Your facility might be perfect." Indeed it might be.

When I return to my room, a message awaits from Joan. A booker for ABC–TV's "Nightline" has called to find out if I can be on the program tonight. The topic: the controversy between a fundamentalist church school in Nebraska and the state because the school officials refuse to permit their teachers to be certified by the state. Nebraska law requires teachers to be certified.

I call the booker and state my position on the case. She says they would like me to be on. I am to be at the Los Angeles studio by eight o'clock. I get to L.A. on time and make it to my hotel minutes before ABC's limo arrives to whisk me to the North Hollywood studio. Some names spark imagination and fantasy: Paris, Rio, Broadway, Hollywood. Despite their magic, reality can be different from image. We whiz past tattered warehouses, peeling apartments, tacky stores. Hollywood's glamour lives, but not in these structures.

Once in the mammouth studio, sitting before a camera in a small office, in front of a cinderblock wall, I listen to the first three quarters of the show. During a commercial break, a voice says to me through the earphone: "Dr. Berendzen, I just wanted to say hello. I'm an AU alum." They are everywhere.

"What was your field?" I ask.

"Communications. And now I'm at ABC."

"Do you have an alumni pledge card yet?"

"No," he laughs. "But I bet I'll get one soon."

By now the show is back. In characteristic style, Ted Koppel has adroitly ferreted out all sides of the issue. Now, he turns to a conservative columnist and me for final, national perspectives about the case. I say the matter is fascinating and instructive but was unnecessary. Surely, ways could have been found for the state and church to work out their difficulties. But both sides are unyielding. The state argues, correctly in my view, that it has the right to require teacher certification. The church leaders assert that they answer to a higher law—that of God. Therefore, they are not required to comply with state law.

I respond that the state has the right, even the responsibility, to demand minimal proficiency for teachers. The state is not attempting to impose religious beliefs upon the church school; rather, the state —that is, the citizenry at large—is attempting to ensure that children are taught by qualified teachers. Earlier in the program, a church member said that they might decide to have a teacher who is not a college graduate, and they demand that right. What should society do if they hire as an instructor someone without even a high school education? Or someone who is devoutly religious but who cannot read or write?

Church supporters point out that children in the church school score as well or better, on average, than Nebraska children as a whole. But I retort that such equivalency measures will not do. For instance, suppose someone never attended medical school or even undergraduate college yet managed to pass, at a minimal level, an equivalency exam in medicine. Should such a person become a certified doctor? My time is brief so I limit my reply. Some forms of equivalency are appropriate. Genuine education, however, properly taught and properly learned, involves several ingredients. Generally, socialization through peer contact is a vital part of elementary and secondary education. Laboratories and homework assignments are, too. Class discussions and question–answer sessions form a part of the intangible educational process. Many benefits of formal, time-consuming education cannot be tested with any single diagnostic. Nor can these attributes be achieved promptly; they require years of subtle assimilation.

I worry that the Nebraska case may be a bellwether. The number of students going to private, church-related schools is increasing rapidly. So this case may be the first in a series. With that observation, the program ends.

Immediately, I call Gail, who has been watching it live. "What did you think?"

"It came off fine. It's just too bad you didn't have more time," she replies.

Because of the east-west time difference, I will be able to see myself on the show later tonight. She says: "Call me after you see it there."

"I'd like to, but it won't be over until very late your time."

"That's okay. In the old days, you called at all kinds of weird hours. And I loved it."

After I watch the show, I call Gail. In grogginess, she says: "It came off fine, don't you think?" My brief moments on this show hardly will make or break education or church-state relations. But I realize several things I wish I had said differently. I point this out to Gail, but she is not impressed. Either she is too kind or I am too critical. Anyway, we say goodnight. She goes to sleep and I go to a twenty-four-hour restaurant to have dinner. Due to the rush from San Francisco, I have not had time to eat.

Halfway through my chicken fried steak, a motorcycle gang arrives, joining the original odd crowd. A man in a corner talks to himself while a man at the counter puts a dozen spoonfuls of sugar in his coffee. A woman from the gang sits next to me. I am not totally stupid, so I rivet my eyes on my steak. Still, my peripheral vision catches a tattoo on her hand. I wonder what she thinks about deterioration of academic rigor. But I do not ask. This is not a fun crowd. Even though I dislike smoke, I do not murmur when she lights a cigar. I do decide to leave, however, before she uses my hand as an ashtray.

WEDNESDAY, JANUARY 18

This morning, I call the homes of several high school students in L.A. who have applied to AU. The admissions office has given me information about the most outstanding ones academically, and they do look strong.

For some reason, all the applicants are female. Boldly, I call the first number: "Hello, is Julie there?" After a long pause, a female voice replies: "No, she isn't. Who's calling?" Attempting to sound as professional and paternal as possible, I explain who I am and ask, "Are you her mother?" Indeed she is, and a protective one at that. After she finds out who I am, she sounds surprised and honored that I have called. We have a delightful chat about her daughter, AU, Washington, and universities in general. That theme holds with each family I call—until I reach a father. Are men more aggressive or is my sample size small? Whatever the case, he asks immediately: "Can she see you in person?"

Shortly before noon, I start my drive to the station from which Michael Jackson—the interviewer, not the singer—broadcasts his national radio program. With several million listeners, he has one of the largest audiences in the country. For almost an hour, he and I discuss academic standards. I maintain that some teachers are unqualified and should be urged out of teaching even though they have tenure. And I argue that we emphasize rote memory, dull facts, and obscure dates without stressing the fourth *R: reasoning*. At the end of the show, a caller from Oregon agrees. He suggests a place to save funds would be through greater efficiency in school administration. There are, he claims, too many administrators and staff members in public schools. Unfortunately, he is right. But more interesting than this is his underlying assumption: that much could be done to improve schools by redeploying existing funds rather than by expending new funds. He does not insist on the federal government or other tax-supported agencies providing vast resources. Most people want to add new monies first.

When I return to my hotel, several people have called me: a friend from London; NBC–TV about an interview; the White House; and the hotel manager sending greetings. The White House?

Thursday, January 19

This morning, in a rental car, I join the rush hour chaos driving from Westwood to downtown L.A. I am to attend a meeting at the Biltmore Hotel of the media commission on which I serve. One of L.A.'s venerable institutions, the Biltmore was famous decades ago, but the city expanded in other directions with new prestige hotels. I have never been to the Biltmore before, so I look for it while reading the map. A block away, I glimpse its sign; traffic is so heavy, though, that my glance is but a second long. As I drive into a parking garage, I think: My intuition about the Biltmore was wrong. It has maintained dignity and stature.

What had I seen that changed my mind? A fleeting sight triggered an ingrained response. As I approach the hotel, I realize what it was: a grand facade and a doorman in top hat. When I realize that just a glance at this made me question my preconceptions, I realize anew the importance of symbols. It is not for nothing that banks occupy stately buildings; that business executives wear "power suits"; that college catalogues show ivy-covered walls and chalk-covered professors.

I step out of the meeting to call the White House. The planning office there inquires about a person who recently joined AU as a research professor. The White House is interested in her studies on child abuse and pornography. And the Justice Department is awarding her a grant to continue her research. The White House wants to know if her research will be forthcoming.

Then I call Bob Norris, who oversees grants, and Anita Gottlieb, director of university relations. They tell me that this research project has become controversial. A congressional committee is investigating the grant-award process, and the press wants to know about that. How did we get into this?

Last summer, Jack Martin—editor of *Texas Business* and an NAB member—referred the woman to AU. And she told Norris and faculty members about her research and a forthcoming grant. The Justice Department told us that, because it wanted her studies performed, it would award us the grant once she was at AU. Occasionally, a researcher will come to a university with a possible grant and ask to be affiliated. The scholar needs the affiliation because—in addition to the colleagial interaction and library resources that it provides—funding agencies award grants to institutions, not to individuals. The university may benefit by overhead from the grant and visibility from the research. Everyone may win—provided the research is worthwhile and the grant is forthcoming. In this case, the research is explosive, yet it seems worthwhile. And the grant is coming. But so, too, is an investigation. I do not understand why. But Norris and Gottlieb are on top of the issue, so I relax—somewhat.

This afternoon, the freshman applicant whom I tried to contact yesterday and her father meet with me for forty-five minutes. A delightful pair, he listens while she asks a barrage of questions. I urge them to visit her first-choice universities. Although catalogues and brochures are informative, they are no substitute for being on campus. The student says she plans to visit AU in April. That is fine with us; April in Washington rivals April in Paris. The city turns into an extended garden and she will be able to see students and professors in action.

At sunset, I drive to famed Rodeo Drive for a special event. Between a Rolls and a Jaguar, I park my rented Ford Tempo. Luigi Leonardi, managing director of the Beverly Hills Gucci store and member of our NAB, is hosting a reception for me. Despite its glitter, the Rodeo Drive shopping strip is only a few hundred yards long. Still, it dazzles. And at its center is located the first, the largest, and perhaps the most impressive store of the group—Gucci.

Gucci glitters. The attentive staff has prepared everything with care, from guest register to harpist, from champagne to caviar. The reception is in the exclusive second floor Galleria, reached with special keys provided only to Gucci's premiere customers. In due course, guests arrive—business executives, the mayor of Beverly Hills, and others. It is a delightful evening, and I make at least one excellent contact for AU.

I thank Luigi and his staff and start to leave when a leather-bound sign catches my eye. It is a quote from Dr. Aldo Gucci in the year

I was born: "Quality is remembered long after the price is forgotten." An excellent motto for his store and for the rest of us.

FRIDAY, JANUARY 20

I visit UCLA on this warm, sunny day. If it is true, as I used to be told in Cambridge, that suffering is essential for the soul, UCLA just does not offer it. Where should Natasha go to college? Fortunately, I do not have to solve that multidimensional problem. Gail and I will make suggestions, but the decision will be hers.

But I do face a pressing question: Should I return to Washington tomorrow or Sunday? If tomorrow, I would have more time with my family and for clearing my desk before Monday. If Sunday, I could drive along the coast to San Diego. For twenty years I have planned to go there but have not made it yet. It is seventy-six degrees in San Diego, eleven degrees in Washington. After agonizing on this all day, I finally decide: I shall return tomorrow.

SATURDAY, JANUARY 21

I bump into three Washington friends on the plane. The man next to me overhears my name and says: "Excuse me, but did I hear you on the radio a couple of days ago?"

"Well, I was on some shows then."

He beams. "You were talking about education. I wondered what you thought about . . . " Over California and Arizona, I answer questions. Over New Mexico, we eat in silence. Over the midwest, the questions start again. By the time we reach Tennessee, he is out of questions and I am out of answers.

Once home, Gail, Natasha, and I have a joyful reunion. And I am brought up to date on critical news: the Volvo has got another problem and Natasha has to have braces.

After dinner, I go to my office to survey a week's mail. Joan has done a commendable job of sorting it, forwarding it, or burning it. Still, the stack remains high. Among the routine items, two stand out. Professor Jim Weaver, the chair of the university senate this year, urges that we reexamine AU's core curriculum, which is based on the theme "America in an Interdependent World." In 1976, when I became provost, I asked the university senate to come up with an appropriate core curriculum for the university at that time. After numerous meetings and months of debate, we agreed on the interdependent world theme. In so doing, we established a solid core program a year

or two before many other universities. Now Jim wants us to reconsider it. I agree.

Although another letter in the pile bears no name or address, its sentiments are unequivocal:

> Are you Russian? You look like one and talk like one .... You're either a Russian or are stupid or ignorant of what the state is doing to children and don't give a damn ....
> You're one of the problems in America.
>
> A Christian

MONDAY, JANUARY 23

Our budget meeting today is troubling. Preliminary registration figures for spring indicate two hundred thousand dollars less than we projected a month ago. This disturbs me because it reminds me how fragile and volatile our finances can be. A government agency may reduce tuition benefits for its employees. Enrollments from a foreign country in English-as-a-second-language may drop unexpectedly. A cold February, a broken steam line, a drop in off-campus enrollments —a hundred things could cause our income to fall. Therefore, we must build our reserves and remain vigilant.

TUESDAY, JANUARY 24

Two reporters interview me for a new AU publication, *The American Scene.* One asks: "As you conclude your fourth year as president, what have been your administration's greatest accomplishments and disappointments?"

As basic as that question is, I have not considered it before. After a moment's pause, I reply:

"For accomplishments:

"First, the marked increase in academic standards—admission requirements, core curriculum, grading practices, exit requirements.

"Second, vast improvements in AU's fiscal posture—increased reserves, endowment, fundraising.

"Third, the distinguished people who have joined the university family. These include new faculty and staff members, trustees, and advisory board members.

"And, fourth, the improved physical plant, with the Quad newly landscaped and energy conservation measures instituted.

"There have been other improvements. But the first three are vital

—academic quality, financial stability, and outstanding people. That's not a bad trilogy.

"On the disappointment side, these come to mind:

"First, I had hoped we would have a naming pledge for the sports center by now.

"Second, I hadn't anticipated the depth of the '82 recession, nor how severely the national economy would jolt the university.

"Third, I had hoped alumni and church contributions would be higher than they are."

Universities often rest upon a three-legged stool of support: the institution's founders; the local business and philanthropic community; the alums. The Methodist Church founded AU and has backed it loyally since. But the church provides only about $300,000 per year out of a $72 million budget. Washington, D.C., is friendly to the university, but it provides no financial support. And Washington traditionally has not been a business center. Moreover, many affluent people who move to Washington do not identify with the city. They grew up elsewhere, were educated elsewhere, intend to go elsewhere. And most AU alums are young. So this university does not have adequate backing from any of the three obvious support groups. That, I am convinced, will change.

WEDNESDAY, JANUARY 25

Milt, the Dons, the deans, and I meet to discuss the forthcoming accreditation visit. I ask them to think of possible chinks in our armor. Where are we weakest? Oddly, none of us can think of much that we have not already discussed at length. We conclude that we are as prepared as we can be.

Even though that is encouraging, the best part of the meeting is what I observe about Milt and the Dons: they are working together again as colleagues and friends.

Triezenberg and I have lunch in the faculty–staff dining room. When he was my assistant, I saw him frequently. Now that he is a line officer, our interactions are less frequent and more formal. I regret this because I enjoy and respect Don; indeed, for almost a decade I have relied on his judgment and insight. During the past few months, he has seemed uncharacteristically tired, even distraught. So I have asked him to lunch today.

His responsibilities are substantial. When he became vice-president, I put him in charge of admissions and financial aid in addition to

development, university relations, athletics, and the campus radio station. Basically, Triezenberg brings in the money; Myers oversees the
money and the physical plant; and Milt oversees the academics and
spends the money. If it all followed the plan, I would oversee everything and deal with the outside. That is how it works—sometimes.

Don and I have a good two-hour conversation, at the end of which
I urge him to call any time he feels beleaguered. Even though he says
he will, I know he will not. But I also know the areas under him are
excelling now, even if it is taking a toll on him.

Barrett Prettyman chairs an afternoon meeting of the trustees'
finance committee. The principal item on the agenda is next year's
budget. By now it has been so thoroughly discussed on campus and
with this committee that there is little left to say. Nonetheless, we
spend two hours saying it, largely because we want to be certain every
part of the budget is examined thoroughly.

Dinner tonight is informal: on trays in the family room while we
watch "M*A*S*H." Just as Radar O'Reilly is anticipating the colonel's next remark, our doorbell rings. It is a student.

"Dr. Berendzen," he says, "I'm sorry to bother you. But I'm an
Eagle reporter and we've just heard exciting news. Would you
confirm it? We hear that trustee Stuart Bernstein has announced that
groundbreaking for the sports center will occur in October."

Stunned, I stammer: "That's the first I've heard of that. Either
Mr. Bernstein is being misquoted or he knows something I don't
know. I'm sure he's being misquoted."

"Okay. I'm sorry to have bothered you. We just wanted to be
sure."

As I shut the door, the phone rings. It is Joan, calling from the
office. "Jill Dutt and an *Eagle* reporter have called. They're both
asking about a recent announcement by Stuart. The reporter would
appreciate your calling her."

I do call her, and she insists that Stuart told her there would be
a fall groundbreaking. I assure her I do not know about this, and I
try to call Stuart. He is not home. I call Triezenberg, explain the issue
to him, and ask him to call the *Eagle.* We do not need a premature
story. I believe strongly in stopping problems before they start.

Thursday, January 26
The congressional committee has asked us to send copies of our
faculty committee's minutes pertaining to the appointment of the

research professor. I ask Milt to consult with Tony Morella, university counsel. We want to cooperate with the committee. We also want to protect academic freedom and privacy. We shall ask for a written request. If they are serious about this, they will send it; meanwhile, we will do our homework.

When I return to my office, I receive a curious telephone message. A reporter for the law school student newspaper wants to know my position on campus recruiting by the Department of Defense. DOD, she says, discriminates against gays. Will we permit them to recruit here? Why do things like this come out of the blue?

My next meeting is as awkward as it is unusual. Last week, a dean took the extraordinary step of writing me, copy to Milt, asking me to overrule Milt's budget allocation for the dean next year. I told Milt I wanted to meet with the dean before making my decision. The dean carefully explains his position to me. He argues that if he is held to what Milt has allotted, the college will encounter significant problems. I ask questions and listen but remain noncommital. I tell him I shall send him a written reply next week.

From that meeting I dash to the Spring Valley shopping center where the university has a satellite office to be inaugurated tonight —the American Institute of Islamic Studies. In my brief remarks, I note that even though no region is more explosive than the Middle East, few Americans know much about the culture, heritage, or religious faith of the majority of its people. Although almost everyone at the ceremony comes from a Judeo–Christian heritage, we share an ancestry with Islam. For these reasons, I decided in the late seventies that AU should have a center of Islamic studies, which would be accessible to policy makers, journalists, and educators. After years of planning and preparation, the center opens tonight. Totally apolitical, its purpose is neither to criticize nor defend; it is to promote understanding.

From there I rush home to shave and change clothes before our next evening event. Gail's home functions usually are in the daytime for a female audience. But this one is in the evening and is for men and women. Tonight's will feature art professors Norma Broude and Mary Garrard. Their talk, illustrated with slides, presents a feminist perspective of art history. The audience, which packs our largest room, includes the Corcoran Gallery of Art's director and many other prominent art scholars and connoisseurs. Gail handles everything from arrangements to introductions. The professors point out that great male artists often have painted from a distinctly male perspective. Female paintings of the same subject were strikingly different. And male historians have omitted from textbooks important works by female artists. This informative talk impresses us all.

FRIDAY, JANUARY 27

Two years ago, I attended a dinner at the home of Charlie Rose, the TV host, where I met Jo Franklin-Trout. With an extraordinary knowledge of the Middle East, she was making a TV documentary about the Arab Gulf states. A few weeks ago, I saw an arresting TV program about Saudi Arabia. It ranged from footage of King Abdul Aziz turning the first oil spigot in Saudi Arabia to interviews with the nation's current leaders. The interviewer, her fair features contrasting sharply with her surroundings, was Jo. Today I have lunch with her to ask if she would be willing to have a private showing with Khashoggi as a special guest. She says she would be delighted.

And then I dig through the afternoon mail. Most of it is routine —interoffice memos, a complaint letter from a father about his son's bill, six research articles by a professor, a request from a journal to write a book review, an invitation to an astrophysics conference, a letter from a trustee urging that his friend's son be admitted to our law school, a prospective freshman's mother wanting to know about our computer facilities. One letter, however, screams out:

> Dear Dr. Berendzen:
> Would you be good enough to help me? Our problem concerns education at home—the subject of the recent TV "Nightline" program in which you participated. My wife and I are concerned that our grandchildren have been taken out of public school by our son and his wife and are studying at their home under a correspondence program, as described in the enclosure.

As I read the enclosure, I feel the poignancy of the grandfather's plight. The flyer begins:

> Our children belong to God, not to the state. [Education] does not belong in the unconstitutional tax-fed, socialistic, anti-God government schools.

It goes on to advise parents:

... don't worry about what your neighbors say if you keep the children out of the government schools. And don't worry about the government authorities. They can be dealt with from our home office, and in other ways as well, if necessary.

Plaintively, the grandfather asks:

As an educator, do you have any helpful comment in this situation?

I call the grandfather but no one answers. I shall try again next week.

SATURDAY, JANUARY 28

We rise early for this big day: Natasha is to take the SATs. As a twelve-year-old seventh grader, no one expects her to have covered much of the math on the test; the vocabulary may be beyond her, too. But Gail and I think the experience will be worthwhile. Even if she scores well, we doubt if we will put her in an accelerated program.

When we arrive at the test center, the handful of other seventh graders look alert and eager, even if nervous. The fathers, however, look like me—disheveled and unshaven. The kids may be bright, but the dads resemble winos. Gail and I watch our little girl take her place in the test room, clutching her pencils. Her wave says: "Couldn't you stay nearby in case I need you? And, leave at once so the other kids won't think I'm a baby."

After four hours, we return to pick her up. The first one out of the room, she gives me one of the hardest math questions. "Since I've never even seen such math before, I just skipped this one," she explains. "I figured at least I could copy the question." I could have done it easily when I was young—perhaps as a college freshman.

As important as the SATs are, for Natasha they are not today's big event. It comes tonight, when she attends a dance following a classmate's bar mitzvah. Gail and I drop her off. Natasha tells us sternly as she flees the car: "Do *not* come before eleven." Dutifully, we arrive at eleven o'clock, just in time to see the last dance. Room lights darkened, strobes flashing, "Thriller" pounding—in the center of the gyrating bodies is our daughter. Meanwhile, in a corner, a girl sobs, consoled by two other girls. Oh, the suffering one must endure at this age.

When Natasha and her girlfriend get into the car, Gail asks, "How was it?" Natasha replies almost inaudibly, "Okay," and rolls her eyes. Oh, God, not eyeball-rolling! We went through that with Debbie. And then it was accompanied by groans. A truly agile adolescent can slump, groan, and eyeball-roll simultaneously.

SUNDAY, JANUARY 29

At noon, I drive to Constitution Hall, near the White House. Today we hold winter commencement. In contrast with the spring commencements, in which each college is separate, this one is all-university. From noon until two o'clock, an alumni chapter hosts a reception in honor of our speaker, Paul Volcker. Then the AU Brass Ensemble plays a fanfare, the procession begins, and several thousand parents and friends rise and applaud in the cavernous hall.

Whereas many universities award degrees en masse, we have each graduate receive a diploma individually. The process today moves as usual, with one exception. As we are lining up to enter the hall, I overhear someone say that we have an unusual graduate today. It sounds like such a touching story that I ask for more information. As we enter the hall, someone whispers details to me.

As the degrees are being awarded, University Marshall Ruth Landman says, "Mary C. Rodriguez, Ph.D. in Sociology." I step to the mike. "Excuse me. I rarely interrupt the proceedings and numerous graduates have special circumstances. But this graduate is unique and I thought you'd like to know about her.

"She has founded and run three centers for financially disadvantaged mothers and their children. After that noble, lifelong career, she came to AU and today obtains her Ph.D. In itself, that's impressive but even more so when you consider that she's seventy-eight years old."

Warm applause I had fully expected. But the thunderous, standing ovation literally stops the show, raises goose bumps, brings tears. It is a moving moment. Dr. Rodriguez blushes and ducks her eyes.

The mood remains effervescent all afternoon. As students' names are called, family and friends whistle and clap. A young graduate's name is called and an entire section of the auditorium erupts with applause. Her glistening smile beaming back to her loved ones says it all: "I made it. We made it. Thank you."

Some graduates whisper to me as they cross, "You must be exhausted from handshaking." Actually, it is not my hand that gives out but my face. By now, I have learned how to cup my hand to avoid its being crushed. But each graduate is an individual, and families flock to the stage to take pictures. Even though hundreds may have crossed already and hundreds are yet to come, for a family there is but a singular graduate. And so I smile and say, "Congratulations," to each one. Being charming for a minute is trivial; doing it for an hour is tough.

My first experience with a commencement came when I was at Boston University and was asked to be a marshall. "What'll I have to do?" I wondered. I had never been to a college graduation, even my own.

"There's nothing to it," I was assured. "All you do is stand at the base of the stage to keep families from rushing the graduates."

What could be easier?, I thought. I stood at the base of the stage, assuming I had a non-job; surely no parent would rush the stage. The first graduate crossed uneventfully. And the second. And the third. But then—with hundreds yet to come—a mother tried to pass me.

"Excuse me, but no one is permitted to pass this point," I said.

"Who the hell are you?"

"I'm a marshall. And my responsibility is to ensure that people don't pass this point . . . ."

"Don't be stupid. And get out of my way," she snapped, pushing me aside.

For the next graduate, a mother and father simultaneously charged the stage. And so it went with the next family, too. At that point I decided my education had not produced a total dummy: I got out of the way and sat on the steps. After all, to many parents, what they see crossing the stage is not merely their beloved child but an anthropomorphic manifestation of forty thousand dollars of college costs. No wonder they cheer that it is over.

At the end of our ceremony, I compliment Landman on pronouncing all the graduates' names. AU used to have each student say his or her own name. But during the campus revolution era, some graduates would seize the mike and give an extemporaneous political speech. That problem ended a decade ago, but another one lingered —under the pressure of the moment, some graduates forgot their own names.

Such a reaction is hardly limited to students. I heard a story, perhaps apocryphal, that a woman riding alone in an elevator was startled when another passenger joined her. Staring in disbelief, she stammered: "Why . . . you're . . . you're . . . Robert Redford!" The actor grinned and said, "That's right, and who are you?" The woman, turning white, murmered: "I . . . I don't remember." To avoid this, our university marshall reads each graduate's name.

Tonight, three trustees—Cy Ansary, Joe Carlo, and Clarence Donohoe—join the university's officers in hosting dinner for the Middle States Accreditation team on this first day of their campus visit. After dinner, Cy and I welcome the team and offer whatever resources they need. I note that this accreditation review, like everything else at a university and in much of life, should be viewed as an educational experience. Of course we are concerned about accreditation; it is vital. But we also want to learn from the team. We look forward to their review.

MONDAY, JANUARY 30

Andy Sherman meets with me to make final plans for our educational forum on February 16th. From the Republicans we shall have Gary Jones, the deputy secretary of education. And from the Democrats we shall have education advisors for Hart, Hollings, Glenn, and Mondale. Andy will welcome the audience and I'll be the moderator. He has arranged everything, and I am impressed by how he approaches our meeting. If only all my meetings with adult professionals were so efficient.

At four o'clock, a large troupe assembles in my office. During the winter break, the university had splendid ambassadors in England— the AU Singers. They received such rave reviews that I have invited them to tell me about their tour.

What a charming group they are. On occasions like this I remember anew that undergrads are young, wide-eyed, and eager to experience life. I also realize that to them the presidency of their university is special. Some may complain about whoever has the top title, but most hold that position, if not the individual filling it, in high esteem. The singers enter my office staring at our pictures of U.S. presidents who have spoken at AU. One student blushes as she shakes my hand and another looks skyward and grins as we pass. To me, I am plain old Richard Berendzen, the fellow who got in trouble sleeping in his faculty office and who blew up his parents' sidewalk as a child. My face is just more leathery. But that is not how some students see me. To them, I realize again today, I am their president. And in person, I am real rather than a picture in a catalog.

I realized this when I assumed this post. I retained the small office I had had as provost. Walls covered with books, astronomical photographs, and Middle Eastern art objects, it is distinctly my room. Private and quiet, it is where I do my reading, writing, and thinking. But I also acquired the president's office, AU's version of the Oval Office. I had it redecorated in a stately, traditional style matching the building's architecture and the university's heritage. The walls are covered with photos from AU's past. Berendzen the individual is not there at all.

The students join me in the president's office. After a few moments of nervousness, they open up. We laugh and discuss experiences in England. After forty-five minutes, I thank them for coming, commend them for their fine performances, and ask if they will sing for me. And that they do, with impressive style. Unrehearsed and scattered around me on chairs, they create a stereophonic harmony rivaling the best choirs I have heard.

So euphoric am I when they conclude that I burst out: "That was great. Will you sing at our next trustees' meeting?" Need I have asked? They squeal and shout: "You bet!"

Tonight I drive to Howard University's impressive TV studio, where I am to tape "America's Black Forum," hosted by Julian Bond, the civil rights leader and Georgia state senator. Before the taping, I am introduced to the other guest—Mary Hatwood Futrell, new president of the National Education Association. She is soft-spoken, in contrast with the hard-hitting image she projects.

Julian tapes a segment with Mary alone. It goes extremely well, largely because they are so articulate. He has good, prepared questions, with even better impromptu ones. She answers him directly, evading nothing and pounding home facts and opinions. Despite my preconceptions about her and the NEA, I disagree with nothing she says except her assertion that funding for public schools should come equally from local, state, and federal sources—a third each. In the U.S., public schools always have been locally controlled and financed. And that is as it should be.

Julian asks me to join them for the second segment, in which he asks me about the administration's recent report on violence in schools: "How bad is violence and is this something that should be of major concern to the American people?"

"The president's recent comments about discipline hit a vital theme," I reply. "You can't have high-quality education without a proper setting. Before you can teach, you must have a semblance of order. For too long, the White House, news media, parents, and society in general ignored this serious issue. In that sense, the president's comments were well made.

"But the recent report by the National Institute of Education about violence seems to be based on out-of-date or faulty information. Violence in schools peaked years ago; the serious problems decried in the government report might have been appropriate then, but not today. Schools nationwide have cracked down, and most report marked improvement.

"There is another meaning to the word *discipline*. And it should be stressed by the president and by everyone else. The term can apply to your major field or to how you conduct your personal life, marshal your resources, utilize your time. In that context, stress on discipline never goes out of date; it needs to be emphasized today more than ever. In fact, the word originally referred to education."

Out of the corner of my eye, I see Mary nodding. Later, Julian asks me: "How do you feel about the home study programs?"

"Like so many other things, they can be good or bad," I answer. "Whichever, we have almost no way to evaluate them or establish standards. Interaction of one child with another cannot be duplicated at home. Nor can one single teacher—mother or father—bring the diversity of scores of teachers in school. A child should encounter variations in personality, perspective, and style."

Again, Mary nods.

As the show ends, we exclaim: "What a shame there wasn't more time. We could've gone on another hour." And that we could. Never have I enjoyed an interview more. The host, the other guest, and the topic itself were hot this evening.

TUESDAY, JANUARY 31
Finally, I reach the grandfather who wrote. We have a lengthy conversation. His options are few, but I offer to help if I can, perhaps with referrals. He thanks me profusely.

And I write my decision to the dean, copy to Milt: I am going to uphold Milt's decision and disapprove the dean's appeal. Finally, I turn to reading. I try to read an hour or two per day, but recently I have fallen behind. So tonight I read for almost six.

WEDNESDAY, FEBRUARY 1
The accreditation team has completed its campus review and meets with Milt, the Dons, and me to give its oral report. Eggers begins by

noting much about AU that impressed the team. And then, as is obligatory in such reviews, he recites weaknesses. None of these surprises us. Although the group is noncommittal, we gather that we will receive reaccreditation without caveats. And I will always remember one team member's comment: "AU is awesome."

My lunch is with Lalo Valdez and Jack Martin. Jack invites me to write a column for *Texas Business* and to attend a business conference in Texas. To get money out of that state borders on impossible. But it is worth a try.

A cancellation gives me an unexpected free hour. Mail should be read; letters should be written. But I remember that the university senate will vote this afternoon on an emotional issue—whether to exclude students from the senate. This academic policy body then would become a faculty senate rather than a faculty-student senate. The faculty want a pristine body, as it used to be here and is today at most universities. I reason that the senate, like most deliberative bodies, must be off schedule. If so, it will get to the key vote just as I arrive. Sure enough, it does.

It has been a long time since I last attended a senate meeting; the provost does regularly. Nothing much has changed, however. What I hear upon entering is: "Is that a friendly amendment?" That is what the senate was doing when I last attended. If it is possible to raise a point of order or introduce an amendment, someone will. In this most political city, both professors and students are master tacticians. In such debates, substance yields to procedure. But the senate does sharpen perspectives and produce good ideas.

Today the faculty remain silent as students decry an all-faculty body. One male student, wearing a short pigtail, asserts: "For a liberal group, your action isn't very liberal." The vote falls along divisional lines. The faculty win easily.

Two decades ago, academic policy bodies were composed exclusively of faculty. In the sixties, a more egalitarian perspective seemed appropriate. AU tried tripartite governance: management shared by administrators, faculty, and students. In the seventies, administrators left the senate; recently, it has been composed of faculty and students. Today, that changes.

This change probably will not affect academic policy, but it will change students' perceptions of campus governance. At AU they have participated more than at most universities. I expect this will continue. I hope so, for they can assume responsibilities and offer worthwhile suggestions. When I arrived at AU, I was surprised to find the extent of student participation in governance. Initially, I thought it inappropriate. But over the years I observed students in action. Some were Machiavellian—but so too were some professors and administrators. Some were incompetent—but so too were some adults. Logically, faculty and administrators should set academic policy, cognizant of students' views. On balance, I have mixed feelings about today's vote.

THURSDAY, FEBRUARY 2

Until three years ago, AU did not have a donors' club. So I founded the President's Circle, with minimum dues of one thousand dollars per year. Tonight I host a dinner at the Mayflower Hotel to thank circle members.

We give an annual award to someone who has supported the university over the years. Tonight, it goes to Dorothy Gondos Beers, professor emerita of history. For twenty-seven years, she was dean of women and a distinguished teacher-scholar. A beloved member of our university family, her former students include Ansary, Bernstein, Ron Nessen (the former White House press secretary), and many others.

After the dinner, a line forms at the coat room. Another function has let out and its guests come for coats, too. A large man with a ruddy complexion, puffing a cigar, edges to the counter—Tip O'Neill. As he stands looking the other way, a man says to me: "Hi, Mr. President." O'Neill's head shoots up, his shoulders straighten, and he whirls around. Sorry, Mr. Speaker, it is the wrong president.

When we arrive home, I read today's *Post*. A report on Black History Month cites the father of black history, Carter G. Woodson: "You don't have time to waste. Work hard and aim high." A line to quote and to live.

SUNDAY, FEBRUARY 5

Two years ago, Gail and I, waiting to board the New York shuttle, noticed a student and mother reading an AU brochure. I introduced myself and asked if I could help them. Surprised, they asked a torrent of questions. At the end, the mother said, "My daughter and I know the university much better having met you and your wife. I'm far more interested than I was before." Neither of us had attempted to sell AU; rather, we had answered questions, calmed fears, and, most of all, humanized the institution. Normally, admissions involves forms, catalogs, and entrance exams. If talking with a senior official was important to this family, might it be to others?

When prospective students and parents come to campus, they are impressed. Student Life arranges a lively program and Milt, the deans, and I talk to the visitors. If this works when they come to us, why not go to them? Admissions officers routinely visit high schools and admission fairs. But last year I proposed sending top administrators to recruit. No one objected: they understood how vital enrollments are. Triezenberg organized our first such "road show"; for a week, I led deans and admissions officers to key recruiting areas. The acceptances by students who attended were substantially higher than our overall pool and their academic averages were higher, too.

Today, we launch our second annual road show. First stop is suburban Philadelphia. Unfortunately, Frank Turaj—the gregarious, irreverent dean of arts and sciences—is ill. Parents and students enjoy him, and we had hoped he would be the first speaker. Frank Jordan, dean of communications and former Washington bureau chief of NBC news, speaks first instead. He launches the program with wit. Bill Peters, Dorothy James (dean of government and public administration), and Bob Cleary follow him. Then Admissions Director Maury O'Connell introduces me, and I talk about public school education. I stress the importance of parents. Two-thirds of my audience are parents, and I want them to know we hope they will remain involved. Then I recite the unparalleled resources of Washington. We have students in internships and cooperative education placements at the Congress, the AFL-CIO, the State Department, the World Bank, the White House. They can obtain an education that prepares them to make a living and lead a life, one that is theoretical and practical, abstract and applied. We take students to the city through internships and bring the city to students through adjunct faculty.

To conclude, I speak personally to students, then parents. To students I say: "Your private reasons for higher education may differ from your public ones. Some of you want to determine who you are in a complex world; how you fit into the sweep of time. Others want to obtain a high-paying job. Others are looking for a mate. Some merely want to get away from home. These motivations are traditional, historic, appropriate. But if you also hope that you can party incessantly, then don't apply to AU. You won't be right for us and we won't be right for you.

"On the other hand, if you would enjoy a campus that resembles a New England college yet is fifteen minutes from the Kennedy Center, then AU might be for you. You should visit us to get a feel for the university; each one is different. At ours, average class size is about sixteen students; only a handful of courses have more than eighty. We are heterogeneous; almost every major ethnic, religious, and political group is represented. If you would benefit from such an environment, then AU might be right for you."

To the parents I say: "At the beginning of my remarks I said that insufficient parental involvement was key to the deterioration in public school education. That is not the case here tonight. Even in a cold drizzle, you came out. Don't stop there. Visit our campus with your son or daughter. This meeting is designed for students, but it's for you as well; you are part of our extended family."

After I speak, Maury and I take questions. Two of them focus on SATs. High school grades and class rank are our primary admissions criteria. They indicate how the student did in dozens of courses over several years; they include evaluations of homework, papers, and tests. By themselves, however, they're inadequate. High school grade inflation has been so rampant that a *B* no longer has much standing. And some students take more challenging courses than others; some have more rigorous teachers than others. To put all seniors on the same basis, we need nationally standardized tests. The admissions office exists to admit, not to exclude. Its task is to determine who is qualified for admission. To admit a student whose file looks weak might please mom, dad, and student at first—but ultimately the student may suffer. Many people wonder why universities use SAT's at all. The main reason is that the scores correlate with students' grades at the end of the first college year; they predict freshman success.

The entourage leaves for our next stop, an inn in central New Jersey. Tomorrow, I will continue on to New York and Long Island, while the others visit New Jersey high schools. In wet snow I pass through Trenton. A large sign proclaims: "Trenton makes. The world takes." It scans well, but the "takes" disturbs me. How about: "Trenton builds; the world buys." As I approach New Brunswick, my car cuts through sleet while the radio reverberates with baroque music. For an hour, I'm bathed in Bach. How did Bach come to be? Or Beethoven—with one parent a TB victim, the other a syphilitic, and his older siblings born ill, malformed, or dead. Did he have strong parental influence? Good schools? Incongruities again.

Our New Jersey meeting goes smoothly with dozens of families talking with each of us. They're not here for data, though. They came to sense the institution. Who makes it work? Who guides it?

Back in my room, I watch a TV tribute to Buddy Holly, the rock singer, on an anniversary of his death. His music transcended his brief life. Perhaps it's only those things that capture the moment and freeze time that truly count—a photograph, a book, a record, a motion picture. Holly's "Peggy Sue" reminds me of my rock-and-roll days. Always too bowlegged to wear jeans, I wore khakis instead. But I did have a navy peajacket and ducktail haircut. For three excruciating months, my parents stared in disbelief. For me, that era ended quickly.

Then I think of current fads; they change but never fade. And so it goes with educational criticism. At every epoch people have claimed that education then was inferior to the past. This has happened every ten to twenty years for generations. Many students today have learned less than they could or should. But with Buddy Holly on my mind, my ducktail becomes more real. I remember how much we *actually* studied then. And I remember fights in school. Have things deteriorated so much? Yes, the evidence is clear: There *has been* a major educational decline. We must tighten the system, raise expectations, provide adequate funding. That's my public posture, but my private one is less resolute. What was *I* like as a twelfth grader?

MONDAY, FEBRUARY 6
When I became president, I introduced the concept of "institutional advancement" at AU. By this, I meant the mobilization of everyone to achieve common objectives. I wanted us to mesh the efforts of many offices—admissions, alumni affairs, academic affairs, the president. On this trip, we do.

Our reception today is in Westbury, Long Island. Jordan starts the evening. He says that he arrived early to visit the field from which Lindbergh flew to Paris. Jordan was born the day Lindbergh took off. But he had never visited the site and this was a good opportunity. "So I found the exact spot from which Lindbergh took off," Frank says. "It's now the lingerie department at Macy's." When I speak, I say: "I was intrigued by Dean Jordan's attempt to explain why people saw him in the lingerie department. You gentle Long Islanders believed him; we jaded Washingtonians look for truth behind the truth."

After the reception, I go to the parking lot to get my rental car. I walk up to a red sedan and insert the key, but it won't turn. This isn't my car. Worse yet, a woman is huddled by the far door. I smile at her through the window. "Sorry to scare you. You see, I have a rental car. . . ." She will not look at me and I doubt that she believes me.

Back in my hotel, I read today's *Post.* A front-page story describes the growing dispute over scholarships based on academic merit. Reporter Larry Feinberg quotes me: "There's a shrinking pool and enormous emphasis on quality." Consequently, the cream of the crop are in demand. Although a bidding war is unseemly, college costs have become so high and the number of academically outstanding students has become so small that merit scholarships can determine where a student will go. Many colleges have courted athletes that way for years. Athletes, however, presumably pay for themselves by attracting other students and fans. Although academically strong students may not do the same, they give the institution a positive image.

But scholarship funds are limited. Most of them come from the federal government, and that money cannot be used for no-need awards; hence, the university must use its own funds. The demands are great already, especially from financially disadvantaged students. Conflicts need not arise, however, if the portion of student financial aid devoted to academic no-need scholarships remains modest; if the portion becomes high, equity questions arise.

At one in the morning, I am lonesome and call Gail. "I'm glad you called," she says. "I started to call you but decided to wait until morning. Debbie called from Dallas to tell us she was robbed."

"Not again. Her apartment was broken into last year."

"This one's worse. She and a friend had just parked their car when a young man maced her companion and pointed a gun at her. He took her wallet and fled. He was extremely nervous, which is what frightened her."

Feeling nauseous, I slump to the sofa. How easily the gun could have gone off. All the caring, all the love, snuffed out in a second. For fifteen dollars. Why? Gail brings me back: "Debbie said don't worry. She's safe, even if shaken."

TUESDAY, FEBRUARY 7

For two hours I creep along the Long Island Expressway to midtown Manhattan's Algonquin Hotel, once the famed meeting place for literati. How can a radio program nowadays originate from a hotel suite? Easy—the interviewer and I sit in the bedroom while the technician sits in the living room. A pounding jackhammer interrupts us. The technician shouts: "Hey. We're taping a radio show. Stop that. Who's your boss?" The worker shouts back. The noise subsides and we finish taping. Ah, New York.

After the interview, I try calling Deborah but miss her. From the Algonquin, I make my way through Manhattan to Tarrytown, where the deans and I will host high school guidance counselors. Along the way, especially in context of Deborah's robbery, I am drawn to the South Bronx. It is only a few blocks out of my way, and I have not been there in years. It seems to be improving. Still, its need jolts me. It is probably unwise to drive through the area, but I am traveling at high speed in a locked car in the daytime. Politicians have not solved the South Bronx dilemma; will anyone? Is it soluble?

My speeches about improving education focus on college-level and college-preparatory programs. But what of the South Bronx? Think of the anguish a parent here must feel. And the frustration a child must feel. How can he or she realistically hope—not to get ahead—but to catch up? Can education help break the cycle of poverty and hopelessness?

Forty counselors attend our luncheon. I discuss public school education as well as AU. And I urge them not to send us students who are less than serious. Some of the counselors seem startled—first to encounter this entourage and then to hear about *not* sending students to AU. But they understand the message.

When I arrive at my Manhattan hotel, I finally reach Deborah. She is okay. Then I call home. "Natasha, a celebration is being held tonight in New York for Michael Jackson."

"Fantastic! He's wonderful. Can you get me his autograph?" I once read in a psychology book that at the age when girls begin to notice males, a ruggedly masculine one would threaten them. So they prefer performers who are male and different from themselves yet have characteristics with which they are familiar. Whatever the general explanation, Jackson's talent and respectability warrant attention.

The deans and I host a reception at the New York Athletic Club for New York area alums. At least a hundred attend, arriving only moments before several hundred parents and prospective students appear. For an hour, alums, deans, admissions staff, and I mingle with parents and students. Most questions I get reflect nervousness over admissions, for AU is getting known for being more selective.

Deftly, Maury O'Connell begins the program. The deans are funny and factual, and then it is my turn. This is my favorite type of audience—large in number, well educated, deeply interested in the subject. They hang on every word, laughing at every humorous nuance. And during serious comments, some parents take notes. The eyes are with me all the way.

Afterwards, we are surrounded by inquisitive parents and students. In contrast with past years, not one family indicates that it is still shopping; they all say AU is their first choice. Triezenberg has come for this large gathering. After the guests leave, he gives me the latest news: freshman applications are 40 percent higher than a year ago. And that was a banner year.

WEDNESDAY, FEBRUARY 8

Bleary-eyed, I ride an early shuttle back to Washington. I have been gone only two days and I have handled as much incoming material as possible by phone; yet my desk is covered. A trustee complains that a friend of his did not get a campus job even though he referred him to us. And a church newsletter says that AU will ignore the sanctity of Holy Saturday, between Good Friday and Easter, by permitting students to hold a rock concert then. In fact, the students hold a concert on an April Saturday each year. Planning months in advance, the student organizers failed to notice that the day this year fell just before Easter. The performers cannot come on another day and the students cannot find a backup group for a different date. For many students, the concert is a major event, the social closing of the school year. But we realize the religious significance of that weekend. How do we solve this dilemma?

Vice-Provost for Student Life Bruce Poynter, Greenberg, and I have decided that the concert can proceed, but we insist that the volume be kept moderate. Our audio technicians can measure that. The students will have a satisfactory concert, although a slightly subdued one, and the neighbors will have a peaceful holiday. At least that is how it should work.

At three o'clock the trustee executive committee proceeds through a heavy agenda. Cy chairs the meeting well; the spirit is positive. Everything goes smoothly until we reach the issue of the sports center. Bender stresses that the trustees—individually and collectively—must shoulder more responsibility. Everyone agrees, but several trustees are feeling pressured. Even though they are devoted and will give, we are pushing fundraising vigorously. Sondra is right, of course, that trustees must lead. Two cardinal support groups for any university are trustees and alums. Both must lead or no one else may follow.

Soon we come to a list of potential recipients of honorary degrees that the deans have suggested for their individual commencements, partly as a way to thank illustrious commencement speakers. After a good discussion, the committee approves recipients for May. Then I raise a question. "Given 1984's emphasis on quality in education and AU's role as a national university, how about our recognizing an outstanding teacher or principal?" The trustees agree that such an award would be appropriate and they urge us to find good candidates.

After the meeting, Cy and a few others join me privately to discuss how to structure full board meetings to make them more stimulating for trustees. The board's load is so great and its meeting time so limited that we must proceed methodically, following Roberts' Rules. This precludes informal roundtable discussion. Hence, trustees may not feel involved personally, even though they want to participate and help. They do not want to be figureheads; nor do they want to intrude into administration.

By now it is almost seven o'clock and Gail calls to remind me that we are due downtown at once. I rush home, shave, chat with Natasha, and then speed to a reception in honor of John Wallach's new TV series about public people in private places. He takes me aside to tell me how we can secure a foundation grant. As Gail and I leave, the Caspar Weinbergers arrive. He asks: "How are things at the university?"

"Remarkably good. If DOD needs a loan, perhaps we can work out something." He laughs and says, "Well, I guess not."

Truth is, I wish we could receive a fraction of the cost overrun on a single weapons system. All of us look to the defense budget with envy. If it went down, my budget would not go up, and the nation needs a strong defense. Still, is there not a way a sports center in Washington could help protect the republic?

THURSDAY, FEBRUARY 9
How do you pack for Boston and Miami simultaneously? Wearing winter clothes and carrying summer ones, I fly this morning from

Washington to Boston. A cab takes me through the tunnel, alongside the Charles River, down Beacon Street, across Commonwealth Avenue, to the Prudential Center. A short but scenic drive, it triggers overwhelming *déjà vu*. As an undergraduate, graduate student, and then professor, I lived here longer than in any other place. And never have I experienced any locale more than Boston. By myself and later with Gail, I explored all of downtown, street by street, building by building. Socrates said of Athens: "It is not I but the city that teaches." With that precept in mind, I arrived as a student fully intending to learn from all available resources, in class and out. And, I assumed, Boston would be a fine teacher. So it was.

From the North End to the Isabella Stewart Gardner Museum, from the Boston Public Garden to the bandshell, we explored it. And we did so at every hour, from before dawn to past midnight. We had spring picnics in bucolic Mount Auburn Cemetery; watched fishing boats return on early Friday mornings; toured a bakery at three o'clock in the morning. Now my responsibilities preclude such adventures. Still, any complex, cosmopolitan city beckons to me. Tourist sights should be seen, of course. But more than that, how does the city work? In my white-collar world, there are no barges or vegetable trucks; in the real world, achievements of hands are as vital as achievements of mind. Sometimes I fantasize about becoming a carpenter. Then, at the end of the day, the new door might be crooked, but, by God, it would be mine—a clear, tangible result of my effort in contrast with the murky, drawn-out response to my meetings and memos.

Basically, jobs deal with ideas, people, or things. As a professor, my world centered on *ideas* and *people.* As an administrator, it centers on *people,* then *ideas.* The significant enterprise of *things* rarely arose when I was a professor; now, it does as I am an administrator. While I was a student, I attempted to savor them all—ideas, people, and things.

The Prudential Center and its surroundings have become an impressive complex. When I arrived as a student, this area was a train yard, blighted and sooty. As I walk today past modern midtown Boston, I realize that none of this existed when I arrived twenty-five years ago. How can I reminisce about a city a quarter of a century ago? Have I become old enough to talk about "how it used to be"?

After checking into my hotel, I walk across Copley Plaza to historic Trinity Church. Quiet and empty on this cold winter afternoon, I find it today as I remember it—stately and peaceful. With no appointments until evening, I sit for an hour alone with my thoughts. Thick stone walls muffle city sounds. My mind rushes back to another time I sat alone in this church as a young undergraduate far from home. And I think of all that came to me in this city, from education and experience to Gail and Natasha. From there I stroll along Newbury Street, looking at the boutiques. Around every corner I see a twenty-year-old student with a thick Texas accent. Or young Debbie chasing pigeons. It borders on sensory overload.

As I walk up the Boston Public Library's marble steps, I remember my first visit. Awed, I explored every public room; on warm spring days, I would sit beside the courtyard fountain. And I read the names chiseled in the facade. From centuries, even millennia ago, they show the effect a single person can have. What special talents did these people possess? What did it take for them to contribute beyond their own lifetimes? Such questions puzzled me then, challenge me now.

Back in my hotel, I call Joan and try to handle the afternoon mail by phone. Then I take a cab to the archetypal academic club—the Harvard Club of Boston. Our function tonight will be held in its spectacular Harvard Hall, with paneled lower walls and stone upper walls laden with heavy tapestries and a massive pipe organ. Truly baronial, the building projects the Harvard image of influence and accomplishment.

Boston alums arrive for a reception, followed by a meeting of several hundred prospective students and parents. This group's response to our presentation is overwhelmingly positive.

Afterwards, I take in a Boston specialty—a seafood restaurant. From all the offerings—cod to swordfish—I select scrod. And it reminds me of the story of a man who had never been to Boston but loved seafood. He arrived at Logan Airport with only three hours until his connecting flight. As he hopped into a cab, he said: "I don't have much time, but I'd like to get scrod." To which the cabbie replied: "I'm asked that all the time, but never before in the past-perfect subjunctive."

FRIDAY, FEBRUARY 10

At the reception last night, Jordan joked about Boston's peculiar accent. As he pointed out, there are strong bonds between Boston and the rest of the nation but common language is not one of them. When

I arrived here from Texas, I could not understand Bostonians. And they could not understand me. Even at my extreme, though, I never sounded the way some Texas males do, singing out in alto: "Why, hi there, Billy Bob and Bobby Ray." How such a high pitch can emanate from burly, Stetson-wearing he-men, I never understood. Perhaps their shorts are tight.

But how do you explain Bostonians? Everyone knows that you can achieve a rough approximation of their language by making vowels hard and dropping *r's* after them. "I paked my ca in Havad yad." What few recognize, however, is that a true New Englander, being a frugal person, conserves those *r's* and sticks them into words that end in vowels. Remember John Kennedy's lilt: "I have an idear about Cubar."

Another Boston curiosity is its driving. In the airport shop I even notice a book explaining the idiosyncratic local driving habits. Only in Boston have I seen cars triple-parked in front of a fire hydrant. And where else in the U.S. do you have to look both ways before crossing a one-way street? Left turns from right lanes are routine; Boston is so notorious for jaywalking that New York cops have been known to shout at pedestrians, "Hey, Boston, get back on the curb."

Most newcomers to Boston are either terrified or mystified by the driving. But I figured it out. As selfish and unpredictable as the driving appears, it is based on mutual rationality; that is, a driver may be rude but he assumes other drivers will react logically. When a driver turns right from the left lane, he assumes the right lane driver, whom he has just squeezed into the curb, will curse but stop. What would happen, I wondered as a student, if you violated that basic premise?

I tested my hypothesis rigorously—during rush hour traffic at the entrance to Callahan Tunnel. There, numerous lanes funnel into two. Engineers could devise a better road system or drivers could cooperate with each other, but that would ruin the fun. In Boston, the person gets through first who has the oldest car or is the least concerned about bent fenders. Each driver knows the rules: stare dead ahead, pretending you see no one to your side. Then, with peripheral vision, watch the distance between your car and adjacent cars as you squeeze into the precious two lanes. The trick is to pretend you do not see the other cars or that you do not care if yours is hit. Even though every driver does this, ultimately someone gives in.

One fateful day I approached the tunnel, determined to try my ploy of apparent irrationality. As only an undergraduate might do, I disheveled my hair, pulled my glasses to the tip of my nose, talked conspicuously to myself, and looked maniacal. Like magic, drivers on both sides stopped and let me pass as if I had a siren.

If Boston's driving borders on the barbaric, other aspects of the city approach nobility. Countless hard-pressed people have found a home and success here. Tony Morella, for instance, son of Boston immigrant laborers, worked his way through college, became a lawyer, aided Judge Sirica during his Watergate deliberations, and now serves as AU's general counsel.

And today's newspaper describes how the Bank of Boston is commemorating its two-hundredth anniversary—by giving a $1.5 million endowment to the Boston public schools. To add even more class to this contribution, the bank does not put its name on the bequest, thereby making it possible for other organizations to contribute, too. If public schools are to meet our expectations, we must establish stronger bonds between them and business, universities, news media, government, and families. The Bank of Boston is setting a fine example of such a partnership.

In three hours the plane takes me from Boston, where it is twelve degrees, to Miami, where it is seventy-seven. I arrive at my hotel just before our luncheon begins for area high school counselors. After lunch, Maury introduces me and I give the only talk. The audience nods enthusiastically as I pound on the need for increased classroom rigor, greater parental involvement, and restoration of the true meaning of discipline—the setting of priorities, the prudent use of time and resources, and the ability to say no to yourself and to others.

SATURDAY, FEBRUARY 11

It hits again tonight, but worse than usual: insomnia. After reading and writing in my room until two o'clock in the morning, I toss and turn until four. I dress and wander the empty lobby, listening to my footsteps echo. Back in my room, in desperation, I watch the only thing on TV at this hour: "The Three Stooges." What is a university president doing in Miami watching this infantile program? By now my stomach is churning, but I have no food bars. Room service and the coffee shop do not open for an hour and a half. I wait. After breakfast I stagger to bed, set the alarm for eleven and at last fall asleep.

I awaken refreshed. While I dress, I think about a TV interview

I saw hours earlier. The guest: Mohammed Ali. Last Father's Day, he came to our home. We wanted to show him Washington, but what is available on Sunday night? He had seen the monuments, and the buildings were shut. Gail and I hit upon taking this champion of fighting to a great symbol of peace. We went on a private tour of the Washington Cathedral. This imposing structure inspires all who see it, Ali being no exception. A religious man, he seemed more at home there than in the ring. He gawked at the vaulted ceilings and massive pillars. A friend with Ali told me privately, "If the Champ could preach here, he'd be more thrilled than when he won the heavyweight crown."

Ali impressed Natasha. His boxing ability did not do so. She had never seen him box; she detests boxing anyway. What she liked were the magic tricks he did for her. Neither his athletic ability nor his verses won her; it was his quiet charm.

Our afternoon meeting with parents and prospective students from South Florida goes well. When it is my turn to speak, I ask if the audience knows about oxymorons. That's when you use two words together that individually mean the opposite, like "jumbo shrimp." Some people would include "airline food," "dormitory living," and "military intelligence." Others might add "Washington wisdom." Calvin Coolidge gave fine examples of the latter, one of which I repeat. When asked why unemployment was high, he replied: "Because so many people don't have jobs." Despite Coolidge, I tell them, Washington has much wisdom to teach and AU draws upon it fully.

In the question-and-answer session that follows, a mother says: "AU sounds like the place for my daughter. Something bothers me, though. I don't want to be impolite, but why do some friends tell me that AU is a party school?"

In the uncomfortable silence, I respond: "That's a fair question. Let me answer it candidly. The image you mention arose primarily because AU, like many other universities, expanded too quickly in the sixties and early seventies. It has always had good programs, good students, good faculty, and good alums. Nonetheless, for some years it expanded rapidly in quantity but not quality. About fifteen years ago, despite AU's strengths in many areas, it got a party reputation.

"In some respects, this was unfair. In others, it was valid: admission standards had dropped, classroom rigor had slackened, a party atmosphere had risen. AU was not alone in this; similar problems afflicted numerous universities. Irrespective of what happened with others, however, AU's task has been to put its own house in order. And that it has done dramatically.

"AU today scarcely resembles AU five years ago, much less ten years ago. Its SATs are up dramatically; it has a new university library; student class time has increased 25 percent; honors programs, a core curriculum, and cooperative education have been introduced; competency-based math and English requirements have been imposed. AU's transformation has been fast and deep. Many of its programs rank among the nation's best. New outstanding professors have joined the faculty. No student I have met nowadays considers it a party school.

"Unfortunately, images linger long after reality changes. That happens with individuals, universities, even nations. A university's image, good or bad, can last for years, even decades. At AU, reality changed years ago, continues to do so now, and will in the future. And the image began to change years ago in the eyes of those who know us best: well-informed counselors, program evaluators, and employers. In time, everyone will know the new AU. Our task is to accelerate that process."

As I wait for my plane, I read two disturbing newspaper articles. One reports a recent finding that incidences of cancer can be lowered by eating less red meat and more high-fiber foods—turnips, broccoli, brussels sprouts. What a world. To avoid cancer, I should eat less of what I enjoy and more of what I detest. Already, I have cut down on sodium, sugar, and caffeine. I eat no desserts and try to avoid additives. But turnips? That is too much.

The other article is more disturbing. It lists characteristics of a person headed towards "burnout": long work hours, propensity to take on too much, little exercise or vacation time, all-consuming focus on your job. And the symptoms of burnout? The feeling that what you do has little consequence. Insomnia. Melancholy. Disillusionment with your achievements and even your professional goals. This seems familiar. How to avoid this? Relax. Get away from the job. Increase exercise and idle time. Talk and laugh more with friends and family. Focus on things other than job and career.

Before becoming too concerned, I realize I have few symptoms and none continuously. Such generic descriptions can sound like anyone's situation. So it is that astrology columns seem plausible to many people. If things are stated broadly enough and the reader is susceptible enough, he will see himself in it. I shall remember the article, but it is nothing for me to worry about. Still, I long to have time to do nothing—just to sleep or read or walk. And why do I keep asking myself if what I do is worthwhile?

MONDAY, FEBRUARY 13

An alum writes, disagreeing with the position I took on ABC–TV's "Nightline." He says no AU faculty member is required by a state or the District of Columbia to be certified. And he says that if such certification were required, academics would fight it on grounds of academic freedom. I write back:

> The American University, like all accredited institutions of higher learning, is reviewed by an accreditation association. This body—composed of peers from other institutions of higher education—carefully reviews our curriculum, teaching resources, library holdings, finances, physical plant, and professors' qualifications. If we did not pass inspection, we would be denied accreditation, which would be tantamount to shutting us. In addition, several departments and programs are reviewed by professional accreditation associations—in clinical psychology, law, communications, chemistry, and so on.
>
> The Nebraska case resembles medical situations in which parents argue, on religious grounds, that their child must not receive medical care even though doctors argue that without it the child may die. The parents say they answer to religious law and the state cannot impose its authority over their freedom with their children. Such cases usually go to court, and invariably, the court rules in favor of the medical authorities. Education cases may follow a similar track.

And the mail brings for adjudication two controversial faculty personnel actions. Milt has ruled against the faculty members, but they have appealed to the faculty grievance committee. Now the matters come to me. Both affected parties are represented by lawyers; unless I rule in their favor, the cases will go to court. Although I am inclined to support the provost, I take my appellate responsibility seriously. Just to read the voluminous files will take hours; both cases raise fundamental issues that are important to the individuals and to the university. Here go my evenings for two weeks.

This afternoon, Milt and I visit the new microcomputer lab in the department of math, statistics, and computer science. Each terminal can do in an hour what my computer took weeks to achieve when I was a graduate student. We listen as a student demonstrates a program he has written. We frown ponderously, suggesting critical attention to every word he says. In truth, the computer revolution came after our school days; like many adults, the most profound thing we can say is, "Un huh. How long did it take you to do that?"

When I was preparing my Ph.D. thesis, I did my data analysis on the Harvard computer. One night I finished a lengthy program. Repeatedly, Gail and I checked it; it was completely debugged. At four o'clock in the morning, I submitted boxes of cards, carefully ordered, for the fateful run. That afternoon I went to pick up the printout. It was not there. Panicked that a careless computer operator had lost my invaluable cards, I rushed to the desk.

"Oh, yes. We made a run for Berendzen. The printout wouldn't fit with the other runs, so we put it against the wall." There it was— boxes upon boxes, floor to ceiling. My "flawless" program had contained an error that led to a feedback loop; worse, my cards had not instructed that if such a loop occurred, the run should stop. And so the computer, running at an odd hour with scant supervision, ground on until the stock of paper was exhausted. I was embarrassed and disappointed. I lugged the printout away, and for years we used it for scribble paper.

As I watch the demonstrations today, I remember this experience, smile, and keep the story to myself.

TUESDAY, FEBRUARY 14

After a lengthy meeting with my cabinet, I come out to find a bouquet of red flowers awaiting me. Gail has sent them for Valentine's Day. What a lovely touch. Before having a chance to admire them, I notice the top item in my mail: the latest enrollment report. Freshman applications are up 4 percent from last year. Only 4 percent? I thought we were far ahead of that. And graduate applications are down 24 percent. How can this be?

Shut in my study, I pour over the figures, hands trembling. Are our applications softening? What of our optimistic projections? I call Maury O'Connell, but he is out of town; I call Triezenberg, but he is downtown. Aside from enrollments, this is Valentine's Day. I call to thank Gail for the flowers, but she is not home. "Please tell her I enjoyed the red roses," I tell the housekeeper.

This afternoon Gail calls to say the flowers are carnations. They are? I did not look carefully. She thinks this is funny. Certainly I know the difference between roses and carnations; carnations are what boys used to wear to school proms. Besides, I am preoccupied with enrollment data. I tell Milt I am extremely concerned. In two weeks I have a meeting scheduled with deans, professors, and others to review graduate enrollments. He will meet with the deans before then. I ask him to stress the importance of improving our data.

Finally, I reach Triezenberg. He assures me that several hundred more freshman applications have arrived since the computer run was made. Our freshman tally is 15 percent ahead of last year, thereby cushioning declines in other areas. That is great, I tell him, but it does not remove my anxieties. I have heard that freshman applications may be up 5 to 10 percent at other private universities. Our 15 percent is exceptionally high. But if they are all up, then either freshman enrollments will decline in state schools or students now are shopping more than in the past. Perhaps they are searching for the best package of scholarships and loans.

We will not have reliable data on transfers until the summer; they usually do not apply until late in the spring. Our transfer enrollment has declined for the past few years, and it could happen again; also, our summer and nondegree enrollments have decreased in recent years. We will not have data on them for several months. Therefore, we may be seeing the best side of the story first—the one about freshmen. To come out well in the fall, we must work vigorously in all areas and build up a substantial lead with freshmen.

The latest enrollment figures also indicate trends that are simultaneously encouraging and disturbing. Applications are up in some humanities programs while down in some professional programs. Perhaps student interests are moving away from strictly job-related studies. If so, that trend is encouraging for the nation. But it is disturbing for the university if it occurs precipitously; then, the university will have to redeploy resources promptly. Will we ever sail calmly?

WEDNESDAY, FEBRUARY 15

I write to everyone who oversees a critical office involved with student recruitment or retention, urging them to be especially vigilant in spotting even slight indicators of enrollment trends, positive or negative. We need better intelligence gathering. If students become disillusioned with dorm life, we should know before there is a mass exodus. If federal agencies cut back tuition benefits for government employees, we should find out before they transfer or drop out. I spread the word that I personally shall spearhead investigations of our forthcoming summer and fall enrollments. In a well-ordered world, that should spark efforts down the line; in the real world, most people will not know or care. But it is worth a try.

Tonight a large group assembles in the School for International Service building. I am to speak on international education as part of an ITT lecture series. After a student introduces me, I begin by reminding this sophisticated audience of how truly interdependent the world has become. Even though everyone knows that the world economy is interlocked, I cite statistics to drive this point home: 40 percent of all U.S. farmland raises crops sold abroad. One U.S. industrial worker out of six produces items sold abroad. And I close with a highly personalized perspective, one coming uniquely from my field of astronomy.

"As seen from the astronomer's orbiting satellite, no geopolitical boundaries are visible. From this vantage point, we do not see the multicolored map of politics, history, or tradition; instead, we see a shared globe of finite and limited resources. And when the astronomer looks outward rather than downward, earth becomes simply planet number three, truly the blue marble in a black eternal night, orbiting a typical star on the periphery of an unexceptional galaxy in an ordinary part of the cosmos. In a universe dotted with more astronomical objects than there are grains of sand on earth, our minuscule planet shrinks almost to nothingness. Yet it remains our home—our origin and our future, our cradle and our grave. Delicate, fragile, irreplaceable—the earth may be small in the grander scheme of things, but it is all we have.

"And one harsh prospect comes joltingly to mind as I consider it from an astronomer's perspective: either we shall learn how to live together on this planet or surely we shall die together on this planet. No single enterprise—whether foreign policy or global education—can ensure international understanding and peace. But in so far as the exchange of peoples and ideas contributes to this, then the true meaning and cardinal value of global education becomes clear."

As I walk home in the cold drizzle, I pass a student. "Hi, Dr. Berendzen," he greets me wistfully.

"How are you doing?"

"Not so good. I just lost an election."

Light from a street lamp glistens on tears welling in his eyes. I turn up my raincoat's collar as we stand in the chill.

"Was it an important race for you?"

"I guess so. Anyway, I just heard about losing. And I'm really upset. How can I tell my parents?"

Before I can reply, he goes on. "There may be a benefit to this. Maybe now I can get an internship or a job doing the same kind of thing."

"Exactly," I respond. "If you had won, you would have little to add to your résumé; this way, you can start building a career."

"I know. I keep reminding myself. But it really hurts . . . "

He cannot go on. Tears come too fast. His voice quakes. I do not want to embarrass him, even in private on this barren sidewalk. No one else sees him. But he knows I do. So I avert my eyes, put my hand on his arm, and say: "After you walk alone awhile, call your parents. They'll understand. Things like this happen to everyone. They happened to Lincoln. To Kennedy. If I might intrude into such company, they happened to me, too. It hurts like hell at first. You feel that friends let you down or strangers misjudged you. And it gives little comfort to remember that in any race someone must lose. But the pain will leave. Your career is unharmed; your reputation is intact; your life will go on."

"Thanks, Dr. Berendzen. Maybe I'll do that. Good night."

I watch as he walks into the haze. And then I continue home.

Natasha asks me what I spoke about tonight, and I give her and Gail a summary, ending with the observation, "My remarks seemed to go over okay, although I probably spoke too long."

"Daddy, you always speak too long."

"That's not true. I watch the audiences carefully, and they always seem . . . "

"I don't care how they seem to you. You are caught up in what you are saying. Everyone—as you always tell me—enjoys hearing himself speak. You do, too."

"Natasha, that's unfair, because you often hear me."

"And that's another thing. You repeat yourself. Let me give you an example."

"You needn't do that. You don't understand that each audience is different, each is fresh. None has heard me before, and I don't repeat the same speech. I combine parts from many preceding speeches and always try to work in new material."

"Sure, they're not all alike. But your word patterns repeat. Do you realize the peculiar way you form sentences? And how you pronounce certain words?"

At this point, mother, the referee, steps in: "That's enough. Natasha, help set the table." After Natasha leaves the room, I shrug and say to Gail: "Are my speeches actually too long? And do I have a peculiar, repetitive style?"

Gail raises her chin but not her voice. "Richard, don't you realize how Natasha idolizes you? She hangs on your every word, memorizes your speeches and articles. Of course, she knows everything you've said. She's that impressed; she loves you that much. She just feels awkward and doesn't know how else to say it."

Oh.

THURSDAY, FEBRUARY 16

A week ago we called a major donor's office and asked for him to call back. He has not done so. Did he get the message? Is he just busy? Or is he disinterested? And what should I do?

If he were the only one, I would be puzzled but patient. As it is, he is more the norm than the exception. Why do so many benefactors act this way? If they are disinterested, why don't they just say so? Even if disappointed, I would understand. Or at least I would know where we stood. Many of them play a cat-and-mouse game—baiting me one day, avoiding me the next.

Our educational forum featuring representatives of the presidential candidates is well attended by representatives for Cranston, Glenn, Hart, McGovern, Mondale, and Reagan. The Hollings aide became ill at the last minute, and the Askew and Jackson offices did not respond to Andy Sherman's letter. The campus and community representation is less satisfying. In a hall that seats hundreds, a few dozen gather. Where are the shouting throngs from two years ago, when headlines told of student financial aid cuts?

Andy opens the program and introduces me; I introduce the speakers and explain the format. Each Democrat is allotted five minutes, followed by the undersecretary of education, representing Reagan, who is allotted ten minutes because he is the only Republican.

Is My Armor Straight?

For the next fifteen minutes, panelists will question one another. Then I shall question them all before opening to questions from the floor. Deadlines for speeches resemble offers in bazaars—rough indicators. The only Democrat to stay within the allotted time is Hart's spokeswoman. Glenn's spokesman fires out concrete proposals, then ends: "Any Democrat would be better than Reagan, who's an educational disaster." Mondale's adds colorful hyperbole: "If Reagan is reelected, in his second term he'll do to schools, teachers, and students what Khomeini did to women in Iran."

After an hour, I ask all panelists the same question: "Mary Futrell, head of the National Education Association—the nation's largest teachers' organization and second largest union—recently said the funding mix for public education should change. At present, about 92 percent of the funding comes from local and state sources; about 8 percent comes from the federal government. She said the ideal mix would be a third, a third, a third. What do you think?"

Reagan's spokesman replies: "There's no such thing as different taxpayers. The funds ultimately come from the same person, just through different tax means. I oppose her suggestion."

Mondale's says: "We might not be able to move immediately to what she suggests, but it sets the ideal. It's a goal we'd work towards."

Then I ask another question: "In a week, all eyes will be on a small New England state. Just for fun, consider some educational statistics about that paradoxical place. Of the fifty states, New Hampshire ranks fiftieth in state tax support for public schools. The average salaries of its public school teachers rank forty-eighth. However, its students' average scores on nationally standardized tests rank at the top. How would your candidates interpret these divergent facts?"

Rarely have I heard more stammering. The first panelists are not sure what to say. Finally, McGovern's spokesman says education would be improved if "Reagan's waste of money on weapons of murder were diverted to improving the lives of children." Mondale's jokes: "Mr. Mondale has deep respect for the people of New Hampshire. It wouldn't surprise him that their children have good test scores."

Obviously, such generic data are difficult to explain. I had thought, however, that this would be an ideal vehicle for the panelists. New Hampshire benefits from having a close family structure, well-educated parents, tightly-knit schools, low violence, small average class size, and a strong sense of community. No one should conclude, of course, that board scores will rise if teachers' salaries fall. But advocates of higher teachers' salaries will have to find other data to show that by paying teachers more, students will perform better. The entry-level salary for many teaching jobs should be higher, and many current teachers should be paid more. Teaching should be transformed into a genuine profession. But aside from money, it needs dignity and support. The former comes from a societal view that education is imperative and teachers are vital; the latter comes from the local community, especially the parents.

As I drive downtown, I am proud of my adopted city. Always a great city, Washington now is becoming a grand one; the sleepy southern town of 1960 has emerged as a world metropolis. It boasts the highest concentration of almost everything to be found anywhere. The greatest density of museums in the world is here. This is the news capital of the world. Almost every nation is represented here along with almost every major U.S. corporation. The wealth and diversity of Washington's arts rival New York's. In sheer majesty, Washington is America's London.

As I rejoice over Washington's wonders, I pass a street person huddled on a sidewalk grate for warmth. With all his belongings in a pushcart, he looks at me as I wait at a stoplight. But he stares past me, focusing on nothing, his eyes as empty as his hope. Why does the nation's capital have such people? Can they not find shelter? Many of them belong in mental institutions. Sociologists say some of them refuse city shelters, preferring freedom in the streets. Aside from where they might go, where did they come from? What went wrong?

My first encounter with such people came when I moved to Boston. If they were in Dallas, I had never seen them. But in the Boston Common, there were hundreds. I was so intrigued by them that, being young and impetuous, I decided to join them for a night. What would I learn? I left my watch at home and took but two dollars with me. Wearing my oldest clothes, I spread newspapers on the ground for a bed, just as my compatriots did. For hours I lay in the dark, listening to them talk and cough. At first, I thought the coughs came from tobacco; then, more sobering possibilities occurred to me. By 3 A.M., with theater patrons long gone and only an occasional policeman in sight, I realized the adventure I had expected involved a hard bed, covered with dew, surrounded by strange and potentially dangerous companions. As the sun rose, I had had enough. In the distance, I heard men shouting over remaining drops in a whiskey bottle. A man glared at me. He knew I was not one of them. I did not look the part, as disheveled as I had attempted to make myself. My hands were too smooth; my shoes too polished; my hair too neat; my clothes too clean.

Quickly, I crept from the park, walked to my car, and drove to the safety, warmth, and comfort of home. Never have I bathed more thoroughly. Never have I enjoyed scrambled eggs more. For me, it was an experience, creating a lifetime memory. For them, it was simply a lifetime, with no memory.

This afternoon, I am interviewed by phone on a radio show in Atlanta. A caller says she used "to teach in the nineteen hundred and thirties." The problem with schools today, she asserts, is that "God isn't in them anymore." The interviewer asks me what I think.

"Whether or not you explicitly have God in the classroom is irrelevant to the key educational issues today—how to improve quality and maintain equity. I'm not so interested in whether children pray in school as I am in whether they read, write, and think in school —and out of school."

Then the interviewer says: "Home study programs are becoming controversial in this area. What do you think about them?"

"They're a reaction by some parents to the failings of the schools. Rather than improve the schools, they give up on them. Still others want a strong religious orientation in their children's education. Why they can't achieve that sufficiently in church and at home, I don't know. But for them, home study programs seem desirable.

"In certain instances, such as for physically impaired persons who can't get to school, such programs are essential. In the main, however, they're dangerous. The child is deprived of the diversity in a public school—laboratories and libraries, field trips and sporting events, school dances and debate teams, and a heterogeneous student body.

"In the nation's early days, education, especially in rural areas, was conducted at home. Then, as the nation progressed, parents toiled to build one-room schools. Eventually, they became our modern public school system. Instead of preparing for the next century, advocates of home study want to return education to where it was a century or two ago."

Next week's mail will explode.

Over dinner, Gail, Natasha, and I have a tense convesation. For days, Natasha has awaited her report card. It arrived today. Overall, her grades are fine. But several teachers repeat the same theme: she should be more careful. Without comment, we give her the card. She ducks her head and reads it. I ask, "What do you think?"

"My grades are good. But I guess I don't check my work enough."

Gail—master mother and talented teacher—points out: "You are in an unusual situation, Natasha. You are bright enough to get outstanding grades almost without effort; when you do try, they are superlative. But you don't always review what you've done. You'd enjoy school more if you'd slow down and be more careful."

Sensing that even so gentle an admonition can traumatize a sensitive twelve-year-old, I add: "We all get careless sometimes, Natasha. Did I tell you about the time I took a physics exam in college and came out with the constant of gravity having different values? As you know, there is only one constant of gravity. But each time I calculated it, I got a different value. So I wrote that, 'the constant of gravity is a variable constant.'

"My professor kept me after class, showed me my statement, and growled, 'What the hell is a *variable constant?*' "

Natasha giggles. As I am about to start reading, Gail says, "Here is today's mail. One is from Frank and Bethine Church. It's rather sad."

Only weeks ago, Frank discovered that he has terminal cancer. Last week Gail sent him a stuffed bear wearing an AU T-shirt. We hoped it might cheer him. He and Bethine have sent us a thank-you card. And they have sent much more. He writes: "I hope you are having a good day sitting in the sun together, looking at the wonders of the world. Your days together are precious." For them, there may not be many more. The rest of us take such moments, such small things, for granted. In their quiet way, the Churches remind us not to do so.

My mind floats back a couple of years ago to one of our faculty stars, Ben Chertok. An internationally renowned physicist, he was engaged in pioneering research on nuclear structure. On leave that semester, Ben was working in Geneva. One evening, he felt ill. The doctor urged Ben to return to Washington for exploratory surgery. He did, and the doctors discovered advanced stages of cancer. Within weeks this charming, brilliant young man decayed before our eyes. I went to the hospital to see him, an experience I shall never forget. I knew his room number, but where was Ben? From a form I would never have recognized came a voice I knew—Ben's. My friend talked softly about the university, physics, his family. He had no pity for himself, only thanks for my having come and best wishes for us all. The next day he was gone. A noble, brave, and brilliant man, his memory will be part of AU always.

His death stunned me. Why him—so talented, caring, young? I anguished for him and his family. And although it seemed selfish, I worried for myself and my loved ones. Ben's mortality and my own suddenly loomed large.

I remember, too, a few years ago when a rash mysteriously appeared on my face. After trying home remedies, I saw a dermatologist. He examined me thoroughly and said he wanted to take a plug from my cheek. He explained that he didn't want to alarm me, but my symptoms resembled those of lupus, which could be serious. Even though he urged me not to be concerned until the tests were back, I rushed to my medical encyclopedias, which described two forms of lupus: "The nose may be wholly eaten away . . . [which] gives the countenance a horrible appearance" and "fever and anemia and a progressive course make the disease fatal." Sobered and sickened, I shared the information with no one but Gail. A few days later, the lab studies returned: benign. My rash soon left as mysteriously as it had come, and it has never returned.

A similar jolt came a few years ago with Gail, when, during a routine examination, her doctor noticed a lump. That it existed at all disturbed us; that the doctor insisted that it be removed immediately traumatized us. I took her to the hospital. We kissed and touched hands as they wheeled her down the hallway and through the swinging doors. For an eternity, I waited alone in her room. Finally, the doctor entered: "It's benign."

A few months later I came home to a grim-faced wife. "The doctor found another lump and it should be removed." And so the process went once more: The early morning. The long wait. The agonizing stay by myself until the doctor appeared. And again, that wonderful word: benign.

More than a year went by. Then, one afternoon, Gail called. The way she said, "Hello," told me something was wrong. Soon her words told me as well: "The doctor found still another lump. I'm to go in next week." As in sleepwalk, we retraced our steps. Was it an eerie dream? No, it was as real as the crunch of our shoes in the morning frost, the clang of the steel hospital bed against the doorway. Finally, the doctor came: benign.

Each time, a cloud lifted, the sun shone, our spirits soared. Each time, we were reminded anew of the fragility of the body and the blessing, not just of life, but of the life we share.

SATURDAY, FEBRUARY 18
The phone rings. I turn to answer it, but Gail says: "Don't bother. It'll be for Natasha." Sure enough, it is.

At least 90 percent of our calls these days are for her. How can she and her friends talk so much? A year ago, she never talked on the phone; now, she does constantly. A phone receiver has become an appendage, as much a part of her head as her nose.

Both Natasha and I agree to sacrifice today for the sake of family. She puts down her phone and I stop my sleeping so we can accompany Gail to a shop where she will select a gown for a special dinner. She is so frugal about herself that I have had to urge her to buy a dress even for this occasion. After all, we are not invited to a White House state dinner every day. Stern critics, Natasha and I veto the first three gowns Gail tries. The fourth one we like.

With that done, we return home, Natasha works on her term paper about Martin Luther, and I start to leave for my office when the phone rings. It is for Gail. I wish she would keep me better informed about what is she is doing. But, given that I am in my office at all hours and consumed in my own things even when I am home, how is she to do that? This afternoon, I discover that Professor Sally Smith, who heads the Lab School for learning-disabled children, asked Gail if she could help secure a prominent Washington woman to chair the school's benefit this year. Sally wants to have Susan Baker, wife of James Baker of the White House. Gail called Susan yesterday and she accepted. Today, Gail gives Sally the good news. It is a fleeting conversation, as I go out the door. But it reminds me of how many ways Gail aids me and AU.

After days of fog, the temperature has risen, the moisture has left. On this springlike day, springlike activities emerge. Students toss a frisbee in front of the library. A group plays croquet on the Quad. And a young couple cuddles on a park bench with the boy's arm around the girl's shoulder. Little do they suspect why I smile in passing.

On one of my first dates as a teenager, I took a girl to a movie. In the darkened theater, I mustered nerve for the big move. I went into such a spasm of yawning that the girl must have thought I was stricken by sleeping sickness. She didn't know this was part of my plot. After five minutes of yawning, I stretched my legs. Then I stretched my arms in an upward V-formation. Ever so slowly, I let my left arm fall to the back of her seat. Patience, I had been told, was a virtue. So, with the speed of a glacier or a nervous but determined adolescent, my left hand crept towards its quary. Previews of coming attractions flashed on the screen. A cartoon went by. The newsreel ended. We were well into the main feature before my arm curled around her shoulder and my hand fell down her side.

Can my heart actually stop beating? I wondered, for I was sure mine had. I knew my breathing had stopped. I could scarcely believe it, but somehow my left hand had fallen on her soft bare skin. I was touching her breast!

How many pulse points does a person have? All of mine pounded like jackhammers. My temples throbbed. My glasses fogged. I did not bother to remove them, for I did not want to disturb the moment. Maybe she had not noticed my hand. But how could that be? If I could feel her, surely she could feel me. Yet she did not move. Could this mean she liked it? The more I considered the possibility, the blinder I became; my fogged glasses became opaque. I fought to keep my breathing from becoming too noisy, as I stretched one leg, then the other.

Then, with cunning and daring, I began to stroke and massage the flesh beneath my fingers. I wanted to turn to see if her glasses were fogged, too. But I was hesitant. Besides, I could see nothing anyway. Finally, she broke the mood.

"Stop that! For ten minutes you've gone crazy rubbing my elbow. You're making it sore. Move your arm. And go get us popcorn."

The popcorn was cold, salty, and soggy. But no more than I was.

TUESDAY, FEBRUARY 21

As I pack to leave once again, the telephone rings.

"The chief and I want to say hello from Brunei."

It scarcely surprises me that they call from Adnan's yacht half a planet away in the obscure nation of Brunei. What would surprise me would be if they called from a bus depot in Cleveland.

Several months ago, Adnan told me he was going to meet with the sultan of Brunei when the nation officially received independence from England. Only a sliver on the coast of Borneo, Brunei may be the least known nation to Americans. Yet it is worth knowing. Small in area and population while rich in oil, it has the highest average per-capita income in the world.

When I was in Kuala Lumpur a few years ago, I heard through diplomatic channels that when Brunei achieved independence, it might seek middle-management training programs. I wrote to the sultan, suggesting that AU could provide such services. But I never received a reply. When Adnan told me he would be meeting with the sultan, I wrote the sultan again and asked Adnan to hand-deliver my letter. Today, Shaheen says he has done so and the sultan is receptive.

After I hang up with Bob, I catch a flight to Colorado. Out of my plane's window, I see the cities and farms of Indiana and Missouri. Then we pass over snow-covered prairies with desolate roads comprising interlocking grids. Scattered homes and farms look like bubbles on a pond—small, fragile, and inconsequential compared with the nature around them. Yet it was in land such as this that Mondale just won his Iowa victory. Could that have been his first step to Pennsylvania Avenue?

Not so much the jewel of the Rockies as the queen of the prairie, Denver is situated at the western edge of the great expanse. How much have I changed since my first trip here? As a research assistant at the Smithsonian Astrophysical Observatory in Cambridge, I was sent to obtain upper-atmospheric data from a research center in Boulder. That was my first business trip.

Don Hoagland—prominent Denver attorney, father of an AU student, and new AU trustee—meets me at the airport. He fills me in about the group I shall address tonight at the Mile High Club. One hundred fifty of Denver's elite gather in black tie and gowns for a gracious dinner. Surrounded by "birds in art," the dinner's ambience is as appealing as its cuisine. I would have preferred speaking about education in general or AU in particular, topics that might have been more beneficial to us. But astronomy is what I was asked to discuss. So I do.

WEDNESDAY, FEBRUARY 22
After taping a radio program on educational standards, I take a cab to the Denver Art Museum from which I can walk back to my hotel. The stroll takes me from the fortresslike museum to a classical park, with the Civic Center on one side and the State Capitol on the other. My attention, however, is diverted by the snarls of a half dozen vagrants. Past them, glittering new business towers loom upward, man-made rivals to the Rockies behind. At the geometric if not philosophic center of all this sits a ragged quartet.

One man yanks a beer can from another. He stuffs it into his bag and pulls the top tight.

"Why do you want those old bottles and cans?" barks the man who just lost his can.

"When I get enough of 'em," the man with the bag explains, "I can sell 'em. It's the only way I've got to make money. There ain't no jobs."

Behind me sits the finest art museum for hundreds of miles. To either side, monuments of government. Dead ahead, gleaming office towers. All about me, statues and benches. And then these men. Another incongruity.

As I walk Denver's glass and steel canyons, I realize that most of these buildings were not here on my first visit. The same is true in San Francisco, Dallas, Atlanta. Most of the towers in our cities' cores were built in just the past two decades. How much was created in such a short time. And during the same period our society at last began to put many things right: civil rights, women's rights, human rights. What a glorious twenty years.

Or was it? That was the same era during which public schools deteriorated, the economy collapsed, and family ties weakened. Twenty years ago, Denver's residents didn't have these buildings—nor did many of them lock home doors at night. Twenty years ago, Denver was not a national center for energy and airlines—nor did a yellow-orange haze engulf it.

Does cause and effect hold here? If we had focused less on erecting new towers and more on improving minds, would our system be better? I doubt it. Just the opposite might have happened. Fine minds need jobs and industrial leadership, which is what the new buildings are about. The educated minds need museums and civic centers and planetariums.

But if all that was built was essential, why did we fail so badly with our most precious resource—our children? Or did we indeed do that badly? Despite poor academic performance in many schools, the U.S. educates a higher portion of its population than almost any other nation. A larger fraction of our financially disadvantaged youth today have more education than at any time before, here or elsewhere. The best of our students compete well with top students anywhere.

Safeway Stores, I read in the *Denver Post,* are donating computers to the public schools. And a unique partnership has been struck between a community government and an elementary school. An after-school computer lab, free to all students from kindergarten through sixth grade, is administered by the community, and that augments the regular school curriculum. This pioneering project may lead to "more direct community involvement for the Denver Public School District."

Every day, in almost every community, such stories appear. A year ago, there were but a handful. The seeds sown by *A Nation at Risk* are blossoming even before spring. By its first anniversary in April, hundreds of local initiatives will be in place. That is precisely what we have needed. Our priorities became skewered for too long. No one consciously wanted to harm public schools; it was just that too few worked to help them. Now, at last, the tide has turned.

In my hotel room, a message awaits: "Call Natasha Berendzen."

"What's up, big girl?"

"Daddy, I'm doing my homework. Could you help me with two questions?"

"Sure. That's what daddys are for."

"Good. The first is to explain how an electric generator works, and the second is to describe how Martin Luther affected the Reformation."

"Uh, I see. I'd love to help you. But I won't do you much good if I tell you answers. Don't you agree?"

"I guess. But can't you just explain about generators and Luther?"

"Actually, it would be hard to do so about generators without our looking together at a diagram. Why don't you look them up in an encyclopedia? As for Luther, the AU library has good books, or I could introduce you to one of our theology professors. For that matter, you could call the Lutheran Church headquarters, which must be in Washington."

"Oh, those are good ideas. Thanks, Daddy."

When she hits me out-of-the-blue at home, I send her on an errand while I look up answers. But I cannot carry a library on a trip. Even though I tell her she is approaching the age at which I will not have all the answers, she does not believe me. Soon she will.

THURSDAY, FEBRUARY 23

Flat. That is the first thing the viewer thinks as he surveys this land. Then he notices how much there is of it. The vast Texas Panhandle stretches endlessly until a curious apparition appears—multilane highways, clusters of houses and shopping centers, and then one of the world's largest airports. If everything about Texas is supposed to be giant, Dallas matches its image.

In a rental car I start the long drive to my parents' home in East Dallas. The flat land, gnarled trees, and Dodge pickups contrast with northwest Washington. And does Washington receive no goods by train? Rarely do I see one there; here, within ten minutes I pass three. Memories of my boyhood race at me: blue, cloudless skies; low, immaculate industrial centers; broad highways and ubiquitous left-turn lanes.

As I approach my parents' home, buildings I remember as massive now look small. The middle-income shopping center where I grew up has been replaced by army-navy stores and pawnshops. But my parents' home remains much the same, except it is now more decrepit. As a child, I considered it middle-class; now, it is distinctly lower middle-class. It needs work. My parents are too old to do it, and they refuse my assistance.

My mother rushes to the door, hugs herself, and squeals: "Earl, Earl, he's here!" My father can't hear. So she grabs him and brings him into the room. Hunched at a thirty-degree angle, he smiles and shakes hands.

The rooms are just as I remember them, except half my memory's size. And then I notice the Bibles—four on one table, one on another, two more on another. On the dining-room buffet are snapshots of Natasha and Deborah. Crowning the wall is a lifesize portrait of Jesus. Old and inelegant, the house is spotlessly clean.

My mother's large bedroom mirror still has a three-foot-long crack from when I, at eight, pretended I was a pirate and threw a tinker-toy dagger at my reflection. The dagger came off in my hand, cracking her mirror. More than a third of a century later, the crack remains.

Small space heaters remain, too. Beside the one in the bathroom sits an ashtray. Ah, what memories. When I was a child, both my mother and father worked. My mother's stern admonition: "Never light a match." Generally, I followed her directives, but one day I accidentally touched cotton against a hot object and watched it dissolve. Fascinated, I put a cotton wad in that ashtray and lit it. Puff! Instantly, it disintegrated, shrinking into a small ball. Entranced, I burned handful after handful until it was gone.

That evening, my mother, crimson-eyed and trembling,

screamed: "Richard, did you burn cotton in the bathroom?" Terrified, I just stammered. Satisfied I had said no, and convinced I would never disobey her, she scowled at my father: "Earl, why did you burn the cotton?"

"Do what?"

If he had not burned it, she had not, and her son had not, who had? In those days, milk companies made home deliveries, actually coming into our unlocked home and placing milk in the icebox.(My daughters cannot believe we used a box cooled with ice before we got a refrigerator.) How much life has changed. Today, there are no such deliveries and no one would leave doors unlocked.

My mother cornered the milkman and bellowed: "What do you mean by burning cotton in my bathroom!"

"Lady, what are you talking about?"

I ducked out the door and spent the day in woods a block away. But I couldn't avoid the truth forever. That evening, as the woods grew dark, I had to go home.

"Richard, look me in the eye. Did you burn that cotton?"

I could not look at anyone: my eyes were too teared. And I could not even say yes: my hiccups were too loud. But at least my guilt was over.

From the bathroom, the three of us go to the backyard and garage. How many hours did I spend shooting baskets through my net? And here is the driveway that served as the pitcher's lane, when I fancied myself a professional hardball player. At least, that spurred me at twelve to try writing my first book—a history of baseball.

I drive my parents to Brownies in the East Grand Shopping Center where I used to eat regularly. Except for some new paint, it remains the same. Even the menu is the same. A full lunch costs $3.75, and every booth has a jukebox. My mother, who has not changed either, rushes up to strangers, saying: "Isn't he beautiful? He's my son."

From Brownies, we walk past my old barber shop, now named Rodrigues's, to Lindops, where my father worked for more than thirty years and where I held my first job. Its wooden floors creak just as they used to. The feel, the smell remain the same. The storeroom, with pipes and wire, is where I uncrated boxes from wholesale houses, where I threaded pipe, cut glass, assembled bikes, where I worked alone, learned responsibility, earned my first paycheck, and seriously wondered: what'll I be when I grow up?

During the half hour we are in Lindops, they make but one sale: $1.75. Typically, as a salesman I spent twenty minutes aiding a customer with the total sale less than five dollars. At week's end, I learned the value of the dollar and the worth of my time.

I drive my parents home and we sadly say goodbye. What an odd pair they are: he, a conservative Republican; she, a liberal Democrat. He always sought stability and security. He was reluctant to take risks but was determined, however great the effort, to fulfill responsibilities. She always sought the good life, convinced that with innovation it could be found. Living for today, she was vibrant. He planned; she dreamed. He plodded; she soared. They were precisely wrong for each other; they were precisely right for each other.

As I drive across Dallas back to my hotel, I marvel again at this extraordinary place, the largest city in the world not built on a navigable seaway. It never should have been. Yet here it is, rising out of the prairie, sprawling across the prairie. From the original one-room log cabin that was its first structure, Dallas now has, arguably, some of the world's finest living. Nonetheless, it is in search of identity. Its public relations imply the chic of Paris, the glamour of Los Angeles, the savoir faire of New York. None of these tags fits. Still, despite the down-home, old-boy flavor—scuffed boots, country music, case of beer in the truck bed—a vast new tract reaches northward for miles. Sprinkled with gleaming shopping centers, it abounds with expensive brick homes, topped by aircraft-carrier-sized roofs.

The silent, beige hotel lobby contrasts sharply with Lindops, which is filled with things to touch and feel. Lindops itself is earthy. When I worked there, never did I dream I would view it so. But it is of real people that do real work. Not antiseptic, homogenized, or glossed, it is rough and abrasive. It is what is inside the machine, on the roof, under the ground. It is the unsightly essentials that make the good life possible.

As I wait to be picked up, I glance at an article about a commission headed by Texas computer magnate H. Ross Perot. Its members argue that Texas schools emphasize athletics over academics. What an astounding discovery. I could have told them about a high school senior with a pregnant wife who applied in 1956 for a freshman scholarship. The applicant pool was narrowed to two. Only one scholarship would be given. The finalists were invited to a selection dinner at a men's club. One—an athlete heralded in the newspapers—instantly caught the judges' eyes. He was lionized, peppered with questions—not about school or his future but about sports and his past. Meanwhile, the young student/husband/father stood alone and watched. When the interview came, he explained as poignantly as he could his academic plans and stressed how much he needed the scholarship. A judge replied, "That's interesting. But are you in major sports?"

"No."

As he left, the men still hovered over the athlete, wrapping arms about his shoulders, inviting him to sit in their boxes at next year's games. A week later, one of the pair received the rejection letter he expected. But it did not matter. He would simply work more hours part-time at Lindops.

I am driven to the Dallas Woman's Club, where Deborah meets me. Given this is Dallas, I should have known what to expect. Still, I am impressed. Enormous in size and luxurious in decor, it is genuine Dallas. And at our dinner table is Caroline Hunt Schoellkopf, reportedly the nation's wealthiest woman. My address in the handsome auditorium is on astronomy.

Afterwards, Deborah drives me back to my hotel where we talk in the lounge. She appears more buoyed than I can remember her in years. As she puts it, "Everything's going great." I am happy for her and proud of her.

After she leaves, I reflect on my native town. In some ways, it seems alien. But there is much I remember and admire. Who would not like clean streets and courteous people? And the money. The omnipresent, conspicuous money. Fundraising here has no equivalent elsewhere. Is it pointless to try doggedly in Washington? Is the dream of a great national university in the capital city truly that noble? Is it obtainable?

I flick on TV, coming in at the end of the popular movie *Flashdance*. The hero is telling the heroine: "When you give up your dream, you die." To rousing, throbbing music, she tries her once-in-a-lifetime audition. She falls. But she rises and tries again. The film ends exhilaratingly. Pure schmaltz. And I love it.

It is late. I am tired. For now, I have answered my own questions.

FRIDAY, FEBRUARY 24

On Christmas Day, 1889, Methodist bishop John Fletcher Hurst set out on a buggy ride in search of the ideal site for the national university. Some days later, he found the perfect place—ninety acres of

rolling hills in far northwest Washington which commanded a pano-
ramic view of the District. Then, on 23 February 1893, by act of
Congress, The American University was chartered. Yesterday
marked the university's ninety-first anniversary.

For many years, AU did not hold a Founder's Day celebration.
Last year, in conjunction with the ninetieth anniversary, Gail and Jan
Ansary organized an elaborate dinner-dance, held in Georgetown
Park, a shopping mall designed in a Victorian-era style. Guests came
in 1890s attire and the evening's proceeds went for scholarships. This
year, the commemoration is much smaller but nonetheless dignified.
The Tokyo String Quartet, a premiere musical group, is in residence
at the university. It performed last night. Gail, who introduced the
group and substituted for me, calls to say that everything went well.
It was an appropriate academic night with a family feeling.

I drive to a radio station, where the interviewer asks me about a
new Perot proposal that parents should be held financially responsible
for their children's progress in school. He says parents and students
should be required to carry out specific objectives. If those are not
met, they would be fined an amount equaling the cost of the schooling
and possibly forfeiting the child's right to attend school. What do I
think?

Perot has gone too far. Why can we not have balance? We go from
one extreme to another. We have had too little parental involvement
and accountability. Now, Perot proposes just the opposite.

The media say Perot wants school attendance to be noncompul-
sory. Again, I disagree. In frustration over the deterioration of public
schools, critics now propose such ideas. Some say that all "incorrigi-
bles" should be dismissed from school so that the majority who are
there to learn will have the opportunity to do so. The difficulty,
however, comes in determining what to do with "troublemakers" or
academically indolent students. Should they be sent to special
schools? Thrown out of school and left on the street? As Fred Hechinger wrote in the *New York Times* several weeks ago, schools need
to be both tougher and better.

It is too bad Perot has gone so far in these proposals because most
of what he has suggested for Texas—despite the controversy it has
stirred—has been bold, imaginative, and right. He wants more rigor
and higher standards, with less fluff.

My lunch is with Jack Martin of *Texas Business,* who has assembled a group of educators and civic leaders to meet me. It will be in the Tower Club, across from Thanksgiving Square. For thirty minutes I criss-cross downtown searching for the square. It is not on my map and two policemen and a pedestrian tell me they have heard of it but do not know where it is. Finally, I find it. What a shame that all Dallasites are not aware of this graceful new shrine. Designed by the renowned Philip Johnson and created as a center for the expression of thanksgiving and praise, it is supported voluntarily. With a half hour before my luncheon, I decide to visit it. On this winter day, no one is in the plaza. At the doorway stands a rough-looking man, unshaven, in dirty clothes. Should I enter alone with him?

Problems can arise anywhere, though surely not in this chapel at noon. I pass the man and discover a silent, inspiring room with spiraling choirloft climbing heavenward. The two of us share the room and the moment. But we are not alone. A third man rises from praying and joins the other man. Who are they? Whatever the answer, one of them waited while the other prayed. Now both of them, in stained and tattered clothes, close the door, leaving me alone.

At the luncheon, I give the group my views about public education and a synopsis of AU. In turn, I hear about Positive Parents of Dallas, a volunteer group that promotes public schools. Similarly, I learn how the Dallas Chamber of Commerce promotes the "Adopt-A-School" program. Although the Dallas public school system, like most, is beset with problems, there is strong support from industry, government, and ordinary citizens. These partnerships are precisely what public education needs.

After lunch I pass the old Majestic Theater, once Dallas's finest. With marble columns and velvet walls, chandeliers and broad staircases, it was in the grand old style. For me as a young boy, going there was special.

One afternoon, when I was about ten, I noticed that there were two box offices—one where I went and a smaller one down the street. The other one was for "coloreds." But if they entered through this separate entrance, where did they sit? I had never seen a black person in the theater. I found that they climbed to the top balcony so they would not be seated with whites.

Intrigued and baffled, a friend and I decided to explore the highest balcony. But as we climbed to it, a black man rose and said softly but sternly: "What are you white boys doing here? Don't you know this is just for colored folk? You've got the best part of the theater. You just turn around and go back to where you belong."

Obediently, we did so. And when I got home, I asked my parents why the theater was divided. My mother explained about segregation. "A lot of people feel strongly that the races must not mix. Your father and I don't, but that's the way it's always been. And I don't know whether it'll change in your lifetime."

Having reached that level of awareness, I soon noted segregation everywhere—dual water fountains, one marked "whites only"; arrows on buses pointing "coloreds" to the rear. In my home, racial matters just did not come up. So to me segregation seemed peculiar. I was not so outraged morally as I was puzzled intellectually. What was its point?

Then one summer day, I had an aisle seat in the middle of a crowded bus. An elderly black woman, perspiration soaking her blouse, boarded the bus laden with packages. There were no seats. So I did what my parents had taught me to do in deference to anyone bearing burdens, but most especially to an elderly person—namely, offered her my seat. She looked at me in disbelief. Equally shocked, the white woman beside me growled: "What do you think you're doing? Do you have no sense?"

I turned to see a black man motion the woman with the packages to take his seat at the back. He smiled at me and said: "She can sit here with us. You keep your seat. And thanks." I rode home quietly, sitting as far from the woman next to me as possible, thinking about all this. I just did not understand the fuss.

Martin Luther King and his supporters jolted the nation. Their accomplishments will last forever. Dallas responded more gracefully than most cities; the Dallas of today differs vastly from the one in which I grew up.

I drive back to my hotel for a reception with prospective students and parents. Texas chauvinism is so strong that most students do not leave the state; also, Texas provides outstanding public and private universities. Still, the world does not end at the Texas border. For the sophisticated student, Washington and AU might provide an intriguing option. The group this afternoon seems to agree.

Then I put my work aside to have a joyous evening with my older daughter. As a child, she was Debbie; now, she is Deborah. Our first stop is the Galleria, Dallas's newest shopping center. With three levels and a large skating rink, it bristles with fine stores: Fifth Avenue has come to Texas. From there, we head for dinner at Keller's Drive-in. A relic from my high school days, it looks like a set in *The Last Picture Show*. Debbie parks her Honda between a sixties Ford and a pickup truck. I order a corndog, a hotdog encrusted in cornmeal mix. As we balance tater tots and greasy napkins on our laps, we laugh and talk, and it feels like old times.

After dinner, she drives us to Showbiz Pizza Place. The ultimate of Americana, it is great for youngsters, but why are we here? Because she discovered that it shows a remarkable movie, *New Magic*. When she was little, I surprised her with unusual things. Tonight, she reciprocates.

We return to my hotel where we sit in the lobby and people-watch. She tells me about apartment hunting, career aspirations, and hopes. At midnight she leaves. Twenty years ago when that happened, I found it almost unbearable; now, I miss her but remember what I admonish the parents of freshmen: "Cut the cord, but keep the contact."

MONDAY, FEBRUARY 27

When I became president, I brought in a financial consulting firm to assist us in selecting a new endowment-portfolio manager. After considering managers nationwide, we selected one in Boston. A fortunate choice, the firm has handled our account extraordinarily well. The consulting firm monitors its performance, and today the trustee investment committee hears from both organizations.

Apparently, we have decided astutely when to change the mix of equity, debt, and cash equivalence in our portfolio, for the review firm, which monitors the performance of about 75 percent of higher education's endowment funds, reports that our recent yield has been the highest of any institution it monitors.

Tonight, history professors Richard Breitman and Alan Kraut will talk at our home about American Jewry's response to the Holocaust. For this profound, timeless subject, we have invited guests to bring their children. Perhaps not a suitable topic for young children, it is ideal for Natasha's age. Afterwards, we invite the sixty guests to partake of borscht, blintzes, and hamentaschen. Our largely Jewish group asks if we prepared the food ourselves. French-Italian Gail, who grew up Catholic before becoming an Episcopalian, grins and says: "What do you think?"

We will never tell.

TUESDAY, FEBRUARY 28

The university's finances look so good that our monthly budget meeting ends in fifteen minutes. We shall, indeed, end the fiscal year with a substantial surplus.

A TV team arrives to interview me about AU's remarkable growth in enrollment and admission standards. Always wary of the media, irrespective of how friendly they seem, I wait for the zinger. But it never comes. The closest to it: "Why did AU suffer more during the recession than some other universities?"

"Because our financial cushion was so small. AU's fiscal reserves have never been large. The university could live okay with that so long as conditions were stable; however, with the unexpected enrollment drop, our reserves eroded quickly."

"Well, then, to what do you attribute AU's turnaround?"

"Hard work on many people's part. We reorganized the administration, increased efficiency, expunged waste, invigorated fundraising and recruitment efforts, and began to enjoy the benefits of our improving academic reputation."

While the camera crew packs, Maureen Bunyan, a TV news anchor and personal friend, calls: "Richard, the Supreme Court just gave its opinion in the Grove City College case. Would you be available in a couple of hours to be interviewed?"

"I've heard about the case but I can't recall the details. Can you bring me up to date?"

"A small, private, liberal-arts college in Pennsylvania refuses to accept tax-supported funds from the state or federal government," she explains, "but its students receive federal financial aid. The case questioned whether receiving those monies meant the whole college must comply with Title IX, the federal law barring sex discrimination. The court decided, six to three, that it didn't."

"Now it comes back," I reply, trying to remember what I have read. Every day I read several newspapers as well as magazines, journals, and newsletters; I try to keep up-to-date in many areas. The test comes, however, in a situation such as this. I plan to eat at my desk, which will give me time for quick research.

"I'll be glad to see you this afternoon, Maureen. Meanwhile, I'll bone up."

I ask University Relations to send me wire-service stories about the decision. I dig through back issues of the *Chronicle of Higher Education* and my education clipping file. And I call a friend and real pro on such matters—Shelly Steinbach, the general counsel for the American Council on Education. As the umbrella organization for higher education, ACE is on top of breaking issues. Sure enough, Shelly is informed about this case and confirms what I have concluded from my reading.

Don Myers and two of his staff join me to review plans for changing campus maps and outside lighting. The two principal entrances have large maps, which are outdated and hard to read. I have asked for them to be redesigned. Then we discuss a new lighting system. I have reviewed dozens of lamp designs and have driven around town to look at street-lamp styles. The one we have settled on—the classic sodium-vapor "Washington lamp"—is like the ones on Pennsylvania Avenue. If we can replace our current potpourri with these handsome fixtures, the campus appearance, day and night, will improve dramatically.

While we review architects' drawings, Joan says Maureen is ready in my big office. Tape rolling, she begins: "How will today's Supreme Court decision affect AU and other universities?"

"In theory, the decision could have dramatic effects. If a university continues to receive federal funds in one unit even if it discriminates in another, then it might be disinclined to comply with Title IX. Also in theory, universities might more easily discriminate against the handicapped.

"In practice, however, I don't foresee any change at AU. The goals of Title IX now are so much a part of the ideology of this campus and most others that I can't see them lessening their resolve because of this decision. We don't provide equal access just because of Title IX. We do so because it's the right thing to do."

When I arrive home and tell Gail my position, she scowls. "A fine husband I have. Now it will be easier for schools that want to discriminate to do so. It isn't good enough to say that existing safeguards are adequate and that universities like AU have no intention of discriminating. Maybe AU doesn't, but that won't stop others."

"For heaven's sake," I try to explain, "it's just not that big a deal. Why do you and some women's organizations make it sound like all equity issues now are dead? If I thought that were the case, I'd oppose it too. But the reporter asked me what was going to happen at AU, and I told her . . . "

"I know what you told her, but I'm not happy with the court's decision or your statement. Natasha, what do you think?"

Nestled in a large chair, Natasha has listened quietly to this unusual exchange. Either she has not followed it or she is unwilling to take sides. "I don't know what either of you is talking about. This is very confusing."

The TV is on and Maureen begins. Spokespersons for the National Organization of Women and other women's groups denounce the court's decision. Maureen then says there is another perspective, switching to me. Gail gives me a piercing look. After my segment, the TV sportscaster says the decision might handicap women's sports. Gail's silent frown erupts into an audible harumph. But the next people interviewed—male and female coaches—say that although the decision could lead to discrimination, they do not expect it to do so.

By now, it is 6:40 P.M.; we rush to change clothes. Minutes later, we kiss Natasha goodnight and drive to the White House to attend a state dinner for the president of Austria. Marine honor guards snap to as we pull up. In the ground floor Diplomatic Reception Room, another marine whispers: "How do you want to be introduced?" East Dallas comes out: "Oh, just Richard and Gail Berendzen will be fine." The marine's frown tells me that is not what he expected. "Well, maybe you should say Dr. and Mrs. Richard Berendzen." Now satisfied, he whirls on his heel and barks: "DR. AND MRS. RICHARD BERENDZEN!"

Gail takes my arm as we promenade down the hallway. At the end of the photo gauntlet, we pause to watch the next guest enter. It is actress Patricia Neal; all cameras flash, as they should. We climb the marble steps, listening to the Marine Band play in the Entrance Hall. Guides are everywhere. Graciously, they point us to the East Room. As we approach it, another marine asks: "How do you want to be introduced?" Now an authority at this, I snap: "Dr. and Mrs. Richard Berendzen." He wheels and shouts it. After such an entrance, what do you do next? If you know no one, then you merely stand. Fortunately, we see friends—the Michael Botwinicks. He is the new director of the Corcoran Gallery of Art. Aides move guests about, and we see other friends—the Bill Cafritzs, the Ed Meeses, Chief of Protocol Selwa Roosevelt, Secretary of the Air Force Verne Orr, and Bill Marriott.

"He's coming," I tell Gail. Seconds later, an aide intones: "The President of the United States and Mrs. Reagan and the President of Austria and Mrs. Kirchschlaeger." They enter to applause and form a receiving line.

Afterwards, we are ushered into the State Dining Room. Someone in the administration hosts each table. Gail is at Barbara Bush's and I am at George Shultz's. That is fine, but who made the seating arrangements? Gail is seated beside Maximilian Schell, her version of Michael Jackson; I am next to Phyllis Diller. Gail smiles smugly.

Soon I discover my dinner companion to be quiet and enjoyable. And attractive. No frizzy hair or harsh features; she is petite and surprisingly beautiful. My preconceived images of Phyllis Diller are shattered, save two: her infectious laugh and spontaneous wit are real.

After the toasts, we move to the Red, Blue, and Green rooms. Selwa introduces me to the Austrian president, and he, Schell, and I have a lengthy conversation. Then Gail and I chat with Bill and Ernestine Bradley. Formerly a basketball star and Rhodes scholar and currently a leading senator, Bill is imposing from height to accomplishments.

Soon the omnipresent aides direct us to the East Room for the evening's entertainment. Peter Nero and Mel Torme give a sparkling review of Gershwin hits. Pat Boone, sitting next to me, seems to enjoy it deeply. Not being jazz fans, Gail and I are only moderately enthused. Graciously, Reagan thanks Nero and Torme and we return to the Entrance Hall. The band strikes up a fox trot, the crowd steps back, and the president and first lady start dancing.

By the second dance, we decide etiquette now accepts all comers to the floor. With light snow falling and fireplace roaring, Gail and I begin dancing. She nudges me gently, our silent signal that I am about to collide with people behind me. In this case, it is the Reagans. Bumping them would be, as my mother would put it, "downright tacky." As we whirl about the room, we watch Dom DeLuise clowning at the sideline and Larry Hagman deep in conversation. Gail leans close to my ear and whispers: "We've done a lot together, haven't we?"

"Indeed we have. And I wonder how much more life will bring us?"

"I don't know. But I feel pretty giddy."

"On that, you're not alone," I whisper, as we glide past Baroness Von Trapp, Ted Turner, Dorothy Hamill, and the vice-president. I had expected the Reagans would stay for only one or two pieces, but on and on they dance. So do we all.

In between dances, Gail and I stare out the Blue Room's windows, across the South Lawn to the illuminated Jefferson Memorial.

Is My Armor Straight?

The view is stunning, the moment special. We pause, holding hands, standing alone, gazing through the window in a room furnished by James Monroe. In the background, the president and his guests dance. It would be maudlin and unoriginal to say that this grand home still houses all those who have lived here—Lincoln and Wilson, Roosevelt and Truman and Eisenhower, Johnson and Ford. Yet, with scant imagination, their presence is everywhere. Did Lincoln stand where we are standing when he agonized over Gettysburg? Roosevelt over Pearl Harbor? Kennedy over Cuba? The past and present merge for us in this precious moment. We squeeze hands and return to the Hall slightly misty-eyed. The Reagans say goodnight and the rest of us stay for a final dance.

When we return home, I flip on TV to hear news about the New Hampshire primary. Gary Hart has won decisively! The race is alive. And what are they all racing for? The right to live four years in the house we just left. And the opportunities the job provides. And the responsibilities it entails. Mostly, the responsibilities.

WEDNESDAY, FEBRUARY 29
My large office fills with deans, directors, and faculty members as we discuss graduate recruitment. The number of inquiries we receive is high, yet the conversion to actual enrollments is too low in certain areas. In other areas competition for admission is vigorous. How can we get higher conversion of well-qualified applicants in all areas?

After considering a dozen approaches, we conclude what we knew at the outset: the best approach is direct, one-on-one. We shall have more faculty, staff, students, alums, advisory board members, and others contact desirable applicants.

That group exits and a new one assembles for my next meeting —on recruitment of nondegree-seeking adults. Adult enrollments have declined for years at most private universities in the area. We are convinced, nonetheless, that we can stop this trend if we offer new, exciting programs and improve support services, especially for returning women.

After the meeting, I ask Anita Gottlieb to issue a press release:

The American University has a historic commitment to equal educational opportunities for women, minorities, and the handicapped. This commitment is unaffected by the Supreme Court decision in *Grove City vs. Bell.* Access to equal educational opportunities to ensure all individuals the chance to become fully integrated members of society is a moral principle that must not be disputed. Today I reaffirm the commitment of The American University to that principle.

A letter arrives asking me to review a manuscript for a scholarly journal. I flip the pages, scan the footnotes. The style and tone set it apart from my usual mail. Instead of broad, conceptual issues, it focuses on a narrow, esoteric one. If the manuscript were never published, the world would not be different. Yet through the accumulation of such articles, scholarship progresses. And, occasionally, a brilliant one will propel an entire field. This is not one of those, but it reminds me of my professorial past. Sometimes I deeply miss being a professor—teaching and studying what you want when you want.

The phone jolts me: "Khashoggi's office called. He can't return from Asia in time for Friday's board meeting." The next call informs me that one of our professors has become gravely ill. And Joan brings me yet another stack of mail. A writer in Paris wants to know if we will host some Afghan musicians who play the delroba and the rouhbab. We just have to pay their airfare and fee. My professorial interlude ends; I am back to administration.

This afternoon I meet with the WDVM–TV producers to discuss the pilots I taped months ago. They want to proceed. We agree that I shall be on call for the evening news about breaking events and I shall tape two-minute commentaries on education to play once or twice per week. By Monday I shall write scripts for the first commentaries. Offhand, I am unsure which topics to discuss, much less what data to include. But tonight I shall start assembling information.

Last week, the undergraduate student government held its annual election. Darryl Jones won the presidency decisively. I ask him to meet me this afternoon so we can get to know one another.

Soft-spoken and articulate, he projects self-confidence and poise. He says that the student government and the administration can work together cooperatively. And he stresses that students want to be involved. I assure him that we all want the same things—high academic standards, solvent finances, solid institutional reputation, moderate tuition increases, more student financial aid, efficient student services, a sports and convocation center. We discuss ways students can assist. I am impressed by this serious young black man from Dallas who has studied business and computers yet majors in philosophy.

Is My Armor Straight?

Gail and I had planned to go this evening to Alej Orfila's farewell reception as OAS secretary general. Afterwards, we were to see Natasha in a play. But I do not feel like going to either. I ask Natasha if she will be disappointed. "It's a dumb play," she assures me. "The teachers planned everything and didn't let the kids have much say." From seventh grade to undergraduate college government, the theme remains the same: "We want a say."

THURSDAY, MARCH 1

Lani Barovick, our staff personnel director, joins my cabinet meeting this morning. We discuss how we should distribute special salary inequity funds in May. Lani has identified almost every area in which pay scales are inequitable. The increases this summer will be a good first step towards correcting these. If our budget next year permits us to repeat the process, we shall remove most of them.

Don Myers and I go to lunch. Although I meet regularly with Milt, the Dons, the vice-provosts, the deans, and others in groups, I rarely meet with them individually. I must try to do so more often. From humble origins in rural Maryland, Don has become an uncanny businessman, and his "creative financing" constitutes a significant form of fundraising. With his management perspective, he finds academics to be puzzling. Professors, in his view, should "market" their "new product line," thereby "improving our income stream." Translated, this means that professors should design attractive programs geared to contemporary needs, inform potential students about them, and thereby enhance enrollments. Actually, he understands academia well.

After dinner at home with Natasha, Gail and I attend a reception at the Greek embassy for Margaret Papandreou, wife of the premier of Greece. We see former acquaintances, but that is not why we are here. Our purpose is to make new contacts. After an hour of eating olive leaves stuffed with rice and chatting with government and media officials, I am ready to leave. I find Gail, who has been talking with Debbie Toll, wife of the University of Maryland president.

"Debbie's writing an article about the role of the university president's wife," Gail says as we depart. "She tells me that she's impressed by what I do and wants to mention it in her essay."

"Splendid."

"Yes, I'm flattered. She's interviewed AU trustees and administrators. Maybe she's just being polite, but she claims the people she talked to told her that when AU selected you, it hired one person but got two. She also said a trustee told her I should be paid. I've not thought much about this, but Debbie says there's a growing movement among presidential wives to ask for a stipend. And a widower president now receives funds to hire someone to carry out his deceased wife's social duties."

"I've heard that," I interject. "It makes sense. The university hires a man to be president, yet everyone assumes his wife will be available, without pay, for a barrage of activities. I wonder how it works when a woman is president of a university? Does her husband do the things you do?"

"I'd like to think that what I do is worth something," Gail responds. "Money is a good way to indicate worth. But just a thanks or my own perception that I've achieved something is a good reward —for the time being."

FRIDAY, MARCH 2

Bob Cleary welcomes the group and introduces me. I begin: "In preparation for this special celebration, I have read what others have said about government and public administration. Here is a sample:

> *Plato:* If anyone at all is to have the privilege of lying, the rulers of the state should be such persons.

> *John F. Kennedy:* My experience in government is that when things are noncontroversial and beautifully coordinated, there's not much going on.

> *Will Rogers:* The government now is not one bit better than the government we got for one third the money twenty years ago.

> *Confucius:* Govern a great nation as you would cook a small fish—don't overdo it."

I go on:

"Fifty years ago, a deep recession gnawed at the nation and dark clouds loomed over Europe. On this campus—that half century ago —public affairs education began. Since then, these programs at The American University have developed and prospered, producing outstanding public leaders.

"Today, government and international relations are more vital than ever before; hence, academic public affairs programs are more vital than ever before. I'm profoundly proud of ours; it has served the nation well.

"So, in context of this celebration's first session—'Preparing for the Next Fifty Years'—may I remind you of another quotation. It's from John F. Kennedy: 'Our task now is not to fix the blame for the past, but to fix the course for the future.' "

As I enter my office, Climis Lascaris calls. "Richard, let me tell you the wonderful news about last night's meeting. Sondra Bender, Roland Rice [a trustee emeritus], Joe Carlo, Don Triezenberg, several young alums, and I met to discuss the sports and convocation center. The alums spoke enthusiastically about their love for AU and their desire to support it. By the time the meeting ended, we had pledges for almost $1.5 million."

Stupendous! For weeks, Don and others have been meeting these alums. This will be joyous news for this afternoon's meeting of the board of trustees. In addition, Triezenberg can announce $1.2 million worth of signed commitments to the endowment. This is a banner day, as months of effort come to fruition.

So enthused am I that I decide to push for an answer from Adnan. Joan calls his New York office and asks for him to call me when convenient. He does call—at about 1:00 A.M. his time in Hong Kong. A student receptionist answers the phone and says I am not here. In fact, I am in my office. That is frustrating, but I have no time to fret because the trustees have arrived.

Ansary calls the meeting to order, Jim Mathews gives the opening prayer, and we begin. Triezenberg reports the endowment gifts and Climis, Sondra, and Roland speak eloquently about our recent fundraising successes for the center. To date we've raised about $5.5 million. When we reach $7 million, we can announce groundbreaking. If the naming pledge were to come, the campaign would be nearly finished.

Unanimously, the trustees pass a resolution that all board members will support the sports and convocation center drive financially. The board ends its executive session in high spirits. The AU Singers enter and charm us with a brief rendition. Then the trustees assemble on the building steps to be photographed for the student yearbook.

Cy gavels the second session to order, this time with faculty and student representatives. After campus representatives speak, the board is to consider today's major agenda item: the 1984–85 budget.

Traditionally, the March meeting has been confrontational, sometimes rancorous. Those days, thank goodness, are gone. Even in good years, though, the March meeting tends to be passionate—and sometimes irrational. Today, regrettably, is no exception.

Paul Schroeder, the first campus person to speak, is as disappointing today as he was impressive in the fall. He disavows the budget, even though until now almost every student leader has supported it. Of course he does not know what just happened in the executive session. But next year's budget is independent of that. His assertions are false; his prose strident.

And the other campus speakers continue this negative mood, their positive comments lost in the overall pall. Each had been asked to talk no more than five minutes. None complies; the time for the four goes over forty minutes. They bring up matters that have nothing to do with the trustees. They emphasize issues that the administration has not heard all year.

The unflappable Cy, always a gentleman, permits the speakers to go overtime. He does not want to stifle dissent. But he whispers to me, "What a shame they take this approach." Barrett Prettyman leads the discussion about the budget. It is approved unanimously. Ansary declares the meeting ended. Last time, students, faculty, administrators, and trustees stayed and talked and laughed. Today, they trail out despondently. One trustee, frowning, says to me, "I'll come to committee meetings. They're worthwhile. But this was ridiculous."

TUESDAY, MARCH 6
Of all the impressive structures in this monumental city, the OAS building is one of the most distinguished. It is here that departing OAS secretary general, Alej Orfila, hosts a luncheon on my behalf today. I am unsure how this particular meeting will help us, but such informal discussions with community leaders have an ever-widening effect.

Back at my office, I sort through mail and phone messages: There are invitations to address the Bergen County School Board Association in New Jersey and to give commencement addresses at Saint Andrews Episcopal School in Maryland and Woodson Public High School in Virginia. Parents I met in Boston write to say they hope their daughter will be accepted. A woman in the Dallas Women's Club writes to thank me for my recent talk there. An alumnus says he would like to become more involved. A professor sends me his latest tome to add to the faculty book collection in my office. A learned society informs me that a professor has done an exemplary job. An investment firm asks me to shift our portfolio management to it.

With that handled, I join guests in my large office. For six decades, Roland Rice has been a dedicated member of the AU community: first as a student, then loyal alum, for years active trustee, now, equally active trustee emeritus. Today, we thank him for his service and present him with a chair bearing the university seal.

At the beginning of the brief ceremony, attended by senior trustees and Roland's family, I point out artifacts in my office: an early architectural plan of the campus, old photographs, faculty books, the university charter. "All of this," I note, "might imply that this university is composed of a campus, legal documents, and books. That's part of it. But beyond buildings and even curricula, the heart of a university is its people. Today we celebrate an exemplary member, one who cares deeply. There is only one word appropriate for his devotion—love."

Roland blows his nose, wipes his eyes. With a soft yet clear voice he tells of the early days, about faculty and students, about kindnesses shown him that he still remembers. And what a memory. Glancing across the room, he notices a classmate from the 1920s and fellow trustee emeritus, Don Bittinger, former chair of the Washington Gas Light Company. Roland smiles and says:

"People here in those days always seemed to know exactly the right thing to say at the right moment. Once, when our football team was feeling down, Don turned to them and quoted Macbeth—I believe it was act five, scene three: 'The Devil damn the black, thou creamed-fac'd loon/ Where gottest thou that goose'd look?' "

This is a good line for athletes and administrators, then or now. As he leaves, Roland says, "I really appreciate the university recognizing me this way." He misses the point: The university has not honored him. For he *is* the university. He and others like him. They are why the buildings and professors and deans are here: to produce accomplished and loyal alums. But more than that, wherever these alums go, *there* is the university.

WEDNESDAY, MARCH 7
Mary Gray, chair of the math, statistics, and computer sciences department, meets with me to discuss our computer programs. Not

surprisingly, she says we need more terminals; to my delight, she adds that our undergraduate computer program is the best in town.

An exceptional person, Mary has a Ph.D. in math and a J.D. in law. She is especially concerned with increasing opportunities for young women in math. I ask her why ten times more boys than girls study computers. Her instant reply: "gadget fascination." Boys, she explains, always have enjoyed tinkering, whether with electric trains, bikes, or racers. Computers are just the latest gadget. How can we interest more girls in them?

After Mary leaves, my thoughts turn from education for children to education for senior citizens. Our Institute for Learning in Retirement—with a minimum age of fifty-five and an average age of seventy—has the most inquisitive, vibrant students I have ever met. In contrast with many who are half a century younger, these did not enroll because their parents forced them. Today, I read about their forthcoming programs and recall the ones I have visited. Recently, I asked an eighty-two-year-old member what she was studying. "Computers," she tersely answered. "Really? Why that subject?" I asked. She patted my arm and said, "Young man, hasn't anyone told you? It's the field of tomorrow. You've got to know it."

Maybe she should talk with school girls about careers—and what they can do in the world.

Triezenberg and his staff have worked so feverishly for the past year that they've had no time for an extended staff meeting. Today they hold a retreat at the Brookings Institution. Don has invited me to join them for lunch. I am delighted to do so for several reasons: Offices under him bring in most of the university's revenues; they are unquestionably important; and they are doing a fine job.

Halfway through lunch, Don begins. During the past year his units have had massive staff turnover. In some, most of the employees are new. Still, they are pulling together well. He asks each director to discuss his or her area. What a story they tell. In my office, with mail and meetings, I may be shielded from some campus tumult but I am also prevented from seeing directly how much we have going well. Gifts are up; applications are up; admission standards are up; alumni interest and support are up. Better management procedures are in place; financial aid is being utilized more effectively; publications are more cost efficient, informative, and attractive; institutional research and planning are more comprehensive and insightful. And next year's prospects are even better.

Is My Armor Straight?

Tonight Gail and I attend a reception at the Swedish embassy for the 1983 American Nobel laureates. Ambassador Wachtmeister graciously says he has invited "the laureates and their Washington intellectual equals." Despite the hyperbole, he does have a diverse and distinguished group. As much as I admire the Washington contingent, I am especially impressed by the laureates.

How does one explain their genius? Genes? Environment? Both? Did anyone guess when they were young what they would achieve? How did schooling affect them? Will America continue to win so many Nobel Prizes, even as the seventies generation comes of age? Is the number of truly talented people constant, impervious to fluctuations in the schools? Does genius develop out of school or does school plant the seed?

FRIDAY, MARCH 9
I truly overdid it last night, reading until after 4:00 A.M. With no early-morning meetings scheduled, I had planned to luxuriate in bed. But in the darkened room I see the telephone light flashing. It is Joan.

"WRC wants to know if you'll go on this afternoon to discuss the latest theory on the extinction of dinosaurs. They need an answer at once."

"Sure."

A few minutes later, when my alarm awakens me at the preset time of 9:30, I vaguely remember a conversation about a radio station and dinosaurs. Did they really ask me to talk about *that* today? Did I really say *yes?*

Once on the show, I am unsure how much to say. Oh, well. After this one, our applications will either soar or plummet.

"Whatever the cause, something profound occurred 65 million years ago, when the 'great death' swept the globe, killing much of the lizard and marine life. Theories to explain it come in many forms, one being that the large-body, small-brain dinosaur was not adaptable or intelligent enough to survive. There are other, more intriguing explanations, too, which Stephen Jay Gould, the paleontologist, has written about recently.

"One argument says the flowering plants that started evolving near the end of the dinosaurs' era contained psychoactive agents, which mammals today avoid because of their bad taste. Dinosaurs, so the argument goes, were incapable of tasting the plants' bitterness and their digestive systems couldn't detoxify the substances. Consequently, they died of overdoses. They OD'd.

"Others claim that dinosaurs' testes produced only over a limited temperature range. When worldwide temperatures increased towards the end of the Cretaceous era, the dinosaurs' testes presumably stopped functioning, effectively leading to a global dinosaurian vasectomy.

"These fanciful explanations are commendable for originality, if nothing else. But they are unlikely on multiple grounds. In addition, they are not amenable to testing. A key question is whether or not the mass extinctions occurred abruptly. If they did, astronomy may provide the answer. Moreover, the catastrophe theories can be checked against astronomical and geological evidence. They're probably the best bets.

"An old favorite of this genre was that a nearby supernova—a massive, exploding star at the end of its life—bathed the earth in enhanced radiation, ultimately killing the large lizards. A newer astronomical theory holds that a comet or asteroid collided with the earth, enshrouding it in a dust cloud, thereby blocking sunlight, suppressing photosynthesis, and eliminating many food supplies. Strong, indirect evidence supports this hypothesis."

Ron Eisenberg, the show's host, asks: "Why, in 1984, should anybody care about such matters 65 million years ago?"

"Whatever happened then, it was one of the most significant events in history. If it hadn't happened, intelligent life today might be ten to fifteen feet tall with green skin—lizards instead of humans. It's worth understanding what made it possible for us to exist.

"And, if the cometary theory is correct, then fine debris from the impact so permeated the stratosphere that large life forms couldn't survive. Consider the recent studies of a massive nuclear exchange. Except for radioactive fallout, the 'nuclear winter' resembles what may have happened those eons ago, leading to the extinction of our ancestors. If so, we should learn from the past and prepare for the future. Dinosaurs could not control their destiny; we may be able to control ours."

SATURDAY, MARCH 10
The press brings two happy items: a half-page photo in this week's *Time* of Gary Hart wearing what appears to be the AU tie we gave

Is My Armor Straight?

Is My Armor Straight?

him last fall, and a ranking in today's *Post* of morning radio programs that places our station, WAMU–FM, first in the city.

MONDAY, MARCH 12

On an otherwise bland day, Madeleine Green of the American Council on Education writes to confirm my opening a conference for new university and college presidents. My talk's title is listed as, "The Faces of the Presidency," and the advertisement claims I shall discuss:

Expectations of the President as
• Educational Leader, Skilled Administrator, and Scholar
• Financial Genius
• Model Citizen and Community Leader
• Fundraiser, Astute Politician, Persuader of Legislature
• Public Speaker
• Friend and Counselor of Students and Faculty.

The program even says I shall explain how to do all this while "keeping a realistic perspective, a sense of humor, and professional and personal survival." That's a talk I would enjoy hearing. I wonder who could give it.

TUESDAY, MARCH 13

At 7:00 A.M., in driving sleet, where would I most want to go? To Newark, of course. With airports shut, the Metroliner remains undaunted, rumbling past Baltimore and Wilmington on its way to Newark's decaying station. In a world of free will, why have I elected to be here on such a day? I know the answer, naturally, and I have no regret about coming. But what a day. Mud puddles and blackened snow are nature's intrusion into the backdrop of ancient buildings and rusting cars. I am met at the station and driven to Kean College in Union, New Jersey, where I am to give a convocation address.

Despite the weather, spirits glow at Kean today. Proud of their institution, administrators, faculty members, and trustees tell me how much they have progressed. A sense of achievement is essential for any institution.

We don academic regalia and enter the main auditorium. After preliminary remarks, I am introduced. I note that the year the college was founded—1855—was propitious for education in the U.S. Besides Kean, Penn State and Michigan State started then. And in New York

State, the Elmira Female College began, becoming the first U.S. institution to grant academic degrees to women. In Watertown, Wisconsin, the wife of a German immigrant opened a school for children of other immigrants: the first U.S. kindergarten.

I remind the audience of significant events in 1958, the year of Kean's move from Newark to Union. The Supreme Court ruled unanimously that Little Rock schools must integrate. Pan Am and BOAC inaugurated transatlantic jet flights. The U.S. launched its first earth satellite. The median family income was $5,087. A Chevrolet sold for $2,080; a gallon of gas, 30 cents; newspapers, 5 cents; hospital rooms, $28 a day; round steak, $1.04 a pound; a year's tuition at Harvard, $1,250.

To help us pay for this, Bank of America introduced a wondrous device—the BankAmericard. First-class postal rates went up for the first time since 1932—to 4 cents. The U.S. Government authorized the National Defense Education Act, allocating $480 million for science, math, and foreign language instruction. The reason for this was Sputnik I. Americans were jolted to realize that the Soviet Union could achieve scientific and engineering feats beyond our current ability.

What, I ask, has happened in education since then? After discussing the pluses and minuses of this unique era, I suggest likely future changes. Some theorists claim that by 1995 about half the U.S. jobs will be in information; most of the remainder will be in service. If so, America in the year 2000 will be dominated by information, communication, and service. Farsighted educators should plan accordingly today.

Computers will be essential. I acknowledge this extraordinary new tool, but with three caveats:

• The field is male-dominated. Even though there is no genetic or psychological reason why girls should be left out, they are. Boys' propensity in the past to tinker with electric trains and bikes may have led to some positive adult skills. Current tinkering with computer programming undoubtedly will benefit them in the future. Computer games, on the other hand, merely waste time; they teach neither computer programming nor mental-muscle dexterity.

• Guilt-ridden parents should not be lulled into thinking they can meet parental obligations by buying their child a home computer. Money alone is not enough. Parents' personal time and attention is irreplaceable.

 • Even in a world of laser beams and silicon chips, the humanities will remain vital.

I note that in the year of Kean's founding, Robert Browning wrote an immortal line: "A man's reach should exceed his grasp." I close with the wish: "May this college and its people reach far and grasp much. Happy Birthday."

To my surprise, they award me an honorary degree. Asked if I would like to respond, I grin and say: "A college as much on the move as this one undoubtedly will send me an alumni pledge card."

The sleet has given way to rain. As the temperature drops, it turns to ice. I call Gail from a Newark airport hotel where I am isolated until the morning thaw. We were scheduled to attend a lavish Washington event tonight, but she and her mother, who's visiting us, will have to go without me. Her mother is going to wear a gown I picked for Gail. I know the gown and I know Gail's mother. The quiet lady from a small town in Massachusetts will make quite a splash.

As they head to the elegant affair in Washington, I gaze out my hotel window at chimneys and factories, trucks and warehouses. Is it true that by the end of the century much of this will go? Last century, our agrarian society became highly industrialized. Now, as implausible as it seems, the nation is moving inexorably towards a new economy. Older, industrialized sectors will readjust painfully. But readjust they must. Those of us with responsibility to prepare future workers and leaders must readjust, too. In a way our readjustment will be at least as difficult, for we must change not our physical plant but our thinking.

And what imposing responsibilities educators bear: to instruct and civilize; to teach facts and ways to learn facts; to spark curiosity and instill a desire to know; to raise questions, more than to give answers; to teach the past while attempting to see the future and prepare for it.

The cold reality of the university clashes as loudly against such idealism as the rain does against my windowpane. The professor's yellowed lecture notes, crafted two decades ago, reflect what he distilled then, not what his students need tomorrow. The professor is not idle in this; he is merely human. He feels the pressure of dean, provost, president—all urging him to do more with less: to assist recruitment, contact alumni, seek grants, publish articles. But what does this have to do with the professor's need to readjust himself and his pedagogy?

By now the night is black; through the haze I no longer see even the nearest factory. As I stare into the dark, Newark becomes the teacher and I the student.

WEDNESDAY, MARCH 14

The rain has stopped and my flight is smooth.

Deans, directors, student-life staff, and others gather in my office for a meeting about international students. Nationwide, the surge in foreign-student enrollment has slowed. Foreign economic difficulties have reduced enrollments from what some of us projected only a few years ago. International students continue to come, but in smaller numbers. They are important members of the AU community, adding diversity that wouldn't be available otherwise. We discuss ways to improve enrollment of and services for them.

Lunch is with Doris McMillon, news anchor at WJLA–TV. Our reason for meeting is that she will cover education. What does that mean? She says she will have occasional spots about education on the evening news. I tell her that when the paperwork is cleared away, I am going to do something similar at another station. We laugh. Beyond that, I am intrigued by this new friend.

After she mentions God several times, I ask, "Are you deeply religious?"

"I'm not born-again; I've always been a Christian. I believe deeply in God. He's what makes all things possible."

And what remarkable things she has experienced. She tells me about meeting, after a three-decade separation, her biological mother. Her white mother had put the half-black baby up for adoption. Black parents had adopted young Doris, ultimately settling in Chicago. Only a few months ago, Doris found her biological mother in Germany. The joyous reunion clearly was important to Doris. And she tells me about her childhood in a military family, as she attended literally dozens of schools. Now she anchors the evening news on a Washington TV station and soon will give its education reports. Not bad achievement for anyone. Amazing achievement for someone who had to overcome so much.

FRIDAY, MARCH 16

After giving opening remarks at a conference on fundraising for the nonprofit sector, I join Gail to visit Natasha's teachers. We all agree that although she is doing well, the next several months may be difficult as she moves into adolescence. Temptations abound to distract her—stereo, phone, friends. Gail tells the teachers that she is setting definite hours for homework and leisure; the two are not to comingle. I add that homework is to be done first, remembering my parents' admonition: First work, then play.

At home tonight, I flick on TV. Phil Donohue is interviewing Hispanic, Chinese, and black spokespersons who argue that TV fails to represent their ethnic groups accurately and sufficiently. Why, I wonder, are so many things called "united" when they are not? For example, the United Nations. For that matter, the United States. Although Americans are bound together, they are different in profound ways. Within a single state, city, or institution, we break into subdivisions. Even now, in technologically advanced America, we remain a community of tribes—Italians, Japanese, West Africans, Northern Europeans. We began as tribes; we continue as tribes. We blend and we integrate; we also remain separate. Is that inevitable? If so, what does it imply about education in a pluralistic society?

SATURDAY, MARCH 17

Gail and I explain to Natasha why and how we want her to arrange her after-school time. I point out that nothing comes easily. When something appears easy, it often reflects extensive prior work. The graceful ice skater or nubile gymnast reveals untold practice. Michael Jackson's brief "Thriller," I assure her, must have required weeks to prepare, choreograph, and practice. The worst thing to do with an adolescent is to say something corny. Nonetheless, I repeat what my mother used to quote to me: 3 Ecclesiastes. "For everything there is a season, and a time for every matter under heaven . . . ."

There is a time for her to study and a time for her to play. They are not the same time. Therefore, she is not to study with stereo playing or phone ringing; when she relaxes, we do not expect her to study or write. And, she is to leave completed homework on the kitchen table so we can see it. Our point is not to correct it but to review it. Sloppy work will not leave the house.

Through this brief but tense conversation, she looks down, saying nothing. At the end, she smiles brightly and goes about her usual business. Could we have succeeded as it seems? Even though she would be the last to admit it, I sense the cliché is true: she truly wants us to care.

After both of them leave the room, I go on reading 3 Ecclesiastes:

281

"A time to be born, and a time to die . . . . A time to weep, and a time to laugh . . . ."

It dawns on me: the first time I heard this was in school—as a school prayer. At the time I wondered if my school wanted to drill these words into my brain, for this passage seemed to be read daily over the PA system. Is this what the school prayer flap is about? I have argued that school prayer is unnecessary. No single prayer likely could be inoffensive to all religious groups without trivializing religion. Moreover, why cannot children pray in private, as the Bible teaches? Why cannot sufficient religious instruction be given at home or church? Those and other objections remain valid, in my view. But what would be wrong with having a period of silence? As Ecclesiastes says, there is a "time to keep silent, and a time to speak." And what would be wrong with having such beauty and wisdom read in school?

SUNDAY, MARCH 18

Natasha shows me her lab report. She and a girlfriend experimented to determine how the speed of water waves varies as a function of the depth. We go over her report, line by line. I remind myself that this is only a seventh grader. And even gentle criticism can upset her. So rather than give directives, I ask questions. "If you read this without having conducted the experiment, would you be able to understand it? Are your units consistent? Do your conclusions confirm your hypothesis?" Intently, she listens, then leaves to rewrite the report. If there is a time for everything, then now is the time for dad to cease for today.

Beyond enrollments and endowments, institutional visability and financial management, there are more fundamental concerns at a university. Academic administrators, caught up in crisis control, can lose sight of the institution's real purpose. Means can obscure ends; procedures can loom larger than purposes. After lunch, I closet myself and embark on a continuing-education program of refreshment and renewal.

Where better to begin than with Cardinal Newman's 1910 classic? Its very name—*The Idea of a University*—sets the compass for my day. My destination is not to find new benefactors or improve the physical plant; rather, it is to remind me of why universities exist.

Twenty years ago, when I first read Frederick Rudolph's, *The American College and University: A History,* I found a wealth of information about the enterprise that was so much a part of my life.

Today, academia is even more vital to me, and, as I reread Rudolph's superlative volume, I appreciate nuances I failed to notice before.

To place higher education in perspective, I browse again through Lawrence A. Cremin's *The Transformation of the School*, the masterwork on the progressive school movement. After that, I read a potpourri of seminal thinkers: John Dewey, Robert M. Hutchins, Richard Hofstadter, David Riesman.

The phone interrupts abruptly. "Wouldn't you like to have dinner? It's almost nine o'clock," Gail informs me.

After dinner, the books and I retire to the family room. Next in the stack is Daniel Bell's *The Reforming of General Education.* Although focused on Columbia College, it provides a splendid history of the movement. Next, I plan to review the major science-and-society treatises. But just as I begin Eric Ashby's *Technology and the Academics,* Gail calls from upstairs: "Richard!" How did it get to be 3 A.M.? My mind buzzes with William James and Alfred North Whitehead, but they will have to wait until next week.

MONDAY, MARCH 19

The National Endowment for the Humanities has sent me a lengthy grant proposal to review. Carefully written and closely argued, it persuades me. My only hesitancy is over the budget—more than $750,000. In the face of a $200 billion federal deficit, is this project vital? That, I conclude, is not for me to determine. Congress approves funding for NEH and other federal agencies. They, in turn, allocate funds for their divisions and examine proposed budgets carefully.

The process of peer review for proposals seeking federal funds is appropriate and constructive; however, the determination of what constitutes an appropriate level of funding and an appropriate federal expenditure is a subtle, imprecise art. Many proposals, such as this one, are genuinely meritorious. But do they warrant as much money as they request? And how do you determine the cost-benefit ratio of new information and ideas? Although this is hard to achieve, the federal agencies, assisted by anonymous academic reviewers, generally do a commendable job.

TUESDAY, MARCH 20

At our luncheon consortium meeting, we discuss: a project on East Asian art history, cooperative library storage, health care insurance, and the handling of hazardous materials on campus.

Tonight, I attend the Arab Women's League dinner in support of humanitarian and philanthropic efforts in the Middle East. The guest of honor is Queen Noor of Jordan. American by birth, Middle Eastern by interest and marriage, she looks decidedly regal, wearing a long rose-colored robe with gold bodice. Dillon Ripley, secretary of the Smithsonian Institution, and I chat as we wait to be introduced to her. Minutes later, she tells me how well her small children ski. We discuss more serious matters, too, such as the fate of the American University of Beirut. The program features an Arabic fashion show. I am impressed, not only by the skillful design, but also by the permeating ethnic pride.

THURSDAY, MARCH 22
A report arrives announcing that our faculty grants and contracts just have reached an all-time high. With pride I read a lengthy list of other recent faculty accomplishments: The Busch-Reisinger Saturday organ concert series, which will be broadcast over National Public Radio, will feature organist Haig Mardirosian; Louise Shelley, School of Justice, has been awarded a Guggenheim Fellowship and has been appointed to the editorial board of *Annales Internationales de Criminology;* Howard M. Wachtel, professor of economics, has published a new textbook; Arnold S. Trebach, School of Justice, has been widely quoted about his research on heroin. And on the list goes.

This afternoon, I stop by WRC–AM to be interviewed for an hour about UFOs. Roughly 95 percent of all sightings can be explained in terms of normal, understandable terrestrial phenomena—birds, planes, reflections, and occasionally hoaxes. Admittedly, the remaining 5 percent are hard to explain. Does that mean that they are inexplicable? Millions of people have accepted the least plausible, most extreme explanations—that UFOs are extraterrestrial visitors. The burden of proof falls upon the proponent, not the critic. It is not my responsibility to prove that UFOs *are not* from beyond earth; it is the believer's to prove that they *are.*

But how about the sightings by "responsible" people? Perhaps the most renowned person to report one was then governor of Georgia. Jimmy Carter said he saw a strange, peculiar object one evening—and he was not referring to his brother. Later, astronomers used computers to determine what natural phenomenon he might have mistaken. Sure enough, he almost undoubtedly saw a bright planet through the evening haze, a phenomenon that has misled many experienced observers. But the tawdry press relishes UFO stories. One of the best I have seen was on the cover of a romance magazine: "How a UFO Saved My Virginity."

FRIDAY, MARCH 23
At 8:30 A.M., Patricia Shaheen calls. "I just wanted to say hello, and please give my love to Gail and Natasha. Here's Bob, who'd like to talk to you."

"Bob, I'm delighted you are on this side of the world again. I'd like to go over several things with you." Finally, I get to the last item on my list.

He interrupts: "The center."

"That's it," I say. "The issue will be the principal topic for the May 4th board meeting. Now's the time."

"I'll be back to you as soon as we've talked with the chief."

Today's *Eagle* is outstanding. The editorship of the student paper and the presidency of the undergraduate student government both change hands today. The *Eagle*'s new head, Alexandra Clough, who is only a sophomore, apparently is a responsible, informed journalist.

The *Post* contains an article of personal interest to me. Fifteen years ago, I had a winter flu, with typical symptoms. After a few days, the flu ended and the symptoms left—all, that is, except a ringing in my right ear. It was maddening. So loud and persistent was it that I tried everything to get rid of it. I went to the doctor. Then to another one. And another one. I was examined by specialists. And more specialists. A year later, financially drained from doctors' visits, I accepted reluctantly what the first doctor had diagnosed: "Your tinnitus probably is incurable. It may leave quickly or it may last indefinitely."

After fifteen years, it is as loud as ever. By now, however, I have accepted it. Only when I am tired or tense does it become a siren in my head that nothing will squelch. There is no escape; it follows me everywhere. The paper says 36 million Americans have the affliction, roughly 2 million severely. I am far from alone. There is little comfort in that, though, or in the remedies the article suggests, all of which I have tried.

Gail and I tell Natasha, *bonsoir,* and drive to the ceremonial Departmental Auditorium on Constitution Avenue. We are ushered to a private chamber where a small group waits to meet French president Francois Mitterrand. Presently, he arrives, looking disturb-

285

ingly ashen. After we chat with several acquaintances, we slip out as Mitterrand starts to speak in French in the main auditorium. In front of us, tiptoeing out is Bob Strauss. I take his arm and say, "Some of us know to sit on the back pew." He grins broadly and replies: "In politics, you've got to learn that." Just ahead of us is Chuck Manatt, Democratic party chief. The Manatts and Berendzens see each other and smile, each knowing the other is leaving early. Such is the nature of Washington schedules.

After dinner I return to my office to work, but it proves impossible. The earth, in its orderly course around the sun, passed the vernal equinox two days ago. Although students may not know that, they sense it: spring has come. Music blares from McDowell Dormitory next to my office so loudly that I give up and decide to walk home.

At least since Socrates, if not before, youth have observed the rites of spring. Tonight is no exception. A couple strolls hand-in-hand, looking dreamily at one another. Young men toss a frisbee. Another student strums a guitar. Black sorority pledges march in unison, chanting. A student, with a foot-high stack of boxes, shouts to an open dorm window: "I've got the pizzas." All this, and it is 1:30 A.M.

SATURDAY, MARCH 24
Birds sing, breezes blow, the sun shines—on this glorious day, I drive alongside the Potomac to the beltway, cross the bridge, and turn towards lush suburban Virginia. Up and down rolling hills, I pass racehorses on the left, white fences on the right. Finally, I come to Madeira School where I am to give the keynote address at a meeting of the Junior League of Washington.

A dedicated group gathers in the auditorium to hear me hammer on education's flaws and needs, stressing how volunteers can help. They ask numerous questions. Public notions abound about such young women, attired in alligators and polo's, sockless in loafers, wrapped in pink and green, festooned with tiny flowers and whales. A fleet of Volvo stationwagons, BMWs, and Audis fills the lot. Beckys and Susans and Karens thank me profusely and rush back to their carefully crafted program. How fortunate schools will be to have their devotion. With all the opportunities available to them, they choose unpaid service.

This afternoon, I shock my family, my neighbors, and my body: I decide to jog. I know it's pointless and even dangerous to do so unless you intend to exercise regularly. I don't. But I feel in the mood for a good run. So I don my gear and trot to the AU track, feeling moderately athletic—until I encounter true athletes. How do they keep so bronze all winter? My white legs resemble loping birch trees. Stoically, I begin by walking a lap. Then I start to jog. After four laps, my legs are rubbery, perspiration drenches my glasses, and my cheeks feel like a July sunburn. Gradually, I slow my pace—about half that of the other joggers—to a walk. Then I collapse and watch a white-haired man who was there when I began breeze by for yet another lap. So he is good at jogging. Can he write a crackerjack memo? Keep awake during the third consecutive meeting? Think of anything to say to a stranger at a boring reception?

Feeling adequately consoled and sufficiently self-deceived, I stroll home. Jogging enthusiasts are right: after a good run, you *do* feel different. In my case, I have a craving for chocolate ice cream. Manfully, I overcome it.

I realize I should exercise regularly. Gail does so at the university's health and fitness center, a cardiovascular facility staffed by professionals. She enjoys it, and both Dons go, too. Milt is an avid jogger. Joan finds time for routine swimming and calisthenics. Only I try to exercise by walking fast and climbing stairs.

When I was provost, we lived in an apartment building in Bethesda. The distance from one end of it to the other was almost a tenth of a mile. One hot evening, I decided I wanted to jog. Why not in the hallway? After all, it was air conditioned, humidity controlled, carpeted, and free from rocks, dogs, and vehicles. And, at one o'clock in the morning, it was empty. So I donned my gear and loped along, following the winding corridors from one end to the other, occasionally passing a returning theater patron who would blink at me in disbelief. For months that went on. I had discovered the perfect jogging track. I bothered no one; no one bothered me. Outside, weather came and went, as I kept to my late-night treks. Ultimately, this routine was undone by my move to the president's residence. I gained a home and lost a body.

SUNDAY, MARCH 25
The International Studies Association is a multidisciplinary society of scholars and decision-makers from more than fifty countries. It is marking its twenty-fifth anniversary with a global assembly in Washington. The opening meeting is held at AU tonight, and I give the first address. Rather than have the audacity to tell them about their own

field, I share perspectives from mine. I give an astronomer's view of the globe, a view from space instead of the political bargaining table. After they depart, I stroll the campus, talking with students. "Say, Prez, are we ever going to get the sports center?" one asks. "We're working on it," I assure him. Then I visit the library. I ask the student guard at the door, "How's it been tonight?" He puts down his art book and says, "It's packed." Not bad for 11:00 P.M. on Sunday.

For the rest of the evening, I return to reading—the recommendations of the Carnegie Commission on Higher Education. Written more than a decade ago, these tomes influenced me then; and they warrant review now.

Eyes itching, body aching, I finally call an end to this round of self-study. How it will affect me professionally, I am uncertain; how it will affect me privately, I already know. I am recharged—not just to build a sports center but to fulfill the AU dream.

From all that I have read, many maxims ring. None, however, more so than Joseph Addison's from centuries ago:

> Education is a companion which no misfortune can depress, no crime can destroy, no enemy can alienate, no despotism can enslave. At home a friend, abroad an introduction, in solitude a solace, and in society an ornament. It chastens vice, it guides virtue, it gives, at once, grace and government to genius. Without it, what is man? A splendid slave, a reasoning savage.

This is why universities exist, why AU exists, why education in America must improve. And it is why I care.

WEDNESDAY, MARCH 28

After making preliminary remarks about the state of the university, I begin my meeting with the deans by asking, "Will each of you please tell us briefly about your unit? In elementary school, we called this Show and Tell or Bring and Brag."

Around the table we go for two hours. Despite my efforts to keep up on campus activities, I am amazed by the new initiatives that I have not heard about. A faculty member has just received a substantial grant. A student has won a significant fellowship. Applications are up in an area that has had poor enrollments for years. Staff members are disgruntled over one thing while buoyed by another. The deans are misinformed about some central administration positions.

Is My Armor Straight?

This is one of the most informative meetings I have attended in months.

After a brown-bag lunch at my desk, I walk through a downpour to a staff personnel office meeting. For half an hour I hear repeatedly, "We need better communication." No doubt we do. That need exists perpetually. For years, we have tried to solve it—using large meetings, small meetings, retreats, newsletters. Today, I suggest yet another approach.

"If you're not already doing so," I suggest, "individual units should invite people every few weeks for a brown-bag lunch. Show your guests your quarters; then, over lunch, explain what you do. Don't bore them. Prepare your remarks. Perhaps use visual aids. And don't do this just with top managers; invite guests down the chart. Also, do it when your unit is *not* in conflict with others. These should be problem-preventing sessions, not crisis-control confrontations."

Everyone supports this idea enthusiastically. What would they say if I suggested that we set fire to our feet? If the president says it, many employees applaud immediately—publicly if not privately. The test will be whether they implement this elementary suggestion.

Whatever the mechanism, we must diminish the classic bureaucratic beliefs: "I'm vital; you're dispensable." "I'm overworked; you're lazy." "I'm inadequately staffed, poorly equipped, underfunded; you're flush."

THURSDAY, MARCH 29
Technologically advanced America slows for few things, but a heavy rain is one. Today's torrents close the New York and D.C. airports, forcing Sally Frame, president of Ann Taylor Stores, to take the Metroliner. Despite the weather, she arrives in time to be our Marketing Club's luncheon speaker and to receive its Marketeer-of-the-Year Award.

As I listen to her discuss merchandising, I realize anew the professional challenges others face. Where should Ann Taylor open its next store? What's the local competition? How will consumers' attitudes change with the economy? With demography?

Sally speaks with ease, conviction, and humor. She knows her field well. I am impressed and proud that she is an AU alum. Ann Beattie, the acclaimed author, spoke on campus last week. The students not only enjoyed hearing her but also delighted in knowing that she is an AU alum. Sally has the same impact today.

When I return to my office, Milt hands me an eight-inch-thick pile: supporting documents for this year's honors awardees. To build pride and acknowledge achievement, a few years ago I invented Honors Convocation. In contrast with similar events elsewhere, we combine accolades for all segments of our community—undergraduate and graduate students, faculty, staff, and alumni.

There is no time to read the file now, for Milt and I are due at a reception honoring Laura Kummer, nursing school dean since 1967, who retires this year. Her colleagues recently requested that checks be sent to establish a Laura B. Kummer Scholarship. Already, several thousand dollars have arrived, a clear tribute to her.

Nina Roscher has arranged the reception well and presents Laura with AU mementos. Laura's faculty colleagues pay her an especially warm tribute. And then Milt, acting as emcee, calls me to the mike.

When I arrived in 1974, I point out, Laura already had served for seven years—almost the average tenure for a dean. Since then, all the deans have changed, except the dean of nursing. Over those years, she has been my one continuing professional colleague. I have enjoyed working with her and admire her as an individual. At this point, I put my arm around her shoulder. Normally, she is understated, even reticent. Not today: "Dick, word is going to get out about us."

"Laura, stop that. They know that you live in Virginia, I live in D.C., and that . . . "

"We're just going to have to stop meeting in Maryland," she grins.

What has gotten into her? Whatever it is, she is having fun. And the warmth she has shown her faculty and students is reflected by the ovation she receives.

FRIDAY, MARCH 30

Today's *New York Times* carries an item about the reception Gail and I will hold tomorrow night. Warren Weaver, the *Times* reporter, interviewed Gail rather than me. And she comes off well. Maybe too well.

"Dr. Berendzen, I'm from CNN–TV," the caller begins. "We read in the *Times* about your reception. Can we cover it?" Would lights and cameras change the ambience or offend guests? Probably not, and TV coverage could give AU excellent visability. So, sure, "You're welcome."

An hour later, the phone rings again: "I'm with CBS and we read about your reception. Can we cover it?" Thirty minutes later: "We're at Channel 9 and wonder if we can tape your reception." By now, I am genuinely nervous about lights and cameras and reporters. Still, this should be quite an experience for our students.

SATURDAY, MARCH 31
Even though Gail has prepared for days, we are up early to work on our assigned tasks. She designs one of her acclaimed centerpieces for the dining room—this one with a Boehm duck inside a large spherical bowl filled with water and dozens of tiny fish. Natasha arranges nametags in the study while I position furniture under a tent behind the house.

At 6:30 P.M., TV crews arrive. Half an hour later, students arrive —some hundred of them. Outstanding through academic achievement or student service, they are among our finest. As they enter, we greet them: "Our other guests look forward to meeting you. Don't be bashful." The students thank us for inviting them and confidently say they're not reticent—until they notice the TV cameras and the other guests. Our invitation just said we wanted to introduce student leaders to national and community leaders, but we did not name them. While Gail watches the door and Natasha gives out nametags, I try to ensure that the two groups do, in fact, converse. Little to worry about. Everywhere, conversations sparkle. We have done our part; now, we just leave them alone. The reward comes as they leave.

"President Berendzen," Josh Ederheimer says, eyes glistening, "I'm majoring in criminal justice. I bumped into someone and read his name tag: William Webster, director of the FBI. He talked to me at length about a career in justice."

Nancy Steorts, chair of the Consumer Product Safety Commission, remarks: "I suggested to some students how they could be involved with the commission." Another student says excitedly: "Aside from the usual references in my economics paper, I'm going to include one saying: 'Private Communication with Paul Volcker.' " Ambassador Layachi Yaker of Algeria clasps my shoulders and asks: "Dick, would you mind if I accepted your students' invitation to talk about the Brandt Commission?" Quietly, Supreme Court Justice Harry Blackmun says: "This has been quite an evening. Students questioned me about decisions I've made on the bench. I was impressed by their arguments."

Fred Fielding, White House general counsel, tells CNN: "This is a great opportunity for students to talk with Washington people. And it's a great opportunity for us to hear from them. It gives us a new perspective." As he leaves, he tells me: "You know, Dick, I attend a lot of functions. But this one I actually enjoyed."

Dick Lescher, U.S. Chamber of Commerce president, says the same as he leaves, while Loret Ruppe, Peace Corps director, challenges students to consider the corps. Senator Alan Simpson, half-glasses perched on his nose, bends his lanky frame in animated conversation with two young women.

My inaugural address comes back to me: "Think of it. Think of a truly great national university, located in the nation's capital city, drawing fully upon those incomparable resources."

The last guest leaves, Natasha goes to bed, and Gail and I clean up until two o'clock in the morning. Finally, we slump onto the sofa, smile, and sum it up without a word: The experiment worked; we shall do it again.

SUNDAY, APRIL 1
After a tortuous bout with cancer, Helen Herzbrun, professor of art and former department chair, has died—a tragic loss to AU and the Washington art community. We shall miss her deeply, for her grace equaled her art. She left instructions for the rest of us: rather than the customary flowers and funeral service, she asked that the collages she made during her final years, while she was racked with the disease, be sold in the campus gallery. Characteristically, she wanted the proceeds to go for scholarships. A special showing occurs this afternoon.

Even though the gallery is located at the remote end of the campus, far from traffic congestion, all parking places near it are filled. Finding the hallway packed, I inch into the gallery. Although I admire her artistic skills, I admire her courage even more. The collages' titles alone tell a story: *A Patch of Blue, Pulse, Storm Brewing*. Yet, through all this she maintained poise, never complained, and even, for a while, kept teaching.

TUESDAY, APRIL 3
Our consortium luncheon proceeds as usual, with one exception. We pass a resolution, to be sent in calligraphy to Father Tim Healy, the president of Georgetown University, commending Georgetown's basketball team on its stunning NCAA championship. Last year, AU's team beat Georgetown's. A narrow, one point victory, it nonetheless

brought joy to our campus. But many of our players graduated and our young team this year was no match for the mighty Hoyas. The Georgetown team and its remarkable coach, John Thompson, deserve the consortium's praise.

Tonight Gail and I attend a dinner celebrating the fifteenth anniversary of Second Genesis, a private, nonprofit rehabilitation program for drug abusers. Mrs. Reagan will receive a special award for her support of this activity. Our friends and trustees are here in abundance—the Benders, Bernsteins, Hodgeses, Lascarises. "Dick, I don't know where the *Eagle* got the idea I said anything about groundbreaking in October," Stuart tells me. "They're just ultraoptimistic," I reassure him.

Howard Bender smiles and asks: "When are we going to New York again? That evening with Khashoggi was really something." And Sondra, eyes beaming, says: "The center's looking exciting, isn't it? We're going to do it, don't you think?" Little does she know. How badly I want to tell her. But I cannot. Not here. Not yet. There are only a few more days to go.

WEDNESDAY, APRIL 4

Last year we started holding a spring reception for scholarship recipients and donors. Individuals, foundations, and corporations fund scholarships, yet they rarely get to meet the recipients. And recipients, it seemed to us, would enjoy thanking donors. We hope such interaction will prompt greater future support. Today we hold this year's reception.

As we leave, Gail digs her nails into my arm. Startled, I keep smiling as we pass students. It would be unseemly if they saw their president wince. Once outside, I shake her hand loose. "What's that about?"

"Indeed, what *was* that about?" she retorts.

"What was what about?"

"You know perfectly well. It's embarrassing to see you gawking at a woman's bosom."

"What bosom?"

"Not just gawking, but downright staring, with your head bobbing."

At last it comes clear: "Boy, do you have things mixed up. I was just trying to read her nametag."

"Read it! Your eyes practically drilled through it."

"You don't understand. With bifocals, I can't read through the top of the glass but I can through the bottom—provided I tilt my head just right and get close enough. But that takes adjusting."

She laughs and says: "Yes, I figured that out. At first it did look funny. Maybe you should carry a magnifying glass."

THURSDAY, APRIL 5

Thornton F. Bradshaw, CEO of RCA, and Frank Stanton, head of the Center for Communications, cochair an award luncheon today at New York's Plaza Hotel. The recipient is Allen H. Neuharth, president of the Gannett Company, the nation's largest newspaper chain. As a founder of *USA Today,* he fully deserves this accolade. Given that I agreed to be a vice-chair for this luncheon—that is, I bought a ticket—I felt I should attend. The group fills the ballroom, but, unfortunately, I know only a few people here.

This evening I spend several delightful hours with Bob and Patricia Shaheen as we watch TV and discuss AU. Bob is lucky to have Patricia, and Adnan is lucky to have them both.

FRIDAY, APRIL 6

After having lunch with Henry Dormann, I fly back to Washington. On the plane I read the *Chronicle of Higher Education,* which reports a recent study showing that although most college and university presidents enjoy their jobs, a fourth "would quit tomorrow, given the chance." The study confirmed the unremarkable cliché that it "can be lonely at the top." The plane is about to land. I put the paper away, gaze out at Washington, and ponder the article.

SATURDAY, APRIL 7

The mail brings me a form letter from the American Association of Retired Persons:

Dear Friend,
If you're over 50, the enclosed temporary membership card . . .

Moreover, I shall receive *Modern Maturity* magazine. Help! Their computer is confused. I am not over fifty. This probably is a fine organization with a splendid magazine. Someday I may join—someday. Meanwhile, take me off the mailing list.

At lunch I join professors from our math, statistics, and computer science department. We reminisce about our own student days when we used primeval instruments—slide rules. For greater precision we used clanging desk calculators. Wasn't that just yesterday? Maybe I should retrieve the offer of *Modern Maturity.*

After a family dinner, Gail works at home, I work in my office, and Natasha explores my building. As we start to leave, she points to the photographs of presidents who have spoken at AU: Wilson, Coolidge, Roosevelt, Truman, Eisenhower, and so on. "Any university that's had them should be able to get Michael Jackson."

SUNDAY, APRIL 8

On past weekends, I have reviewed the history and philosophy of education. Today, I shall read about AU *per se;* in particular, about our faculty.

Charlie McLaughlin of the history department has a grant to continue his definitive research on Frederick Law Olmsted. Linda Lubrano of the School of International Service is finishing an extraordinary book, *The Social, Cultural, and Political Dimensions of Contemporary Science: A Case Study of the Soviet Union.* A husband–wife team in literature—Chuck Larson and Roberta Rubenstein—are on sabbatical. He, an authority on Third World literature, and she, an expert on twentieth-century women writers, are writing new books.

Herb Striner, former business college dean and now university professor, has brought out a new economics book. He argues that to improve productivity, we must have "respect for individuals." Nick Long, professor of education, directs the Rose Demonstration School for emotionally disturbed children. A top school of its type, Rose provides on-site training for AU students as well as unique aid for troubled children. Nick's work reflects AU's commitment to the city.

MONDAY, APRIL 9

"All the world tonight is divided into two parts—those who are watching the Academy Awards and those who are here. I salute this obviously superior group.

"No less an authority on communications and politics than Groucho Marx once observed: 'Only in America can the people go on the air and kid political leaders and can political leaders go on the air and kid the people.'

"Tonight, we'll discuss more serious relationships between the press, government and the public." And so I introduce tonight's program in a series that AU sponsors on communications, business, and government. The organizer and moderator is Nick Kotz, adjunct professor and Pulitzer Prize winner. His panelists include Marvin Kalb, chief diplomatic correspondent for NBC News; Senator Nancy Kassebaum; and James Fallows, Washington editor of the *Atlantic.*

The standing-room-only crowd of students, professors, and media professionals listens intently and participates actively. C–SPAN televises the program nationally, while closed-circuit TV shows it to an overflow campus crowd.

TUESDAY, APRIL 10

Light streaming through stained glass windows falls on monumental stone pillars. The frailty of man contrasts with the durability of his handiwork here at Frank Church's memorial service in the Washington Cathedral. Military buses bring scores of congressmen, senators, and ambassadors as they and hundreds of family members and friends pay last homage to this extraordinary man.

George McGovern, the first speaker, is the most touching. As he reminds us of Frank's broad, effervescent grin, tears come to every eye. When McGovern finishes, Gail squeezes my hand. Our wet stare says it all: We remember Frank fondly; we anguish with Bethine; we recall his last letter to us; and we reaffirm our joy in living.

From this pensive, mournful morning, I return to my management tasks. The trustees' physical plant committee, chaired by Ed Carr, hears Myers's detailed presentation of our revised plans for the center. The new model excludes a theater and arts areas. This will disappoint our arts faculty and students, but we fully intend to provide them with outstanding facilities. At present, however, we are constrained by contract from divulging, except to the board, that we may acquire a major new facility by summer of 1986: using tax-exempt bonds, we will buy an eight-acre satellite campus, only a few blocks from AU, located on the Metro. By fall, those confidentiality requirements will be lifted. And then we can announce this major expansion.

The principal discussion this afternoon is about the exciting new design for the center. The trustees ask questions and make suggestions. Overall, they are thrilled by it. After two hours of enthusiastic discussion, punctuated by exclamations ("This'll give us a tremendous new resource!" "Look how attractive it will be!"), someone asks: "How will we pay for this expanded version?" Myers tries to deflect the question, but the trustees keep hammering. Then Stuart says, "I don't see how these numbers fit, unless you guys know something we don't know." Stu, you're on to it. But today we can't say so. Myers says the full financial discussion will occur at Thursday's executive committee meeting. Bob Kogod—the naming donor of our business college and an astute business executive—sums up the finances succinctly, concluding there is a substantial gap between what we have and what we need, but he assumes we will explain how we propose to fill it. And he adds, "I imagine they've got a way." Today the committee sees what we hope to build. On Thursday we shall tell them how.

For the past few months, because we were tired and had so many other things to do, Gail and I have cut back on social events. As useful as they are for expanding the university's circle, we just grew weary of them. Tonight, however, is an exception. It is the annual dinner of the International Neighbor's Club to which Gail belongs. The club's members include the wives of most of the key White House staff members, senators, congressmen, ambassadors, media figures, and a few others. Apparently, Gail and I fit into the "other" category.

She enjoys her membership, having made many close friendships. Tonight we ask Milt and Sonia to be our guests. As I drive downtown, Milt runs through a day's worth of meetings with me while the wives sit in silence. Finally, Gail says, "Can't you settle this in the office?" And Sonia adds instantly, "Yes, remember, we're here, too." Properly chastised, Milt and I stop discussing lawsuits, student plagiarism, staff personnel problems, and curricular changes. We listen as Gail and Sonia talk about the presidential race.

Dinner tonight is in an extraordinary place: Statuary Hall in the Capitol. Millions of tourists visit it every year, but only a handful of dinners have been held here. Tip O'Neill, complying with a request from his wife, arranged for the dinner to be held in this dramatic room, surely one of the most patriotic settings anywhere. For years, this was where the U.S. House of Representatives met; today, the House Chamber is just down the corridor.

I watch Milt and Sonia at another table being gracious ambassadors for AU. What a handsome couple they are. Both with dark good looks, white strands in their hair flecking the black. They smile with their eyes while holding hands like high school sweethearts.

After dinner, Jeanne Simon, wife of the Illinois congressman and chairwoman of tonight's event, thanks O'Neill for permitting us to dine in this exceptional place and then adds, to everyone's delight,

"You're welcome to go into the Speaker's office. His door's open, which doesn't happen often." A melodious sound then comes from all directions. The acclaimed U.S. Air Force Strolling Strings charm us with Pachebel's Canon and rouse us with a hoedown.

As we four walk to the car, I note the U.S. flag waving over the Capitol, and Gail observes the moon gleaming behind the dome. It has been quite a night. If we could whistle John Philip Sousa, we would leave the car and march home.

WEDNESDAY, APRIL 11
The Claremont Graduate School in California is studying significant changes in faculty conditions in the U.S. during the past fifteen years. Claremont selected thirty-eight institutions for site visits and AU is one. For two days, the interviewer has met with faculty and administrators; now she meets with me. Academics, I tell her, readily acknowledge that societal and political attitudes have changed, yet they are dismayed to find that their own enterprise has, too. Industry has been forced to achieve economies and improve efficiencies. So have universities, but many wonder why.

A generation ago, professors assumed that someone—it hardly mattered who—would provide a full classroom. Their role was to teach and conduct research. But just as war is too important to leave to generals, recruitment is too important to leave to admissions officers. Nowadays, everyone who cares about the university must participate. And increasingly, professors are being asked to provide academic and career counseling. While they have assumed these additional burdens, the inflation of the seventies and the recession of the eighties have eroded the purchasing power of their salaries. Not surprisingly, faculty morale on many campuses has declined.

Professors want dignity and dollars. They do not want increasing burdens and shrinking resources. They want to participate, as appropriate, in institutional decision-making, especially when it is related to academic matters. I tell the interviewer that our faculty morale is high. What deficiencies we have could be solved readily with one ingredient—more money.

As the interviewer leaves, my phone rings:

"I have an unusual request to make or opportunity to offer, depending on how you look at it. In June, a fundraising event will occur in Washington for the military academies. We wonder if it could be held at AU. The key speaker will be Richard Nixon."

"Richard Nixon?" I stammer. "This will be a major Washington return for him?"

"I suppose. Anyway, he believes in this fundraiser. What do you think? We need an answer immediately."

After a pause, I reply: "I don't like making a unilateral decision on this, but given your time constraint, I'll give my answer: no.

"First, we don't have an adequate facility—a convocation center. But besides that, Nixon wouldn't be here for a bona fide university-related reason. He wouldn't have been invited by our faculty or students. He wouldn't participate in a university function. He wouldn't even be here during our school year. If a legitimate body in our university invited him, I would defend his right to come. On this visit, however, he'd simply be using AU as a lecture hall. The city is filled with those—in the Kennedy Center, Convention Center, and hotels."

"I understand," the caller replies. "We'll try a hotel."

With that done, I read a terse, arresting letter from Orange County, California: "I am interested in purchasing your school for cash." No thanks. Would he like to purchase our competitors? That has promise.

At 12:30 P.M., I arrive at WRC–TV to tape "The Fred Thomas Show," to be shown tomorrow morning. Thomas asks me wide-ranging questions, particularly about who should go to college and why. I stress that not everyone needs a college education. We should dignify service jobs. Still, the riches of education benefit everyone.

Joe Carlo—former high school administrator and deeply devoted AU alum—chairs the trustees' academic affairs committee meeting. In contrast with our financially oriented board committees, this one is vital yet ill defined. Trustees want to be involved with academic matters, but their purview is limited. Day-to-day academic matters lie with the faculty, department chairs, deans, and the provost. The board sets overall policy; the rest of us implement it. The trustees want to be informed and to assist; they want to anguish over difficult problems with us and to share in decision-making. But they do not want to intrude.

Today, Carlo, Vince Reed (vice-president of the *Washington Post* and former D.C. superintendent of schools), and Fred Ness (past-president of the Association of American Colleges and former college president himself) analyze the university's honorary degree policies. Then we hit them with an unexpected bomb.

The Judge Advocate General's Office at the Department of the Army just informed our law college dean that public law "prohibits use of DOD appropriations at any institution of higher learning which by policy bars military recruiting personnel from the premises of the institution." If our law college prohibits a JAG recruiter from campus facilities because DOD will not recruit homosexuals, DOD funding for the entire university, not just the law college, will end. For the law college, such a cutoff would be inconsequential, but for the rest of the university, it would be catastrophic. Our distinguished Foreign Area Studies Handbook series would end, as would faculty contract research in several departments. Also, we would lose student financial aid.

After vigorous discussion, the board committee recommends that Tony Morella should request a deadline extension for when we must reply. We shall inform the dean that this is a university issue, not a college one. Tony will determine our obligations and will consult with general counsels at other universities that have encountered this situation.

The tugs on this case, legal and emotional, are strong and sometimes contradictory. On one side, none of us will permit the university to lose several million dollars each year; on the other side, should we be forced to accept a recruiter who discriminates against anyone? Irrespective of financial repercussions, we would not accept a recruiter who discriminated against blacks, Hispanics, women, the elderly, Catholics, Poles or handicapped people. But federal laws protect those populations. We do, in fact, provide equal oppor-tunity in our educational programs and activities; we do not discriminate on the basis of race, creed, color, national origin, handicap, or sex. In so doing, we comply not only with our beliefs but also with federal law. The law, however, does not include sexual orientation.

As the meeting ends, Carlo breaks the tension by reading a clipping of answers given recently on college science exams:

- A magnet is something you find crawling over a dead cat.
- Geometry teaches us how to bisex angels.
- For fainting, rub the person's chest; or if it is a female, rub her arm above the hand.
- To collect fumes of sulpher, hold a deacon over a flame in a test tube.

THURSDAY, APRIL 12

Goldie Hawn is filming in D.C. She is a former AU student and I will try to contact her. Also, I learn today that Barry Levinson, who directed *Diner,* majored in broadcast journalism at AU. He has just finished making *The Natural.* I will try to contact him, too.

The board's executive committee, plus the university officers, fill my large office. The turnout is excellent, as is appropriate for today's critical meeting. Cy and I confer briefly. Then he calls the meeting to order. "I'd like to turn to our president for a statement." The emotions are high; time, short; matters, weighty. I make my remarks pithy and pointed.

"I'm happy to report that the state of the university is extremely good. You around this table contribute substantially to our accomplishments. Specifically, you, individually and collectively, help us as never before with the annual fund and with the sports center drive. In that context, I have an announcement to make. Before doing so, may I urge that what I'm about to say not be disclosed until the appropriate time. To do so prematurely or incorrectly could jeopardize everything.

"I'm delighted to inform you that Adnan Khashoggi has agreed to give $5 million. In gratitude, you could name the center for him."

The room erupts. Thundering, sustained applause. Glowing faces, warm handshakes. Sondra Bender scarcely can keep in her chair. Stuart beams: "We've got it! After all these years, we've got it!" Bob Linowes, puffing a long cigar, grins, and says: "I don't know how you did it, Dick. But I'm delighted. Congratulations."

Questions shoot about the room: How can we ever thank him adequately? Will he be at the board meeting? How much more do we need to raise? Can we announce on May 4th? Dick, how long have you known? To the latter, I confess: "I've had a hunch for a month; I've known definitely for about two weeks." They kid me that I kept it to myself so long, although they recognize the importance of confidentiality. We must not have a premature leak. Everything must be in writing and the board must accept the gift. Even with Adnan's gift, we will have to work hard to announce on the 4th. We will not make a premature announcement. When we announce, it will be real.

After the group settles down, we continue with a thorough review by Myers of the revised architectural plans for the center. All agree: they are stunning. A splendid facility, it will have a handsome arena, other sports facilities, a large indoor parking lot, a board of trustees meeting room, other offices, and even a shopping arcade.

After the trustees leave, Myers, Triezenberg, and I meet to make further plans for the 4th. Then I have more phone conversations with New York. By now, it is 8:00 P.M. and I am painfully aware that this is Gail's birthday.

"Hello, Bunny. Your bum husband didn't forget. I'm just snowed under."

"That's okay, Love. I know how important the meeting was today. Did it go all right?"

"Fine. I just hope everything is okay with our pledges. I'll feel more secure when Adnan's is spelled out. The board must know exactly what he'll provide and it must accept it officially. Until that's done, everything's speculation. Pregnant speculation, admittedly. But speculation nonetheless."

FRIDAY, APRIL 13

Milt joins me for lunch in the faculty–staff dining room. While walking there, we are stopped half a dozen times for impromptu meetings. We expected this. If we had wanted privacy or efficiency, we would have gone off campus. Over lunch, he brings me up to date on the academic program reviews we initiated last year. They are progressing surprisingly well. The faculty and deans take them seriously. Actually, we may be able to drop some graduate programs, shift our resources, and improve other programs.

When I return to my office, a welter of messages and mail awaits me: Three calls from trustees about yesterday's meeting. Two others from New York. A request to review an astronomy text. A parent's six-page letter about his son's bill of $12.30. A donation from someone I met casually six months ago. A lawyer's letter threatening to sue over a faculty personnel matter. Two letters criticizing an administrator; a memo from him. A neighbor complaining that students park in front of her home. A welfare worker asking us to devote more resources to the disadvantaged. Three job applicants. A trustee urging that his partner's son be admitted. A student group inviting me to its picnic. An undergrad asking to interview me for a class assignment.

At 3:30, Milt, the Dons, Tony Morella, and I meet to plan the board meeting and retreat. Setting the agenda is straightforward: we follow the actions of the executive committee. Arranging the entire day is more complicated.

Advisory board members will join us at lunch. At two o'clock, in time for the evening news, we'll hold our news conference. On this joyous day, I want all appropriate campus representatives to be present. Normally, they would not attend a board retreat. So, which of them should we invite and how can we do so without rousing their suspicions? Finally, we are confident that the plans look good.

But it is now 8:00 P.M. Gail and Natasha already have gone to the campus production of *Chicago.* Given that this is the president's night at the performance, we all want to be there. The family will stand in for me until I shave and trot over. When I arrive, the room is darkened. I sit by myself at the edge. That is just as well, for the play includes salty language and provocative scenes. It is fine for college students, but borderline for a twelve-year-old. Natasha, nonetheless, survives the evening well; her mother looks frazzled.

This reminds me of a friend whose young son asked: "Dad, what's a faggot?" Panicked, my friend began a lengthy, fatherly discourse on sexual preferences. Finally, the boy said: "Dad, that's interesting, but I don't see what it's got to do with my reading. In *Joan of Arc,* it says they're going to burn her on faggots of iron."

SUNDAY, APRIL 15
This afternoon Milt, Bruce, Carmen, and I attend the annual initiation ceremony of the Mortar Board Honor Society. As each initiate's name is called, that person's résumé is read. They are stunning. While maintaining exemplary grade-point averages, they have tutored handicapped children, served in Big Buddy programs, led blood drives, labored in soup kitchens. They have received prestigious scholarships, participated in social and political causes, excelled in the arts and in athletics. And their names alone illustrate AU's pluralism: Aldestein, Aponte-Pons, Chang, Fiorazo, Parnett, Puri, Schlesinger, Waterfield.

On this day of student recognition, I join Gail for the annual Student Leadership Awards program. Last year the program went on interminably as each awardee elaborated about his program and thanked everyone, starting with his grandmother. Tonight, however, the program zips along. To my surprise, the students call upon some administrators for brief remarks: Milt first, followed by Bruce, and, finally, me. Everyone is lighthearted tonight and barbs fly back and forth. A group such as this could not laugh at such jokes unless they knew one another and cared about one another. When Paul Schroeder comes to the mike and is thanked for his outstanding stewardship of student government, he launches into an impromptu comic routine. He is made of many parts, one being quick wit. At the outset, he quips: "This has been an odd evening. It's the only night Dr. Berendzen hasn't talked about the 'great national university.' " The students cheer. Okay, I will tone down my pep talks.

The students are charming and humorous. And, again, their diversity becomes clear. The AU sailing club now is one of the finest in the nation. The black student union is highly active and increasingly is joining other student groups in cooperative ventures. The Residence Hall Association has been more productive this year than ever before. The *Eagle* has achieved a new level of professionalism. The Greek organizations have become responsible members of our community. The honor societies have more members than ever. And on the list goes. I also learn about groups I had not known we had: the Thai Student Association, Dungeons and Dragons, the Gaelic League, and the Society for Creative Anachronisms.

MONDAY, APRIL 16
For years Jim Weaver has been a campus mainstay. Elected to chair the new faculty senate, he also has chaired the economics department and is one of the campus's most respected voices. Two years ago, Milt and I easily selected him to be the first recipient of the Teacher-Scholar of the Year Award.

Today he joins me for lunch. Jim's positions are as firm as his voice is soft. His view of campus governance may be romantic for the mid-eighties, a kaleidescope from the sixties. Nonetheless, his wisdom makes him worth hearing; more than an economist, he is a humanist. And he cares passionately about the university.

Over lunch, he urges me personally to be involved in recruitment of star faculty. That, he says, is the best way to secure illustrious professors. Faculty want the president's aid in recruiting a star, but they do not want him to pick whom to invite or to participate otherwise. Jim's point is valid, nonetheless. Given that an institution depends upon the quality of its people, I want to do what I can to help.

TUESDAY, APRIL 17
"Jobs in the Year 2000" is today's topic on "Morning Break" on WDVM–TV. Two futurists and I are the guests; Carol Randolph is the host. One guest says future employment will fall into "dumb jobs"

and "smart jobs." Although he never defines these terms, I find them distasteful. I stress that our nation is becoming increasingly techno-logical, with growing emphasis on information transfer. Hence, many future jobs will require knowledge of computers, electronics, word processors, and other wizardry. "But," I caution, "life is more com-plex than that. Even in the year 2000, goods and services will remain vital. And someone will have to assemble microchips and robots. The one thing we can say with certitude about the future is that it won't be what we expect it to be. It is imprudent, therefore, to orient educa-tion based upon past job opportunities.

"Some people claim that cable TV will change the way we see movies, talk with friends, bank, and even shop. But electronic marvels cannot replace the innate desire of one human to be with other hu-mans. The world of tomorrow could liberate us while confining us. In the future, we hear, we won't need to leave home to work, play, or shop. But will we accept such imprisonment? Proper education for today and for the future is specific yet broad, professional yet general. Liberal and liberating, it should enable the students to adapt readily to a changing world."

After the show, students from the audience ask: "I'm fairly good at singing. Should I try a career in that?" "Nobody in my family has gone to college. Do I need to?" "I'm pretty smart, y'know. But I don't do well on tests, y'know. Whadda you think I oughtta do after high school?" "Would I have a good career if I combined a bachelor's in marketing with a law degree and an M.D.?" Charming in their nai-veté, they encircle me for half an hour. That I can help them, I doubt; that they spark a hundred thoughts for me is unquestionable.

When I return to my office, I worry about Adnan's gift. Maybe he will not give what I thought he would. I do not know the details; I am confused and concerned. I know he will come through because he said he would. But I have not heard directly from him. And I have seen nothing in writing. I sit in my armchair, my temples pounding, my vision blurring. This has meant so much to so many for so long, it just cannot go wrong now.

Besides Adnan, where is everyone else? Lots of people talk; few put it in writing. We must have many $100,000 gifts. Where are they? Dare I go forward without irrevocable pledges? Meanwhile, the cam-pus expectations are almost uncontrollable. The students assume that one or two donors will send me a check and all will be accomplished.

Never mind zoning. Or building permits. Or cash flow. Never mind that a donor publicly pledges $100,000, only for us to discover privately that he will pay it at $5,000 a year for twenty years. The pledges are helpful, but they alone will not pay a construction firm. We need upfront capital. It is coming, but will we have enough by May 4th? On top of that, how will Khashoggi's name go over?

No time to worry now, for Gail and I are due at a luncheon at the embassy of Spain, at which Lalo Valdez will be awarded a citation for his work on behalf of Hispanics in America. Courteous and charming, he is a splendid representative for the United States, for Hispanic people, and for the American dream.

After signing innumerable certificates for students, faculty, and staff prize winners, I have dinner at home before walking to WAVE–TV, the student station at AU. Student journalists interview Darryl Jones and me. As usual, Darryl is quiet and thoughtful. His maturity and presence are well beyond his years. His speech reflects what he is—a philosophy major.

I am so impressed by the TV staff that I stay to watch part of the next show—an aerobics class. The young woman hosting it literally hops onto the set and bends, runs in place, swings her arms, all while giving instructions and smiling into the camera. Move over, Jane Fonda.

WEDNESDAY, APRIL 18
"Remember the bishops' recent statement about nuclear war?" Father Paul Lavin, our Catholic chaplain, begins. "Now, they're preparing other statements, one pertaining to education. I've been asked to talk to you."

"I'll help if I can."

Father Lavin goes on, "What forces do you see affecting higher education in the future?"

"Not in rank order, they would have to include demography, the economy, population shifts, and Americans' attitudes about academia vis-a-vis other social institutions, including the home.

"The demographic decline remains, even though some private university enrollments may rise next September. Overall, the number of high school graduates will decline until the early 1990s.

"Also, education's recent roller-coaster ride of success and failure has been closely linked to the national economy. When the boom slackens, as it inevitably will, higher education will be an indicator. When the national economy is bullish, parents and students have more disposable income and view higher education as affordable, a necessity rather than a luxury. When the economy turns bearish, parents and students alike lose confidence and view education as expendable."

Father Lavin asks, "What recommendations should the bishops make?" Among others, I suggest, "to urge the building of bonds between higher education and other institutions—secondary schools, industry, government, the news media. Those traditional linkages disintegrated in the sixties. They should be restored.

"And given that this will be the bishops' statement," I go on, "they should comment on value-free education, the vogue in the early seventies. The premise then was that society has no absolutes; hence, one person's values aren't necessarily superior to another person's. The role of education, so went the prevailing view, was to teach facts, not value judgments.

"Although that reasoning has merit," I continue, "if we continue to have value-free education—in universities and schools and at home —then eventually we may have a society free of values."

After Father Lavin leaves, I call home.

"Natasha? Is that you?"

"Yes."

"I was calling for Mommy. Is she around? Does she exist?"

"Of course she exists, Daddy. Everything exists."

"Are you sure?" I ask. "In fact, are you positive that you exist?"

"Of course I do."

"How do you know? Maybe you're just a dream. Perhaps you'll awaken to discover that you're an old man on a park bench and what you've thought was life was actually his dream." Silence from a twelve-year-old is a rarity. For twenty seconds, I get it. Then she starts: "That's ridiculous. How could so many dreams fit together? We can't all be products of dreams."

"Might we be an hallucination of someone on drugs?" I challenge. "Or maybe the world is an elaborate mechanical toy devised by Gargantuan species. That doesn't seem likely, but could you prove it untrue?" More silence. Then: "I don't know whether I could or not. It's kind of a neat idea, though. But are you trying to say that houses and cars and other objects don't exist?"

"Do you remember the hologram I showed you recently? You

thought you saw an eagle-shaped object when what you actually saw was an illusion. Was that eagle real?"

"Well, I guess it depends on what you mean by *real*. What I saw wasn't what I thought I saw, but it was a real hologram."

"Natasha, I'd love to go on with you about epistemology, but I must talk to Mommy. When I get home, I'll give you something to read by Gorgias."

"What a weird name," Natasha laughs.

"Yes, he sounds like an egotist or a wrestler. Actually, he was a Greek philosopher. You won't like this, but he argued that there's no evidence that anything exists."

"I guess so. But I'm convinced I exist, and I can hear Sparky bark. I think he thinks he exists. And I'm sure Michael Jackson . . ."

"Okay. We'll take this up at home. I'll give you a Gorgias essay to read. It's not easy reading, but you'll have fun thinking about it."

"Actually, Daddy, I'm too busy to think about it today."

"I'll bet you that between now and dinner you'll think of Gorgias."

"No, I won't," she replies.

"I guarantee you will. Tolstoy and his brother had an exclusive club. It had only two members—just the two of them. To join, they had to—for half an hour, on their honor—not think of a polar bear. Do you think you could?"

"Sure. I practically never think of polar bears. Why should I during that thirty minutes?"

"Try it, Natasha. You can't do it."

Four hours later, Gail calls: "Richard, you can't survive on food bars. Natasha's finished her homework and we've had dinner. Are you *ever* coming home?"

"I'm overwhelmed with work between now and the 4th. And I'm almost sick over the possibility that we won't get the pieces together. By the way, how'd Natasha do on her effort to . . . "

"That's another thing. Why do you give her such challenges? At length, she told me about how she wasn't supposed to think about polar bears or somebody named Gorgeous. That's all I heard over dinner. I'm tired of polar bears and Gorgeous. Anyway, she hasn't been able to do the challenge. She's trying to figure out why she can't think of nothing."

"You might ask her if *nothing* actually exists," I suggest. "It seems to, but if you consider . . . "

"Stop! You two go on like that forever. Leave me out of it. Come home, eat a decent meal, and let your family see you in person." But does home really exist? Do I? Will the center?

THURSDAY, APRIL 19

At 10:00 A.M., I reach Myers. "Don, can you accompany me on the 3:00 P.M. New York shuttle? I just learned that I'm supposed to meet someone—it may be Shaheen, financial advisors, or Khashoggi himself. I'm not sure who'll be there, but this could be *the* meeting. I need your help."

"Of course I'll go. What's it about?" I tell him what I know and ask him to be at my office by 2:00 P.M. with all materials about the center.

Ambassador Yaker of Algeria hosts a consultation lunch for me at his embassy. In his gracious toast he explains about AU as an international institution. In my response, I thank him for his hospitality, invite the distinguished guests to know us better, and conclude by noting that a former inhabitant of that house—Lyndon Johnson as vice-president, before the house was sold to Algeria—commented when he moved to the Oval Office: "From where I sit, all the problems of this nation, all the problems of the world, come down to a single word. And that word is education." I thank the ambassador and rush to meet Don by 2:00 P.M.

We hit New York in rush hour. What an odd term *rush hour;* it should be called *slow hour.* As we creep towards Manhattan, Don and I review our financial strategies. At 5:00 P.M. sharp, we ascend the elevator to Adnan's apartment. Bob and Patricia greet me warmly and I introduce them to Myers. We are ushered into Adnan's living room. The man himself joins us, and I realize: this *will* be the meeting. Moments later, two top Wall Street financial advisors arrive. Adnan begins: "Professor, we're excited about the project. For two nights I've banged my head on the wall trying to think how to get the finances to work out for you. We've come up with good ideas, ones that may go further than you expected. Our Wall Street friends here will explain."

He leaves the room as the analysts begin. The techniques they propose are valid and creative. What else would we expect of Adnan? But I still do not understand how our dollars will fit. Despondently, I slump in the sofa. "This is dandy," I grumble. "But it won't cover interest payments. Unless more money comes from somewhere, we're dead in the water."

The analysts go on talking as Patricia leaves the room. Moments later, Adnan returns. "What's the problem?" he asks. "I said this will work and it will. I'll make it work. As for interest payments, I'll take care of them."

That's it! For the first time, I have heard it from him personally. Now we are talking about details; the substance is there. We will work out the mechanics, get it in writing, discuss it with the board, and have Adnan sign. That is much to achieve in two weeks. But we are on our way.

As I attempt to thank him, he smiles and says, "It's okay. I believe in what you're doing at the university. I'm glad to help. It'll work. Don't worry." Don and I exchange cards with the Wall Street men and depart for LaGuardia.

When we arrive in Washington, our cab blows a tire a dozen blocks from campus. Don and I trod along Foxhall Road at 10:00 P.M. carrying overnight bags, for we were unsure whether we would come back tonight or in the morning. Tired, hungry, and cabless, we snicker at our circumstances and smile about our prospects.

FRIDAY, APRIL 20
Due to a cancellation, I have an hour free. I walk the campus, from the admissions office to the student center to the library, past the dorms, and back to my office. On this beautiful Good Friday, buds are opening and everyone I meet is warm and optimistic. In the spring, Washington is undoubtedly this nation's most beautiful city. The tourists know the cherry blossoms; the residents know the dogwoods, azaleas, and tulips.

Our scenic campus is awakening, and traditional spring campus life is returning as well. A class meets on the Quad while three students have a heated discussion on a park bench. Two other students give out handbills while another rushes up to say: "Dr. B., I hope you'll be at the concert. It's really going to be exciting." I assure him that I will drop by, just as I do every year. The annual spring concert —viewed by many undergrads as *the* event of the year—will be held outdoors tomorrow in the Woods-Brown Amphitheater. For months, student organizers have planned it. Fortunately, the forecast could not be better: sixty-five degrees, light breeze, no rain.

Is My Armor Straight?

As I head up the hill to my office, another student passes me: "If you want a concert seat, you'd better stake it out now. Do you realize the Pretenders are coming?" I smile wanly, not knowing how to reply. No, I had not known the name of the group. Even if I had, I would not have known what that suggests. As the student goes past me, he shouts back, "The Pretenders are *big!* Even my New England friends are coming." That is great. This event is always important for students, but this year they are more excited than usual. And it is fun to see how thrilled they are over having friends visit.

As I enter my office, however, unsettling thoughts come to me: How big is this event becoming? Why did several students mention it? Why did so many say they had friends coming from out of state? We have never had that before.

Because of another cancellation, my lunch is free. So I do the unexpected and exceptional. "Hi, Bunny, would you like to join your husband for lunch at the faculty–staff dining room?"

"Really? I'd love to."

After lunch, Gail heads home and I walk back to my office. A student walking beside me says: "Dr. Berendzen, you're welcome to come to my room if you want a good view of the concert. With the crowd I hear about, there won't be room on the ground." I thank him but decline. And I wonder anew about the event.

Every university has exceptional faculty members, truly unforgettable people. One of the most preeminent of ours, Abdul Aziz Said, meets with me this afternoon.

A man of many parts, Abdul was born in Syria but was educated in America. He is of two worlds, two cultures, two eras. Political scientist and philosopher, humanist and romantic, he is a professor like none other. Rolling waves of black and gray hair, mustache, European tailoring, and exotic accent all add to his mystique. Omar Sharif with a Ph.D. He is an imposing figure, physically and mentally. When he calls himself "just a humble boy from the desert," faculty colleagues roar. Facts and legends about him abound. Twenty years ago when a group of Jewish students wished to found a fraternity, this Syrian-American became their faculty advisor. And a few years ago when I asked a senior about her most memorable professor, she told me:

"As a freshman, I wanted to take a course from the famous Professor Said. I arrived early and sat in the front row. Time came for the class, but there was no professor. We waited one minute, then two. Students began to shift in their seats. I wondered if I was in the right room. Another minute went by. The front of the room contained only a table, with no chair. After another moment, a nondescript young man carried a pillow to the table. Could this be the fabled Said? He placed the pillow on the table and left. Another minute passed. Then I sensed Said even before I saw him. We all turned in our seats to look at the doorway. A tall man with full hair and a lanky frame strode in, a long black cape about his neck. He walked directly to the table, took off the cape, whirled it onto the table, lept onto the table himself, crossed his legs, folded his arms, and said in a deep baritone: "I'm Abdul Aziz Said. Let us begin.' "

Students do not always understand his blend of mysticism and political theory, but they never forget him. He inspires them or transfixes them.

After my meeting with Abdul, Gail calls to say that the son of one of her friends is coming from Ohio for our concert. Then my phone starts ringing. "I'm in North Carolina and want to find out if tickets for your concert are free." "I'm an alum in New Jersey. A lot of us are driving down for the concert. Any chance we could stay in a dorm?" Something is wrong. We had never had such inquiries before.

The phone rings again. "Don Myers here. I just got the note you sent me about having enough security at the concert. You mention offhandedly that it's a shame it comes at this critical time for our zoning. It's more than a shame; it could be deadly. I'm hearing bizarre stories today. One office was contacted by somebody out-of-state who wanted to know where to park seven buses. They plan to bring bus-loads!"

"Yes, Don, I'm getting worried, too. I hadn't realized until minutes ago, when I read the *Eagle,* that the students project a crowd of 15,000—which is 7,000 more than last year. Last year's concert came off well; it was fun for everybody. Best of all, it was almost totally an AU event, with only a few off-campus people. But if the 15,000 estimate is even close to accurate, then most of the additional 7,000 will be non-AU."

"Exactly. And if they park in the residential areas, we'll *never* get zoning for a sports center or anything else. Do the students realize the dynamite they're playing with?"

"I doubt it. Nor do they realize the danger to themselves of such a crowd. They're just trying to put together an enjoyable spring weekend without appreciating what might happen. Let's meet in Poynter's office in fifteen minutes."

Shortly after 5:00 P.M., I join Poynter, Neuberger, Myers, and Gary Wright, the director of intercultural and community affairs. "Does anyone have a reliable estimate of tomorrow's attendance?"

"Nothing precise," Bruce replies. "But we've got scary indicators. The phones are ringing off the hook." Even as he speaks, two lines ring simultaneously. Carmen goes on: "The student offices may be getting even more calls than we are. For several days we've gotten increasing numbers of calls, but since noon today it's gone wild."

For an hour, we consider logistics. How many security guards? Ambulances? Who is going to control the noise level? How many portable toilets? Twelve. For beer drinkers? Thirteen hundred per toilet? Then, I make a simple calculation. "Look, if we assume 7,000 more people than last year, and if we assume two or three people per car, then we'll have at least 2,000 more cars than last year. And last year our lots were full. Where will the additional cars go?"

"You know where they'll go," Myers replies hotly. "They'll spill into the neighborhood, parking in front of homes and stores for blocks, in front of driveways and even on lawns. The non-AU crowd comes for a free concert; they couldn't care less about AU or its neighbors. But we do, and we must maintain good ties."

I ask, "Can we bring in Peter Martin to join us?"

As Student Union board chair, Martin has been principal organizer of this extravaganza. His office is down the hall from Bruce's and within five minutes he joins us.

"Peter, could you give an educated guess about tomorrow's attendance?"

"Twenty thousand," he replies.

Twenty thousand! How, we ask, do you get such a figure? He explains that not only are the student office phones ringing constantly but he also is hearing stories about people bringing carloads of friends. Peter tells us that announcements of the concert have been aired over Washington and New York radio stations and even over national TV. In addition, the lead group—the Pretenders—were modestly known when he invited them but recently had a highly successful album. Now they have a national name. Word is spreading uncontrollably that there will be a free Pretenders' concert tomorrow at AU.

Recently, when the Pretenders went on tour, they sold out at all stops. They *sold* out. But ours is free. The more we talk, the more concerned we become. After an hour, I say: "This is more serious than I'd expected. We must protect the university's people, property, and image. Let's bring in every student leader we can find."

Carmen and Bruce start phoning and within fifteen minutes about twenty students file into Bruce's office. I begin: "Thanks for coming on short notice. As a family, we face a crisis. As a family, let's try to solve it or at least minimize it. I'm not the best person to chair this meeting; I've had little experience with the concert. But someone must do so, so I will. Let me stress that nothing has been determined, no action has been taken. We're here to decide together what we should do—in our mutual best interest."

We start by asking how many they think will come. "Twenty-five thousand." "No, 40,000." "Not over 20,000." Estimates vary greatly, but no one expects under 15,000; 20,000 to 25,000 is accepted without pause. When I note that 25,000 implies 4,000 to 6,000 thousand more cars, the room grows silent. A student suggests that they could park in residential areas. Myers groans, while other students point out that will not work. Aside from relations with the community, the entire neighborhood cannot hold that many cars. Could we find parking at a shopping center and bus people back? At which shopping center? And on Saturday before Easter? Could we move the entire concert? Where?

When I point out that 20,000 is substantially greater than the capacity of the Capital Centre, everyone looks stunned. Our amphitheater will hold 2,000 comfortably. For a concert, we can squeeze in 6,000 to 8,000. But if we had 15,000, most attendees would not be able to see the stage or hear the music. Students' cars would be in great jeopardy. And, worst of all, we could not ensure safety.

For almost two hours, we search for ways to save the day. Could we put the Pretenders on early, ending the entire concert by 2:00 PM.? Could we give false statements to radio stations, announcing the concert is cancelled, so as to discourage non-AU people? Could we say, "President Berendzen has replaced the Pretenders with Liberace?" (That might lead to a rush of blue-haired grandmothers.) Could we park cars on our field? Could we ask D.C. police to regulate traffic in the community? Could we hire more security guards and attempt to cordon off the campus?

Gary Wright speaks forcefully: "We have to look at this in perspective. Should we try to have a five-hour concert, as much fun as it might be, or cancel it and preserve the university? We can't guarantee that the concert will proceed safely; it could get out of control. Even if it didn't, a large crowd might destroy the campus and ruin our relations with neighbors for years."

I had not entered this meeting with the notion that the concert would be canceled; to the contrary, that was almost unthinkable. I look sympathetically at the students who have worked diligently for tomorrow, as they agonize over one of the most difficult decisions they have ever faced. Finally, I say: "We've exhausted our imaginations. The concert is approaching. Whatever we're going to do, we've got to do it now. Unless there's something constructive to add, I'm calling the question.

"Can we continue as we've proceeded throughout this meeting?" I ask. "As a family, we have a problem. As a family, we seek a solution. I don't have it; nor do I know of anyone who does. Maybe together we can find it.

"I seek your advice. I'd like to go around the room to hear your opinions. But I don't want to put anyone on the spot. If you'd prefer to abstain, do so."

Peter Martin is unequivocal: "Even though I've put months into preparing this event, there's no question about it. We've got to cancel." Darryl Jones says nothing but turns his thumb down. Poynter and Myers, next in the circle, instantly say "cancel." Mitch Hertz, the new head of the Residence Hall Association, quietly concurs. And so the litany goes, with two students abstaining and two, who desperately want to keep the event, arguing that the crowd estimates may be high or that we somehow can control the situation. Despite the few dissents, the overwhelming consensus is to cancel.

How ironic. This event, more than any other, is student-run. They decide that the event itself is worth having. They pick the date, select performers, make arrangements, and handle advertising. And now they decide to cancel it. Not only does this remarkable group realize how much their fellow students want the event, they also know they stand to lose $50,000 if it is canceled. Contracts for big-name performers stipulate that they are paid whether they perform or not. I reassure the students that the university will help absorb the loss.

With the recommendations in, the consensus clear, and the circumstances compelling, I address the group. "Although I deeply wish the concert could occur, I regret that I must accept the recommendation almost all of you make. On this, as on everything, a single person must assume responsibility. I do so."

Carmen prepares a statement that we have canceled the concert. Peter— a courageous statesman—says he personally will make the announcement at Woods-Brown to several hundred people who are camping there already.

After dinner, I stop by to ask Peter if students took it well or if they blamed him unfairly. I find Bruce and Carmen before I find him. They are being blasted by two students who cannot understand why this cardinal event was canceled. Then I see Peter. He tells me that his announcement was met with a cascade of beer bottles. A heavy-drinking group—mostly non-AU people—shouted obscenities and threw things at the stage. Security has the area under control, but a couple of thousand angry dorm students have joined the protesters in the amphitheater. Peter urges me not to go near it.

In twenty minutes, he and I appear live over the student TV. We explain the situation and Peter courageously points out that we had to balance the value of a five-hour concert against the institution's future. We both say there was no choice but to cancel. WAVE–TV will run our interviews all night. That should help explain to dorm residents what happened. It may even mollify them.

Once outside the studio, however, I wonder. Groups mill about, some laughing and talking, others drinking and shouting. It is unclear who is a student and who is from off-campus. Wearily, I notice six males across the street. One of them heads my way. I steel myself for the worst.

"Dr. Berendzen, it was a courageous decision. The administration and the student leaders did the right thing. I've worked on this for months and it hurts like hell to see it canceled. But we had to do it. There's no way AU could have held such a crowd."

To youth today, a once-a-year major concert is a cherished thing. Yet these students show maturity, wisdom, and courage. While I see it this way, many students do not. In their minds, only one villain could have been responsible for such a dastardly deed—Berendzen. And so I hear taunts, shouts, slurs, curses. I pass three large, scruffy males who do not resemble students. When a dorm resident says, "Hi, President Berendzen" as she passes, this trio looks at me intently. I pass them. Then I feel it. A dull thud to my upper shoulder, knocking me forward. I whirl around and see the trio running. With my shoulder aching, I check to see what hit me. It was a beer bottle. What, I wonder, would have happened if it had hit six inches higher, at the base of my skull? Should I contact Security? Might that provoke more violence? I decide to let the matter pass. To find the threesome in the dark with so many people on campus would be impossible. And even if we succeed, what would we have achieved?

My attempts at consoling and explaining by now are spent, and I've become more of a lightning rod than a pacifier. So I head home. Yet another group of students comes up with the suggestion I have heard three times in two hours: "We understand the cancellation. Frankly, we are grateful. There could have been 35,000 people; some of our friends who know about such events projected 50,000. But some type of get-together is important to students. Could we hold a picnic next Friday night, maybe with a small band? It's the last night after classes before exams."

"Of course," I reply.

SATURDAY, APRIL 21

My house rumbles. Through the window I see a motorcycle gang roar by. Despite our radio announcements, many would-be concert-goers arrive. Young people with hair in four-inch-long spikes stalk the campus perimeter. Security guards fortify all campus entrances, and, for a few hours, they block access to all who do not have AU IDs. What a curious melange sits across the street—men with coolers of beer and women with pink and purple hair: the off-campus contingent we feared.

Shortly, they disperse, Security thins, and the campus returns to normal—more or less. While the library is packed, students stand in clumps outside. As I walk along the mall, one says loudly to her companion: "It's all that bastard Berendzen's fault." Further on, another says to me: "I hope you're happy ruining what would've been the greatest day of my life." A bodiless voice shouts: "Pig!"

Once in my office, I set about the work I had planned to skip this afternoon. The phone rings. Foolishly, I answer it. I should know better on a Saturday. "Hello."

"Is this Berendzen?"

"Yes."

"Who the hell are you, canceling our concert?"

"The university has the responsibility to ensure safety. A crowd the size everyone projected could have become a mob that would . . ."

"Don't hand me bullshit. You're just a . . . "

I hang up. Ten seconds later, the phone rings again. This time, I ignore it. It rings at least fifty times. I turn off the bell, but even in my silent study, the flashing lights of incoming calls blink. Finally, I head home.

Three students cross the road to speak to me and I prepare for their blast. But they surprise me: "It was the right decision. AU isn't Madison Square Garden and we shouldn't try to hold a major concert."

"Especially one that's free," I interject. "Thanks for saying so."

No doubt my haggard look reveals more than my words, for one of them adds: "You're probably getting a lot of noise from angry students. Mostly, they're unhappy because they'd been counting on a big, unifying event. It's not the music they miss so much as the chance to be together, perhaps the last time for seniors."

"Given that," I ask, "would a picnic or concert with lesser known performers next Friday evening fill this void?"

"It would help."

As I walk home, I wonder what we should arrange for Friday. If we announce today, we might reduce the current disappointment. But we also might be misunderstood by the off-campus crowd, who would think we had shifted the big concert to Friday. Despite the temptation, we shall keep quiet until next week.

MONDAY, APRIL 23

WAMU–AM, the student radio station, asks if I am willing to appear tonight. Although I have to rearrange my schedule, I agree to do so, for the concert issue remains impassioned. Communication, I believe, is the solution. If students hear the facts, most will understand; many will concur.

I arrive at the station and meet Bruce, Carmen, and a student who was at the Friday meeting. A student interviewer starts the program. "Is it true," she begins, "that you canceled because of neighbors' complaints?" "No," I respond. "Not a single neighbor protested. I doubt if any knew about the crowd."

So far so good. Now come live phone questions. The first caller angrily complains about the cancellation and then shouts: "F_ _ _ Berendzen!" The moderator, blushing, slams the *off* switch and barks: "If your intention is to be abusive, don't call. We'll cut you off. The program is a forum for opinions and information, not crude language or insults."

The next several callers roar disapproval, but do so civilly. Then a caller adds a new twist: "When are you going to apologize to us?" I start to answer, but Bruce speaks first: "Dr. Berendzen is capable of answering for himself, but I'd like to respond, if I may. We acted to protect the students and the university. To have done otherwise would have been irresponsible. Many of your own student leaders recommended this decision to the president. It was the right decision. If we hadn't taken it, we might be trying to explain tonight why we'd allowed a disaster to occur."

After another twenty minutes, the show ends. The WAMU staff —all courteous and gracious—thank us for coming. As I start to leave, one whispers: "You'd better wait. There are some rough-looking fellows outside. We've called Security to escort you."

What is this? I cannot walk on my own campus? This is silly. When I leave the building, I see no one. Heavy mist hangs in the air, giving the campus an eerie, London-like appearance. I round the corner and find a security car and guard waiting. No one else is in sight. I wave the guard on. Then I notice several students. One of the largest strides my way. He thrusts out his hand and says, "I'm with you. You saved my university. And you may even have saved a number of AU students." I thank him and continue on through the mist.

As I pass in front of the Broadcast Center, yet another beefy frame heads my way. This one has no warm hand, smile, or praise. He blocks my path and starts: "I want to tell you what I think about the cancellation." That is as far as he gets. I look him squarely in the eye and rumble out a single word: "Move." He does, and I go home.

TUESDAY, APRIL 24

Confusion reigns over our center pledges. What is their present value? If the payments are spread out too long, we shall have cash-flow problems. As Myers and I analyze the data this morning, we conclude painfully that we cannot fund it. Meanwhile, students assume the only reason for canceling the concert was that the center is imminent.

As I try to determine how to save the center's fragmenting finances, I hear that some students at Friday's meeting now disavow their votes. Can this be? Can students who acted nobly and courageously four days ago now have no integrity?

Maybe I am sleepy. Or hungry. Whatever the cause, I am exhausted. Never have I felt more spent. With my tinnitus screeching, my head is ready to burst. My eyes ache, my temples throb.

I call Triezenberg to ask how he sees funds coming for the center. He is as disillusioned as I am. People keep telling us what we want to hear, but they won't put it in writing. I tell him: "Don, I'm fed up. Yesterday, a student asked me about the design for the center complex. I told her that it will be twice the size of Mary Graydon Center and three times the cost of the library, yet its construction costs won't fall on tuition. She shrugged and said, 'Yeah, so?' "

"It does get discouraging," Don agrees.

"Discouraging, hell!" I snap back. "I've had it. I'm tired of donors equivocating while adolescents scream. I'm tired of faculty who don't care about anything but pay raises and alumni who only want better jobs. I'm tired of worrying about neighbors' sensibilities while the same people won't support their local university. I'm tired of everyone who wants something but will contribute nothing—of people who criticize but won't help.

"In fact, Don, I'll tell you how fed up I am. I'm thinking about not attending on the 4th. It's the trustees' meeting. Let them handle it. Then, after the commencements on the 13th, I'm thinking of resigning."

There is silence. Even though I realize I have gone too far, I do not retreat. Calmly, Don replies: "I don't blame you for feeling down. I do, too. But as a stubborn Dutchman, I'm determined to find the money. Still, I won't try to pep you up. There's not much I can say. Unfortunately, you're right."

As we hang up, Myers calls.

"Dr. Berendzen," he begins. "Darryl Jones and other students are here in my office. We've agreed on the concert costs. In accord with your instructions, I have said the university will pay up to half the loss. And I also have offered funds for the Friday night event, in accord with your instructions. Do these arrangements sound satisfactory?"

Never has Don spoken to me so formally before. Clearly, he is trying to tell the students that I approve these expenditures and that the administration genuinely cares about their welfare, which is true. This is good strategy, but I'm not in the mood. I grumble back: "Don, I don't give a shit one way or another." His voice drops. "Very well, Dr. Berendzen. With your concurrence, we'll proceed with this arrangement. Thank you." We hang up.

Joan brings me the mail. A parent complains about a professor. A professor demands a raise. A staff member dislikes his office. An alum complains: "You have some nerve. You sent me a solicitation letter but you still haven't built the sports center. When you get off your ass and do that, I'll consider giving." The final item in the pile is an unsigned, obscene letter about the concert cancellation.

When Joan returns to my office, I lean back and say: "I've had it. Either this university is falling apart or I am. I think I'll not attend on the 4th but just send a one-sentence letter: 'I resign.' " Joan's jaw drops slightly; she whitens and says tentatively: "Things really have gone crazy. You look awfully tired."

As she returns to her office, I think how unfair it is to scare her and the Dons. Although they are professionals, their jobs derive from mine. Although they care about the university, they also care about themselves. Such blasts must frighten them. Even as I think this, Joan buzzes to say that Poynter has returned my call.

"Bruce, do we have a single student with integrity?"

His momentary silence echoes the others. Then the constantly mellow Bruce replies: "Dick, don't let the crazies get you down. There are always hotheads and loudmouths, but they're in the minority. The great majority are really very responsible, and they . . . "

"Bruce," I butt in, "you always say that we only hear from a noisy minority. That's probably true. But where are the others? Why are they *always* quiet? Why do the ones who speak out to me privately become silent when they're with peers? I understand the pressures on them. But some of their slipping and sliding goes beyond the pale. A student last Friday told me that cancellation was the only prudent choice; today, with students listening, he took exactly the opposite position."

"I know, Dick. But, believe me, you're just hearing an unrepresentative minority."

"I used to believe that," I confess. "Now, I wonder. Probably I'm just tired. Such generalizations are stupid. But, I swear, they just seem like spoiled brats. Between them and equivocating donors, I scarcely know which way's up."

With the phone back on the hook, I tell Joan I am going out.

For the first time in years, I go home at midday. Gail stares disbelievingly, smiles pertly, and asks: "Hi, Love. Why are you home?" "I've truly had it. I'm tired or something. I just don't know. I'm thinking seriously about resigning." She blanches and says, "Oh, Richard. You're pushing too hard. Why don't you . . . "

"I don't want to talk. I'd like to be alone."

I walk into the sunroom—a charming, tranquilizing place that guests enjoy. This is the first time I have sat here at midday or by myself. I turn on a Simon and Garfunkel tape, the Pretenders of 1970. I stare out at trees, listen to "Bridge over Troubled Water," and feel sorry for myself.

After a few minutes, remorse sets in and I head to the faculty–staff dining room for lunch. A student passes and says, "Hi." I ignore him. As I see his smile fade, I turn to apologize. But on this, my day of exhaustion and self-pity, I keep walking.

A few people glance at me as I sit alone at the end of the room. Rarely do I eat here so late; never do I do so alone. My eyes fixed on my plate, head buzzing, thoughts ricocheting, I notice someone at my table. "I've never had the opportunity to meet you before, President Berendzen. I'm a senior and graduate in a few weeks. I just wanted to say that during the four years I've been at AU, the university's improved tremendously. It's getting better and better. I'm deeply proud of it. And I'm grateful to you." My mouth opens but no words come out. I choke back my wavering voice and blot my eyes as if they were tired. The student and I shake hands. With a cracking voice I say: "More than you'll ever know, I appreciate that."

He leaves and I look across the empty room. Where did he come from? Why was a student alone in the faculty-staff dining room? Did the Dons send him? Gail? Joan? Bruce? Impossible. No one knew I was here. Then I realize that I did not ask his name. If there ever was a student whose name I would like to know, this is the one.

As I walk back to my office, Myers passes me on the sidewalk. He puts his arm around my shoulder and says with a laugh, "Mr. President, hang in there."

THURSDAY, APRIL 26

On a splendid spring day such as this, surely all is right with the world. Low humidity, a temperature of seventy degrees, bright sunshine, soft breeze, blossoming trees—nature contributes, but so, too, do our students. Today is Israel Day and students have set up displays of food and handicrafts. From posters to books, from clothes to music, the central Quad is filled with Israel. Two students beam as they hand me Jewish pastry. Another student asks me: "Do you like it?"

"Yes, I really do."

"Have you had it before?"

"Not in the U.S."

The young woman's eyes narrow slightly, and she asks: "Where, then?"

"Israel."

"Really? Where in Israel?"

"Jerusalem."

Her eyes brighten as she cradles the word: *Jerusalem.*

I drop by a luncheon meeting of emeriti professors. As I stop to chat at each table, I think back to eating pastry on the Quad. This is all too much like being a politician. Maybe that is part of my job, too.

The emeriti are in good spirits. "Dick, thanks for shutting that concert," one of them says. "It could have destroyed the university and the neighborhood."

With my zeal momentarily restored, I return to my office, where a new stack of complaints and crises awaits me. Again, the center's funding seems murky. Myers and I have another long discussion and we wonder anew if everything will come together by the 4th.

At 6:30 P.M., I go home, lie in bed, and stare at the ceiling. Gail turns off the light and says: "Why don't you sleep?"

"I can't. We're supposed to be there by 7:00 P.M. and neither of us is dressed. Sondra worked hard on this. You know how difficult chairing a big ball can be."

"Yes, and the Heart Fund is worth supporting," Gail says, "but the Benders would understand if we didn't go. I'm worried about you. I've never seen you look so tired before."

"I'll be okay once I eat. We owe it to Sondra to go."

And so we do go. Howard and Sondra greet us in the receiving line. He beams and pumps my hand. Resplendent in a heart-red gown, Sondra looks radiant. She kisses us hello before we meet the next jovial person in line—Willard Scott, TV personality and AU alum. As usual, he has a dozen lightning-fast quips.

Within moments, we see many of our friends—the Bernsteins, the Dick Dubins, the John Masons. As much as I enjoy chatting with them, I feel dizzy. Finally, I say to Gail: "I must leave. I don't know whether it's lack of food or sleep, but I'm woozy. Please give my regrets to our table." Gail does so while I lean against a wall.

Never has bed felt better. And, somehow, I go to sleep before midnight.

323

FRIDAY, APRIL 27

Again, nature blesses us. And what a special day this is. Hundreds of admitted freshmen and their parents are our guests for an introduction to AU. So far, 28 percent have paid deposits; 72 percent have not. The latter group may decide to do so or to accept admission elsewhere. Today could be decisive.

Milt, who has had a two-week bout with flu, is at the breakfast for freshmen and their parents. So, too, are the usual troops—Poynter, Neuberger, O'Connell. And so is Triezenberg, who took the red-eye back from California to be here. He made a two-day trip there in a push for funds before the 4th.

At 9:30 A.M., students file into a large lecture hall to hear Greenberg and Turaj, while parents file into another one to hear me. What to tell them? Rather than pontificate about educational theory, I will give them vignettes from my past couple of weeks. In so doing, perhaps I will illustrate what our university is about. So I tell them about the Nixon inquiry, the concert cancellation, the Quad yesterday, and a recent TV interview. But I am so tired and unprepared that I stumble in my syntax. My sentences get entangled after the second clause, third semicolon, fourth dash. As part of my brain scrambles for the next idea, another part wonders why I ramble.

The morning mail brings a barrage of problems, and Myers and I have another discussion about the center's seesaw financing. In desperation, he states: "Unless we can get more donors on this in writing with reasonable pay periods, we'll have to postpone the center meeting. I don't give the 4th more than fifty-fifty odds. It could be a success or a disaster."

On that ambivalent note, I read an editorial in today's *Eagle:* "AU will finally get its Sports Center. We know they're going to announce it. . . . The question is, why haven't the students been informed . . . why should others know before the students who support the university?" The editorial goes on to say that if a sports center is not completed by 1986, "the jobs of all the AU administrators are in jeopardy."

After lunch, I stop by the library. As I head back to my office, a student walks beside me. "I hear the sports center won't be finished until late 1986. A lot of good that'll do me. I'm a junior. Can't it be built faster or are you screwing up on that like you did with the concert?" I start to explain about zoning, contracts, and construction time. But I shrug and give what is probably a better reply: "Life's filled with disappointments. Try to bear up."

Late this afternoon, I begin feeling vertigo again. Given that we have an important night ahead, I decide to leave early. Before doing so, however, I stop by Milt's office to review the week. He says some faculty sound "squeaky" . . . that is, grumpy. How can this be, given such an excellent year? By all measures, this has been one of AU's best. Logically, we should be exuberant. But few are, least of all me.

Then I launch into a diatribe, telling a silent and ashen Milt: "I've had it. I'm disillusioned with this institution. People who work for its improvement seem to be outnumbered tenfold—or a thousand fold—by those who tear it down."

"University administrators," he observes, "often stay only a few years. They get fed up or burned out. The next place they go probably won't be much better. But at least they'll have a brief honeymoon before they discover the weak spots there."

"I'm baffled, Milt. I'm unsure whether it's me or the institution. I've never seen it look rotten before. For the first time since I came here—close to a decade now—I genuinely don't care. I'm tempted to tell Khashoggi to save his money and scotch the project. When a petulant child pounds the floor and screams, do you buy him a bike? I'm tired of bellyaching kids, whining professors, and evasive donors. My skin's wearing thin; my patience is going."

I do not tell him that in only two weeks I have lost nine pounds. Obviously, something is wrong. But when can I fix it?

Tonight the Shaheens are fellow guests with us at a dinner honoring Robert Byrd, senator and AU alum. The host, Ed Morgan, is a mutual friend. Although we talk to the Shaheens about many things, the conversation always returns to the center. They will discuss final details with Adnan early next week. They assure me everything is fine and I believe them. If we can get the other donors lined up, the pieces may yet fit by the 4th.

As Gail and I drive home, I swing by my office. We do this so often and at such odd hours, that she does not even ask why tonight. From the hill by my office, we see thousands of people spreading into the amphitheater. Apparently, our Friday night event has been well attended. But has it been well liked? If the hour were not so late and if I were not so tired, I would try to find out before venturing into what could be a hostile crowd.

"Hey, look, it's Berendzen." Some students shout; others stare; a few whisper. Quietly, Gail says: "Don't get far from me." And I murmer back: "You'd be safer if you weren't so near."

But then three students walk up, big grins on their faces. "This has been great. It's one of the best nights we've ever had."

As I look about, the truth of this is evident. The crowd fills the amphitheater, a light breeze blows, and laughter engulfs the area. As Gail and I walk slowly through the crowd, at least two dozen students say: "It's a great night." "It's far better than the concert would have been." "The best part of tonight is that it's strictly AU without tens of thousands of other people." "The concert would have been a disaster." "Thanks for this evening."

As Gail and I descend the amphitheater's steps, a young couple smiles. He asks: "Are you a professor?"

"Not exactly," I reply. "I'm the president."

Even in the dark, his blush glistens. "Oh, my God. I'm sorry. I didn't know."

"That's okay. Are you a student here?"

"Yes, sir. A freshman."

I grin and say: "You mean, you *were* a student here."

The young woman with him laughs; he blushes even more. As we leave, we hear him stammer: "My gosh, I didn't know who he was."

A student hands us a beer-company painter's hat—popular attire tonight. Gail holds hers; I don mine, thinking vaguely about the famous picture of Calvin Coolidge in an Indian headdress. For the second day in a row, I feel like a politician.

Another student hands me a bottle of beer, which I reluctantly sip —I hate beer. The students' fervor tonight is so contagious, their excitement so real, that Gail and I are swept up in it. For half an hour, we watch them dance and laugh. On the way back to our car, students wave and shout: "Hi, Mr. President. Thanks for this wonderful night. We appreciate it."

SATURDAY, APRIL 28
At 9:00 A.M., the tenth- and twenty-fifth-anniversary alumni classes pour through our front door for their annual reunions. Anita Gottlieb's office has arranged the day, starting with the reception and ending with our annual spring ball tonight. While Natasha pours coffee, Gail greets people at the door and I mingle with the group.

Fifteen minutes after the group leaves, the fiftieth-anniversary class arrives. I tell them: "I've heard about your escapades." They laugh. I go on: "When you're on campus today, don't tell the students about them. I have assured them that students used to be serious. You mustn't ruin the image." They clap. And later they smile as I tell them about their university's accomplishments.

As the last of the fiftieth-anniversary group leaves, I ask Anita: "Am I needed at lunch? Milt will be there."

"No," she shrugs. "We had you on the program as a courtesy. You don't have to go."

"In that case, I'd like to skip it. I'm not feeling well, and I must perk up before evening."

From noon until 5:oo P.M., I do something I didn't think I could do anymore: take a nap. But I can.

Tonight, we go to the spring ball, which I invented when I was dean. My intent was to come up with a community-building event at the end of the academic year that all sectors of our community—from freshmen to fiftieth-year returning alums—would enjoy. Gail and I dance portions of only two pieces before I say: "It's early, but I'd like to leave."

SUNDAY, APRIL 29

I awaken at 7:oo A.M., eat breakfast, go back to bed, and don't budge until 2:oo P.M. Then I read newspapers, watch TV, go for a walk, take another nap, look at Natasha's latest report card (all *A*s—apparently her recent effort paid off), and talk with Natasha and Gail about a design for a new AU flag. After a hearty dinner, I go for another walk. I reread "If," tinker with cameras, listen to Kenny Rogers' records, and stare at the stars.

MONDAY, APRIL 30

I am supposed to take an early shuttle to New York for a luncheon in my honor and return immediately for the annual athletic awards dinner on campus. I awaken feeling better but not well and with phone calls and telexes flying about the 4th. With reluctance, I cancel the luncheon. I apologize to my host—the gregarious head of the New York Public Library system, Vartan Gregorian.

An old friend from Boston, Vartan is remarkable. His office resembles a nineteenth-century poet's after a storm. Books stacked helter-skelter, papers everywhere, he sits in the whirl, coat off, tie down, hair disheveled, his mind absorbed in eloquent prose or fundraising spectaculars. In the short time he has been at the New York Public Library, he has brought new life to that faltering but great institution.

Our friendship links in curious ways. Several years ago, Gail and I were guests at a dinner and belly-dancing show at the Hotel Méridien in Cairo. As we listened to exotic music and watched a sultry dancer with the unforgettable name of Fe Fe Abdul, across the room we spotted Gregorian and Marty Meyerson, then, respectively, provost and president of the University of Pennsylvania. They also were guests of the University of Cairo. The next day, while Vartan and Marty had meetings, their wives were taken to see the great pyramids. Gail and I, too, were driven out to see them. The four of us arrived together at the base of the largest Giza pyramid. Being inquisitive Americans, we wanted to explore the interior. So we started on what seemed to be an endless climb. Finally, we reached our destination: the burial crypt deep inside. A guide, the three wives, two other women we didn't know, and I stood in silence in the heart of that historic, massive strructure.

The silence ended abruptly when the guide launched into an expansive explanation of hieroglyphics. Then, without warning, the single room-light went out, as did the lights down the long stairway. For a few moments, we joked in the dark. The guide, either nervous or irrepressible, babbled on as if nothing had happened. "Here you see a symbol depicting . . . "

Finally, in the blackness, our banter ended. A woman stammered that she was claustrophobic. While the guide lectured undeterred in the blackened room, I took Gail's hand and we made our way to the opening. The other women joined hands and found Gail's in the dark. I started down the long, steep steps. With uneven rises and stone worn away over the years, they are dangerous in the light; in the dark, they border on treacherous. Gail came down next. I placed her foot on each step, while she did the same with the women above her. Meanwhile, the guide's unending narrative and the claustrophobic woman's plea, "I've gotta get out of here," still echoed in the closed chamber.

Slowly, we inched down, step by step, bumping knees, bruising knuckles, trying to keep from falling while moving as quickly as possible from the closed chamber to fresh air. After what seemed like a dynasty of descending—probably ten minutes—the lights flickered on as mysteriously as they had flickered off.

Is My Armor Straight?

Vartan and Marty missed all this. However, they did join us when we rode camels. I tried to rent regalia from a camel owner. He told me he had none, so I suggested that he rent me his own—one size fits all. As I mounted the camel and tossed the headdress around my shoulder, a crowd of camel drivers cheered: "Lawrence! Lawrence!" For a few moments, as the camel swept over the dunes and into the desert, I felt genuinely exhilarated. But Walter Mitty dissolved quickly when I saw a half-dozen camel owners running behind. They were not going to let me steal the camel or get lost. No need to worry, for the camel did the navigating. He went as far as he wished, stopped abruptly, and loped back to where he had begun.

All this brings me a grin today, as I revise my plans and work feverishly to be ready by Friday.

The mood at the athletic dinner surprises me. Given the sports center rumors, I assumed everyone here—true sports afficionados—would be exuberant. To my amazement, they are not. Why?

From there, I rush to the Kay Spiritual Life Center for a reception in honor of the new B'nai B'rith Hillel advisory board. These volunteers will expand the outreach and increase the resources of Hillel. I thank them for supporting this worthy cause.

Gail and I again excuse ourselves early and trot through mist to the house. I bound into the bathroom and apply my makeup. As she shouts, "I'll watch you," I dash to the car and drive to WJLA–TV, where I am to appear on a show about teachers.

The other panelists—primarily teachers' union officials and school administrators—argue that teachers' salaries must be higher. I do too. But I also stress that teachers' colleges must improve, that review procedures for current teachers must be tightened, that schools must build bridges to the rest of society, and that parents must shoulder more responsibilities. The format is too crowded for me to wedge in all I would like to say. Overall, I find the discussion discouraging. The union leaders pander to their current and potential members. A school board member argues that high academic achievement is not essential for teachers. A teacher asserts that merit pay will discriminate against women and minorities. And an administrator expounds in jargon about educational research.

What distresses me is that so many educators and administrators are preoccupied with the wrong things—their income, peculiar pedagogical philosophies, and meaningless methodology—while education's staggering problems go unanswered.

329

TUESDAY, MAY 1

The Dons, Milt, Tony Morella, and I meet all morning to prepare for the board meeting. Assuming that the monies come, how should we proceed? Should we talk individually with committee chairs before Friday? But how can we talk with trustees when we do not know the details?

I want to involve students and faculty as much as possible on the 4th, but how do we do so? They will want to know architectural details, which we either do not know or cannot disclose. Very soon, we must go to the zoning commission and the neighborhood residents' associations. Everyone—from students to faculty to trustees to neighbors—will want to be the first to review the plans.

Following an afternoon of meetings, I call Myers at 6:00 P.M. "What have you heard from Shaheen?"

"Nothing," Don replies. "I'd hoped he'd called you."

"No, I'm going to call him now." And so I do.

"How are you feeling, Doc?"

"I'm not sure, Bob. It's Tuesday night and I'm uncertain about the numbers and we don't have Adnan's letter."

"You worry too much. Everything will be fine. . . . It *is* getting close to Friday, though. I'll see if I can hurry things along."

Triezenberg calls: "Cy has pledged $250,000 for the center complex." Delighted, I tell him, "That's great. I knew he'd come through. Aside from the money, his leadership will help a lot."

When I arrive home, Gail and Natasha have everything prepared. Tonight we host a dinner to support a bipartisan program that encourages and enables women to go into politics. Around town, people host such dinners while others have bought tickets to attend them. To assist in luring ticket buyers, each host has been assigned a few "special guests." One of ours is Senator Bob Packwood of Oregon. When Natasha hears he is coming, she is thrilled. She wants to meet him but would prefer Howard Baker, because she's supposed to "be" Baker at GDS. Each student has been assigned to "be" a prominent politician. Natasha is Baker; one of her classmates is Packwood. Each student is to read up on his or her "namesake" and to obtain information about that person's political views, preferably by interviewing the political figure.

Gail asks Bob if he would mind Natasha's questioning him for her classmate. "Of course not." With slight shyness, Natasha takes notes while he answers her questions: "What are your views on school prayer?" "What should be the minimum drinking age?" Gail and I watch from a distance, wanting to be sure she does not impose. She shoots questions; he answers; she responds with a follow-up question. Finally, we extricate him, so he can mingle with the guests. "Natasha, I enjoyed this," he tells her. "If you didn't get all the information you need, call my office. I'll be glad to see you." Normally, she is cool about everything. But tonight she beams.

WEDNESDAY, MAY 2

The morning mail brings details about staff recognition day, to be held on May 16th on my building's lawn. Each year, Milt and I hold a picnic at which we give awards to outstanding employees from across the university. It is a splendid, homey time. And it gives us a rare opportunity to thank people publicly who work diligently all year.

This afternoon, Milt, the Dons, Tony, and I return to planning for the 4th. The funding *still* is not clear. Nonetheless, we continue to talk with individual trustees, prepare a draft press release, and compile a list of campus people to invite. We proceed as if we *will* announce the center, even though on this Wednesday evening we do not have the architect's plans in hand, the funding secured, or the commitments in writing. Two weeks ago when we did not have such items, I was distraught. Now I am numbed and stoic. We are doing all we can; there is nothing else to do. We shall make it or we shall not. If we do, terrific; if we do not, we shall know that we tried. Even the center is not worth a stroke.

The phone rings. I flip on the conference speaker so we all can talk to Bob Shaheen and Adnan's financial advisors. Their proposed wording for Adnan's letter sounds perfect. There are only minor details left to settle.

As the meeting ends, Milt says: "I look forward to going tonight, but just don't tell my grandmother." This will be a first for him and for some other guests. Shaikh Saud Al-Sabah, ambassador of Kuwait, hosts a dinner in my honor. He holds it in the new Kuwaiti Educational and Cultural Center. A glistening glass box, sitting on a proud promenade near several other Middle Eastern diplomatic facilities, the building symbolizes the dynamic nation. Low in population and awash in oil and trade, Kuwait for a decade has enjoyed one of the world's highest per-capita GNPs.

The ambassador and his wife greet Gail and me warmly. And I watch with pleasure as Milt, Sonia, law dean Tom Buergenthal, and several others enjoy the evening. The Al-Sabahs, ever gracious hosts, care for us attentively while introducing me to major Gulf envoys.

In his after-dinner remarks, the ambassador says: "My country will support Dr. Berendzen and The American University. We shall talk with him about how we can do this. We hope our Gulf neighbors also will offer support."

I talk briefly about my visits to Kuwait. But I do not tell about my Kuwaiti TV experience. They once taped a show with me describing the evolution of the universe. Due to the subject matter, the tape had to be reviewed by Kuwait's highest religious court. Muslim authorities studied it to determine if it were sacrilegious. They decided it was not, but thought that it would be controversial at that time given the religious fervor in nearby Iran. Consequently, they approved my tape but waited to show it. So, for a while, I was banned in Kuwait.

I thank our host for an exceptional evening. Milt, Sonia, Gail, and I chat as we leave. "What a charming and elegant night," Milt remarks. "In the history of U.S. education, this must be extremely rare."

"Probably unique," I reply. "When else has Kuwait assembled Gulf diplomats to hear a university president talk about his institution? And wasn't the statement exciting about forthcoming support?"

THURSDAY, MAY 3

The usual group assembles in my office this morning for our final meeting for tomorrow. But by 1:00 P.M., we still have a dozen loose ends. While we eat hamburgers at the conference table, we revise the press release, prepare draft board resolutions, make sure that appropriate guests are invited, and wonder again, will it come together?

After getting a haircut, I return to my office where Myers is reviewing slides for the architectural presentation. "Don, where do we stand with Adnan?"

"Wall Street and I have gone back and forth on the last details. And we've now reached definite agreement."

"That's great, but when do we get Adnan's letter?"

"Beats me," Don replies. "As I understand it, they've telexed A. K. in Spain the financial details plus his proposed letter to you. Now they're waiting for him to approve it."

"I thought he was in Saudi Arabia."

"That was yesterday. Now he's in Spain."

Just then, Shaheen calls. "We've sent papers down to Wall Street by helicopter and we've telexed Spain. Don't worry." But by 6:10 P.M. I am concerned. Where is Adnan's okay? And where is the letter? If I do not have it in hand, will the board proceed? Myers and I pace back and forth. Finally, I say: "There's only one thing to do. I'll tell Bob we must have the letter tonight. He can send someone with it or we'll send someone to get it." So I call.

"Bob, how do you want to handle this?" He thinks for a moment and replies: "Could you send someone to New York tonight?"

"I suppose, although I don't know who it'll be. Whoever it is must catch the 7:00 P.M. shuttle here to get to LaGuardia by 8:00 P.M. If you could send the letter to the airport, then our person could catch the 9:00 P.M. shuttle and return here by 10:00. That's the last one into Washington. Otherwise, our person will have to spend the night there and bring the letter on tomorrow's 7:00 A.M. shuttle."

"I'll have a car take the letter to LaGuardia," Bob says, "If you'll find someone to come to New York. Call me as soon as you have someone."

Who to ask? While Don asks Security to come to my office with a car to drive whomever we find, Joan comes out of her office wearing exercise clothes, prepared for her weekly class. Don and I exchange glances. "How would you like to go to New York?" he asks.

"Oh, sure," she replies. But our expressions tell her it is no joke. "We're serious," I assure her. "It's crazy, but are you willing to catch the seven o'clock shuttle and try to return on the nine o'clock?" Without hesitating, she says, "Sure."

While she changes and Don gets the security car, I call Bob. Before I can say anything, he starts: "We've got a problem. Well, not so much a problem as a glitch. Our telex arrived in Spain, but the chief hasn't seen it yet."

"Do you mean," I ask, "that Adnan hasn't signed off on it?"

"That's right, and I can't release the letter until he does. I don't know why he hasn't seen the telex, but he hasn't. It's now 12:30 A.M. his time. Don't worry, though. It'll all come together."

"I believe you, Bob. But the *Washington Times* ran an article today saying that we're announcing the center tomorrow. Where they got the story, I don't know. Many statements in it are untrue and they say nothing about Khashoggi. The reporters apparently contacted no one in authority. Nonetheless, it's in print and it probably will trigger other press."

"I hadn't known about that," Bob replies. "but I'm doing all I can. I understand the timing. Patricia, Nabila, and I will be there by noon tomorrow. I'll take care of the letter. I guarantee it." With that, we hang up. Don and I shrug. Joan changes back to exercise clothes. And I dash home.

To raise funds for the Washington Ballet Society, we are hosting a dinner at home tonight. I fly into the bathroom, shave so fast I cut my face, then breeze into the bedroom to dress. Given that this is for the ballet, I pick my navy blue suit rather than brown sports clothes. As I rush to meet the first guest, Gail blanches and says: "This is black tie." I grunt, whirl around on the steps and rush upstairs. Off comes the blue suit; on goes the tux. Winded and hungry, I make it to the door in time to greet the next arrival, who says: "You're kind to have us. And congratulations on the sports coliseum."

"What?"

"Your sports coliseum," he goes on. "The radio just said that tomorrow you'll announce that AU is building a massive sports coliseum."

After two dozen guests have arrived, I notice a strange dichotomy: brown socks in my black tux-shoes. Gail chortles as I leap upstairs two steps at a time to change clothes for what seems like the twelfth time.

When the last guest leaves, I sit with my papers to prepare once more for tomorrow. Most of all, I wait for the phone—for Shaheen to tell me that he has received final approval. But it never rings.

Then silence merges with blackness as a storm knocks out a power line. For several minutes I sit in the dark waiting for the lights to come on. But they do not. With a flashlight, I go upstairs and dig out my travel alarm clock. I must be up early. For what, however, I am uncertain. As I lie in the dark, lightning sends flashes across the room, thunder rumbles the house. It seems like the world is ending.

FRIDAY, MAY 4

As I start to take a shower, I ask Gail to listen for Shaheen's call. But it does not come. At 8:30, I leave for the Madison Hotel, the site of the board meeting and retreat. This morning's *Post* says, pending board approval, AU will announce that it is building a sports and convocation center.

Last night's storm has ended. A spring morning has come in its stead. Dogwoods and azaleas bloom. Joggers trot by. The bright sun and warm weather bring out pastels and smiles on everyone we pass. Could the weather be a portent?

As I enter the room where the trustees are to assemble at 9:00 A.M., Joan hands me a phone slip.

"8:45 A.M. Bob Shaheen called. He's on his way to Washington with the letter."

I pour myself a glass of orange juice, wink at Triezenberg, and greet arriving trustees. Quietly, Bill Moss says: "I told you I'd pledge for the center by today. Put me down for $100,000." Cy calls the meeting to order and proceeds expeditiously through routine agenda items. Then we come to the big one: the center. After introducing it, he turns the floor to me. I review AU's forty-year quest for such a facility. I remind the board that the center is not just for athletics but also for convocations and addresses by world leaders. Its construction will add a sparkling facility while leading to the demolition of delapidated ones. It will yield attractive new parks. In short, it will transform the university.

Then I report what they already have heard through rumors: gifts from Khashoggi, the Benders, and the late John Reeves, formerly a prominent Methodist and chair of the AU board. They applaud and listen attentively as Triezenberg gives further details and Myers describes architectural plans.

Before the question is called, I say: "The decision is yours, but I strongly recommend that you pass four resolutions. First, name the Reeves Aquatic Center in appreciation of the gift from the John Reeves estate. Second, name the Bender Arena in honor of Howard and Sondra Bender's gift. Third, name the entire facility the Adnan Khashoggi Center, in appreciation of Adnan's gift. And fourth, state publicly the board's intention to proceed with creating the center and authorize the administration to develop plans for occupancy by late 1986." The first three resolutions pass immediately. Just before the vote is taken on the fourth, I speak again:

"Although I don't want to make too much of it, I'd like to point out an extraordinary feature of this endeavor. Consider carefully the three key names—Khashoggi, Bender, Reeves. The American nation is diverse and pluralistic. As befits its name, The American University is too. Such ecumenicism as the center exhibits is rare and ennobling. It is, I believe, a tribute to our community and our university. I'm proud to be associated with such an institution."

No one responds—at least not orally. One man dabs his eye while a woman clears her throat. A half dozen nod in agreement; they know precisely what I mean.

Cy calls the question. The vote is unanimous. The center is born.

Trustees, beaming, shake hands with one another and with the administrators. "I didn't think we'd see this day," an old-timer remarks. "I remember a few years ago when we wondered if we could raise $100,000. Now you talk about millions." I am unsure which is greater today: joy or pride. It hardly matters.

As trustees go to lunch at the Vista Hotel next door, I await the arrival of Shaheen and company. I still do not have the letter. They were supposed to be here by noon; it's now 12:15. Then I see Patricia and another young woman coming up the staircase. The other woman is not just anyone. Startlingly beautiful, she must be Nabila Khashoggi.

In a few moments, Bob joins us. "How'd it go, Doc?"

"Splendidly."

"Even without the letter?"

"I assured them that you'd given details over the phone, that Adnan had approved them, and that the document was on the way. They accepted that."

"Great. Now, can we have you and Nabila on a quick TV interview, to be sent by satellite to Europe and the Middle East?"

In a private room, a crew tapes while I tell Nabila how important her father's gift is to the university and the city. Nervous before the camera, she listens shyly, saying little. But her smile says enough.

Afterwards, I rush to the Vista where advisory board members join trustees for a buffet lunch. From the ambassador of Nepal to the superintendent of the D.C. public schools, from the head of one of Taiwan's largest industries to the general managers of Washington TV stations, we have a potpourri of leaders and friends who have agreed to assist the university.

After lunch we return to the Madison, where the ballroom has been converted for a press conference. TV lights glare as guests take their seats behind cordoned-off sections. Large, colorful architectural plans line the room. While students, professors, trustees, and advisory board members read the press release and study the sketches, I head to the restroom to dash out my notes. Usually, I have privacy doing this in a restroom, but not today. Ed Carr, who is leaving as I enter, beams and says, "Congratulations. This is terrific." And Bob Kogod sees me outside the door, grasps my shoulders, and grins. "Dick, I'm delighted."

Without notes, I rush back to the ballroom where the program is about to begin. Cy calls it to order, introduces me, and I begin:

"When any dream is fulfilled, it's a joyous occasion. When the dream has lingered for generations, then its fulfillment is truly a celebration. Many people help to make a dream come true, but a handful turn fantasy into reality." With that, I acknowledge all our trustees and alumni supporters, stressing Reeves, the Benders, and Khashoggi.

I go on: "Unfortunately, Mr. Khashoggi cannot be here today. But he has sent an able and charming emissary, his daughter, Nabila Khashoggi. Will she please join me at the rostrum?"

This doe-eyed, long-legged beauty stands at my side, gazes at the audience, and melts Washington. Whatever the sternest critic might have felt about the man Khashoggi, after seeing Nabila, it must be forgotten. With a soft voice, she reads her father's gracious letter to me, explaining why he is pleased to contribute. Every eye is on her, flicking from her model's face to her inch-long diamond. Most of all, her grace charms us all.

I respond by noting that his gift will transform the university. He has done more than make a magnificent bequest to a single institution. He has built a center; fulfilled a dream; touched time.

The entire program lasts but thirty minutes. It has taken decades to prepare. I thank everyone for coming and invite them to examine the architectural plans. The room erupts. Students flock around Nabila and Sondra while professors and trustees study the drawings. I rush about, trying to arrange photographs of Jim Weaver and Darryl Jones with Nabila and Sondra. Roland Rice engrosses student reporters with stories about the early days, explaining how the center has been needed since his youth. I feel a pull on my elbow. "Fantastic, Dick," exclaims a beaming Frank Turaj. "This is great and I'm proud."

I rush home, change clothes, and meet Gail. When we return to the hotel, people are arriving for the reception—trustees, advisory board members, and alumni donors. During dinner, I am seated next to Nabila. What an exceptional young woman she is. The head of two companies, she has business dealings on three continents, lives in the south of France, commutes between New York and Geneva, actively supports projects dealing with child abuse and world hunger, is devoted to her five brothers, is a Michael Jackson fan, will appear on the July cover of *Town & Country*, and is friends with recording artists and movie stars, writers and executives, diplomats and kings. All this, and she is only twenty-two.

After dinner, I go to the rostrum and begin: "This has been a great day for AU." Bob Kogod—who has pledged $500,000 towards the center—jumps to his feet, applauding vigorously. Others at his table cheer; soon the entire room does.

"There's one person who couldn't be here tonight," I continue, "but we want to thank him sincerely—Adnan Khashoggi." There is sustained applause.

"The center's largest feature is the gym, a place for major sporting events and convocations," I explain. "With pride, we've named it the Bender Arena, after Howard and Sondra Bender, our friends and staunch supporters." They smile and wave. As I wait for the applause to subside, my mind rushes back to a winter evening two years ago when they told me they'd support the center drive, starting payments at once. They did so without promise of anything. From the moment Sondra joined the board, she became an unfaltering center champion, urging and cajoling other trustees. For months, no other contributions came. Yet, she never lost faith, never slackened her zeal. Resolutely, she believed in something that might never be. That had class.

After thanking the Benders, I ask Nabila to join me at the rostrum. She gives greetings from her father. When she finishes, I request: "May we raise our glasses?" From inside the rostrum, I pull out two champagne glasses I hid earlier and give the toast: "To all who dream. And to those precious few who make dreams come true."

At home, the whirlwind stops. The room, the world is silent. TV lights off, applause ended. Now I sit alone and replay the day, the week, the month. Ironies strike me. A man born in Mecca, a third of the planet away, gives the naming gift. The person who did not get a scholarship in Dallas because he was not an athlete spearheaded the drive to get AU's athletic facility. People who shouted the most for the center ultimately gave the least. When all was said, a few dedicated people made it happen.

I was right in my tribute to Adnan: He has "touched time." And he was right in his statement: Our friendship shall be "bound in stone." This transforming structure will last the decades, touching the lives of tens of thousands. The power of words is beyond description, as all scholars know. But we academics need to remember what others take for granted: physical things count, too. It is good and noble that we raise standards and improve our image. But these indices are like clouds: they are real, but you cannot grasp them. The center is different. It symbolizes success. It will be real. Like the things of Lindops, it will be hard and rough; it will make noise. It will stand long after memos have yellowed and speeches have blown in the wind.

SATURDAY, MAY 5

After fifteen years, Jo Williams retires this year. In posts in the Division of Student Life, School of Communication, and Career Center, she has advised and helped hundreds of students. Tonight some of them hold a surprise party for her.

Gail and I arrive not knowing what to expect. This is exam time; students are extremely busy. An *Eagle* editor is at the entrance. Soon I see students who graduated three, seven, fifteen years ago. The hallways are packed. Reservations closed a week ago when the two hundred-person seating capacity filled.

For the first time in years, I am not on the program. This time, thank goodness, I am simply part of the crowd. The attraction is Jo and the head table is made up of people who have worked closely with her, each of whom pays tribute to this exceptional person.

When she arrived at AU in 1969, students had occupied the president's building just four months earlier. Since then, she has been advisor, companion, and surrogate mother to generations. She has had students home for dinner. She has counseled them late into the evening. She has gotten them internships and has written hundreds of letters of reference. Lest anyone think young people ungrateful, tonight shows the truth. And it is not just the warmth that touches me but the skill with which the affair was planned. Students arranged skits and songs, and, with Frank Jordan's help, collected money for Jo's surprise gift: a trip to Rome.

Tony Perkins, who graduated last year, is the evening's emcee. Now a stand-up comic, he clearly has found his calling. At the outset he intones: "President Berendzen told me a few minutes ago, 'Due to a large crowd tonight, he regrets . . .' " That is as far as he gets before the room erupts with laughter and applause. This keen-witted young black man then comments about the center: "Isn't it ironic that an Arab gentleman gives money to a Methodist university attended by

a large number of Jewish students so tall black guys can play basketball?"

MONDAY, MAY 7

The phone rings only twice. No telexes arrive. The mail contains just
six items. Exams are ending; students are leaving. The center is announced; the event is over. And this is my quietest day in a year.

I clear my desk and silently sit for a moment in my study. As my
eye scans from my books to the photograph of the Whirlpool Galaxy
to the artist's sketch of the center, Lao Tzu's words from the sixth
century B.C. come back to me: "Of a good leader they will say, 'We
did this ourselves.' "

And that is just fine with me.

WEDNESDAY, MAY 9

The American Council on Education asks if I will participate in June
in its national identification program for women. I had hoped to have
a few days for myself then, but I tell them okay. "Late Night America," the public broadcast system TV program, calls from Detroit to
ask if I will appear in June. The topic: "Quality in Public Education."
I accept. A lawyer asks if I will give a welcoming address to newly
naturalized citizens. I would be delighted.

As I pass through Joan's office on the way to the photocopier, I
notice that she looks flushed. She says over the phone, "Well, Sir, I
don't know about that. I'll see if he can talk with you." She puts the
caller on hold, stares at her desk, and says: "When I attempted to
screen this call, he said he was angry because you're having an affair
with his daughter." What is this? I take the call only to discover that
I know the man. A lawyer, he is calling on behalf of his client who
has a complaint against the university. When I ask about the story he
gave Joan, he laughs: "That routine will get around a secretary every
time. It works like a charm." He is a lawyer? And a former senator?

THURSDAY, MAY 10

This evening, Gail, Natasha, and I have an important family meeting:
to plan Natasha's epochal thirteenth birthday party. The thirteenth
is special, the more so for her because many of her friends are Jewish.
For months she's attended their bar mitzvahs and bat mitzvahs.

"Those functions are much more than a birthday party," Natasha explains. "The first part is a religious ceremony with parents and lots of others. I've attended so many that I've memorized it. Could I have one? They're really nice."

"No, Natasha," I reply. "That wouldn't be kosher, so to speak."

"Although the religious part is important, the entire day is special," Gail explains. "Perhaps we could get ideas from the bat mitzvahs that you could use."

"Yes, although you wouldn't have the religious part, we might have something similar to the rest of it," I propose. "One of the most charming aspects is that it brings generations together; it bonds.

"How would it be," I go on, "if you invite your friends for a dance to your music? And Mommy and I invite your friends' parents to attend our party at the same time? We'll dance to good music—that is, from the fifties and sixties. We'll be in the sunroom, while you're in the basement."

"Great," Natasha grins. "But there's one rule," I add. "You kids can't horn in on our good music." She grunts: "Big chance." Gail suggests, "After the dance, we can get the kids and parents together for a backyard picnic." Satisfied, Natasha starts preparing invitations.

She also mentions that it is time for softball again. Last year, I taught her how to play, but it was painful. Her batting was okay and her catching fair, but her throwing was dreadful. What is it about the female anatomy that makes a girl throw funny? Her entire team needed practice. It took sheer parental devotion to get Gail and me to watch last year's game. Natasha's team lost, eighty-seven to three. The mystery is how they got the three.

This year, however, her playing is better. She hits well and runs quickly. But her throwing—elbows go everywhere, the ball goes anywhere. Gail tells her, "You can do it. After all, your mother was outstanding in softball." That we have heard before, but today we learn more.

"Bunny, what position did you play?" I ask. "You've never told us."

With pride she says, "I was shortstop on the Christ the King Lassies."

"Wow," Natasha exclaims. "That's an important position."

"That's what they told me, but not many balls came my way. Mostly, people ran into me."

"How'd that happen?" I ask. "Where exactly did you play?"

"Between home and first base."

Natasha and I exchange glances. "Mommy, you mean this great softball career you've told us about for years amounted to your being shortstop between home and first base?"

"That's where they put me. I thought it was odd, but the coach said that's where I belonged."

FRIDAY, MAY 11

Gail calls. "I need your advice," she begins. "An alumnus saw me in the front yard as he was driving by, so he stopped. He was enthusiastic about the sports center and said alums now would like to help. I suggested that he talk with Triezenberg, but he said the alumni office's approach was dull. He urged—almost demanded—that we hold receptions in our home to which hundreds of alums would be invited. After an hour of drinking and chatting, you'd tell them about the center and ask for money."

"What did you say?"

"I told him that you and Don were planning wide-scale solicitations, but he insisted that his idea was the only way to do it. As he left he said, 'My wife and I will arrange your house for the receptions.'"

"I didn't want to offend him," she goes on, "but he was arrogant. How do you want to handle it?"

We agree that I will call him and try to point him to other ways to help. I appreciate his zeal, if not his approach.

The mail brings a different attitude. A New York alumnus writes: "We're all excited about the new sports center. I'm so proud of AU. Some AU person is in the media every few days, and I know the standards are rising." And another letter says: "I'll be at the graduation with bells on. I'm so thrilled by what the university has done for my granddaughter, I just wanted to say thanks."

As the term winds down, I am tired but exhilarated. And for two hours, I inspect the campus in preparation for the big weekend, when families arrive and graduates leave.

SATURDAY, MAY 12

Six centuries ago, Deschamps wrote, "Better honor than shameful wealth." There is not much danger of the latter at a university where most employees deserve more pay and many students scrape by. But honor, we can provide, even if only on this single day.

For those times when I wonder why academic life is worth it, today gives the ringing reply. It comes not from the ceremony but from the people; not from pageantry but from the achievement. Parents, husbands, wives, children, and friends beam as I begin Honors Convocation. They gasp and then applaud as Milt and I read the accomplishments of this year's winners.

What a group: Alan Kraut for his teaching of history; an entire committee for their revisions of the arts and sciences curriculum; Chinh Kien Nguyen, a senior who has made almost all *A*s while majoring in chemistry.

Although the applause for them all is warm, the hall especially rings for one staff member. Marion Logue, university archivist, retires this year. When Milt finishes reading her citation, she walks slowly to the rostrum. I go down the steps to meet her. With her white-haired head tilted back, she looks up at me, tears in her eyes. As I help her to the rostrum, the applause swells—for she is our memory, our living institutional history. She has seen it all and known everyone. Now, after more than three decades, she leaves. But as she has remembered AU's past, we shall remember her.

After we honor distinguished alums, the ceremony ends—and the best part begins: a reception for the honorees and their loved ones. Squirrels scamper up the trees outside my office while the crowd mingles on the rolling lawn. Washington spring is in full glory. The best part, however, is the pride of the families. Even forty-year-olds who have won honors today want me to meet their parents.

I put my academic regalia in my car and drive to a student reception where Andy Sherman and Paul Schroeder live. Again, proud parents grin. And I do too. If AU is the students' alma mater, then I am the surrogate father. And so is Jim Weaver, who speaks for all dedicated professors when he says to me this evening, "This group of students has everything—intelligence, compassion, even common sense."

SUNDAY, MAY 13
Because we do not yet have a convocation center, in the spring we must hold commencements for our five colleges separately. This permits them to be individualistic, but it exhausts the provost, the university marshall, and me because we must zip about the city to attend them all; Sonia and Gail do too.

The Lucy Webb Hayes School of Nursing starts the day with an on-campus ceremony. "Today is a special day," I begin, "as we recognize a special group—it's Mother's Day."

"Some years ago," I continue, "the president of Harvard was asked how it was that his institution had gained the reputation of being one of the nation's great storehouses of knowledge. 'Probably,' he replied, 'it's because freshmen bring us so much knowledge and seniors take away so little.'

"That may have been the case there, then; it isn't the case here, now."

Milt, Ruth Landman, and I dash from campus to Constitution Hall downtown where the College of Arts and Sciences (CAS) fills the several thousand seats. From there, we rush back to my office and eat fried chicken. Then we join the Kogod College of Business Administration (KCBA) at the Washington Hebrew Congregation. Then we make another dash to Constitution Hall for the College of Public and International Affairs (CPIA), followed by a return sprint to the Washington Hebrew Congregation for the Washington College of Law commencement.

Someday a traffic cop is going to stop us. I can imagine his report: three people wearing medieval garb, one carrying a mace. For us it is a rush. Yet at each ceremony we must appear calm and collected. We hear only one address—Ted Koppel's to CAS. John Kenneth Galbraith's to CPIA and Donald Regan's to KCBA illustrate AU's diversity. We bestow honorary degrees on those three plus one other: Jack Kneble, AU alumnus and former secretary of agriculture. Each ceremony has its own style, from nursing's two musicians to CPIA's Scottish band, complete with kilts and bagpipes. At the CAS ceremony, I award a presidential citation to Jay Sommer, a member of the National Commission on Excellence in Education. A language specialist, he is also a genuine American success. After surviving the Holocaust, he came to the United States and became a National Teacher of the Year.

Despite the rush, one moment at each ceremony is special. The dean asks the graduates to rise, the provost presents the groups to me, and I walk to the mike. Because the ceremonies are complex, we have scripts; they become stage productions. At this point, however, I put mine aside.

"Parents, think back to when they were born. And when they started first grade and when they packed to go to college. Remember the phone calls, the dirty laundry at holidays, the checks—maybe mostly the checks. And remember your hopes for them—that they will have more than you had, will go farther than you've gone. And remember your belief—that education is the way.

"And, you graduates, think back to taking the SATs, reading college catalogues, waiting for admissions letters. Remember moving in and meeting your dorm mate. Remember the library and the basketball games, the Quad and the study lounges.

"In our hectic world, one minute can seem like every other minute; one day like every other day. But not all moments are alike. This one is special. You've waited a long time for it. Savor it. And remember it always."

Then I turn to the script: "By authority of the Congress of the United States, vested in the Board of Trustees of The American University and by that board delegated to me, I hereby confer upon you the degrees for which you have been certified and recommended."

Tonight, my office is dark; the campus, silent. With my crimson robe slung over my shoulder, I walk home. I pass parents photographing a graduate still in his regalia. I pass quiet dorms, the parking lot from which the Khashoggi Center will rise, a darkened library. For a moment I pause at the corner of the Quad and think back to the jeering protesters who crowded here a year and a half ago and to the cheering parents I saw a few hours ago. And I think back to what I said in my inaugural speech about the founding dream of The American University: "It will come true!"

As I continue on past Clark Hall, I recall the summer schedule. Physical Plant must reroof Anderson Hall and repair steamlines. Triezenberg and I must secure more center funding. Myers and I must prepare to purchase the off-campus facility. Milt and I must discuss the core curriculum. I must start my recruitment efforts. I must meet with individual trustees. And then I must . . .

INDEX

P

Pacino, Al, 194
Packwood, Bob, 329–30
Papandreou, Margaret, 268
Paraskevaides, George, 135, 136, 155
Percy, Chuck, 29, 103
Perkins, Tony, 338–39
Perot, H. Ross, 256–57, 258
Peters, Bill, 54, 225
Peters, John Punnet, 84
Pfeiffer, Ed, 81, 82
Powell, Jody, 37
Poynter, Bruce, 12, 230, 302, 312, 313, 314, 315, 317, 318, 320, 323
Press, Billie, 131
Press, Frank, 81, 131
Prettyman, Barrett, 32, 109, 110, 214, 271

R

Radziwill, Lee, 64
Randolph, Carol, 155, 303
Reagan, Nancy, 171, 264, 266, 292
Reagan, Ronald, 21–22, 34, 47–48, 129, 243, 244, 264, 265, 266
Reed, Vince, 298
Reeve, Christopher, 112
Reeves, John, 334, 336
Regan, Donald, 343
Rense, Page, 14
Rice, Roland, 270, 272, 336
Richards, Renee, 99–100
Ride, Sally, 119, 123
Ripley, Dillon, 283
Rodriguez, Mary C., 218
Romano, Lois, 30
Roosevelt, Archie, 44
Roosevelt, Selwa, 40, 44, 264
Roosevelt, Theodore, 266, 294
Roscher, Nina, 119, 126, 150, 162, 289
Rose, Charlie, 216
Rubenstein, Roberta, 294
Ruppe, Loret, 291

S

Sadat, Anwar, 117, 171
Sadat, Madame Anwar, 171
Sagan, Annie, 131–32, 133
Sagan, Carl, 51–52, 131–32, 133
Said, Abdul Aziz, 310–11
Sampson, Jim, 200
Sandberg, Mike, 81
Sasser, James, 34, 35
Schell, Maximilian, 265
Schieffer, Bob, 13
Schnall, Maxine, 166
Schoellkopf, Caroline Hunt, 257
Schroeder, Paul, 47, 95, 108–109, 271, 302–3, 342
Schubert, Leo, 57
Schuckel, Harry, 199
Scott, Willard, 322
de Sepulveda, Bernardo, 138
Shaheen, Bob, 43, 45, 106, 110, 111, 115, 156, 251, 284, 293, 308–9, 324, 329, 330, 332, 333, 334, 335
Shaheen, Patricia, 106, 111, 155–56, 284, 293, 308–9, 324, 333, 335
Shane, C. D., 192
Shelley, Louise, 283
Sherman, Andy, 5, 95, 97–98, 220, 243, 342
Shouse, Kay, 12
Shultz, George, 40, 157, 265
Shultz, Obie, 40
Simon, Bill, 123
Simon, Jeanne, 296–97
Simon, Rita, 15
Simpson, Alan, 291
Sirica, John, 65, 235
Sirica, Lucy, 65
Smith, Mrs. William French, 47
Smith, Sally, 249
Smith, William French, 47, 172, 178
Sommer, Jay, 343
Spivak, Joel, 2, 5
Stanton, Frank, 293
Stark, Koo, 112
Steinbach, Shelly, 263
Steorts, Nancy, 290

ABOUT THE MAKING OF THIS BOOK

The text of *Is My Armor Straight?*
was set in Times Roman by Com
Com, a division of The Haddon
Craftsmen, of Allentown,
Pennsylvania. The book was printed
and bound by Fairfield Graphics of
Fairfield, Pennsylvania. The
typography and binding were
designed by Tom Suzuki of Falls
Church, Virginia.